WITHDRAWN
UTSA LIBRARIES

P9-DTS-031

The Science of
Clinical Psychology

The Science of Clinical Psychology

Accomplishments and Future Directions

*Edited by Donald K. Routh
and Robert J. DeRubeis*

American Psychological Association
Washington, DC

Copyright © 1998 by the American Psychological Association. All rights reserved. Except as permitted under the United States Copyright Act of 1976, no part of this publication may be reproduced or distributed in any form or by any means, or stored in a database or retrieval system, without the prior written permission of the publisher.

Published by
American Psychological Association
750 First Street, NE
Washington, DC 20002

Copies may be ordered from
APA Order Department
P.O. Box 92984
Washington, DC 20090-2984

In the U.K., Europe, Africa, and the Middle East, copies may be ordered from
American Psychological Association
3 Henrietta Street
Covent Garden
London WC2E 8LU
England

Typeset in Goudy by EPS Group Inc., Easton, MD

Printer: Braun-Brumfield, Inc., Ann Arbor, MI
Jacket designer: Design Concepts, San Diego, CA
Technical/production editor: Valerie Montenegro

Library of Congress Cataloging-in-Publication Data
The science of clinical psychology : accomplishments and future directions / edited
  by Donald K. Routh and Robert J. DeRubeis.—1st ed.
      p.   cm.
    Includes bibliographical references and index.
    ISBN 1-55798-520-0 (cb : acid-free paper)
    1. Clinical psychology.   2. Clinical psychology—Forecasting.   I. Routh,
  Donald K.   II. DeRubeis, Robert J.
    [DNLM: 1. Mental Disorders.   2. Psychopathology.   3. Psychology,
  Clinical.   4. Research.   WM 140S416 1998]
  RC467.S433   1998
  616.89—dc21
  DNLM/DLC
  for Library of Congress   98-39998
                                                                              CIP

British Library Cataloguing-in-Publication Data
A CIP record is available from the British Library.

Printed in the United States of America
First edition

Library
University of Texas
at San Antonio.

CONTENTS

CONTRIBUTORS

Amy K. Bach, *Center for Anxiety and Related Disorders at Boston University, Boston, MA*

David H. Barlow, *Center for Anxiety and Related Disorders at Boston University, Boston, MA*

Carrie E. Bearden, *Department of Psychology, University of Pennsylvania, Philadelphia*

Thomas N. Bradbury, *Department of Psychology, University of California, Los Angeles*

Tyrone D. Cannon, *Department of Psychology, University of Pennsylvania, Philadelphia*

Lucy Canter Kihlstrom, *Institute of Personality and Social Research and Center for Mental Health Services Research, University of California, Berkeley*

Robert J. DeRubeis, *Department of Psychology, University of Pennsylvania, Philadelphia*

Cynthia Flynn, *Department of Psychology and Human Development, Vanderbilt University, Nashville, TN*

Edna B. Foa, *Department of Psychiatry, Allegheny University of the Health Sciences, Philadelphia, PA*

Martin E. Franklin, *Department of Psychiatry, Allegheny University of the Health Sciences, Philadelphia, PA*

Judy Garber, *Department of Psychology and Human Development, Vanderbilt University, Nashville, TN*

William G. Iacono, *Department of Psychology, University of Minnesota, Minneapolis*

Matthew D. Johnson, *Department of Psychology, University of California, Los Angeles*

Philip C. Kendall, *Department of Psychology, Temple University, Philadelphia, PA*

John F. Kihlstrom, *Department of Psychology, University of California, Berkeley*

Erika E. Lawrence, *Department of Psychology, University of California, Los Angeles*

Lester Luborsky, *Department of Psychiatry, University of Pennsylvania, Philadelphia*

Richard M. McFall, *Department of Psychology, Indiana University, Bloomington*

Ronald D. Rogge, *Department of Psychology, University of California, Los Angeles*

Donald K. Routh, *Department of Psychology, University of Miami, Coral Gables, FL*

Linda G. Russek, *Department of Psychology, University of Arizona, Tucson*

Gary E. Schwartz, *Department of Psychology, University of Arizona, Tucson*

Martin E. P. Seligman, *Department of Psychology, University of Pennsylvania, Philadelphia*

Susan A. Tracey, *Center for Anxiety and Related Disorders at Boston University, Boston, MA*

Teresa A. Treat, *Department of Psychology, Indiana University, Bloomington*

Richard J. Viken, *Department of Psychology, Indiana University, Bloomington*

ACKNOWLEDGMENTS

The editors gratefully acknowledge the assistance of the following colleagues in reviewing early drafts of the chapters published in this book: Joseph Barrash, Robert M. Bilder, Paul H. Blaney, David Cole, Barbara Cornblatt, Joseph A. Durlak, Stephen V. Faraone, James V. Hinrichs, Sheri L. Johnson, Thomas Joiner, Nadine Kaslow, Alan E. Kazdin, Annette M. LaGreca, Arnold A. Lazarus, Russell Newman, Thomas H. Ollendick, Michael Pogue-Guile, Lynn P. Rehm, Patrice Saab, Wendy Silverman, Douglas K. Snyder, and George Stricker.

INTRODUCTION

DONALD K. ROUTH

The main aim of this book is to try to set an agenda for research in clinical psychology for the new century. The field is now over 100 years old. It has developed into a broad discipline concerned with the scientific study of psychopathology and with the assessment and treatment of persons with emotional, cognitive, and behavioral problems. It has been called the most common psychological specialty in the world (Sexton & Hogan, 1992). The fields of abnormal psychology and psychotherapy, which are key parts of present-day clinical psychology, have ancient origins. The study of psychopathology can be traced back at least as far as the medical writings attributed to Hippocrates, dating from the 5th century B.C.E., and also to the work of philosophers such as Democritus who were not physicians (Routh, in press). The precise origins of psychological approaches to healing, though elusive, are no doubt even more ancient.

Of course, the involvement of psychologists in the study of psychopathology and its treatment had to wait until the late 19th century, when a formal discipline of psychology developed, but research on psychopathology soon became a part of this new field. The neurologist Jean Charcot

Marion Routh, Beth A. Beisel, and Sheri L. Johnson made helpful comments on an initial draft of the manuscript.

appointed Pierre Janet to direct a psychology laboratory at the Salpetriere Hospital in Paris in 1890, to study patients with "hysteria." Alfred Binet was another French psychologist who worked with Charcot and was greatly influenced by him. The German psychiatrist Emil Kraepelin spent time working with the psychologist Wilhelm Wundt at the University of Leipzig. Kraepelin was an influential figure in the development of descriptive psychopathology and of psychopharmacology. He later carried out psychological research in his psychiatry service at the University of Munich.

In the United States, beginning toward the end of the 19th century, there was a great interest in abnormal psychology and psychotherapy among many of the early psychologists, including William James, G. Stanley Hall, and Boris Sidis. James presented the Lowell lectures on exceptional mental states in Boston in 1896 (Taylor, 1982) and was interested in research on automatic writing. Hall at one point served as the lay superintendent of a mental hospital in Maryland and later taught psychology to psychiatry residents at Worcester State Hospital in Massachusetts. Morton Prince, a psychologically oriented physician, studied a famous case of a woman with multiple personality. He established the *Journal of Abnormal Psychology* in 1906 and founded the Harvard Psychological Clinic in 1926. What might be termed the Boston school of abnormal psychology and psychotherapy was active in the 1890s and at the turn of the century, though it tended to be absorbed by the psychoanalytic movement after the first decade of the new century.

As is well known, Lightner Witmer founded the world's first psychology clinic at the University of Pennsylvania in 1896 at the University of Pennsylvania (Witmer, 1897) and was one of the first to advocate the use of psychology to help people rather than only to carry out research. The first known use of the term *clinical psychology* was in a 1907 article by Witmer in the inaugural issue of *Psychological Clinic*, the journal he edited.

Research on psychopathology, including its assessment and treatment, has greatly accelerated during the past hundred years. In fact, more research in this field has probably been published during the 20th century than in all previous centuries (Routh, in press). Research funding is available both from various private foundations and from the National Institutes of Health in the United States, the Medical Research Council in the United Kingdom, and other such governmental organizations. Thus, clinical psychology, psychiatry, and other disciplines involved in research in this domain are in a relatively healthy state. For example, there has been a resurgent interest in genetic factors in psychopathology in relation to the worldwide Human Genome project. The 1990s, designated as the "Decade of the Brain" in the United States, have included rapid strides in the neurosciences and have involved use of the new neuroimaging technology in the study of psychopathology. Prevention research, previously seen only as a theoretical possibility, has begun to move into actuality.

This book focuses on research in clinical psychology, including causes and risk factors for psychopathology and physical health problems, assessment and treatment, and the effective delivery of mental health services. It includes chapters by several of the most promising clinical psychology researchers of our day on these topics and therefore should be of interest to scientists, professors, graduate students, and scientifically oriented practitioners of clinical psychology. This introduction explains how the book came into being and provides some context for the chapters to follow. The inspiration for it was a celebration of the centenary of the founding of the first psychology clinic at the University of Pennsylvania. The celebration occurred in Philadelphia on October 25–26, 1996, approximately a hundred years after Lightner Witmer founded his clinic there. By doing so, he is considered by many to have founded the field of clinical psychology as well.

This book considers what directions might be most fruitful for clinical psychology research to pursue in the 21st century. Chapters 1 to 5, grouped under the heading of Causes and Risk Factors, immediately make it clear that the field of clinical psychology is linked with various allied scientific fields, including, of course, psychiatry, but also many others, such as genetics, neurology, developmental and cognitive psychology, psychometrics, and internal medicine. The topic of depression, the subject of two of the chapters in this section, was already familiar to Hippocrates 2,500 years ago as what was then labeled melancholia. Chapters 6 and 7, in the second section, Assessment, are devoted to aspects of assessment, which also has its origins in ancient time, including over 1,000 years of formal examinations for "Mandarin" civil service of ancient China. Chapters 8 to 11, under the section Interventions, are devoted to psychological interventions, which date back at least to 1882, when the French neurologist Jean Charcot demonstrated the experimental production and removal of "hysterical" symptoms in his patients. As Foa and Franklin (chap. 10, this volume) note, devising and validating such psychological interventions may be one of the most important emerging roles for the clinical psychologists of the next century.

According to Wilson (1998a, 1998b), modern science is characterized by "consilience," defined as "the interlocking of causal explanations across disciplines" (Wilson, 1998b, p. 2048). In this way, physics, chemistry, and the biological sciences are not only linked with each other but now also have many areas in which they interface with the social sciences and the humanities. Wilson advocated that this process go much further, with the social sciences and the humanities adopting the established generalizations of biology and psychology instead of attempting to operate independently as they have in the past. He listed four disciplines that now inhabit the borderland between the established natural sciences and the emerging ones: cognitive neuroscience, behavioral genetics, evolutionary psychology and anthropology, and environmental science (including human ecology). Although not specifically mentioned by Wilson, clinical psychology is clearly a part of this same border territory. Thus, to carry out effective research in the future, clinical psychologists will have to become familiar with and attempt to build on the findings and methods of any other scientific fields related to the problems they study.

CAUSES AND RISK FACTORS

In his chapter on identifying genetic risk for schizophrenia, Iacono (chap. 1) endorses the established scientific consensus that genetic factors probably play some role in schizophrenia. This is a category of psychopathology that was identified in the 19th century by Kraepelin, who called it *dementia praecox*. The particular genetic mechanisms involved in schizophrenia have so far eluded investigators, including Eugen Bleuler, the psychiatrist who named the disorder. One promising scientific advance was the identification of aberrant smooth pursuit eye movement as a "trait" marker for schizophrenia. This neuropsychological difficulty is often found in individuals with schizophrenia, remains with them even when the disorder is in remission, and is often found in their nonschizophrenic close relatives as well. With the enormous strides now being made by molecular genetics, including the Human Genome project, it does seem likely, as Iacono says, that the next few decades will greatly clarify the role of genetic factors in schizophrenia. In this area of investigation, it would be highly useful to discover one or more "endophenotypes" with behavioral features resembling schizophrenia. Thus, as we learn more about the actual effects of particular genes, we may end up refining the clinical diagnosis of variants of the schizophrenia spectrum to align them with such endophenotypes.

It is certainly true that the discovery of other genetic disorders that involve behavioral features has led to a complete regrouping of the behavioral problems involved. A recent example of such a discovery is provided by Fragile X syndrome (Hagerman, 1996). This X-linked disorder is one of the most common causes of mental retardation. Its behavioral phenotype is however complex and includes abstract reasoning problems, IQ decline as the individual becomes older, as well as overall mental retardation, instability of mood, aggression, right-hemisphere deficits, executive function deficits, and, at the mild end, shyness and social sensitivity (Hagerman, 1996).

Chapter 2, by Bearden and Cannon, considers neurodevelopmental origins of schizophrenia. Like Iacono's chapter, it is concerned with a highly interdisciplinary area of research. Psychologists have known for some time from neuroimaging research that the brains of individuals with schizophrenia tend to have enlarged ventricles and other more subtle types of neuropathology. Bearden and Cannon review research, including their own, suggesting that some of these brain abnormalities date from early in fetal development, for example, a failure of neuronal migration, and others from obstetric complications. This evidence, combined with behavioral observations suggesting attentional problems in children who later develop schizophrenia, leads one toward reconceptualizing schizophrenia as a developmental disorder rather than one with its onset only in adolescence or young adulthood.

The study of neurodevelopmental factors in any disorder is hampered by limitations in our knowledge of normal brain development and function. Such research has been greatly facilitated by the development of modern, noninvasive neuroimaging technology, including the computed tomography scan, magnetic resonance imaging, the positron emission tomography scan (which provide precise spatial localization), and complementary developments in electrophysiology (which permit equally precise temporal resolution). As noted already, the 1990s have been characterized as the decade of the brain, and leading researchers such as Francis Crick (1990) have identified the human brain as the most important present scientific frontier. Thus it seems likely that the next century will provide excellent opportunities for the study of neural development in relation to psychopathology.

Chapter 3, by Garber and Flynn, explores the psychosocial origins of the depressive cognitive style of negative thoughts about the self, the world, and the future, and the tendency to make global, stable, and internal attributions of negative events. In reviewing prospective developmental studies, they indeed find some evidence supportive of these hypotheses. In addition, they review research suggesting that changing such cognitive styles can prevent depressive symptoms. Even though Garber and Flynn are particularly interested in psychosocial risk factors for depression, they do not deny the possibility of genetic factors or of patterns of electrophysiological asymmetry in the frontal lobes of the brain as relevant factors. Garber and Flynn's own recent research project on the development of depression focused on predictors of adolescents' depression, such as their mothers' cognitive styles, mothers' parenting styles, and mothers' negative life events. They found some linkage between mothers' self-worth and that of the adolescents in their study. Mothers' attributional styles and negative life events were also found to be predictive.

As already noted, depression is one of the oldest topics in psychopathology. Since the time of Hippocrates, the principal scientific hypothesis was that some biological substrate (originally, black bile) was mainly responsible for this disorder. The study of depression in children and adolescents and of psychosocial hypotheses concerning its cause are relatively recent developments and ones in which clinical psychology researchers have had a prominent role. Intervention studies showing that specific changes in cognitive style were linked to changes in the prevalence of clinical depression would seem to be a particularly promising research strategy here.

Chapter 4, by Barlow, Bach, and Tracey, is mainly concerned with the covariance structure of anxiety and depression. It is well known that anxious people are often depressed, and vice versa, but what is the precise relationship between them? According to Barlow and his colleagues, statistical analysis confirms the existence of superordinate factors of positive and negative affect, as other researchers such as Lee Anna Clark and David Watson have suggested. Narrower psychometric factors are then found for depression and for different varieties of anxiety disorder, which all share the phenomenon of autonomic arousal. Barlow et al. also review literature on the causes of anxiety and depression and consider both psychosocial factors such as one's ability to control the environment and neurobiological aspects, including the hypothalamic–pituitary–adrenocortical axis.

Other researchers, such as Davidson (1992), have suggested the differential involvement of the left- and right-cerebral hemispheres in regulating affect. According to Davidson, the left-frontal hemisphere is more involved in elation and depression and the right-frontal hemisphere more in anxiety and relief from fear. It seems likely that we will be hearing a lot more about this new field of "affective neuroscience" over the next few decades.

The final chapter in this section of the book, by Schwartz and Russek (chap. 5), addresses the important issue of psychosocial factors in physical health. They report findings from a 35-year follow-up of individuals who participated in the Harvard Mastery of Stress Study. Eighty-seven percent of persons in this study who, when they were in college, rated their mothers as low on parental love and caring had diagnosed physical diseases at midlife, as compared with only 25% of subjects who had rated both parents as high on parental love and caring. Schwartz and Russek's chapter also includes an appendix about a "dynamical energy systems approach" that is sure to be controversial. It will be interesting to see, after several decades, whether they are correct. After all, they laughed at Edison!

ASSESSMENT

The assessment of psychopathology has been an important part of clinical psychology throughout its existence. In fact, before World War II, assessment was probably the main professional activity of clinical psychologists. The present book, being concerned mainly with future research issues, does not include chapters devoted to the standard assessment tools commonly used in the field and marketed commercially, such as the Wechsler Adult Intelligence Scale or the Minnesota Multiphasic Personality Inventory.

One of the assessment chapters was written by Lester Luborsky (chap. 6), still an active psychotherapy researcher after five decades in the field. In fact, in his chapter, Luborsky mentions that as a child, in 1926, he was taken to Witmer's psychological clinic at the University of Pennsylvania and given what was probably the Binet test. He says he was patted on the head and his mother reassured him that he would be fine, as indeed he turned out to be. Luborsky's present chapter deals with the assessment of processes observable within actual psychotherapy sessions. His measure of the *symptom-context theme* links events in the therapy session that reliably precede the emergence of a particular symptom, for example, stomach pain. His measures of a *core conflictual relationship theme* appear to assess Freud's original concept of transference. In his chapter, Luborsky demonstrates the interrater reliability of both measures and suggests uses to which they may be put in psychotherapy research.

The other chapter in this section, by McFall, Treat, and Viken (chap. 7), in my opinion does a service to clinical psychology by pointing out the major discrepancy between what passes for "cognitive" in the clinical area and what is denoted by the same word as understood by cognitive psychologists. Assessment procedures for depression such as that developed by Beck, and the therapies labeled "cognitive" and "cognitive–behavioral," tend to rely on the rather old-fashioned method of introspection, such as "What are your thoughts and feelings" or "Why do you think you failed that exam?" In ordinary (nonclinical) cognitive psychology, subjects are often not asked such questions at all. Instead, they are observed doing some task or engaging in some social activity, and a testable model is constructed of the hypothetical cognitive (and affective) processes that might underlie the observed performance. Experimental procedures are devised to test these hypotheses. Thus, to take a simple example, we need not ask subjects if they were mentally rehearsing a series of digits (such as a telephone number) they were asked to recall. Instead, we observe that there is a "primacy" effect in the serial learning curve, that is, they remember the earlier digits better than those in the middle of the list. This can be eliminated if we provide filler activities that would block such rehearsal in between the presentations of digits. Alternatively, we can teach young children who show no primacy effect in serial learning to engage in overt rehearsal, and we can show that this produces the same type of serial position curve seen with older children and adults. Clinical psychologists who are not accustomed to using such methods need to become more familiar with experimental research testing cognitive models. Their own investigations should greatly benefit from breaking down these barriers to intellectual exchange.

INTERVENTIONS

The National Institute of Mental Health (NIMH), founded at the end of World War II, is perhaps the most important single source of funding for research done by clinical psychologists and others in this field in the United States. Seligman's chapter (chap. 8) points out that its name might be considered a misnomer. Perhaps it should have been called the National Institute of Mental Illness, since most of the research it supports investigates psychopathology and how to treat it. Seligman argues convincingly that this Institute should devote more of its funds to supporting positive mental health and to preventive activities.

Seligman goes on to report two promising research activities aimed at promoting optimism and warding off depressive symptoms. The first of these studies selected a subgroup of a freshman class at the University of Pennsylvania with the most "pessimistic" scores on a questionnaire and thus at risk for depression in reaction to predictable life events such as poor performance on class exams. Half of these students were randomly assigned to workshops teaching them to be effective in disputing catastrophic thoughts and in other skills thought to be relevant in preventing depression. Initial follow-up findings showed that these workshops led to a 50% reduction in the rates of moderate to severe depressive symptoms compared with untreated controls.

Similarly, Seligman and his colleagues are carrying out research with school children in Philadelphia to try to prevent depressive symptoms. The children are selected on the basis of mild symptoms of depression and on the basis of parental fighting, both known to be risk factors for later depressive episodes. The children are randomly assigned to groups receiving either cognitive and behavioral skill training (using skits, cartoons, and role playing in a pleasant setting including refreshments) or to control groups. Like the workshops with college students, these done with children appeared to reduce the rate of moderate or severe depressive symptoms by about half. This brief chapter certainly whets the researcher's appetite to see the detailed versions of these studies, which are already beginning to appear in print.

Some of Seligman's recent speeches and writings echo those of a previous American Psychological Association president, George Albee, who emphasized prevention, but with some major differences. Albee's provocative rhetoric was based on a pessimistic appraisal of the efficacy of remedial approaches and the idea that there were never going to be enough therapists to go around. Albee also tended to reject biological approaches to psychopathology outright. Seligman is not just making speeches trying to convince us of the importance of prevention but is also producing research on this topic. In addition, Seligman's present research is firmly grounded in his previous experimental work with learned helplessness in animals. Unlike Albee, Seligman also advocates the use of pharmacological treatment approaches as well as psychological ones. Together with psychiatrist Donald F. Klein, he attempted to found an innovative electronic journal devoted to research on both kinds of intervention. As already noted, the present author agrees with Edward O. Wilson that what we need is "consilience" rather than competition across disciplines.

The third intervention chapter, by Foa and Franklin (chap. 10), continues with the theme of cognitive–behavioral treatment, in this case applied to obsessive–compulsive disorder (OCD). Foa and her colleagues have mounted an extensive program of controlled treatment outcome research on OCD, in both adults and children. The most essential parts of the psychological treatments they have found to be effective are exposure and response prevention, that is, exposure to stimuli or images that evoke obsessional thoughts and prevention of the compulsive responses that have habitually followed. More than the other investigators whose chapters appear in this volume, Foa and her colleagues are also quite interested in pharmacological treatments for OCD, for example, clomipramine and other serotonic antidepressants. Their present view is that both the psychological treatments and the pharmacological ones are effective against OCD, but there is insufficient research so far on how these treatments interact or whether there is some optimal way to combine them.

The final chapter in the intervention section is by Bradbury, Johnson, Lawrence, and Rogge (chap. 11) and concerns marital dysfunction. These investigators begin by pointing out some relevant general statistics. In the United States, about 90% of the population get married, but about half of these marriages end up in divorce. Marital therapy, for example, the behavioral couples therapy that has been the subject of controlled research by clinical psychologist Neil Jacobson and his colleagues, has established itself as having some efficacy. However, Bradbury et al. note that the effect sizes in marital therapy are relatively small, and consumer surveys have found the public to be more dissatisfied with the services of marriage counselors than with those of other mental health professionals. As a result of these facts, it is argued that our research agenda should focus on the prevention of marital dysfunction rather than its treatment, and should include longitudinal studies so that marital satisfaction could be tracked over time.

The treatments sampled in this chapter represent a strong bias toward cognitive–behavioral approaches, an area in which clinical psychology researchers have played a prominent role in recent years. There are other approaches with significant traditions of controlled outcome studies. Some of these could have been represented as well. For example, there is Hans Strupp's (1993) research on brief psychodynamically oriented psychotherapy. There is the type of "interpersonal psychotherapy" used successfully in treating depression in the NIMH clinical trials. There is also the example of applied behavior analysis as represented by O. Ivar Lovaas's studies of interventions with young children with autism (e.g., McEachin, Smith, & Lovaas, 1993). A final example might be the controlled studies of pharmacological interventions, such as C. Keith Conners's research on the effects of stimulant medications on children with attention deficit hyperactivity disorder (Conners & Eisenberg, 1963). There is simply not room in any single book to represent every such approach.

SERVICE DELIVERY

The final chapter, by Kihlstrom and Canter Kihlstrom (chap. 12), rounds out the book in considering clinical psychology as a field involving both science and practice. Many of the original doctoral students of Witmer's program at the University of Pennsylvania worked in schools, hospitals, and community clinics rather than universities. After World War II, the U.S. Veterans Administration (later the Department of Veterans Affairs) became the world's largest employer of clinical psychologists. In the last two decades, the modal clinical psychologist has become a psychotherapist in private practice. The livelihood of many such practitioners has been threatened by recent developments in managed care, which has come to be seen by many as "the enemy." Kihlstrom and Canter Kihlstrom describe this situation and indicate how they think clinical psychology can respond to it in an adaptive fashion. Using their knowledge of psychology and their research training, clinical psychologists cannot only maintain but also increase both their autonomy and the respect they receive both from colleagues and consumers.

All mental health practitioners have direct clinical experience. Primary care physicians, psychiatrists, and nurses have varying amounts of medical knowledge and training. Clinical psychologists are distinctive in their training in research, in quantitative methods, and in the behavioral sciences. They are also well read in the literature of psychopathology, assessment, and psychosocial interventions. Thus, no one is better prepared than a clinical psychologist to devise and study psychosocial interventions to determine their efficacy, effectiveness, and cost effectiveness. Psychologists must realize, however, that many of the activities involved in the assessment and treatment of mental health problems are shared by several professional groups. Cost factors dictate that those services that can be carried out by those with more modest levels of education and training be delegated to them.

REFERENCES

Conners, C. K., & Eisenberg, L. (1963). The effects of methylphenidate on symptomatology and learning in disturbed children. *American Journal of Psychiatry, 120*, 458–464.

Crick, F. (1990). *What mad pursuit?* New York: Basic Books.

Davidson, R. J. (1992). Anterior cerebral asymmetry and the nature of emotion. *Brain and Cognition, 20*, 125–151.

Hagerman, R. J. (1996). Physical and behavioral phenotype. In R. J. Hagerman & A. Cronister (Eds.), *Fragile X syndrome: Diagnosis, treatment, and research.* (2nd ed., pp. 3–87). Baltimore: Johns Hopkins University Press.

McEachin, J. J., Smith, T., & Lovaas, O. I. (1993). Long-term outcome for children with autism who received early intensive behavioral treatment. *American Journal on Mental Retardation, 97*, 359–372.

Routh, D. K. (in press). Hippocrates meets Democritus: A history of psychiatry and clinical psychology. In C. E. Walker (Vol. Ed.), *Foundations: Vol. 1.* M. Hersen & A. Bellak (Series Eds.), *Comprehensive clinical psychology.* Oxford, UK: Elsevier.

Sexton, V. S., & Hogan, J. D. (1992). Epilogue. In V. S. Sexton & J. D. Hogan (Eds.), *International psychology: Views from around the world* (pp. 467–477). Lincoln: University of Nebraska Press.

Strupp, H. (1993). The Vanderbilt psychotherapy studies: Synopsis. *Journal of Consulting and Clinical Psychology, 61*, 431–433.

Taylor, E. I. (1982). *William James on exceptional mental states: Reconstruction of the 1896 Lowell lectures.* New York: Scribner's.

Wilson, E. O. (1998a). *Consilience: The unity of knowledge.* New York: Knopf.

Wilson, E. O. (1998b, April). Integrated science and the coming century of the environment. *Science, 279*, 2048–2049.

Witmer, L. (1897). The organization of practical work in psychology. *Psychological Review, 4*, 116.

Witmer, L. (1907). Clinical psychology. *Psychological Clinic, 1*, 1–9.

I

CAUSES AND RISK FACTORS

1

IDENTIFYING GENETIC RISK FOR PSYCHOPATHOLOGY

WILLIAM G. IACONO

One of the most exciting developments in the life sciences in the last 20 years has been the ability to use molecular genetic techniques to search the human genome for genes that may predispose people to develop various forms of psychopathology. The identification of a predisposing gene has obvious etiologic significance. By understanding what the gene does, scientists should eventually be better able to discover how best to treat the afflicted and perhaps even how to minimize the chances that susceptible individuals succumb to the disorder. In the last decade, the popular press has repeatedly trumpeted research findings from the best science journals that have announced linkage between different chromosomal regions and various disorders, including schizophrenia, bipolar disorder, and alcoholism. However, despite all the optimism accompanying these reports, these findings have become notoriously difficult to replicate. Although it is likely that the genetic riddle underlying these disorders will eventually be solved, it is not clear that conventional molecular genetic research strategies will yield this solution any time soon.

The preparation of this chapter was supported in part by Grant MH49738 from the National Institute of Mental Health.

3

In this chapter, I will explore some of the reasons for this state of affairs. I will also examine how psychologists might improve the odds for success in the search for psychopathology-relevant genes. In the process, I hope to show that despite their lack of expertise in molecular biology, psychologists nevertheless have the opportunity to make important contributions to this research venture. For purposes of illustration, I will draw primarily from schizophrenia research, focusing on investigations carried out with collaborators in my laboratory. However, the themes and arguments developed here apply as well to virtually all of the major psychopathological disorders.[1]

WHY IS THE SEARCH FOR PSYCHOPATHOLOGY-RELATED GENES DIFFICULT?

The search for the gene for Huntington's disease (HD), a neurological condition determined by an autosomal dominant gene, provides a useful illustration in contrast to the problems encountered in the search for genes associated with psychopathology. With HD, the mode of transmission is known. Because the disease is 100% penetrant, all the gene carriers can be expected to succumb to the disease, which can be detected easily clinically, if the individual lives long enough. To demonstrate genetic linkage, one must show that a segment of DNA in a specific region of a chromosome is transmitted together with the disease from one generation to the next. Because those at risk for HD have often reproduced before it was known whether they were gene carriers, many with HD have children, 50% of whom can be expected to succumb to the disease.

Because psychopathology differs in many important ways from HD, gene finding in psychopathology research has been hampered by a variety of problems. In this section, I will note how some of these differences have stood in the way of progress, using as an illustration the problems that must be faced in the search for schizophrenia-relevant genes.

The Problem of Phenotype Definition

HD is easy to diagnose in symptomatic individuals, especially if it is known that the family history for the disease is positive. Hence, the phenotype for HD is relatively well defined, a situation that is quite different from that for schizophrenia.

Although the reliability of diagnosing schizophrenia is as high as that

---

[1]It is not an aim of this chapter to make the case that susceptibility to schizophrenia (or other forms of psychopathology) is heritable. Most serious investigators of this disorder find the evidence that genes play a role in the etiology of schizophrenia to be overwhelming (e.g., see Gottesman, 1991).

for the diagnosis for just about any form of psychopathology, it still eludes precise definition. The operational criteria found in our current diagnostic systems, *ICD-10* (International Classification of Diseases, 10th ed.; World Health Organization, 1992) and the *Diagnostic and Statistical Manual of Mental Disorders* (4th ed.; *DSM–IV*; American Psychiatric Association, 1994), as well as in *DSM–IV*'s immediate predecessors, the third edition and third revised edition (*DSM–III* and *DSM–III–R*; American Psychiatric Association, 1980, 1987), are all similar but not identical, and therefore identify overlapping but different groups of individuals as affected. Exactly what constitutes the schizophrenia "spectrum," that is, the collection of disorders that shares the genetic diathesis for schizophrenia, is not agreed on. The one candidate spectrum disorder about which there is the most agreement, schizotypal personality disorder, is both less reliably diagnosed and more difficult to define than schizophrenia. Knowing that one member of a family has a diagnosis of schizophrenia does not make it certain that other family members showing signs of psychological disturbance have either schizophrenia or one of its spectrum disorders, a fact that makes blinded assessment of psychopathology and the inclusion of nonpsychiatric comparison groups essential to family studies of schizophrenia.

The resulting ambiguity regarding the exact nature of the phenotype adds considerable noise to efforts to identify genetic material linked to the disorder. For instance, if a DNA marker fails to be associated with occurrences of schizophrenia in a given family, it can be either because the marker is not linked to schizophrenia or because one or more members of the family constitute either a false positive (i.e., an individual identified as having the phenotype who in fact does not have schizophrenia or a spectrum disorder) or a false negative (i.e., an individual who should have been identified as a case but who was not). Of the two types of error, false positives have typically been seen as perhaps more serious, because they tend to undermine linkage by showing that the appearance of the disorder is not appropriately "marked" by the DNA. False negatives are not seen as damaging because modeling parameters can be adjusted to account for the incomplete penetrance of the disorder. However, it is the inability to identify gene carriers, not the false identification of cases, that makes psychopathology linkage research extremely difficult, because most families contain no more than one affected member, a phenomenon that makes it impossible to use these typical families in any linkage study.

Although we should take heart in the success of other gene searches for complex diseases (like Alzheimer's dementia or Parkinson's disease), which, like schizophrenia, are difficult to define or are heterogeneous, schizophrenia differs from these other disorders in two important respects: (a) We do not know anything definitive about the pathophysiology of schizophrenia, and (b) we have no objective means (like microscopic evidence of neurofibrillary tangles or substantia nigra degeneration) to ensure that any given individual actually has or does not have the disorder.

Identifying Gene Carriers

Gene carriers for HD are easy to identify, because eventually almost all of them can be expected to develop the disorder. As noted earlier, gene carriers for schizophrenia are difficult to identify, in part because the phenotype cannot be precisely defined. However, there is another, perhaps more serious issue regarding the difficulty identifying those who carry genetic risk for schizophrenia.

We know from behavior genetic studies of a wide variety of psychopathological afflictions that disorder concordance rates in identical twins are well under 100%. For instance, in schizophrenia research, the monozygotic (MZ) twin concordance rate is just under 50% (Gottesman, Shields, & Hanson, 1982). This means that most of the time, those who possess the hypothesized genotype for susceptibility to schizophrenia do not express the phenotype and cannot be identified through clinical assessment. It is possible to assume that in MZ twins discordant for schizophrenia, the observed disorder represents a form of schizophrenia for which genes play no role. The work of Gottesman and Bertelsen (1989), however, renders this conclusion unlikely. They followed up the offspring of identical twins discordant for schizophrenia and found that the risk for schizophrenia was virtually identical for both the clinically affected and unaffected twins. The morbid risk for schizophrenia in both offspring groups was 17%, substantially higher than the comparison group rate of 2%. This investigation thus indicated that the absence of the schizophrenia phenotype was consistent with being a gene carrier for this disorder.

In Gottesman and Bertelsen's (1989) study, unaffected gene carriers could be identified by virtue of their having a cotwin with schizophrenia. Because most of those with this illness do not have identical twins, there is no way to identify who among their unaffected biological relatives is at genetic risk.

Reproductive Fitness

Only about 20% of those with schizophrenia have even one first-degree biological relative with the disorder (Gottesman et al., 1982, p. 98). This finding, coupled with the fact that many of these relatives are nevertheless likely to be gene carriers, means that although they are potentially informative, most families of schizophrenia patients cannot be used to study genetic linkage because it is not possible to determine if genetic material is passed on with the disorder if only one member of the family is affected. This means that family studies of schizophrenia that look for linkage must concentrate their efforts on "multiplex" families, those with many affected members. For schizophrenia, these families are the exception rather than the rule, a fact that leaves open the question of how representative they are of schizophrenia generally. Their rarity also often leads to the use of small samples, a fact that no doubt contributes to failures to consistently show a linkage effect from study to study when the genetic effect size is small (see, e.g., Gershon & Cloninger, 1994).

Genetic Heterogeneity

Although schizophrenia shows considerable heterogeneity in phenomenology, course, and treatment response, this variability does not necessarily translate into etiologic heterogeneity. Nevertheless, many schizophrenia scientists believe it is likely that there exists more than one variant of schizophrenia and that schizophrenia may be more analogous to epilepsy or mental retardation than it is to HD. The possibility that genetic variants of schizophrenia exist further complicates and adds noise to linkage studies, because (a) there is no a priori means for determining whether a given family has one genetic variant or another, and (b) each variant would be expected to show different linkage.

Mode of Transmission

The search for the HD gene was greatly facilitated by knowing how it was genetically transmitted. We do not know how schizophrenia risk is inherited, except to say that it is unlikely that a single gene acting alone could account for the majority of cases (e.g., McGue & Gottesman, 1989). If vulnerability to schizophrenia is polygenic, with the additive effect of many genes determining who is affected, then investigations based on currently available techniques may fail to find linkage. If a mixed model of genetic transmission in which there exists at least one gene of major effect (i.e., a gene that accounts for a substantial fraction of the variance) could be shown to account for schizophrenia risk, linkage studies would be appropriate. The search for schizophrenia-relevant genes would be facilitated if an empirically supported model for the mechanism of transmission was available and that model was consistent with the existence of a hypothetical major gene.

HOW TO FACILITATE THE SEARCH

It is not my intent to argue that current linkage studies are unlikely ever to be fruitful or that there is any one solution to the many problems inherent to this line of research. Indeed, there is reason to be optimistic that as molecular and quantitative genetic methodology is improved, we will eventually succeed in this formidable enterprise (see, e.g., Sherman et al., 1997). Instead, it is my position that it is possible to facilitate the search for psychopathology-relevant genes by adopting an approach that complements existing methods and that is supported by a considerable empirical literature (especially for schizophrenia). This complementary approach is not proposed as a panacea, and I acknowledge at the outset that it is not without its own limitations, some of which are noted below.

As highlighted in the preceding sections, impediments to linkage studies include poor phenotype definition, inability to identify gene carriers who show no clinical signs of manifest illness, the absence of affected relatives, possible genetic heterogeneity, and uncertainty regarding the likely mode of genetic transmission. All of these problems could be dealt with if it were possible to reliably identify those vulnerable for psychopathology without having to rely on the presence of manifest symptomatology. In this section, I will highlight how we might accomplish this ambitious objective.

The Endophenotype

Ideally, what is needed is the ability to identify the "endophenotype," some measurable endogenous quality of the individual that is itself a product of the psychopathology predisposing genotype. The concept of the endophenotype, a term coined by John and Lewis (1966), was introduced to psychopathology researchers by Gottesman and Shields (1972). Technically, it refers to some biological attribute, like a biochemical detectable in body fluids, that reflects the effect of the gene. An example would be the amount of phenylalanine in those with the genes for phenylketonuria (PKU). Because of their inability to metabolize this amino acid, homozygotes have high levels of this substance, heterozygotes have elevated levels, and nongene carriers have low levels. In this chapter, I have followed the lead of Gottesman and Shields (1972), who expanded the concept of the endophenotype to include more indirect indicators of the gene's presence, including those derivable from behavioral measures.

The desirability of identifying such an attribute has been noted repeatedly by schizophrenia researchers (e.g., Erlenmeyer-Kimling, 1987; Gottesman & Shields, 1972; Iacono & Clementz, 1993; Iacono & Ficken, 1989; Keefe, Silverman, Siever, & Cornblatt, 1991; Meehl, 1990). When the endophenotype is present, the odds that an individual is at genetic risk are greatly enhanced. The search for endophenotypes assumes that susceptibility genes for psychopathology are active or "switched on" before manifest symptoms appear. Fortunately, there is ample evidence of support for this assumption, especially as it is applied to the study of schizophrenia. The ideal qualities of an endophenotype are summarized in Exhibit 1.

EXHIBIT 1
Criteria for Evaluating Variables as Candidate Endophenotypes for Psychopathology

Identifiable deviation
Low base rate in the general population
Specific to a diagnostic subgroup
Show properties of a trait
   Retest stability in affected and at-risk individuals
   Present in remission
Identify at-risk individuals without manifest psychopathology
   Adults
   Children
Predict who develops psychopathology
Family studies show:
   Transmissible—runs in families
      Present in well relatives
      Absent in relatives with unrelated disorders
      Present in relatives with related disorders
      Evidence for simple pattern of genetic transmission

The endophenotype represents a deviation in some psychologically relevant attribute that typically cannot be identified through routine clinical assessment or observation. Examples might include, but are not limited to, high scores on inventories designed to measure psychopathology-relevant traits (e.g., schizotypy questionnaires), a psychophysiological deviation (e.g., an electroencephalogram [EEG] abnormality), or an anatomical variant (e.g., ventricular enlargement). For the attribute to have any utility as an endophenotype, it should occur infrequently in the general population and be relatively specific to a diagnostic subgroup. It is not necessary that all individuals with a disorder have the endophenotype, in part because the disorder may be etiologically heterogeneous. Likewise, because different disorders may share etiologic roots in common (e.g., be part of a spectrum), it is not necessary that the endophenotype appear in only those with a single diagnosis. However, if it were to appear commonly in two different, unrelated disorders (e.g., schizophrenia and bipolar disorder), it would fail to serve the purpose of identifying genetic risk for one of them.

The endophenotype should identify individuals at risk, including adults without manifest psychopathology (e.g., the siblings and parents of affected individuals) and children (e.g., their offspring) who have yet to enter the age of risk but who ultimately could be expected to succumb to their genetic predisposition. Longitudinal studies of both adults and children would help establish the ability of the endophenotype to predict who succumbs to disorder. Because little is known about the stability of expression of candidate endophenotypes from childhood through adulthood, caution is required before a deviation associated with genetic risk in adults is applied as though it has similar significance in children.

The endophenotype should have trait properties. Although it need not be thought of as immutable, ideally it should be stable over time in both at-risk and affected individuals, and it should be present in formerly affected persons now in remission.

A candidate endophenotype could satisfy all of the requirements listed thus far and yet not actually be associated with genetic risk for psychopathology. For instance, assume that maternal exposure to influenza during the second trimester of fetal development increased one's risk for developing Disorder X and also resulted in an EEG abnormality detectable at age 13. An environmental factor would thus account for both heightened risk and the presence of a psychophysiological deviation. If this deviation was uncommon in the general population, occurred mainly in those with Disorder X, identified those who eventually develop the disorder, and was consistently observed over repeated occasions, including during acute episodes and remission, all of the criteria enumerated thus far would be met. However, genes would account for none of them. A variable with these properties would nevertheless serve as a marker of vulnerability for this disorder. Having such a marker would obviously have enormous value, but it would not assist in the identification of gene carriers.

The remaining criteria in Exhibit 1, which require carrying out family studies, help establish the link between the candidate endophenotype and genetic risk. The endophenotype should show evidence of genetic transmission by appearing in the relatives of probands who have the disorder of interest. Because many of these relatives would be unaffected gene carriers, well relatives should be considerably more likely than "normal" people to possess the trait. As partial proof that the endophenotype is "marking" those with the disorder, all individuals in the family with the disorder (or one of its spectrum variants) should have the endophenotype. Likewise, members of the family with unrelated disorders, who would thus not necessarily possess the genotype, would not be expected to show the endophenotype. Finally, the ideal endophenotype will itself show a simple pattern of genetic transmission, suggesting the presence of a major gene. If neither the manifest disorder nor the characteristic marking its genotype showed such a pattern, the probability that linkage to the genotype could be demonstrated would be greatly reduced.

Types of Endophenotypes

Because there are different ways in which genes are likely to influence the development of risk for psychopathology, endophenotypes are likely to index different types of genetic risk. In one type, the endophenotype identifies an important illness-related gene. Hypothesized endophenotypes of schizophrenia, which many believe to be a brain disease, may be of this type.

It is also possible for the endophenotype to index the presence of an extreme deviation on a genetically influenced dimension that underlies a disorder, or even that is common to several disorders. For instance, deficits in inhibitory control or working memory may constitute part of the genetic predisposition for antisocial personality and substance use disorders. In such a case, the endophenotype would not identify an illness gene but the presence of an extreme variant of a psychological trait or heritable ability that increases risk for these forms of psychopathology. Molecular genetic studies of continuously distributed quantitative traits have been able to identify so-called quantitative trait loci in plants, and a recent report demonstrated the promise of these techniques for behavioral research by identifying loci that may influence emotionality in the mouse (Flint et al., 1995). Applying this technology to human traits would have a greater probability of payoff if there were endophenotypic indicators of the traits.

Advantages of Having an Endophenotype

An endophenotype associated with genetic risk for a disorder would confer a number of benefits. Reliance on the *DSM* approach for identifying affected individuals would be lessened. In ambiguous diagnostic cases, the presence or absence of the endophenotype could be used to improve diagnostic accuracy. Indeed, having an endophenotype would provide a tool for refining the diagnosis; the endophenotype would become the criterion against which the validity of the diagnostic criteria could be measured. It could also be used to assess and reduce heterogeneity. For instance, if only a third of those with a disorder had the endophenotype, etiologic homogeneity would be increased by selecting that third for study. The form the endophenotype takes should provide clues for understanding the etiology of the disorder. Ultimately, it could also serve to assist in the development of preventive interventions that could be targeted at those deemed at risk because they have the endophenotype.

The chief advantage of the endophenotype is that it provides a means for identifying gene carriers, thus simplifying the search for susceptibility genes. Much of the remainder of this chapter will be devoted to showing that the deviant eye tracking of schizophrenia patients appears to be an endophenotype for this illness. Although patients with schizophrenia often do not reproduce, and although they have few affected relatives on average, they do have relatives (they all have parents and most have siblings), and typically their relatives have intact ocular motor systems. The eye tracking of these individuals can be assessed, and the quality of their performance can be used as a proxy for manifest schizophrenia to assist in the search for schizophrenia-related genes.

EYE TRACKING IN SCHIZOPHRENIA

If a person follows a slowly moving target (such as a swinging pendulum) accurately, that person's eye movements should reproduce target motion. Individuals accomplish this task by generating smooth pursuit oculomotion, which locks the eyes on target, matching its velocity. Those who do not perform well have difficulty generating smooth, continuous movements with their eyes. Instead, their tracking contains many saccades, or abrupt, discontinuous movements of the eyes, that often represent an attempt to correct for position error when the pursuit system lags too far behind the target. Performance on this simple task and its variants takes as little as 30 seconds to complete and is easily quantified using techniques with well-documented validity (e.g., see Clementz, Iacono, & Grove, 1996).

In the last 25 years, over 400 published articles on eye tracking in schizophrenia have appeared in the scientific literature. A comprehensive evaluation of these reports is beyond the scope of this chapter. However, recent reviews (Iacono, 1993; Iacono & Clementz, 1993; Levy, Holzman, Matthysse, & Mendell, 1993) support the following conclusions:

- The ability to perform pursuit tracking tasks is a trait that is relatively stable over time in both normal and schizophrenia subjects.
- The rate of deviant tracking among those with schizophrenia is substantially higher than normal.
- The unaffected first-degree biological relatives of schizophrenia patients have been shown repeatedly in laboratories around the world to have difficulty with pursuit tasks.
- Although the findings regarding the ability of patients with mood disorders to produce pursuit eye movements are mixed, it is evident that the first-degree biological relatives of mood disorder patients do not show eye-tracking dysfunction.

These findings suggest that deviant eye tracking is a strong candidate endophenotype for schizophrenia. But could it reflect the influence of a major locus genotype?

Modeling the Genetic Transmission of Eye-Tracking Dysfunction

Evidence of Admixture

For a polygenic trait reflecting the additive influence of multiple genes of roughly equivalent effect, the biological relatives of schizophrenia probands would be expected to produce a normal distribution of eye-tracking scores. If eye-tracking dysfunction reflects a single gene influence on schizophrenia risk, then one might expect this quantitative trait to be distributed as a mixture of normal distributions rather than as a single normal distribution among the relatives of those with schizophrenia. This expectation follows because those with and without the genotype would belong to different groups, each with a distinctly different, although perhaps overlapping, performance distribution.

The IQ scores of the offspring of parents who are carriers of the recessive gene for PKU provide an illustration of this effect (Holtzman, Kronmal, van Doorninck, Azen, & Koch, 1986). The PKU infant, lacking a liver enzyme, cannot metabolize phenylalanine, a common amino acid, leading to irreversible brain damage unless the intake of foods containing this substance is restricted early in life. Those offspring without a double dose of the gene show normally distributed IQ scores covering the normal range. By contrast, those carrying the recessive gene pair have substantially lower IQs on average. The distribution of their IQs overlaps that of their unaffected siblings, with those affected who received dietary treatment having the greatest likelihood of obtaining normal scores. The resulting distribution of IQs is thus bimodal, with affected individuals concentrated in the lower IQ mode.

What form does the distribution of eye-tracking performance data take? To answer this question, my colleagues and I examined the distributions of the eye-tracking scores of schizophrenia probands and their first-degree relatives in two different studies using families drawn from different regions of North America—British Columbia (Canada), Minnesota, and New York. The data were evaluated using admixture analysis, a statistical procedure that can be used to determine if the resulting distributions are better accounted for by one or multiple mixing normal distributions. In the first of these studies, a mixture of two distributions was evident for both schizophrenia patients and their relatives (Iacono, Moreau, Beiser, Fleming, & Lin, 1992). Bipolar probands with psychotic features and their first-degree relatives were also included in this investigation. Neither of these groups showed admixture, and their eye tracking did not differ from that of a normal comparison group. Hence, the observed effects appeared to be specific to schizophrenia families. A second study replicated the effects observed by Iacono et al. (1992) for schizophrenia patients and their relatives (Clementz, Grove, Iacono, & Sweeney, 1992).

Other investigators have reported similar findings. Blackwood, St. Clair, Muir, and Duffy (1991) showed that the eye tracking of schizophrenia patients and their unaffected relatives was bimodal. Gibbons et al. (1984) carried out an admixture analysis on a combined group consisting of the relatives of schizophrenia patients, the relatives of patients without schizophrenia, and normal individuals. After demonstrating that the data could be accounted for by a mixture of two distributions, they showed that 72% of those in the component associated with deviant eye tracking were schizophrenia relatives. Three other investigations have reported that the distributions of eye-tracking data from schizophrenia patients suggest the existence of two mixing distributions (Ross, Ochs, Pandurangi, Thacker, & Kendler, 1996; Ross et al., 1997; Sweeney et al., 1993). Hence, admixture in the eye tracking of these patients and/or their relatives has been demonstrated in seven different investigations.

These findings in the relatives of schizophrenia probands are consistent with the hypothesis that a major locus gene affects eye tracking. The finding of admixture in the patients themselves suggests the existence of two schizophrenia groups, one of which has deviant tracking. These data thus offer some empirical support for the conjecture that schizophrenia is etiologically heterogeneous, and that deviant eye tracking is likely to contribute to our understanding of genetic susceptibility for only a subgroup of patients. Indeed, the data of Iacono et al. (1992) and Clementz et al. (1992) suggest that only about 50–60% of schizophrenia families contain at least one member with eye-tracking dysfunction. Findings from these investigators also indicated that probands with deviant pursuit tend to have relatives with similar eye-tracking performance, a finding that is consistent with the supposition that this trait runs in families (Iacono et al., 1992).

Fitting Genetic Models to Eye-Tracking Data

To further evaluate the possibility that a single gene is responsible for some substantial portion of the variance in eye-tracking performance, my colleagues and I carried out a complex segregation analysis using pooled data from Iacono et al. (1992) and Clementz et al. (1992). This is a statistical procedure used to evaluate the mode of inheritance of a particular phenotype by testing the fit of competing genetic models to family data. Segregation analysis is especially well suited to elucidate single-gene effects.

A more complete explication of the technique and the results can be found elsewhere (Grove, Clementz, Iacono, & Katsanis, 1992; Grove & Iacono, 1994; Iacono & Clementz, 1993). In brief, three major genetic models were fit to the data: (a) a mixed model, positing the existence of a Mendelian major gene and polygenes; (b) a model in which a Mendelian major gene acts alone; and (c) a model in which polygenes act alone. The model-fitting results showed that only the first of these models provided an acceptable fit to the data. Although these results do not confirm the mixed model, they do clearly refute the other two models. Hence, the results of the segregation analysis suggest that there are both single-gene and polygenic effects on eye tracking. The hypothetical major gene in the mixed model accounted for 68% of the variance in eye tracking and tended toward recessivity.

Holzman, Matthysse, and their colleagues (Holzman et al., 1988; Matthysse, Holzman, & Lange, 1986) have also shown, in two independent samples, that the smooth pursuit eye tracking of families with schizophrenia fits a quantitative model suggesting that a major gene accounts for much of the variance in eye-tracking performance. Although there are important differences in the findings of these researchers and those of Clementz, Grove, and Iacono (see Iacono & Clementz, 1993, for a discussion of these differences), it is important to note that different research teams using different populations and methods have converged on a common conclusion, namely, that a single gene may play a significant role in the regulation of eye-tracking performance in families with schizophrenia.

These findings receive further support from Arolt et al. (1996). Following the lead of other investigators who found evidence supporting linkage of schizophrenia to chromosome 6 (Moises et al., 1995; Schwab et al., 1995; Straub et al., 1995; Wang et al., 1995), Arolt et al. examined whether eye tracking is linked to DNA markers on this chromosome. Such linkage was indeed found, making this the first study to demonstrate such an effect for a schizophrenia endophenotype and adding yet another study to the empirical literature that suggests a single gene is partly responsible for eye-tracking performance.

Taken in the aggregate, these findings suggest that in the families of schizophrenia patients, (a) the distribution of eye-tracking data suggests two mixing distributions, (b) eye-tracking data fit genetic models positing the action of a major gene, and (c) eye-tracking performance is linked to genetic material on chromosome 6. These are provocative findings that, like the recent linkage studies of schizophrenia that reported positive results (Moises et al., 1995; Schwab et al., 1995; Straub et al., 1995; Wang et al., 1995), warrant replication and extension.[2]

Further Enhancement of the Phenotype

A goal of this chapter is to show that scientists may be able to move beyond using manifest symptoms of psychopathology to identify genetic susceptibility to the disorder. Identifying candidate endophenotypes provides an example of our ability to refine a phenotype through the "bootstraps effect" (Cronbach & Meehl, 1955). Beginning with an imperfect index of schizophrenia risk, one can develop means for identifying risk (the endophenotype) that are better than the criterion phenotype (the diagnosis) used to evaluate the construct validity of the endophenotype.

---

[2]Although these linkage studies are of considerable interest when considered together, they do not confirm linkage between schizophrenia and genetic markers on chromosome 6. These investigations did not all report linkage to the exact same regions of this chromosome, nor did they all successfully fit the same genetic models to their data, and some of the studies reported in this issue of *Nature Genetics* ruled out linkage between areas of chromosome 6 and schizophrenia for which the other investigations reported linkage. Also, although Arolt et al. (1996) found linkage for eye tracking on this chromosome, they did not find linkage for schizophrenia in the families they studied.

Eye tracking seems to have a solid footing as an endophenotype for schizophrenia risk. But can more be done to enhance phenotype definition? Findings from a variety of studies suggest that the answer to this question is yes.

Holzman and his associates (e.g., Holzman et al., 1988) have relied on eye-tracking data to advance a pleiotropic (one gene with multiple, different manifestations) model of schizophrenia in which the genotype is posited to express itself as manifest schizophrenia, deviant smooth pursuit, or both. This pleiotropic model followed logically from family data in which the schizophrenia probands did not show evidence of eye-tracking dysfunction, but their relatives did. A similar finding was reported by Iacono et al. (1992). These results leave open the notion that there may exist other manifestations of the genotype besides schizophrenia and deviant tracking. Were such a pleiotropic gene to exist, then a multivariate approach, relying on several endophenotypes simultaneously, may have the greatest likelihood of assisting in the search for schizophrenia-related genes (e.g., see Erlenmeyer-Kimling, 1987; Grove et al., 1991; Iacono & Grove, 1993).

Several studies from our laboratory suggest that schizophrenia patients and their relatives with eye-tracking dysfunction differ from those with normal pursuit in several ways. For instance, schizophrenia patients with deviant tracking tend to show impairment on conventional neuropsychological tests that putatively tap frontal lobe functioning (Katsanis & Iacono, 1991), a finding that has also been reported by others using both conventional and experimental neuropsychological tests (Bartfai, Levander, Nyback, Berggren, & Schalling, 1985; Grawe & Levander, 1995; Litman et al., 1991; Malaspina et al., 1994; Scarone, Gambini, Hafele, Bellodi, & Smeraldi, 1987; Van den Bosch, Rozendaal, & Mol, 1987). Katsanis and Iacono (1991), as have other investigators (Ross, Thaker, et al. 1996; Sweeney et al., 1994; Sweeney, Haas, & Li, 1992), also found negative symptoms of schizophrenia to be associated with poor tracking. The eye-tracking scores of the first-degree relatives of schizophrenia probands are positively correlated with the presence of schizophrenia-spectrum personality disorders (Clementz, Reid, McDowell, & Cadenhead, 1995; Thaker, Cassady, Adami, Moran, & Ross, 1996) and indexes of schizotypy associated with social–interpersonal oddities (Clementz et al., 1992; Clementz, Sweeney, Hirt, & Haas, 1991; Grove et al., 1991). Other researchers have shown that schizotypal personality disorder is associated with eye-tracking dysfunction (Siever et al., 1994), perhaps only for those schizotypal individuals who also have relatives with schizophrenia (Thaker et al., 1996). Attentional dysfunction, as measured by a degraded stimulus version of the continuous performance test, also appears to be associated with poor eye tracking (Grove et al., 1991). These findings led Iacono and Grove (1993) to present a model of schizophrenia in which a major gene is responsible in part for a number of abnormalities commonly observed in those with schizophrenia and their families, including the presence of negative symptoms in affected individuals, irregular eye tracking, social–interpersonal schizotypy, neuropsychological deficits, and attentional dysfunction.

There are many reports, just in the last 10 years, indicating that the relatives of schizophrenia patients are impaired on a wide variety of tasks that can easily be administered in psychological laboratories, including working memory (Park, Holzman, & Goldman-Rakic, 1995), antisaccadic eye movement tasks in which subjects are asked to move their eyes in the opposite direction of target movement (Clementz, McDowell, & Zisook, 1994; Katsanis, Kortenkamp, Iacono, & Grove, 1997), conventional neuropsychological tests (Cannon et al., 1994; Faraone et al., 1995; Keefe et al., 1994), the p50 wave of the cerebral event-related potential (Freedman et al., 1997), indexes of thought disorder (Kinney et al., 1997), and backward masking (Green, Nuechterlein, & Breitmeyer, 1997). It remains to be determined whether performance on these tasks represents alternative manifestations of the hypothesized genetic factor influencing eye tracking and schizophrenia. Should one or more of these measures appear to be associated with schizophrenia and eye tracking, then they can be added to the multivariate definition of the phenotype. If they do not show such an association, perhaps they will be useful for the identification of genetic risk in the families for which eye tracking does not appear to be informative.

CONCLUSION

The research approach outlined here follows from some simple theoretical considerations about psychopathology generally (and specifically about schizophrenia) that are data driven. The first is that there is a genetic predisposition for many forms of psychopathology. The second is that this genetic susceptibility is detectable in advance of the onset of symptoms of the disorder, and that it is in fact detectable in individuals at genetic risk who will never develop the disorder. These notions provide the rationale for the research approach, the goal of which is to identify gene carriers and eventually psychopathology-related genes.

Exactly where to begin the search for the endophenotype—that is, what variables one decides are likely candidates—is also driven by theoretical considerations. However, because most theories of psychopathology are not well supported by empirical findings (certainly not as well as the hypothesis that there is a genetic diathesis for many forms of psychopathology), considerable good fortune will be required to develop reasonable candidate endophenotypes. For this reason, replication is important to the search process, and this replicability should extend to most of the endophenotype criteria listed in Exhibit 1. In addition, the candidate endophenotype should inform us about the nature of the psychopathology being studied, such that its existence can be used to generate testable hypotheses about etiology and associated features.

REFERENCES

American Psychiatric Association. (1980). *Diagnostic and statistical manual of mental disorders* (3rd ed.). Washington, DC: Author.

American Psychiatric Association. (1987). *Diagnostic and statistical manual of mental disorders* (3rd ed., rev.). Washington, DC: Author.

American Psychiatric Association. (1994). *Diagnostic and statistical manual of mental disorders* (4th ed.). Washington, DC: Author.

Arolt, V., Lencer, R., Nolte, A., Muller-Myhsok, B., Purmann, S., Schurmann, M., Leutelt, J., Pinnow, M., & Schwinger, E. (1996). Eye tracking dysfunction is a putative phenotypic susceptibility marker of schizophrenia and maps to a locus on chromosome 6p in families with multiple occurrence of the disease. *American Journal of Medical Genetics (Neuropsychiatric Genetics), 67*, 564–579.

Bartfai, A., Levander, S. E., Nyback, H., Berggren, B.-M., & Schalling, D. (1985). Smooth pursuit eye tracking, neuropsychological test performance, and computed tomography in schizophrenia. *Psychiatry Research, 15*, 49–62.

Blackwood, D. H. R., St. Clair, D. M., Muir, W. J., & Duffy, J. C. (1991). Auditory P300 and eye tracking dysfunction in schizophrenic pedigrees. *Archives of General Psychiatry, 48*, 899–909.

Cannon, T. D., Zorilla, L. E., Shtasel, D., Gur, R. E., Gur, R. C., Marco, E. J., Moberg, P., & Price, R. A. (1994). Neuropsychological functioning in siblings discordant for schizophrenia and healthy volunteers. *Archives of General Psychiatry, 51*, 651–661.

Clementz, B. A., Grove, W. M., Iacono, W. G., & Sweeney, J. A. (1992). Smooth-pursuit eye movement dysfunction and liability for schizophrenia: Implications for genetic modeling. *Journal of Abnormal Psychology, 101*, 117–129.

Clementz, B. A., Iacono, W. G., & Grove, W. M. (1996). The construct validity of root-mean-square error for quantifying smooth-pursuit eye tracking abnormalities in schizophrenia. *Biological Psychiatry, 39*, 448–450.

Clementz, B. A., McDowell, J. E., & Zisook, S. (1994). Saccadic system functioning among schizophrenia patients and their first degree biological relatives. *Journal of Abnormal Psychology, 103*, 277–287.

Clementz, B. A., Reid, S. A., McDowell, J. E., & Cadenhead, K. S. (1995). Abnormality of smooth pursuit eye movement initiation: Specificity to the schizophrenia spectrum? *Psychophysiology, 32*, 130–134.

Clementz, B. A., Sweeney, J. A., Hirt, M., & Haas, G. (1991). Phenotypic correlations between oculomotor functioning and schizophrenia-related characteristics in relatives of schizophrenic probands. *Psychophysiology, 28*, 570–578.

Cronbach, L. J., & Meehl, P. E. (1955). Construct validity in psychological tests. *Psychological Bulletin, 52,* 281–302.

Erlenmeyer-Kimling, N. (1987). Biological markers for the liability to schizophrenia. In H. Helmschen & F. A. Henn (Eds.), *Biological perspective of schizophrenia* (pp. 33–56). New York: Wiley.

Faraone, S. V., Seidman, L. J., Kremen, W. S., Pepple, J. R., Lyons, M. J., & Tsuang, M. T. (1995). Neuropsychological functioning among the nonpsychotic relatives of schizophrenic patients: A diagnostic efficiency analysis. *Journal of Abnormal Psychology, 104,* 286–304.

Flint, J., Corley, R., DeFries, J. C., Fulker, D. W., Gray, J. A., Miller, S., & Collins, A. C. (1995). A simple genetic basis for a complex psychological trait in laboratory mice. *Science, 269,* 1432–1435.

Freedman, R., Coon, H., Myles-Worsley, M., Orr-Urteger, A., Olincy, A., Davis, A., Polymeropoulos, M., Holk, J., Hopkins, J., Hoff, M., Rosenthal, J., Waldo, M. C., Reimherr, F., Wender, P., Yaw, J., Young, D. A., Breese, C. R., Adams, C., Patterson, D., Adler, L. E., Kruglyak, L., Leonard, S., & Byerley, W. (1997). Linkage of a neuropsychological deficit in schizophrenia to a chromosome 15 locus. *Proceedings of the National Academy of Sciences, 94,* 587–592.

Gershon, E. S., & Cloninger, C. R. (1994). *Genetic approaches to mental disorders.* Washington, DC: American Psychiatric Press.

Gibbons, R. D., Dorus, E., Ostrow, D. G., Pandey, G. N., Davis, J. M., & Levy, D. L. (1984). Mixture distribution in psychiatric research. *Biological Psychiatry, 19,* 935–961.

Gottesman, I. I. (1991). *Schizophrenia genesis: The origins of madness.* New York: Freeman.

Gottesman, I. I., & Bertelsen, A. (1989). Confirming unexpressed genotypes for schizophrenia: Risks in the offspring of Fisher's Danish identical and fraternal twins. *Archives of General Psychiatry, 46,* 867–872.

Gottesman, I. I., & Shields, J. (1972). *Schizophrenia and genetics: A twin study vantage point.* New York: Academic Press.

Gottesman, I. I., Shields, J., & Hanson, D. (1982). *Schizophrenia: The epigenetic puzzle.* New York: Cambridge University Press.

Grawe, R. W., & Levander, S. (1995). Smooth pursuit eye movements and neuropsychological impairments in schizophrenia. *Acta Psychiatrica Scandinavica, 92,* 108–114.

Green, M. F., Nuechterlein, K. H., & Breitmeyer, B. (1997). Backward masking performance in unaffected siblings of schizophrenic patients: Evidence for a vulnerability indicator. *Archives of General Psychiatry, 54,* 465–472.

Grove, W. M., Clementz, B. A., Iacono, W. G., & Katsanis, J. (1992). Smooth pursuit ocular motor dysfunction in schizophrenia: Evidence for a major gene. *American Journal of Psychiatry, 149,* 1362–1368.

Grove, W. M., & Iacono, W. G. (1994). Comment on Levy et al. "Eye tracking and schizophrenia: A critical perspective." *Schizophrenia Bulletin, 20*, 781–786.

Grove, W. M., Lebow, B. S., Clementz, B. A., Cerri, A., Medus, C., & Iacono, W. G. (1991). Familial prevalence and co-aggregation of schizotypy indicators: A multitrait family study. *Journal of Abnormal Psychology, 100*, 115–121.

Holtzman, N. A., Kronmal, R. A., van Doorninck, W., Azen, C., & Koch, R. (1986). Effect of age at loss of dietary control on intellectual performance and behavior of children with phenylketonuria. *New England Journal of Medicine, 314*, 593–598.

Holzman, P. S., Kringlen, E., Matthysse, S., Flanagan, S. D., Lipton, R. B., Cramer, G., Levin, S., Lange, K., & Levy, D. L. (1988). A single dominant gene can account for eye tracking dysfunctions and schizophrenia in offspring of discordant twins. *Archives of General Psychiatry, 45*, 641–647.

Iacono, W. G. (1993). Smooth-pursuit oculomotor dysfunction as an index of schizotaxia. In R. L. Cromwell & C. R. Snyder (Eds.), *Schizophrenia: Origins, processes, treatment, and outcome* (pp. 76–97). New York: Oxford University Press.

Iacono, W. G., & Clementz, B. A. (1993). A strategy for elucidating genetic influences on complex psychopathological syndromes (with special reference to ocular motor functioning and schizophrenia). In L. J. Chapman, J. P. Chapman, & D. Fowles (Eds.), *Progress in experimental personality and psychopathology research* (Vol. 16, pp. 11–65). New York: Springer.

Iacono, W. G., & Ficken, J. (1989). Psychophysiological research strategies. In G. Turpin (Ed.), *Handbook of clinical psychophysiology* (pp. 45–70). London: Wiley.

Iacono, W. G., & Grove, W. M. (1993). Schizophrenia research: Toward an integrative genetic model. *Psychological Science, 4*, 273–276.

Iacono, W. G., Moreau, M., Beiser, M., Fleming, J. A. E., & Lin, T.-Y. (1992). Smooth-pursuit eye tracking in first-episode psychotic patients and their relatives. *Journal of Abnormal Psychology, 101*, 104–116.

John, B., & Lewis, K. R. (1966). Chromosome variability and geographic distribution in insects. *Science, 152*, 711–721.

Katsanis, J., & Iacono, W. G. (1991). Clinical, neuropsychological, and brain structural correlates of smooth-pursuit eye tracking performance in chronic schizophrenia. *Journal of Abnormal Psychology, 100*, 526–534.

Katsanis, J., Kortenkamp, S., Iacono, W. G., & Grove, W. M. (1997). Antisaccade performance in patients with schizophrenia and affective disorder. *Journal of Abnormal Psychology, 106*, 468–472.

Keefe, R. S. E., Silverman, J. M., Roitman, S. E. L., Harvey, P. D., Duncan, M. A., Alroy, D., Siever, L. J., Davis, K. L., & Mohs, R. C. (1994). Performance of nonpsychotic relatives of schizophrenic patients on cognitive tests. *Psychiatry Research, 53*, 1–12.

Keefe, R. S. E., Silverman, J. M., Siever, L. J., & Cornblatt, B. A. (1991). Refining phenotype characterization in genetic linkage studies of schizophrenia. *Social Biology, 38,* 197–218.

Kinney, D. K., Holzman, P. S., Jacobsen, B., Jansson, L., Faber, B., Hildebrand, W., Kasell, E., & Zimbalist, M. E. (1997). Thought disorder in schizophrenic and control adoptees and their relatives. *Archives of General Psychiatry, 54,* 475–479.

Levy, D., Holzman, P., Matthysse, S., & Mendell, N. (1993). Eye tracking dysfunction and schizophrenia: A critical perspective. *Schizophrenia Bulletin, 19,* 461–505.

Litman, R. E., Hommer, D. W., Clem, T., Ornsteen, M. L., Ollo, C., & Pickar, D. (1991). Correlation of Wisconsin Card Sorting Test performance with eye tracking in schizophrenia. *American Journal of Psychiatry, 148,* 1580–1582.

Malaspina, D., Wray, A. D., Friedman, J. H., Amador, X., Yale, S., Hasan, A., Gorman, J. M., & Kaufman, C. A. (1994). Odor discrimination deficits in schizophrenia: Association with eye movement dysfunction. *Journal of Neuropsychiatry and Clinical Neurosciences, 6,* 273–278.

Matthysse, S., Holzman, P. S., & Lange, K. (1986). The genetic transmission of schizophrenia: Application of Mendelian latent structure analysis to eye tracking dysfunctions in schizophrenia and affective disorder. *Journal of Psychiatric Research, 20,* 57–76.

McGue, M., & Gottesman, I. I. (1989). A single dominant gene still cannot account for the transmission of schizophrenia. *Archives of General Psychiatry, 46,* 478–479.

Meehl, P. E. (1990). Toward an integrated theory of schizotaxia, schizotypy, and schizophrenia. *Journal of Personality Disorders, 4,* 1–99.

Moises, H. W., Yang, L., Kristbjarnarson, H., Wiese, C., Byerley, W., Macciardi, F., Arolt, V., Blackwood, D., Liu, X., Sjorgren, B., Aschauer, H. N., Hwu, H.-G., Jang, K., Livesley, W. J., Kennedy, J. L., Zoega, T., Ivarsson, O., Bui, M.-T., Yu, M.-H., Havsteen, B., Commenges, D., Weissenbach, J., Schwinger, E., Gottesman, I. I., Pakstis, A. J., Wetterberg, L., Kidd, K. K., & Helgason, T. (1995). An international two-stage genome-wide search for schizophrenia susceptibility genes. *Nature Genetics, 11,* 321–324.

Park, S., Holzman, P. S., & Goldman-Rakic, P. S. (1995). Spatial working memory deficits in the relatives of schizophrenic patients. *Archives of General Psychiatry, 52,* 821–828.

Ross, D. E., Ochs, A. L., Pandurangi, A. K., Thacker, L. R., & Kendler, K. S. (1996). Mixture analysis of smooth pursuit eye movements in schizophrenia. *Psychophysiology, 33,* 390–397.

Ross, D. E., Thaker, G. K., Buchanan, R. W., Kirkpatrick, B., Lahti, A., Medoff, D., Bartko, J. J., Goodman, J., & Tien, A. (1997). Eye tracking in schizophrenia is characterized by specific ocular motor defects and is associated with the deficit syndrome. *Biological Psychiatry, 42,* 781–796.

Ross, D. E., Thaker, G. K., Buchanan, R. W., Lahti, A., Medoff, D., Bartko, J. J., Moran, J. J., & Hartley, J. (1996). Association of abnormal smooth pursuit eye movements with the deficit syndrome in schizophrenic patients. *American Journal of Psychiatry, 153,* 1158–1165.

Scarone, S., Gambini, O., Hafele, E., Bellodi, L., & Smeraldi, E. (1987). Neuro-functional assessment of schizophrenia: A preliminary investigation of the presence of eye tracking (SPEMs) and quality extinction test (QET) abnor-malities in a sample of schizophrenic patients. *Biological Psychology, 24,* 253–259.

Schwab, S. G., Albus, M., Hallmayer, J., Honig, S., Borrmann, M., Lichtermann, D., Ebstein, R. P., Ackenheil, M., Lerer, B., Risch, N., Maier, W., & Wilden-auer, D. R. (1995). Evaluation of a susceptibility gene for schizophrenia on chromosome 6p by multipoint affected sib-pair linkage analysis. *Nature Ge-netics, 11,* 325–327.

Sherman, S. L., DeFries, J. C., Gottesman, I. I., Loehlin, J. C., Meyer, J. M., Pelias, M. Z., Rice, J., & Waldman, I. (1997). Recent developments in human be-havioral genetics: Past accomplishments and future directions. *American Jour-nal of Human Genetics, 60,* 1265–1275.

Siever, L. J., Friedman, L., Moskowitz, J., Mitropoulou, V., Keefe, R., Roitman, S. L., Merhige, D., Trestman, R., Silverman, J., & Mohs, R. (1994). Eye movement impairment and schizotypal psychopathology. *American Journal of Psychiatry, 151,* 1209–1215.

Straub, R. E., McLean, C. J., O'Neill, F. E., Burke, J., Murphy, B., Duke, F., Shink-win, R., Webb, B. T., Zhang, J., Walsh, D., & Kendler, K. S. (1995). A potential susceptibility locus for schizophrenia on chromosome 6p24–22: Ev-idence for genetic heterogeneity. *Nature Genetics, 11,* 284–293.

Sweeney, J. A., Clementz, B. A., Escobar, M. D., Li, S., Pauler, D. K., & Haas, G. L. (1993). Mixture analysis of pursuit eye-tracking dysfunction in schizo-phrenia. *Biological Psychiatry, 34,* 331–340.

Sweeney, J. A., Clementz, B. A., Haas, G. L., Escobar, M. D., Drake, K., & Frances, A. J. (1994). Eye tracking dysfunction in schizophrenia: Characterization of component eye movement abnormalities, diagnostic specificity, and the role of attention. *Journal of Abnormal Psychology, 103,* 222–230.

Sweeney, J. A., Haas, G. L., & Li, S. (1992). Neuropsychological and eye move-ment abnormalities in first-episode and chronic schizophrenia: Evidence for progressive deterioration of deficits. *Schizophrenia Bulletin, 18,* 283–293.

Thaker, G. K., Cassady, S., Adami, H., Moran, M., & Ross, D. E. (1996). Eye movements in spectrum personality disorders: Comparison of community sub-jects and relatives of schizophrenic patients. *American Journal of Psychiatry, 153,* 362–368.

Van den Bosch, R. J., Rozendaal, N., & Mol, J. F. M. A. (1987). Symptom cor-relates of eye tracking dysfunction. *Biological Psychiatry, 22,* 919–921.

Wang, S., Sun, C., Walczak, C. A., Ziegle, J. S., Kipps, B. R., Goldin, L. R., & Diehl, S. R. (1995). Evidence for a susceptibility locus for schizophrenia on chromosome 6pter-p22. *Nature Genetics, 11,* 41–46.

World Health Organization. (1992). *The ICD-10 classification of mental and behav-ioural disorders: Clinical descriptions and diagnostic guidelines.* Geneva: Author.

2

NEURODEVELOPMENTAL ORIGINS OF SCHIZOPHRENIA

CARRIE E. BEARDEN AND TYRONE D. CANNON

Schizophrenia research has long attempted to identify etiologic factors that might disturb cerebral function immediately before the onset of diagnostic psychotic symptoms. Throughout most of this century, research has been guided by the Kraepelinian concept of schizophrenia as a dementing disorder with onset in early adult life and a progressive clinical deterioration over the course of the illness. From this conceptual framework, it seemed reasonable to assume that in most cases the brain was relatively normal until the onset of the illness in early adulthood, and that any pathological changes resulting from the illness would become more apparent as the illness progressed. This model was consistent with many adult-onset brain disorders, including Alzheimer's disease and infectious encephalopathies. This view of schizophrenia as a neurodegenerative disorder persisted despite the fact that Kraepelin (1919) himself postulated that some cases of schizophrenia probably resulted from early insults that caused cerebral maldevelopment, and despite clinical observations that cognitive deterioration was not present in every case (Bleuler, 1911/1950).

However, in the past decade there has been a radical conceptual shift in thinking about the etiology of schizophrenia. Numerous lines of evidence suggest that earlier events play a significant role. These recent advances point to a prenatal or perinatal origin of at least some of the brain abnormalities in schizophrenia, suggesting that the primary pathological process in schizophrenia occurs during development, long before the onset of clinical symptoms of the illness. Evidence for a neurodevelopmental origin of schizophrenia comes primarily from four lines of inquiry. First, postmortem neuropathology studies have found evidence of heterotopic displacement of neurons in the frontal and temporal cortices and hippocampal formation, indicating a disturbance of early brain development. Second, in vivo neuroimaging studies have observed neuroanatomical changes in young, first-episode patients and have failed to detect evidence of progressive deterioration over the course of illness. Moreover, structural and functional brain abnormalities qualitatively similar to those seen in patients with schizophrenia have also been observed in their unaffected first-degree relatives, suggesting that such abnormalities may be mediated by an underlying genetic predisposition to the disorder. Third, a large number of prospective studies have reported associations between prenatal and perinatal complications and an increased risk for schizophrenia, suggesting that conditions that adversely affect the fetal brain play a role in the development of schizophrenic illness. And finally, numerous prospective studies of high-risk samples and total birth cohorts, as well as retrospective studies of adult schizophrenics, have shown that future schizophrenics have evidence of early impairment, indicating that signs of brain compromise exist early in development in preschizophrenic individuals.

This chapter will review each of these areas in turn, to explore the case for viewing schizophrenia as a neurodevelopmental disorder.

NEUROPATHOLOGY STUDIES

Postmortem analysis of brain tissue from patients with schizophrenia allows the unique opportunity to examine markers of neurodevelopmental and neurodegenerative anatomical changes at the cellular and molecular levels. To understand the importance of such markers in the pathophysiology of schizophrenia, we first present a brief overview of the processes of normal brain development.

Normal Brain Development

The fetal brain develops from the embryological ectoderm as a result of an elaborate, mostly orderly series of changes. The formation of the primitive neural tube is the first step in the formation of the nervous system, followed by proliferation or neurogenesis of cells. Even at the earliest stages, particular cells are targeted for specific locations in the brain. Neurons reach their target locations through a process of cellular migration, which involves either a displacement of formerly generated layers of cells or the guiding of individual cells to their destinations by nonneural support cells known as radial glial fibers. Once a cell reaches its target location, it begins to extend processes to make synaptic connections with other cells. At this point, cells begin to differentiate. This final stage of brain development, involving anatomical and functional differentation, continues at least into the second decade of life.

Although the most dramatic changes occur during gestation, significant changes continue after birth, and most likely continue to some degree throughout the life span. A key principle of brain development is that, because of the "exuberance" of neuronal proliferation, many more neurons and synaptic connections are formed than will be present in the adult brain (E. G. Jones, 1991). Thus, although no new neurons are created beyond about the third month of life (Rakic, 1985), postnatal changes involve the modification of cellular elements and major regressive changes in neuronal populations. In both human and nonhuman primates, synaptic density remains at higher than adult levels for a period of several years, throughout puberty, and then begins a slow but steady decrease (Huttenlocher, 1979; Rakic, Bourgeois, & Goldman-Rakic, 1994). Moreover, many studies suggest that cerebral development is not continuous but proceeds in spurts and plateaus that are synchronized across all brain regions (Epstein, 1986; Hudspeth & Pribram, 1990). Each growth spurt seems to involve a wave of nerve growth factor resulting in the production of a surplus of synaptic connections, followed by a pruning of excess connections (Feinberg, Thode, Chugani, & March, 1990; Thatcher, 1992). This process, also known as concurrent cortical synaptogenesis, in which synapse formations show a sharp spurt and subsequent drop across all areas of the cortex, may mediate the development of many cognitive capacities that emerge in infancy and childhood (Goldman-Rakic, 1987).

Neuronal migration seems to be sensitive to a number of genetic and environmental insults and may be easily disrupted. Evidence of faulty neuronal migration include ectopic neurons, hypocellular areas, and other cytoarchitectural anomalies. The causes of migratory abnormalities are many; possibilities include neurotoxins, viral infections, and genetic mutations. As discussed in the following section, the particular neuropathological abnormalities found in schizophrenia suggest that the illness may involve a disruption of neuronal migration.

Neuropathological Abnormalities

Several postmortem neuropathological studies have reported ectopic changes in the brains of schizophrenic patients, suggesting a prenatal pathogenesis of the disorder. Ectopic or heterotopic cells are cells that are developmentally displaced as a result of disturbances in cellular migration or gestation. In particular, findings of heterotopic prealpha cells in the parahippocampal gyrus (Falkai, Bogerts, Roberts, & Crow, 1988; Jacob & Beckmann, 1986), disturbances of pyramidal cell orientation in the anterior and medial portions of the hippocampus (Falkai et al., 1988; Kovelman & Scheibel, 1984), reduced depth of the granule cell layer in the dentate gyrus (McLardy, 1974), and anomalous distribution of NADPH-d containing neurons in frontal and temporal cortex (Akbarian, Bunney, et al., 1993; Akbarian, Vineula, et al., 1993; Stevens, 1982) imply a failure of neuronal migration during fetal life. Anomalous cytoarchitecture has been reported in the hippocampus, parahippocampal gyrus, entorhinal cortex, and cingulate and prefrontal cortices (Arnold, Hyman, Van Hoesen, & Damasio, 1991; Benes, 1987; Benes, Sorensen, & Bird, 1991; Bogerts, Falkai, & Greve, 1991). Because migration of these cells is largely complete by birth, this suggests a developmental rather than degenerative pathology. Although the exact source of these anomalies is unknown, such findings imply a disturbance in one or more of the basic processes underlying brain development during gestation.

Altered cell densities and gray matter volumes have also been reported in the same brain regions (Benes, Davidson, & Bird, 1987; Benes et al., 1991; Bogerts et al., 1990; Brown et al., 1986), as well as in the basal ganglia, thalamus, and nucleus accumbens. Most of these studies point to decreased numbers of neurons in these locations, although increases in neuronal counts were reported in the basal ganglia in some studies (Dagg, Booth, McLaughlin, & Dolan, 1994; Selemon, Rajkowska, & Goldman-Rakic, 1993).

The anatomical findings most directly relevant to neurodevelopmental models of schizophrenia concern the evidence of cytoarchitectural disorganization of the cortex, as these data point specifically to a defect of cortical development during the second trimester of gestation. It is less definite that reduced gray matter volume and altered cell density are associated with prenatal developmental disturbance. Such findings could also result from excessive neuronal elimination or from a neurodegenerative process in adulthood. However, if this were the case, one would expect to see substantial glial scarring in these regions, as this is the normal reaction of the brain to injury or inflammation in all but the first few months of life. However, gliosis—an increased density or number of glial cells—is an unusual finding in schizophrenia. There is an apparent absence of gliosis in brain regions showing cytoarchitectonic anomalies (Waddington, 1991). While two recent studies showed periventricular and thalamic gliosis (Bogerts, Falkai, & Greve, 1991; Bogerts et al., 1990), this may indicate a secondary cascade process or slightly later effect of those putative events underlying early to middle gestational phenomena. In addition, other markers of neurodegenerative disease, such as neurofibrillary tangles and senile plaques, which are extremely prevalent in the brains of Alzheimer's patients, are not elevated in patients with schizophrenia (Arnold, Franz, & Trojanowski, 1994). Thus, the preponderance of evidence suggests that subtle deficits in brain structure are present at or before birth in individuals destined to become schizophrenic (Bogerts, 1991; Conrad, Abebe, Austin, Forsythe, & Scheibel, 1991; Falkai & Bogerts, 1986; Falkai et al., 1988; Weinberger, 1995).

Implications and Future Directions

Although postmortem neuropathological studies provide compelling evidence of anomalous brain development in schizophrenia, it is important to keep in mind the limitations of this work. First, it is currently unknown what the role of these cytoarchitectural changes (such as abnormal cellular positioning) may be in the development of schizophrenic symptoms. Second, although some of the findings of postmortem studies are consistent with a prenatal origin, the relationship between these subtle abnormalities and the more large-scale neuroanatomical deficits seen in living patients (such as reduced gray matter volume and ventricular enlargement) remains to be determined. And finally, because autopsy studies examine only a small number of cases, for which family, birth, and developmental history are not known, it is unclear whether these individuals are representative of the majority of schizophrenics. Moreover, these studies are not well suited to determine the causes of the neuropathological abormalities or to address their functional implications for individuals predisposed to the disorder.

IN VIVO IMAGING STUDIES

The advent of modern neuroimaging techniques such as computed tomography (CT), magnetic resonance imaging (MRI), and positron emission tomography has facilitated in vivo examination of the schizophrenic brain reliably and noninvasively. As reviewed below, these studies provide widespread support for the hypothesis that a critical part of the etiology of schizophrenia involves structural or functional brain deficits or both.

Structural Abnormalities

The most consistently replicated findings in structural neuroimaging studies of schizophrenic patients are ventricular enlargement (reviewed in Cannon, 1991), decreased volume in limbic structures (including the amygdala and hippocampus), thalamus, and temporal cortex, with some studies also reporting decreased frontal volume and increased basal ganglia volume (reviewed in Gur & Pearlson, 1993). Although abnormalities are seen in both hemispheres of the brain, there appears to be a general trend for pathological markers to be more pronounced in the left hemisphere than the right (e.g., Weinberger, 1995). This pattern has prompted some to speculate that development of the left hemisphere may be delayed during the second trimester of gestation, rendering it more vulnerable to adverse events (e.g., Crow, Ball, & Bloom, 1989).

Pathomorphology in First-Episode Patients

If the structural brain abnormalities seen in schizophrenia are at least partly neurodevelopmental in origin, such abnormalities should be present early in life among those individuals who become schizophrenic in adulthood. Because there have been no studies to date assessing brain structural changes in high-risk individuals before the onset of schizophrenia, it is unknown whether neuroanatomical abnormalities are detectable in childhood or do not become manifest until closer to onset of disorder. However, ventricular enlargement and reduced temporal and frontal lobe volumes have been reported in young, never-medicated, and first-episode patients, indicating they are present at least as early as the beginning stages of the illness (Cannon, 1991; Gur et al., 1998; Murray, O'Callaghan, Castle, & Lewis, 1992; Weinberger, DeLisi, Berman, Targum, & Wyatt, 1982).

A recent MRI study of 24 first-episode schizophrenics, in which all subjects had experienced a full psychotic syndrome for less than 30 weeks, found that patients had significantly more total cerebrospinal fluid (CSF) than controls, accounted for by higher levels of intersulcal CSF and ventricular CSF. Although there were no differences in total volume of brain tissue, patients had a significant regionally specific decrement in frontal lobe tissue compared with controls (Nopoulos et al., 1995). Degreef et al. (1992) also found volumes of all segments of the ventricular system, as measured by MRI, to be significantly larger in 40 first-episode patients than in controls (differences ranged from 17% to 40%). Measures of the temporal horn areas were consistently correlated with a broad range of schizophrenic symptoms. Findings of increased CSF and decreased gray matter volume in frontal and temporal areas have recently been reported in a Philadelphia cohort of first-episode patients (Gur et al., 1998).

In another study of first-episode schizophrenia patients, Bilder et al. (1995) found volume reductions in the mesiotemporal lobes (anterior hippocampus). Furthermore, these volume reductions were correlated with deficits in neuropsychological measures of executive and motor control, thus supporting the hypothesis that neurodevelopmental defects of integrated fronto-limbic control system are important to the pathophysiology of schizophrenia.

Lack of Neuropathological Progression After Illness Onset

Imaging studies have noted little evidence of progressive ventricular enlargement in schizophrenia above that associated with normal aging (Cannon, 1991). Breslin and Weinberger (1991) reviewed evidence demonstrating that ventricular enlargement occurs early in the course of illness and is not related to duration of illness in a majority of studies. This suggests that ventricular enlargement is not a progressive phenomenon accompanying the course of the disease or a by-product of institutionalization. Moreover, as discussed earlier, postmortem studies in general have not found evidence of neurodegenerative processes in frontal areas or general signs of neuronal atrophy (Hoffman & Dobscha, 1989).

At present, only a few longitudinal neuroimaging studies of the same patients over time have been conducted. The majority have failed to detect a difference in the rate of brain tissue loss between schizophrenics and controls over a period of 1 to 8 years (Degreef et al., 1992; DeLisi et al., 1991; Nasrallah, Olsen, McCalley-Whitters, Chapman, & Jacoby, 1986), although a few have detected progressive tissue loss in patients with schizophrenia (DeLisi et al., 1995; Woods et al., 1990). Thus, it may be that there is some degree of progressive deterioration in at least a subgroup of schizophrenic patients. However, such deterioration is not inconsistent with a primary neurodevelopmental process, as anomalies of early cellular migration may result in abnormal cell elimination later in life as a result of secondary processes.

The only study to date to examine brain volumetric measures longitudinally in first-episode patients (Gur et al., 1998) found differences in brain structural changes over time between schizophrenic patients and controls. At intake, both first-episode and previously treated patients had lower whole brain, frontal lobe, and temporal lobe volume than did controls. The existence of brain abnormalities in first-episode patients suggests that the pathology may have been present before clinical presentation. At follow-up, $2\frac{1}{2}$ years later on average, a reduction in frontal lobe volume was found in patients (particularly in first-episode patients) but not in controls, whereas temporal lobe reduction was seen in both patients and controls. More important, first-episode patients showed more pronounced volume reduction in both frontal and temporal lobes than did previously treated patients. This finding suggests that neuroanatomical changes are more pronounced early in psychosis and that a secondary pathological process also occurs around the time of onset.

Consistent with neuroanatomical findings, there is little evidence of significant cognitive decline during course of disorder, beyond that expected because of normal aging processes. Heaton et al. (1994) found that neuropsychological impairment in schizophrenia was unrelated to current age, age at onset, or duration of illness, and that early onset young schizophrenic, early onset older schizophrenic, and late onset groups did not show significant differences in the level or pattern of impairment. All patients with schizophrenia differed from normal controls and Alzheimer's patients in the pattern of neuropsychological functioning. Nopoulos, Flashman, Flaum, Arndt, and Andreasen (1994) found that in new or recent onset schizophrenics (first hospitalization within the past 5 years), cognitive function remained stable in most domains and showed no evidence of deterioration at 1–2 year follow-up. Gur et al. (1998) recently reported similar findings of no significant overall change in cognitive performance in first-episode or previously treated patients at 2–3 year follow-up. These findings suggest that if schizophrenia is a progressive neurodegenerative disorder, the rate of cognitive decline is so subtle that it is nondetectable in most studies.

Structural Abnormalities in Unaffected Relatives

That there is a substantial genetic component in schizophrenia is a matter of little debate. Estimates of the degree of heritability based on concordance rates in twins are on the order of 80% (Cannon, Kaprio, Lonnqvist, Huttunen, & Kokenvuo, 1998; Kendler & Diehl, 1993). Biological relatives of schizophrenia patients also have elevated rates of sub-psychotic or "schizotypal" symptoms, such as magical thinking and suspiciousness. Moreover, there are equivalent risk rates for schizophrenia among the offspring of discordant monozygotic (MZ) twins (Gottesman & Bertelsen, 1989), indicating that there are individuals who possess a genotype that predisposes to schizophrenia but do not manifest the disorder phenotypically.

If some of the neuroanatomical abnormalities seen in schizophrenia patients reflect an underlying genetic predisposition to the disorder, first-degree relatives of these individuals should display some degree of the same deficits as compared with controls. Consistent with this notion, one study found individuals with schizophrenia and their unaffected siblings had significantly larger ventricles compared with normal controls, indicating there may be a genetic contribution to increased ventricular size in schizophrenia (Weinberger, DeLisi, Neophytides, & Wyatt, 1981). DeLisi et al. (1986) also reported a significant relationship between ventricular size and schizophrenia within families, even after controlling for the contributions of several environmental sources of brain pathology.

However, recent evidence suggests the genetic vulnerability to schizophrenia may be particularly relevant to regional brain tissue volume. Suddath, Christison, Torrey, Casanova, and Weinberger (1990) did not find significant differences between discordant MZ twins in volume of prefrontal gray or white matter, temporal lobe white matter, and right temporal lobe gray matter, suggesting a genetic origin for these specific structural brain abnormalities.

Pathophysiology of Structural Brain Abnormalities

In a subsample from the Copenhagen high-risk project, Cannon, Mednick, and Parnas (1989) examined the independent contributions of genetic and perinatal influences to CT measures of structural brain abnormalities. Cortical and cerebellar abnormalities were found to form a single factor that was significantly related to genetic risk for schizophrenia (measured by schizophrenia spectrum illness in the fathers) but was unrelated to pregnancy or delivery complications or birth weight. This implies that fetal neural developmental abnormalities are part of the phenotypic expression of the genetic predisposition to schizophrenia, and that a genetically based disturbance of second-trimester fetal brain development may be responsible for these neural developmental anomalies. Enlargement of the third and lateral ventricles formed a separate factor that was predicted primarily by the interaction of genetic risk for schizophrenia and delivery complications. That is, individuals at elevated genetic risk evidenced greater ventricular enlargement if they suffered delivery complications. Subjects with schizophrenia had significantly more periventricular damage than subjects with schizotypal personality disorder and no mental illness. This suggests that, if the fetal brain is made vulnerable by genetically provoked developmental disruption, it may suffer more severe periventricular tissue damage secondary to delivery complications. Delivery complications may predispose genetically vulnerable individuals to schizophrenic breakdown by adding periventricular damage to existing multisite neural developmental deficits. Thus, this study provides evidence of two types of structural brain damage in schizophrenia, each associated with a different set of etiologic predictors, suggesting there are largely independent etiologic processes underlying the two deficits. In a replication that strengthened these findings, Cannon et al. (1993) found that there was a main effect of genetic risk on overall CSF–brain ratio that was linear and dose dependent. That is, low-risk subjects showed the least number of abnormalities, super high-risk (those with two schizophrenic parents) showed the most, and high-risk subjects fell exactly in between. In addition, the presence of delivery complications was associated with greater ventricular enlargement, but only among those at elevated genetic risk.

Functional Abnormalities in Schizophrenics and Relatives

A pattern of selective deficits in learning and memory has been shown not only in adult schizophrenics (Saykin, Gur, Gur, Mozley, & Mozley, 1991) but also in first-episode, neuroleptic-naive schizophrenics (e.g., Saykin et al., 1994) and in their unaffected siblings. Goldberg et al. (1990) found that unaffected twins of schizophrenic subjects performed more poorly than did normal control twins on 20 of 24 neuropsychological tests, with the largest differences on measures of verbal memory, attention, language, and abstraction. Furthermore, in a Philadelphia cohort of 15 schizophrenic patients and 16 of their nonschizophrenic siblings, Cannon et al. (1994) found both patients and their sibling to be impaired neuropsychologically compared with normal controls, with the siblings' performance intermediate between that of the patients and controls on all measures of functioning. The shapes of the deficit profiles of patients and siblings were similar, as both groups scored lower on tests sensitive to frontal and left temporal lobe function (verbal memory, language, abstraction, and attention) than on tests sensitive to right-hemisphere and parietal lobe function (spatial reasoning, spatial memory, and sensorimotor function). The fact that both schizophrenic patients and their unaffected siblings show a similar pattern of neuropsychological impairment is evidence that this pattern may be indicative of a genetic vulnerability to schizophrenia, rather than an effect of the illness. The problems displayed by schizophrenic patients and their siblings in acquisition of newly presented material implicate the medial temporal lobes (e.g., Squire, 1987), an area that structural neuroimaging studies suggest may be particularly relevant to the pathophysiology of schizophrenia (e.g., Andreasen, Ehrhardt, Swayze, & Alliger, 1990; Cannon, 1991; Gur et al., 1998). Because of the many reciprocal connections between medial temporal lobes and frontal cortical regions, abnormalities in one or the other may be reflected and amplified in tasks calling for coordinated action of both structures.

Implications and Conclusions

Neuroimaging and neurobehavioral studies of adult schizophrenics have provided consistent evidence of structural and functional brain abnormalities in these patients. Given that many of these abnormalities appear in young, first-episode patients as well as in unaffected first-degree relatives, such abnormalities appear to reflect an underlying vulnerability to schizophrenia. The findings from the Copenhagen high-risk study suggest that genetic factors and obstetric complications (OC) may interact in producing some of the characteristic structural brain abnormalities seen in schizophrenia. As we discuss in the following section, a number of prospective studies have found cognitive, behavioral, and neuromotor deficits in children destined to become schizophrenic in adulthood, suggesting that underlying brain abnormalities may be present before the onset of illness, and thus may be indicative of disturbances of early brain development.

However, some studies have reported findings consistent with a degenerative process in some of these markers during the adult course of the illness. It is presently unknown whether there is some degree of deterioration in all cases or whether such changes are confined to a particular subgroup of schizophrenic patients. Methodologically rigorous longitudinal neuroimaging studies of large, well-characterized patient populations are required to resolve this issue. However, it is important to keep in mind that there may be secondary effects of insults to the brain in utero; thus, signs of progressive deterioration, if present, do not rule out a primary neurodevelopmental etiology.

DEVELOPMENTAL PRECURSORS OF SCHIZOPHRENIA

Retrospective studies, as well as high-risk studies of the offspring of schizophrenic mothers, have demonstrated the existence of neurological, cognitive, and behavioral abnormalities before onset of schizophrenic illness. Such studies offer substantial evidence that early brain compromise may be less dormant and more evident functionally than was previously believed. Early childhood data reveal patterns of early cognitive impairment, as well as neurological and behavioral abnormalities in preschizophrenic individuals, ranging from early social withdrawal to hyperactivity (e.g., Cannon & Mednick, 1993). Although the vast majority of schizophrenics show no signs of outright psychotic symptomatology until adolescence or early adulthood, there is substantial evidence that the pathological processes that predispose to the disorder are evident earlier in life in more subtle forms.

Premorbid Cognitive and Behavioral Impairment

In the domain of cognitive development, children with an elevated risk for schizophrenia exhibit impairments in learning and memory functions (Driscoll, 1984; Erlenmeyer-Kimling & Cornblatt, 1987; Klein & Salzman, 1984; Rutschmann, Cornblatt, & Erlenmeyer-Kimling, 1986), attention (Erlenmeyer-Kimling, Golden, & Cornblatt, 1989; Weintraub, 1987), language (Gruzelier, Mednick, & Schulsinger, 1979; Hallett, Quinn, & Hewitt, 1986; Harvey, Weintraub, & Neal, 1982), and other information-processing domains (Erlenmeyer-Kimling & Cornblatt, 1987). Although impairments in specific domains are of particular theoretical interest, there is also evidence that the cognitive deficits in high-risk individuals are quite generalized. In a meta-analysis of the literature, Aylward, Walker, and Bettes (1984) concluded that preschizophrenic children showed deficits on standard IQ tests in comparison with matched groups of peers or siblings with no psychiatric disorder. Moreover, such deficits were shown to predict an early-onset, poor-prognosis form of illness.

In a total birth cohort of approximately 10,000 subjects in Philadelphia, we examined childhood cognitive deficits as predictors of adult psychiatric outcome (Cannon, Bearden, Hollister, & Hadley, 1997). Subjects were evaluated prospectively with standardized IQ tests at 4 and 7 years of age. Individuals who later became schizophrenic showed significant cognitive impairment at age 4 and continued to show cognitive impairment at age 7. We found that the odds of schizophrenia and of being an unaffected sibling of a schizophrenic both increased linearly across decreasing levels of functioning at both assessments. Within families, preschizophrenics were found to have lower test scores than their unaffected siblings, and this disparity was related to a history of perinatal hypoxia in the preschizophrenics. Preschizophrenics thus show cognitive deficits as early as age 4. Because their nonschizophrenic siblings show qualitatively similar deficits, this dysfunction may be indicative of a genetic predisposition to the disorder. Moreover, perinatal hypoxia may magnify this dysfunction in increasing the risk for phenotypic schizophrenia. Furthermore, there was a significant linear trend in the distribution of IQ scores, indicating that preschizophrenics were significantly overrepresented in the lowest quintile of cognitive performance and progressively more underrepresented among the upper quintiles. This result strongly suggests that cognitive impairment is not limited to a subgroup of individuals who later become schizophrenic. P. B. Jones, Rodgers, Murray, and Marmot (1994) reported a similar finding in a British sample of preschizophrenics.

In the behavioral domain, there is considerable heterogeneity in the type of early behavioral disturbance displayed, which might be expected in light of the heterogeneity in the clinical manifestations of the disorder. In the Stony Brook High Risk Project (Weintraub, 1987), children of parents with schizophrenia had lower social competence, were perceived by peers to be abrasive and withdrawn, and were rated by teachers as more behaviorally deviant than their classmate controls. In this study, different subsets of children displayed acting-out problems, withdrawn behavior, and attentional and cognitive deficits, but because the samples have not been followed up in adulthood, it cannot yet be determined whether such subgroups have distinct clinical outcomes. However, there is some evidence to suggest that individuals with schizophrenia display signs of childhood behavior analogous to their adult symptomatology: Schizophrenics who develop prominent negative symptoms (i.e., apathy, anhedonia, social withdrawal) are likely to exhibit poorer premorbid social adjustment than those who do not (Cannon & Mednick, 1993; MacGlashan & Fenton, 1992; Pogue-Guile & Harrow, 1984). In addition, Cannon and Mednick (1993) found that positive symptoms (i.e., hallucinations, delusions, thought disorder) were correlated with early acting-out behavior and conduct disorder. Foerster, Lewis, Owen, and Murray (1991) also found childhood schizoid and schizotypal traits and poor social adjustment in some schizophrenia patients. Those patients who were abnormal as children had an early onset of psychosis characterized by either a family history of schizophrenia or a history of OCs or low birth weight.

Findings with regard to neurologic and motor abnormalities in the offspring of schizophrenic patients are less consistent. Marcus, Hans, Mednick, Schulsinger, and Michelsen (1985) found significantly more impairments in motor functioning in high-risk children than low-risk children. Motor and developmental lags at age 1 were associated with an elevated genetic risk for schizophrenia in the Copenhagen Obstetrical Project (Mednick, Mura, Schulsinger, & Mednick, 1974). Walker, Savole, and Davis (1994) found that viewers of home movies of a preschizophrenic child and their unaffected sibling were able to identify the preschizophrenic child younger than age 8 at above-chance levels. Preschizophrenics differed from their siblings in facial expressions of emotion and had significantly more neuromotor abnormalities and poorer motor skills than their healthy siblings and preaffective disorder patients. Fish (1977) found evidence of early neurological disturbance and pandysmaturation (PDM) in offspring of women with schizophrenia. PDM refers to a generalized neurointegrative disorder, including transient lags in physical growth, presence of irritability, and delay and disorganization of gross motor and/or visuomotor development between birth and age 2. These infants had unusually quiet behavior, including hypotonia, absence of crying, and underactivity, which may represent earliest manifestations of attentional disturbances in high-risk subjects. Fish, Marcus, Hans, Auerbach, and Perdue (1992) also reported significant correlations between PDM and later psychiatric status. However, in the New York High Risk Project, measures of neuromotor deviance did not differentiate high-risk subjects from normal or psychiatric controls, whereas attentional deviance clearly did (Erlenmeyer-Kimling & Cornblatt, 1987). It may be that while early cognitive and social–behavioral deviance are relatively common among high-risk individuals, early motor impairments may characterize a smaller, but more severely impaired subgroup. This is consistent with Neumann, Grimes, Walker, and Baum's (1995) report of a "neurodevelopmental" subgroup of preschizophrenics who are characterized by greater neuromotor deficits, more severe behavioral problems during childhood, and an earlier age of onset.

Because premorbid functional deficits in high-risk individuals have been observed in a variety of domains, it is possible that a combination of premorbid functional indicators is most predictive of schizophrenic outcome in adulthood. Consistent with this hypothesis, several high-risk studies found multiple functional deficits to be linked to an elevated risk for schizophrenia (e.g., Fish, 1977; Marcus et al., 1985). In a replication analysis of the Jerusalem Infant Development Study, Fish et al. (1992) found a small subgroup of schizophrenic offspring characterized by the most severe neurologic deficits, abnormal cognitive functioning, OCs, and low birth weight. Similarly, the Emory University Project found that children of mothers with schizophrenia, as a group, had more problems overall compared with children of depressed or normal mothers; they had lower IQs, more deficits in social competence, and were greatly overrepresented in the group of children with multiple indexes of dysfunction (Goodman, 1987). The New York High Risk Study (Erlenmeyer-Kimling et al., 1989) found that membership in a taxon identified by deviant scores on measures of IQ, motor performance, and sustained visual attention was predictive of psychiatric hospitalization in young adulthood. In a similar taxometric analysis, Tyrka et al. (1995) identified a latent class of individuals characterized by deviant scores on six premorbid behavioral indicators (i.e., social withdrawal, social anxiety, passivity, flat affect, peculiarity, and poor prognosis), and this classification proved to be a sensitive and specific predictor of an adult schizophrenia-spectrum disorder.

Implications and Conclusions

These studies provide substantial evidence that numerous and varied signs of early functional deviance may aggregate in individuals who are predisposed to develop schizophrenia as adults. Although the prospective high-risk design eliminates the potential for reporting bias that is present in retrospective studies of adults with schizophrenia, such studies are nevertheless limited in that it is unclear to what extent the findings obtained on offspring of schizophrenic parents are generalizable to the total population of schizophrenic patients. Furthermore, few of these studies have continued for a sufficient period of time to determine which individuals in the sample actually became schizophrenic in adulthood, and the few that have obtained long-term outcome data have very small sample sizes. Total birth cohort studies are clearly an improvement on the high-risk studies for these reasons; however, a complete test of a neurodevelopmental model would necessarily include neuroimaging assessments of subjects. Any signs of cognitive, behavioral, or neuromotor deviance, although suggestive of an underlying neural defect, do not completely prove its presence.

OBSTETRIC COMPLICATIONS

Patients with schizophrenia are more likely to have experienced obstetric complications, or OCs, during pregnancy or delivery than those without schizophrenia (Lewis, 1989; McNeil, 1988; McNeil & Kaij, 1978; Mednick, Cannon, & Barr, 1991). In their review of the literature and pilot survey, Lewis and Murray (1987) concluded that schizophrenic patients more frequently have a history of OCs than do both normal subjects and other psychiatric patients. Furthermore, OCs may be related to specific structural abnormalities characteristic of schizophrenia; enlarged cerebral ventricles found on CT and MRI scans in a proportion of schizophrenic patients are associated with a history of OCs (Lewis & Murray, 1987). Studies of MZ twins discordant for schizophrenia have all found that the affected twin had larger ventricles than the nonaffected twin, suggesting a nongenetic origin for these deficits (DeLisi et al., 1986; Reveley, Reveley, & Murray, 1984; Suddath et al., 1990). It is possible that the occurrence of OCs may be the critical factor. Thus, OCs may be one of a number of early environmental factors causally associated with ventricular enlargement.

A key question is whether obstetric influences alone, in the absence of a genetic predisposition, are sufficient to produce schizophrenia, whether OCs act additively or interactively with genetic factors in increasing liability to schizophrenia, or whether OCs are themselves consequences of genetic factors. If OCs are able to cause schizophrenia independent of a genetic predisposition to the disorder, one would expect that all individuals with a history of such complications would become schizophrenic. However, this does not appear to be the case; although fetal hypoxia and other OCs are reliably associated with an elevated risk for schizophrenia in population-based cohort studies, over 97% of the individuals exposed to such complications do not become schizophrenic (Done et al., 1991). In Denmark, Parnas et al. (1982) found that offspring of schizophrenic mothers who suffered delivery complications had a higher risk for schizophrenia compared with high-risk offspring without OCs and low-risk offspring (children of normal parents) who experienced a similar number and degree of such complications, suggesting that the effects of OCs were only pathogenic among those with an elevated genetic risk for schizophrenia.

It also does not seem likely that OCs, including low birth weight, are a consequence of genetic predisposition to the disorder, as studies conducted in Scandinavian countries that maintain comprehensive, prospective antenatal and birth records completed at delivery have failed to support this hypothesis. If OCs were caused by a genetic predisposition to the disorder, unaffected siblings and offspring of schizophrenics would have elevated rates of OCs; however, these individuals are no more likely to have a history of OCs than unaffected individuals from the general population (Cannon, 1997).

Thus, we are left with the gene–environment interaction and simple additive influences models. All studies using objective birth records have found that high-risk individuals who suffered OCs are more likely to become schizophrenic than those who did not (reviewed in Cannon, 1997). Moreover, in a prospective longitudinal high-risk study, Cannon and Mednick (1993) found that high-risk offspring with OCs were significantly more likely to develop a schizophrenia outcome than high-risk offspring who did not suffer OCs, yet there was no increased risk for schizophrenia among low-risk controls with the same number and severity of OCs as the high-risk schizophrenia. This supports a gene–environment interaction model, as it indicates that, *only* in the presence of a genetic vulnerability is the experience of OCs associated with schizophrenia outcomes.

Specificity and Mechanisms of OCs in Schizophrenia

In a comprehensive review of the OC literature appearing before 1988, McNeil (1988) concluded that, of the different types of OCs found to be associated with schozhnira, labor and delivery complications—in particular, those related to perinatal hypoxia—have the most robust association. Furthermore, a recent review of studies conducted since then, which compared rates of OCs among schizophrenics and various comparison groups, including unaffected siblings, psychiatric controls, and normal controls, reached the same conclusion (Cannon, 1997).

In a prospective longitudinal study, we found that those birth complications specifically related to perinatal hypoxia were significantly linearly related to risk for schizophrenia and had a significant linear decrease in risk for being an unaffected sibling (Cannon, Hollister, Bearden, & Hadley, 1997). We examined markers of fetal hypoxia and other OCs as predictors of adult psychiatric outcome in the total birth cohort of the Philadelphia Perinatal Project. Gestations and births were monitored prospectively with standard research protocols. The odds of schizophrenia increased linearly, whereas the odds of being an unaffected sibling of a schizophrenic patient decreased linearly, with an increasing number of hypoxia-associated OCs. This effect was also present when modeling the odds of schizophrenia within families. It is important to note that there was no relationship between hypoxia-associated OCs and other psychiatric disorders, and there was no association between schizophrenia and other prenatal or perinatal complications whose primary impact on the fetus was not hypoxia (e.g., labor stimulants, intrapartum shock). These data are consistent with the notion that a genetic factor in schizophrenia may confer a heightened susceptibility to the pathogenic effects of fetal oxygen deprivation, and they argue against a model in which OCs result from genetic predisposition to schizophrenia or increase the risk for the disorder independent of genetic background. These findings support a model in which hypoxia-related OCs represent random environmental events which, when they occur in a genetically vulnerable individual, add to or multiply the risk for phenotypic expression of schizophrenia. Thus, OCs that cause perinatal hypoxia may cause nonspecific damage, which interacts with a more specific, focal genetic vulnerability in the offspring of schizophrenics. That is, genetic factors may predispose to defective proliferation or neuronal migration in brain development, thus rendering specific brain areas more vulnerable to anoxia at birth (Torrey et al., 1993).

Hypoxic complications in general may threaten brain function during the entire life span by invoking neuronal damage that may play a role in later cognitive dysfunction (Nyakas, Buwalda, & Luiten, 1996). Birth asphyxia can be considered a major cause of perinatal brain injury, as it is known to impair oxidative phosphorylation, resulting in many adverse effects on the fetal brain, including anaerobic glycolysis and lactic acid production (Penrice et al., 1996). Hippocampal regions, especially the CA1 region, have been found to be particularly vulnerable to the effects of hypoxia (Kuchna, 1994). This finding is of interest, given the neuropathological and neuroimaging findings of hippocampal abnormalities in schizophrenia (e.g., Akbarian, Vineula, et al., 1993; Benes, 1994). However, in the absence of a predisposing genetic configuration, fetal hypoxia is unlikely to lead to schizophrenia; even in the most severely asphyxiated infants who require prolonged efforts to invoke breathing, the lifetime prevalence of schizophrenia is no greater than 6% (Buka, Tsuang, & Lipsitt, 1993; Cannon, 1997).

Pregnancy Complications

Pregnancy complications in general are less reliably associated with schizophrenia than are labor and delivery complications (Cannon, 1997; McNeil, 1988). Fetal exposure to influenza and rhesus incompatibility have emerged as two of the most prominent types of pregnancy complications. A large number of well-designed population and cohort studies have reported increased rates of schizophrenia among individuals exposed to influenza epidemics during gestation, particularly during the second trimester (Barr, Mednick, & Munk-Jorgensen, 1990; O'Callaghan, Sham, Takei, Glover, & Murray, 1991). The mechanism of this association is presently unknown; it may reflect a neurotoxic effect of influenza on fetal brain development, an effect related to maternal immunological response to infection, or a third factor (Cannon, 1997). Rhesus hemolytic disease involves a number of mechanisms that are potentially disruptive to fetal development, including fetal oxygen insufficiency (Hollister & Cannon, 1998; Hollister, Laing, & Mednick, 1996). Nevertheless, only about 2–3% of the schizophrenic population have a history of such complications (Cannon, 1997; Hollister et al., 1996), indicating that such factors play a much smaller role in the etiology of schizophrenia than do labor and delivery complications.

Implications and Conclusions

The evidence from epidemiologic studies argues against a model in which OCs can cause schizophrenia on their own, even in the most extreme cases. Nor is there evidence that such complications covary with a genetic predisposition to the disorder, as rates of OCs in unaffected relatives of schizophrenic patients are no higher than those in the general population (Cannon, 1997). However, prospective high-risk studies have consistently shown that high-risk individuals with a history of OCs, particularly fetal hypoxia, have a higher risk for schizophrenia than those without such a history and show greater severity of its neuropathological features. Moreover, these complications are not associated with an elevated risk for schizophrenia among individuals with no known genetic predisposition to the disorder. Thus, these studies support a gene–environment interaction model, in which some component of the genetic diathesis to schizophrenia renders the brain particularly vulnerable to the adverse effects of oxygen insufficiency at birth. Nonetheless, to definitively rule out a model of simple additive influences, in which the combined, yet independent effects of a genetic vulnerability and birth complications lead to schizophrenia, researchers need to conduct further genetic studies to isolate the specific genes involved and to demonstrate that labor or delivery complications are associated with schizophrenia only in those individuals who carry a predisposing genotype.

Given the high proportion of schizophrenics with a history of perinatal hypoxia (i.e., 20–30%), hypoxia-related birth complications may represent the single most important environmental factor contributing to liability to schizophrenia (Cannon, 1997). If so, it may be possible to prevent schizophrenia in genetically vulnerable individuals with careful prenatal and perinatal monitoring and early intervention.

SUGGESTED LATENCY MODELS

The latency between the hypothesized prenatal and perinatal origin of schizophrenia and its onset in adult life poses perhaps the most difficult issue for a neurodevelopmental model to explain. There is a marked lack of research on the actual process by which a static lesion early in life can cause later psychotic symptoms. Why should early neural dysfunction not produce the thought disorder, delusions, and hallucinations characteristic of the schizophrenia syndrome until nearly two decades later?

Speculation about the answers to these questions has come primarily from two perspectives. First, Weinberger (1987) postulated that environmental or genetically programmed events in utero disrupt the establishment of fundamental aspects of brain structure and function, and that it is the interaction of this fixed, structural defect with normal maturational processes of adolescence and early adulthood that triggers schizophrenia. Second, an alternative model, espoused by Feinberg (1982/1983) and others (e.g., Keshavan, Anderson, & Pettegrew, 1994; Pogue-Guile, 1991), is that there is a secondary pathological process—that is, an abnormality in these maturational processes—that occurs around the time of onset, thus potentiating the disorder. Thus, this model posits that schizophrenia involves an abnormality in synaptic pruning processes during adolescence. This view is supported by recent anatomical studies that have found evidence of excessive elimination of axons and dendrites in schizophrenia (Pettegrew, Keshavan, & Minshew, 1993). In a recent reformulation of Feinberg's (1982/1983) hypothesis, Keshavan et al. (1994) proposed that the normal peripubertal reorganization of cortical connections, involving synaptic pruning, may be abnormal in schizophrenia, resulting in excessive pruning of the prefrontal cortex and possibly a reciprocal failure of pruning of certain subcortical structures, such as the basal ganglia. The timing and rate of synaptic production and elimination may be genetically programmed, which is consistent with a genetically mediated origin of the structural pathology in schizophrenia. According to the late-developmental genetic hypothesis, schizophrenia-specific abnormalities develop postpubertally as a result of defects in genes that control normal brain development during this period (Feinberg, 1982/1983). However, in contrast with early developmental theories of the origin of schizophrenia, this theory suggests that the manifestations of a genetic anomaly in schizophrenia do not occur until adolescence, close to the onset of the disorder.

For a hypothesis of a secondary pathological process to be correct, it is not necessary to postulate the lack of a previous pathological process in the perinatal period. Some have speculated that early environmental insults (e.g., birth complications) can be viewed as nonspecific stressors that may increase the risk for schizophrenia in genetically vulnerable individuals to the extent that they produce relevant brain sequelae that persist until postpubertal onset of schizophrenia (Pogue-Guile, 1991).

Alternatively, according to the early developmental (Weinberger, 1987) model, this process may be normal but results in psychosis because of its effects on already anomalous neuronal cytoarchitecture. Although the original model does not postulate a particular mechanism by which such a process might occur, Benes (1989) hypothesized that the development of symptoms in adolescence is due to myelination of key linkages in brain circuitry that permit the expression of a previously latent defect. On the basis of the dual findings of increased myelin staining only by the second decade in associative cortical areas and increased myelination in subicular and presubicular (central corticolimbic) regions during late adolescence, Benes (1994) posited that schizophrenia may involve a defect in central corticolimbic circuitry, which only becomes functionally manifest upon normal myelination of these linkages. Weinberger (1995) speculated that prefrontal cortical dysfunction goes "online" during adolescence, because of a secondary induction of mesolimbic dopamine that drives positive symptoms of schizophrenia. Walker et al. (1994) also hypothesized that normal maturational events in the central nervous system moderate the expression of congenital neuropathology, possibly owing to developmental changes in dopamine levels.

Hormonal changes may also play a role in determining age at onset. Seeman and Lang (1990) advanced the hypothesis that estrogens, either directly or indirectly, modify symptom expression and account for many of the observed gender differences, including age at onset. A variety of animal studies have depicted the involvement of sex hormones in neuronal and synaptic proliferation and pruning (e.g., Keshavan et al., 1994). Hormonal changes during adolescence might interact with a preexisting brain structural defect to allow behavioral expressions that are unlikely to occur prior to puberty. Furthermore, stress and other psychosocial factors that arise during later development may assist in triggering the onset of the disorder in vulnerable individuals.

A final possibility is that neurodevelopmental disturbances establish a vulnerability to schizophrenia but are then followed by gradual neurodegenerative changes that reach a particular threshold for the expression of schizophrenic symptomatology in early adulthood.

These models are not mutually exclusive, and it is quite possible that all of these factors play some role in triggering the onset of outright psychosis. Although each represents a reasonably plausible explanation for the latency of onset, all of these models remain to be tested empirically.

CONCLUSION

The research summarized in this chapter tends toward the interpretation that individuals who become schizophrenic as adults have suffered some form of early cerebral maldevelopment. Although this assumption is based on inconclusive and circumstantial evidence, there are nevertheless a number of converging lines of inquiry that would suggest that subtle deficits in brain structure are present at or before birth (Bloom, 1993; Bogerts et al., 1990; Conrad et al., 1991; Falkai et al., 1988; Weinberger, 1995) and are manifested as behavioral and cognitive deficits in genetically vulnerable individuals. Although it remains possible that neurodegenerative features are present in at least some cases of schizophrenia, the largely static nature of the structural findings and the apparent absence of gliosis are much more consistent with the possibility of a neurodevelopmental abnormality. Thus, it seems more appropriate to view schizophrenia as fundamentally a disorder of brain development in utero, whose outright clinical expression may involve a complex interaction of early genetic and environmental insults with functional developmental processes later in life.

REFERENCES

Akbarian, S., Bunney, W. E., Potkin, S. G., Wigal, S. B., Hagman, J. O., Sandman, C. A., & Jones, E. G. (1993). Altered distribution of nicotinamide-adenine dinucleotide phosphate-diaphorase cells in frontal lobe of schizophrenics implies disturbances of cortical development. *Archives of General Psychiatry, 50,* 169–177.

Akbarian, S., Vineula, A., Kim, J. J., Potkin, S. G., Bunney, W. E., & Jones, E. G. (1993). Distorted distribution of nicotinamide-adenine dinucleotide phosphate-diaphorase cells in temporal lobe of schizophrenics implies disturbances of cortical development. *Archives of General Psychiatry, 50,* 178–187.

Andreasen, N. C., Ehrhardt, J. C., Swayze, V. W., & Alliger, R. J. (1990). Magnetic resonance imaging of the brain in schizophrenia: The pathophysiologic significance of structural abnormalities. *Archives of General Psychiatry, 47,* 35–44.

Arnold, S. E., Franz, B. R., & Trojanowski, J. Q. (1994). Elderly patients with schizophrenia exhibit infrequent neurodegenerative lesions. *Neurobiology of Aging, 15,* 299–303.

Arnold, S. E., Hyman, B. T., Van Hoesen, G. W., & Damasio, A. R. (1991). Some cytoarchitectural abnormalities of the entorhinal cortex in schizophrenia. *Archives of General Psychiatry, 48,* 625–632.

Aylward, E., Walker, E., & Bettes, B. (1984). Intelligence in schizophrenia: A meta-analysis of the research. *Schizophrenia Bulletin, 10,* 430–459.

Barr, C. E., Mednick, S. A., & Munk-Jorgensen, P. (1990). Exposure to influenza epidemics during gestation and adult schizophrenia: A 40-year study. *Archives of General Psychiatry, 47,* 869–874.

Benes, F. M. (1987). An analysis of the arrangement of neurons in the cingulate cortex of schizophrenic patients. *Archives of General Psychiatry, 44,* 608–616.

Benes, F. M. (1989). Myelination of cortical hippocampal relays during late adolescence. *Schizophrenia Bulletin, 15,* 585–603.

Benes, F. M. (1994). Myelination of a key relay zone in the hippocampal formation occurs in the human brain during childhood, adolescence, and adulthood. *Archives of General Psychiatry, 51,* 477–484.

Benes, F. M., Davidson, B., & Bird, E. D. (1987). Quantitative cytoarchitectural studies of the cerebral cortex of schizophrenics. *Archives of General Psychiatry, 43,* 6031–6035.

Benes, F. M., Sorensen, I., & Bird, E. D. (1991). Reduced neuronal size in posterior hippocampus of schizophrenic patients. *Schizophrenia Bulletin, 17,* 597–608.

Bilder, R. M., Bogerts, B., Ashtari, M., Wu, H., Alvir, J. M., Jody, D., Retier, G., Bell, L., & Lieberman, J. A. (1995). Anterior hippocampal volume reductions predict frontal lobe dysfunction in first episode schizophrenia. *Schizophrenia Research, 17,* 47–58.

Bleuler, E. (1950). *Dementia praecox or the group of schizophrenias.* New York: International Universities Press. (Original work published 1911)

Bloom, F. E. (1993). Advancing a neurodevelopmental origin for schizophrenia. *Archives of General Psychiatry, 50,* 224–227.

Bogerts, B. (1991). The neuropathology of schizophrenia: Pathophysiological and neurodevelopmental implications. In S. A. Mednick, T. D. Cannon, C. E. Barr, & M. Lyon (Eds.), *Fetal neural development and adult schizophrenia* (pp. 153–173). Cambridge, England: Cambridge University Press.

Bogerts, B., Falkai, P., & Greve, B. (1991). Evidence of reduced temporolimbic structure volumes in schizophrenia. *Archives of General Psychiatry, 48,* 956–958.

Bogerts, B., Falkai, P., Haupts, M., Greve, B., Ernst, S. T., Tapernon-Franz, U., & Heinzmann, U. (1990). Postmortem volume measurements of limbic systems and basal ganglia structures in chronic schizophrenics: Initial results from a new brain collection. *Schizophrenia Research, 3,* 295–301.

Breslin, N. A., & Weinberger, D. R. (1991). Neurodevelopmental implications of findings from brain imaging studies of schizophrenia. In S. A. Mednick, T. D. Cannon, C. E. Barr, & M. Lyon (Eds.), *Fetal neural development and adult schizophrenia* (pp. 199–215). Cambridge, England: Cambridge University Press.

Brown, R., Colter, N., Corsellis, J. A. N., Crow, T. J., Frith, C. D., Jagoe, R., Johnstone, E. C., & Marsh, L. (1986). Postmortem evidence of structural brain changes in schizophrenia: Differences in brain weight, temporal horn area, and parahippocampal gyrus compared with affective disorder. *Archives of General Psychiatry, 43,* 36–42.

Buka, S. L., Tsuang, M. T., & Lipsitt, L. P. (1993). Pregnancy/delivery complications and psychiatric diagnosis: A prospective study. *Archives of General Psychiatry, 50,* 151–156.

Cannon, T. D. (1991). Genetic and perinatal sources of structural brain abnormalities in schizophrenia. In S. A. Mednick, T. D. Cannon, C. E. Barr, & M. Lyon (Eds.), *Fetal neural development and adult schizophrenia* (pp. 174–198). Cambridge, England: Cambridge University Press.

Cannon, T. D. (1997). On the nature and mechanisms of obstetric influences in schizophrenia: A review and synthesis of epidemiologic studies. *International Review of Psychiatry, 9,* 387–397.

Cannon, T. D., Bearden, C. E., Hollister, J. M., & Hadley, T. (1997). A prospective cohort study of childhood cognitive deficits as precursors of schizophrenia. *Schizophrenia Research, 24,* 99–100.

Cannon, T. D., Eyler Zorrilla, L. T., Shtasel, D., Gur, R. E., Gur, R. C., Marco, E. J., Moberg, P., & Price, R. A. (1994). Neuropsychological functioning in siblings discordant for schizophrenia and healthy volunteers. *Archives of General Psychiatry, 51,* 651–661.

Cannon, T. D., Hollister, J. M., Bearden, C. E., & Hadley, T. (1997). A prospective cohort study of genetic and perinatal influences in the etiology of schizophrenia. *Schizophrenia Research, 24,* 248.

Cannon, T. D., Kaprio, J., Lonnqvist, J., Huttunen, M., & Kokenvuo, M. (1998).

The genetic epidemiology of schizophrenia in a Finnish twin cohort: A population based modeling study. *Archives of General Psychiatry, 55,* 67–74.

Cannon, T. D., & Mednick, S. A. (1993). The schizophrenia high risk project in Copenhagen: Three decades of progress. *Acta Psychiatrica Scandinavica, 370,* 33–47.

Cannon, T. D., Mednick, S. A., & Parnas, J. (1989). Genetic and perinatal determinants of structural brain deficits in schizophrenia. *Archives of General Psychiatry, 46,* 883–889.

Cannon, T. D., Mednick, S. A., Parnas, J., Schulsinger, F., Praestholm, J., & Vestergaard, A. (1993). Developmental brain abnormalities in the offspring of schizophrenic mothers: I. Contribution of genetic and perinatal factors. *Archives of General Psychiatry, 50,* 551–564.

Conrad, A. J., Abebe, T., Austin, R., Forsythe, S., & Scheibel, A. B. (1991). Hippocampal pyramidal cell disarray in schizophrenia as a bilateral phenomenon. *Archives of General Psychiatry, 49,* 531–537.

Crow, T. J., Ball, J., & Bloom, S. R. (1989). Schizophrenia as an anomaly of development of cerebral asymmetry. A postmortem study and a proposal concerning the genetic basis of the disease. *Archives of General Psychiatry, 46,* 1145–1150.

Dagg, B. M., Booth, J. D., McLaughlin, J. E., & Dolan, R. J. (1994). A morphometric study of the cingulate cortex in mood disorder and schizophrenia. *Schizophrenia Research, 11,* 137.

Degreef, G., Ashtari, M., Bogerts, B., Bilder, R. M., Jody, D. N., Ma, J., Alvir, J., & Lieberman, J. A. (1992). Volumes of ventricular system subdivisions measured from magnetic resonance images in first episode schizophrenia patients. *Archives of General Psychiatry, 49,* 531–537.

DeLisi, L. E., Goldin, L. R., Hamovit, J. R., Maxwell, E., Kurtz, D., & Gershon, E. S. (1986). A family study of the association of increased ventricular size with schizophrenia. *Archives of General Psychiatry, 43,* 148–153.

DeLisi, L. E., Hoff, A. L., Schwartz, J. E., Shields, G. W., Halthore, S. N., Gupta, S. M., Henn, F. A., & Anand, A. K. (1991). Brain morphology in first-episode schizophrenic-like psychotic patients: A quantitative magnetic resonance imaging study. *Biological Psychiatry, 29,* 159–175.

DeLisi, L. E., Tew, W., Xie, S., Hoff, A. L., Sakuma, M., Kushner, M., Lee, G., Shedlack, K., Smith, A. M., & Grimson, R. (1995). A prospective followup study of brain morphology and cognition in first episode schizophrenic patients: Preliminary findings. *Biological Psychiatry, 38,* 349–360.

Done, D. J., Johnstone, E. C., Frith, C. D., Golding, J., Shepherd, P. M., & Crow, T. J. (1991). Complications of pregnancy and delivery in relation to psychosis in adult life: Data from the British perinatal mortality survey sample. *British Medical Journal, 302,* 1576–1580.

Driscoll, R. M. (1984). Intentional and incidental learning in children vulnerable to psychopathology. In N. F. Watt, E. J. Anthony, L. C. Wynne, & J. E. Roif (Eds.), *Children at risk for schizophrenia: A longitudinal perspective* (pp. 320–326). New York: Cambridge University Press.

Epstein, H. T. (1986). Stages in human development. *Developmental Brain Research*, *30*, 114–119.

Erlenmeyer-Kimling, L., & Cornblatt, B. A. (1987). The New York High Risk Project: A followup report. *Schizophrenia Bulletin*, *13*, 451–460.

Erlenmeyer-Kimling, L., Golden, R., & Cornblatt, B. A. (1989). A taxometric analysis of cognitive and neuromotor variables in children at risk for schizophrenia. *Journal of Abnormal Psychology*, *98*, 203–208.

Falkai, P., & Bogerts, B. (1986). Cell loss in the hippocampus of schizophrenics. *European Archives of Psychiatry and Neurological Science*, *106*, 505–517.

Falkai, P., Bogerts, B., Roberts, G. W., & Crow, T. J. (1988). Measurement of the alpha-cell migration in the entorhinal region: A marker for developmental disturbances in schizophrenia? *Schizophrenia Research*, *1*, 157–158.

Feinberg, I. (1982/1983). Schizophrenia: Caused by a fault in programmed synaptic elimination during adolescence? *Journal of Psychiatric Research*, *17*, 319–334.

Feinberg, I., Thode, H. C., Chugani, H. T., & March, J. D. (1990). Gamma distribution model describes maturation curves for delta wave amplitude, cortical metabolic rate and synaptic density. *Journal of Theoretical Biology*, *142*, 149–161.

Fish, B. (1977). Neurobiologic antecedents of schizophrenia in children: Evidence for an inherited, congenital neurointegrative defect. *Archives of General Psychiatry*, *98*, 203–208.

Fish, B., Marcus, J., Hans, S. L., Auerbach, J. G., & Perdue, S. (1992). Infants at risk for schizophrenia: Sequelae of a genetic neurointegrative defect. *Archives of General Psychiatry*, *49*, 221–235.

Foerster, A., Lewis, S. W., Owen, M. J., & Murray, R. M. (1991). Low birth weight and a family history of schizophrenia predict poor premorbid functioning in psychosis. *Schizophrenia Research*, *5*, 13–20.

Goldberg, T. E., Ragland, J. D., Torrey, E. F., Gold, J. M., Bigelow, L. B., & Weinberger, D. R. (1990). Neuropsychological assessment of monozygotic twins discordant for schizophrenia. *Archives of General Psychiatry*, *46*, 867–872.

Goldman-Rakic, P. S. (1987). Development of cortical circuitry and cognitive function. *Child Development*, *58*, 601–622.

Goodman, S. (1987). Emory University Project on children of disturbed parents. *Schizophrenia Bulletin*, *13*, 411–422.

Gottesman, I. I., & Bertelsen, A. (1989). Confirming unexpressed genotypes for schizophrenia: Risks in the offspring of Fischer's Danish identical and fraternal discordant twins. *Archives of General Psychiatry*, *46*, 867–872.

Gruzelier, J., Mednick, S. A., & Schulsinger, F. (1979). Lateralized impairment in the WISC profile of children at risk for psychopathology. In J. Gruzelier & P. Flor-Henry (Eds.), *Hemisphere asymmetries of function in psychopathology* (pp. 105–110). Amsterdam, The Netherlands: Elsevier Science.

Gur, R. E., Cowell, P. C., Turetsky, B. L., Gallacher, F., Cannon, T. D., Bilker, W., & Gur, R. C. (1998). A followup MRI study of schizophrenia: Relationship of neuroanatomic changes with clinical and neurobehavioral measures. *Archives of General Psychiatry, 55*(2), 145–152.

Gur, R. E., & Pearlson, G. D. (1993). Neuroimaging in schizophrenia research. *Schizophrenia Bulletin, 19*, 337–353.

Hallett, S., Quinn, D., & Hewitt, J. (1986). Defective interhemispheric integration and anomalous language lateralization in children at risk for schizophrenia. *Journal of Nervous and Mental Disease, 174*, 418–427.

Harvey, P., Weintraub, S., & Neal, J. (1982) Speech competence of children vulnerable to psychopathology. *Journal of Abnormal Child Psychology, 10*, 373–388.

Heaton, R., Paulsen, J. S., McAdams, L. A., Kuck, J., Zisook, S., Braff, D., Harris, J., & Jeste, D. V. (1994). Neuropsychological deficits in schizophrenics: Relationship to age, chronicity, and dementia. *Archives of General Psychiatry, 51*, 469–476.

Hoffman, R. E., & Dobscha, S. K. (1989). Cortical pruning and the development of schizophrenia: A computer model. *Schizophrenia Bulletin, 15*, 477–489.

Hollister, J. M., & Cannon, T. D. (1998). Neurodevelopmental disturbances in the etiology of schizophrenia. In M. Ron & A. S. David (Eds.), *Disorders of brain and mind* (pp. 280–302). New York: Cambridge University Press.

Hollister, J. M., Laing, P., & Mednick, S. A. (1996). Rhesus incompatibility as a risk factor for schizophrenia in male adults. *Archives of General Psychiatry, 53*, 19–24.

Hudspeth, W. J., & Pribram, K. H. (1990). Stages of brain and cognitive maturation. *Journal of Educational Psychology, 82*, 881–884.

Huttenlocher, P. R. (1979). Synaptic density in human frontal cortex: Developmental changes and effects of aging. *Brain Research, 163*, 195–205.

Jacob, J., & Beckmann, H. (1986). Prenatal developmental disturbances in the limbic allocortex in schizophrenics. *Journal of Neural Transmission, 65*, 303–326.

Jones, E. G. (1991). The development of the primate neocortex: An overview. In S. A. Mednick, T. D. Cannon, C. E. Barr, & M. Lyon (Eds.), *Fetal neural development and adult schizophrenia* (pp. 153–173). Cambridge, England: Cambridge University Press.

Jones, P. B., Rodgers, B., Murray, R. M., & Marmot, M. (1994). Child developmental risk factors for adult schizophrenia in the British 1946 birth cohort. *Lancet, 344*, 1398–1402.

Kendler, K. S., & Diehl, S. R. (1993). The genetics of schizophrenia: A current, genetic–epidemiologic perspective. *Schizophrenia Bulletin, 19*, 261–285.

Keshavan, M. S., Anderson, S., & Pettegrew, J. W. (1994). Is schizophrenia due to excessive pruning in the prefrontal cortex? The Feinberg hypothesis revisited. *Journal of Psychiatric Research, 28*, 239–265.

Klein, R. H., & Salzman, L. F. (1984). Response contingent learning in children at risk. In N. F. Watt, E. J. Anthony, L. C. Wynne, & J. E. Roif (Eds.),

Children at risk for schizophrenia: A longitudinal perspective (pp. 371–375). New York: Cambridge University Press.

Kovelman, J. A., & Scheibel, A. B. (1984). A neurohistological correlate of schizophrenia. *Biological Psychiatry, 19*, 1601–1621.

Kraepelin, E. (1919). *Dementia praecox and paraphrenia.* Edinburgh, Scotland: Livingston.

Kuchna, I. (1994). Quantitative studies of human newborn hippocampal pyramidal cells after perinatal hypoxia. *Folia Neuropathologica, 32(1)*, 9–16.

Lewis, S. W. (1989). Congenital risk factors for schizophrenia. *Psychological Medicine, 9*, 5–13.

Lewis, S. W., & Murray, R. M. (1987). Obstetric complications, neurodevelopmental deviance, and risk of schizophrenia. *Journal of Psychiatric Research, 21*, 413–421.

MacGlashan, T. H., & Fenton, W. S. (1992). The positive–negative distinction in schizophrenia: Review of natural history validators. *Archives of General Psychiatry, 49*, 63–72.

Marcus, J., Hans, S. L., Mednick, S. A., Schulsinger, F., & Michelsen, N. (1985). Neurological dysfunction in offspring of schizophrenics in Israel and Denmark: A replication analysis. *Archives of General Psychiatry, 42*, 753–761.

McLardy, T. (1974). Hippocampal zinc and structural deficits in brains from chronic alcoholics and some schizophrenics. *Journal of Orthomolecular Psychiatry, 4*, 32–36.

McNeil, T. F. (1988). Obstetric factors and perinatal injuries. In M. T. Tsuang & J. C. Simpson (Eds.), *Handbook of schizophrenia: Vol. 3. Nosology, epidemiology and genetics* (pp. 319–344). New York: Elsevier.

McNeil, T. F., & Kaij, L. (1978). Obstetric factors in the development of schizophrenia: Complications in the births of preschizophrenics and in reproduction by schizophrenic parents. In L. C. Wynne, R. L. Cromwell, & S. Matthyse (Eds.), *The nature of schizophrenia: New approaches to research and treatment* (pp. 401–429). New York: Wiley.

Mednick, S. A., Cannon, T. D., & Barr, C. E. (1991). Obstetric events and adult schizophrenia. In S. A. Mednick, T. D. Cannon, C. E. Barr, & M. Lyon (Eds.), *Fetal neural development and adult schizophrenia* (pp. 115–133). Cambridge, England: Cambridge University Press.

Mednick, S. A., Mura, E., Schulsinger, F., & Mednick, B. (1974). Perinatal conditions and infant development in children with schizophrenic parents. In S. A. Mednick, F. Schulsinger, J. Higgins, & B. Bell (Eds.), *Genetics, environment, and psychopathology* (pp. 231–248). North Holland, Amsterdam: Elsevier.

Murray, R. M., O'Callaghan, E., Castle, D. J., & Lewis, S. W. (1992). A neurodevelopmental approach to the classification of schizophrenia. *Schizophrenia Bulletin, 18*, 319–332.

Nasrallah, H. A., Olsen, S. C., McCalley-Whitters, M., Chapman, S., & Jacoby,

C. G. (1986). Cerebral ventricular enlargement in schizophrenia. *Archives of General Psychiatry, 43,* 157–159.

Neumann, C. S., Grimes, K., Walker, E. F., & Baum, K. (1995). Developmental pathways to schizophrenia: Behavioral subtypes. *Journal of Abnormal Psychology, 104,* 558–566.

Nopoulos, P., Flashman, L., Flaum, M., Arndt, S., & Andreasen, N. (1994). Stability of cognitive functioning early in the course of schizophrenia. *Schizophrenia Research, 14,* 29–37.

Nopoulos, P., Torres, I., Flaum, M., Andreasen, N. C., Ehrhardt, J. C., & Yuh, W. T. (1995). Brain morphology in first episode schizophrenia. *American Journal of Psychiatry, 152,* 1721–1723.

Nyakas, C., Buwalda, B., & Luiten, P. G. (1996). Hypoxia and brain development. *Progress in Neurobiology, 49,* 1–51.

O'Callaghan, E., Sham, P., Takei, N., Glover, G., & Murray, R. M. (1991). Schizophrenia after prenatal exposure to 1957 A2 influenza epidemic. *Lancet, 337,* 1248–1250.

Parnas, J., Schulsinger, F., Teasdale, T. W., Schulsinger, H., Feldman, P. M., & Mednick, S. A. (1982). Perinatal complications and clinical outcome within the schizophrenia spectrum. *British Journal of Psychiatry, 140,* 416–420.

Penrice, J., Cady, E. B., Lorek, A., Wylezinska, M., Amess, P. N., Aldridge, R. F., Stewart, A., Wyatt, J. S., & Reynolds, O. R. (1996). Proton MRS of the brain in normal preterm and term infants and early changes after perinatal hypoxia-ischemia. *Pediatric Research, 40(1),* 6–14.

Pettegrew, J. W., Keshavan, M. S., & Minshew, N. J. (1993). P-nuclear magnetic resonance spectroscopy: Neurodevelopment and schizophrenia. *Schizophrenia Bulletin, 19,* 35–53.

Pogue-Guile, M. F. (1991). The development of liability to schizophrenia: Early and late developmental models. In E. F. Walker (Ed.), *Schizophrenia: A life course developmental perspective* (pp. 227–298). San Diego, CA: Academic Press.

Pogue-Guile, M. F., & Harrow, M. (1984). Negative and positive symptoms in schizophrenia and depression: A follow-up. *Schizophrenia Bulletin, 10,* 371–387.

Rakic, P. (1985, March). Limits of neurogenesis in primates. *Science, 227(4690),* 1054–1056.

Rakic, P., Bourgeois, J. P., & Goldman-Rakic, P. S. (1994). Synaptic development of the cerebral cortex: Implications for learning, memory, and mental illness. *Progress in Brain Research, 102,* 227–241.

Reveley, A. M., Reveley, M. A., & Murray, R. M. (1984). Cerebral ventricular enlargement in nongenetic schizophrenia: A controlled twin study. *British Journal of Psychiatry, 144,* 89–93.

Rutschmann, J., Cornblatt, B., & Erlenmeyer-Kimling, L. (1986). Sustained attention in children at risk for schizophrenia: Findings with two visual continuous performance tasks. *Journal of Abnormal Child Psychology, 14,* 365–385.

Saykin, A. J., Gur, R. C., Gur, R. E., Mozley, D., & Mozley, L. (1991). Neuro-psychological function in schizophrenia: Selective impairment in learning and memory. *Archives of General Psychiatry, 48*, 618–624.

Saykin, A. J., Shtasel, D. L., Gur, R. E., Kester, D. B., Mozley, L. H., Stafiniak, P., & Gur, R. C. (1994). Neuropsychological deficits in neuroleptic-naive, first-episode schizophrenics. *Archives of General Psychiatry, 51*, 124–131.

Seeman, M. V., & Lang, M. (1990). The role of estrogens in schizophrenia gender differences. *Schizophrenia Bulletin, 16*, 185–194.

Selemon, L. D., Rajkowska, G., & Goldman-Rakic, P. S. (1993). A morphometric analysis of the prefrontal areas 9 and 46 in the schizophrenic and normal human brain. *Schizophrenia Research, 9*, 151.

Squire, L. R. (1987). *Memory and the brain.* Oxford, England: Oxford University Press.

Stevens, J. R. (1982). Neuropathology of schizophrenia. *Archives of General Psychiatry, 39*, 1131–1139.

Suddath, R. L., Christison, D. A., Torrey, E. F., Casanova, M. F., & Weinberger, D. R. (1990). Anatomical abnormalities in the brains of monozygotic twins discordant for schizophrenia. *New England Journal of Medicine, 322*, 791–794.

Thatcher, R. W. (1992). Cyclic cortical reorganization during early childhood. *Brain and Cognition, 20*, 24–50.

Torrey, E. F., Taylor, E., Bracha, H. S., Bowler, A. E., McNeil, T. F., Rawlings, R. R., & Quinn, P. O. (1993). Prenatal origin of schizophrenia in a subgroup of discordant MZ twins. *Schizophrenia Bulletin, 20*, 423–431.

Tyrka, A., Cannon, T. D., Haslam, N., Mednick, S. A., Schulsinger, F., & Schulsinger, H. (1995). The latent structure of schizotypy. *Journal of Abnormal Psychology, 104*, 173–183.

Waddington, J. L. (1991). Neurodynamics of abnormalities in cerebral metabolism and structure in schizophrenia. *Schizophrenia Bulletin, 19*, 55–69.

Walker, E. F., Savole, T., & Davis, D. (1994). Neuromotor precursors of schizophrenia. *Schizophrenia Bulletin, 20*, 441–451.

Weinberger, D. R. (1987). Implications of normal brain development for the pathogenesis of schizophrenia. *Archives of General Psychiatry, 44*, 660–669.

Weinberger, D. R. (1995). Schizophrenia as a neurodevelopmental disorder. In S. R. Hirsch & D. R. Weinberger (Eds.), *Schizophrenia* (pp. 293–323). Cambridge, MA: Blackwell Science.

Weinberger, D. R., DeLisi, L. E., Berman, G., Targum, S., & Wyatt, R. J. (1982). Computed tomography scans in schizophreniform disorder and other acute psychatric patients. *Archives of General Psychiatry, 48*, 85.

Weinberger, D. R., DeLisi, L. E., Neophytides, A. N., & Wyatt, R. J. (1981). Familial aspects of CT scan abnormalities in chronic schizophrenic patients. *Psychiatric Research, 4*, 65–71.

Weintraub, S. (1987). Risk factors in schizophrenia: The Stony Brook High Risk project. *Schizophrenia Bulletin, 13,* 439–448.

Woods, B. T., Yurgelun-Todd, D., Benes, F. M., Frankenburg, F. R., Pope, H. G., & McSparren, J. (1990). Progressive ventricular enlargement in schizophrenia: Comparison to bipolar affective disorder and correlation with clinical course. *Biological Psychiatry, 27,* 341–352.

3

ORIGINS OF THE DEPRESSIVE COGNITIVE STYLE

JUDY GARBER AND CYNTHIA FLYNN

Depression is an important public health concern that affects approximately 12% of men and 20% of women in their lifetime (Weissman, 1987). Prevalence of diagnosed major depressive disorders is relatively low during childhood (<3%), whereas the rates during adolescence and young adulthood have been reported to be as high as 20%, particularly in women (Fleming & Offord, 1990; Lewinsohn, Hops, Roberts, Seeley, & Andrew, 1993). At times, depression can be debilitating and even life threatening to the individual, and it can take a serious toll on society in terms of disruptions in productivity and interpersonal relationships. Mood disorders are associated with suicidal ideation and attempts (Brent et al., 1993) and with problems in academic, occupational, and social functioning that persist beyond the depressive episode (Puig-Antich et al., 1985; Weissman, Klerman, Prusoff, Sholomskas, & Padian, 1981). Moreover, follow-up studies indicate that patients who recover from an episode of major depression

This work was supported in part by a FIRST Award from the National Institute of Mental Health (R29-MH4545801A1) and a Faculty Scholar Award (88-1214-88) and Grant 95070390 from the W.T. Grant Foundation. We would like to acknowledge the cooperation of the Nashville Metropolitan School District, and Drs. Binkley and Crouch, and we thank the parents and children who participated in the "Development of Depression" project.

are at increased risk for recurrent episodes (Harrington, Fudge, Rutter, Pickles, & Hill, 1990; Keller, Lavori, Rice, Coryell, & Hirschfeld, 1986; Kovacs et al., 1984). Children and adolescents with early onset depression also are at risk for other accompanying dysfunction, such as tobacco and substance abuse, early pregnancy, school dropout, and poor work history (Christie et al., 1988; Kandel & Davies, 1986). Thus, there is a serious need to identify the factors that contribute to the development of depressive disorders in order to ameliorate and prevent both the short- and long-term consequences of this major mental health problem.

During the past 25 years, there have been several important advances in our knowledge about the diagnosis, course, prognosis, etiology, and treatment of mood disorders in adults (e.g., Paykel, 1992). Over the last decade, our understanding of depression in children and adolescents also has increased (Birmaher, Ryan, Williamson, Brent, & Kaufman, 1996; Birmaher et al., 1996). One of the remaining challenges for clinical psychology in the next century will be to build on this knowledge to develop and test interventions aimed at preventing and treating depression across the life span.

A critical step toward this goal will be to identify early precursors of depression that can be the target of primary prevention. Several depression prevention programs have been developed and initially tested. These interventions aim to alter children's cognitive style (Clarke et al., 1995; Gillham, Reivich, Jaycox, & Seligman, 1995; Jaycox, Reivich, Gillham, & Seligman, 1994) and to increase their general knowledge about depression (Beardslee et al., 1992). The basic premise of cognitive prevention programs is that negative cognitions contribute to the onset and maintenance of mood disorders, and therefore if we can prevent the development of the depressogenic cognitive style, we can prevent depression.

An intriguing question for the field is what is the origin of this cognitive style. The present chapter addresses this issue. First, cognitive models of depression and the evidence supporting them are reviewed briefly. Next, several processes underlying the development of the cognitive vulnerability are proposed. Finally, we review the results of a study designed to test some of the hypotheses generated from these proposed developmental models.

COGNITIVE MODELS OF DEPRESSION

There are basically two cognitive theories of depression. The first was proposed by Beck (1967, 1976, 1984), who asserted that the thinking of depressed individuals is characterized by a *negative cognitive triad*: negative views of the self, the world, and the future. In addition, depressed individuals process information in a distorted manner, which serves to maintain this negative cognitive triad. Thus, the content of depressed persons' cognitions is predominantly negative, self-derogating, and self-blaming, and they project this negative view into the future, leading to hopelessness (Kovacs & Beck, 1978).

The second major cognitive model of depression is the *hopelessness theory* (Abramson, Metalsky, & Alloy, 1989), which is a revision of the reformulated *helplessness model* (Abramson, Seligman, & Teasdale, 1978). According to the hopelessness theory, the proximal sufficient cause of the hopelessness subtype of depression is the expectation that highly desirable outcomes will not occur or that highly undesirable outcomes will occur, and that the person is helpless to change this. Moreover, such hopelessness is hypothesized to result from individuals' making inferences that (a) the causes of negative events are global and stable; (b) the consequences of such events are negative; and (c) the events imply negative characteristics about the self.

Both cognitive theories (Abramson et al., 1989; Beck, 1976) are diathesis–stress models in which the negative cognitive style is the diathesis. That is, when faced with important negative life events, individuals who have the cognitive propensity to interpret the causes of these events in a particular way (i.e., global, stable, internal), to have a negative view of themselves, and to develop negative expectations of the future are more likely to become depressed than are individuals who do not have these cognitive tendencies. The combination of both negative life events and this cognitive style is considered to be a sufficient cause of depression.

Thus, at least three types of cognitions are hypothesized to be important to the etiology of depression. Both models emphasize that a negative view of the self and negative expectations about the future are core parts of the cognitive vulnerability. In addition, the hopelessness theory posits that the tendency to make global, stable, and internal attributions regarding the causes of negative events also is a central feature. Therefore, the current review focuses on understanding the origins of these three cognitions: self-worth, hopelessness, and attributional style. Before exploring the development of these cognitions, however, we briefly review evidence supporting these cognitive models.

Evidence of Cognitive Vulnerability to Depression

Is there evidence of a cognitive vulnerability to depression? A thorough review of the literature concerning cognitions and depression is beyond the scope of this chapter. Rather, we highlight here five kinds of studies that have been conducted to examine the existence of a cognitive vulnerability to depression: correlational, predictive, stability, prevention, and offspring.

Correlational Studies

Although there has been some controversy about the extent of support for the cognitive models (e.g., Coyne & Gotlib, 1983; Haaga, Dyck, & Ernst, 1991), the empirical literature generally has shown that depressed and nondepressed adults differ in ways predicted by the models, particularly with respect to attributions, future expectations, self-schema, and dysfunctional attitudes. Studies also have found that depressed children and adolescents show the hypothesized depressogenic attributional style, negative expectations and hopelessness, cognitive distortions, and cognitive errors (see Garber & Hilsman, 1992, for a review).

Such covariation could be because cognitions are a concomitant, cause, or consequence of the depressive syndrome (Barnett & Gotlib, 1988). Negative cognitions could be the result of the underlying depressive process and hold no particular causal status. Depressions that are clearly caused by a biological process, such as Cushing's disease, have been found to be characterized by some of the same kinds of negative cognitions found in other depressions (Hollon, 1992). Thus, at least in some forms of depression, negative cognitions could simply be a symptom of the depressive disorder.

Alternatively, the experience of depression itself could lead to depressogenic cognitions, and thus they could be a consequence of the depressive syndrome. This hypothesis has found mixed support (Lewinsohn, Steinmetz, Larson, & Franklin, 1981). Lewinsohn and colleagues (Lewinsohn et al., 1981; Rohde, Lewinsohn, & Seeley, 1994) have not found that depression permanently affected cognitive style in either adults or adolescents. In contrast, Nolen-Hoeksema, Girgus, and Seligman (1992) found that children who experienced relatively higher levels of depressive symptoms had more pessimistic explanatory styles over time than did their less depressed peers. Moreover, explanatory style became more pessimistic over time in the group of children with higher levels of depressive symptoms, even after their level of depression declined. Nolen-Hoeksema et al. (1992) concluded that "a period of depression during childhood can lead to the development of a fixed and more pessimistic explanatory style, which remains with a child after his or her depression has begun to subside" (p. 418). Given the differences in the ages of the subjects studied in the Nolen-Hoeksema et al. versus Lewinsohn studies, it is possible that evidence of a "scarring" effect of depression on cognitive style is more apparent earlier in development.

Thus, although the frequently replicated finding of covariation between negative cognitions and current depression is certainly consistent with the cognitive models, the alternative that cognitions are a concomitant or consequence of a depressive state cannot be ruled out from cross-sectional studies showing differences between depressed and nondepressed persons. Rather, experimental or prospective studies showing that negative cognitions temporally precede and predict depressive symptoms would be more compelling.

Prospective Studies

Short-term longitudinal studies examining the contribution of cognitions to the prediction of depression have been both supportive (e.g., Cutrona, 1983; Metalsky, Joiner, Hardin, & Abramson, 1993) and non-supportive (e.g., Cochran & Hammen, 1985; Lewinsohn et al., 1981). Abramson et al. (1989) argued that one reason these longitudinal results have been mixed is that some studies tested a *cognitive–trait theory* in which only the relation between the cognitive variables and depression was assessed, rather than testing a *cognition–stress interaction theory* in which both the cognitive predisposition and negative life events are considered in interaction with one another. Whereas a cognitive–trait theory would predict that all individuals who have the depressogenic cognitive predisposition should become depressed, the cognitive diathesis–stress model improves predictability by suggesting that cognitively vulnerable individuals will become depressed *when* they are faced with important negative life events.

Recently, several prospective studies have tested the cognitive diathesis–stress model of depression in college students (Metalsky, Halberstadt, & Abramson, 1987; Metalsky & Joiner, 1992; Metalsky et al., 1993) and children (Hilsman & Garber, 1995; Nolen-Hoeksema et al., 1992; Panak & Garber, 1992; Robinson, Garber, & Hilsman, 1995). Metalsky and colleagues (Metalsky et al., 1987; Metalsky & Joiner, 1992; Metalsky et al., 1993) have found across three different studies that the interaction of cognitive style and negative life events predicted increases in self-reported depressive symptoms, and one study (Metalsky & Joiner, 1992) found that hopelessness mediated this relation. Garber and colleagues (Hilsman & Garber, 1995; Panak & Garber, 1992; Robinson et al., 1995) similarly have found in three different short-term longitudinal studies using different stressors (grades, peer rejection, and school transition), and different time periods that cognitions (attributions, self-worth) measured before the stressors moderated the effect of the stressors on depressive symptoms in children. Thus, studies that have explicitly tested the cognitive–stress interaction have been finding support for the cognitive model and for the existence of a cognitive vulnerability.

Stability of Cognitive Style

Some researchers have argued that if cognitive style is a vulnerability to depression, then it should be a stable characteristic present both during and after depressive episodes (Barnett & Gotlib, 1988). The most common research design used to test this has been to compare the cognitions of never depressed, currently depressed, and formerly depressed individuals. If negative cognitions are a stable characteristic of depression-vulnerable individuals, then persons in the "remitted" group should continue to report a more negative cognitive style than never-depressed individuals, although possibly not at the same level as those who are currently depressed.

Some studies of adults have found that, compared with nondepressed controls, formerly depressed individuals continue to report more negative cognitions even after their depression has remitted (e.g., Eaves & Rush, 1984; Garber, 1995; Teasdale & Dent, 1987), although most studies have found that the cognitions of remitted persons are not significantly different from nondepressed controls (Fennell & Campbell, 1984; Hamilton & Abramson, 1983; Lewinsohn et al., 1981; Persons & Miranda, 1992; Rohde, Lewinsohn, & Seeley, 1990). Similarly, the few studies in children and adolescents have not found cognitive differences between remitted and nondepressed individuals (Asarnow & Bates, 1988; McCauley, Mitchell, Burke, & Moss, 1988). Gotlib, Lewinsohn, Seeley, Rohde, and Redner (1993) did find that the cognitions of remitted adolescents did not return to normal levels, although neither did their levels of depressive symptoms.

Taken together, these mixed findings have been used to argue against there being a stable cognitive style that serves as a vulnerability to depression (Barnett & Gotlib, 1988; Segal & Dobson, 1992). Recently, however, Just, Alloy, and Abramson (1998) noted several limitations of these kinds of "remission" studies. They suggested that such studies do not consider that (a) treatment could have altered formerly depressed patients' cognitions; (b) the formerly depressed group might have been heterogeneous with regard to cognitive style; and (c) cognitive style might need to be activated to be assessed properly. Thus, the stability of the cognitive vulnerability needs to be studied further.

Prevention Studies

The basic idea of prevention studies is that if an intervention program aimed at changing cognitive style shows lower rates of depression in the treated versus the untreated group, then this is consistent with there being a cognitive vulnerability that is a risk for depression. Seligman and colleagues (Gillham et al., 1995; Hollon, DeRubeis, & Seligman, 1992; Jaycox et al., 1994; Seligman, this volume) have found that a cognitive prevention program that focuses particularly on changing attributional style successfully reduced the rates of depressive symptoms in children and college students.

Several studies (e.g., Blackburn, Eunson, & Bishop, 1983; Evans et al., 1992) have found that depressed adult outpatients treated with cognitive therapy have a reduced risk for subsequent relapse compared with patients brought to remission pharmacologically. Even more interesting is that posttreatment attributional style scores have been found to significantly predict relapse. That is, patients who did not show change in attributional style were most likely to relapse following successful treatment (Hollon, Evans, & DeRubeis, 1990). Thus, changing cognitive style appears to prevent increases in depressive symptoms as well as relapse of depressive episodes.

Offspring of Depressed Parents

Another strategy for studying cognitive vulnerability is to examine the cognitions of individuals who are known to be at risk for depression, such as the offspring of depressed parents. There is clear evidence that children of depressed parents are at increased risk for developing mood disorders themselves (Downey & Coyne, 1990; Weissman et al., 1987). If negative cognitions contribute to the development of such mood disorders, then these "high-risk" individuals would be more likely to exhibit a cognitive vulnerability than children whose parents have not experienced mood disorders.

Only a few studies have explicitly tested this hypothesis. Jaenicke et al. (1987) compared children whose mothers had a history of unipolar depression, bipolar affective disorder, and medical illness and normal controls and found that offspring of unipolar mothers reported significantly lower self-esteem and a more depressogenic attributional style than did children of medically ill and control mothers. Goodman, Adamson, Riniti, and Cole (1994) similarly found that children of depressed mothers reported significantly lower perceived self-worth than did children of well mothers.

Finally, Garber and Robinson (1997) compared the cognitions of offspring of depressed mothers (high risk) to those of children of mothers without a history of psychiatric diagnoses (low risk). They found that the high-risk children, particularly offspring of mothers with a more chronic history of depression, reported a significantly more negative cognitive style than did low-risk children. Even when children's current level of depressive symptoms was controlled, high- and low-risk children continued to differ with regard to their attributional style and perceived self-worth. Thus, children who are at risk for depression, but who have not yet experienced depression themselves, have been found to report a more depressogenic cognitive style that might be a vulnerability to later depression.

In summary, evidence from correlational, predictive, prevention, and high-risk studies indicates that there is a cognitive style that may be a vulnerability to depressive symptoms and disorders in children, adolescents, and adults. More adequate studies examining the stability of this cognitive vulnerability need to be conducted (Just et al., 1998). An important next question is what are the normal developmental processes involved in the construction of cognitions about the self, future, and causes of events, and how might these normative processes go awry?

NORMATIVE DEVELOPMENT

All individuals formulate schema about themselves, their competences, interpersonal relationships, the causes of events, and their outlook for the future. We turn to basic cognitive and social development to understand the origins of these beliefs. The primary social–cognitive constructs derived from cognitive theories of depression are self-worth, attributions about the causes of events, and expectations about the future. The question for the present discussion is how do these cognitions develop, and how does cognitive style become negative for some people but not others.

Self-Worth

Self-worth can be defined as the overall level of regard that one has for the self as a person (Harter, 1993). James (1890/1963) described self-worth as perceived competency in domains that are considered important by the individual. Cooley (1902/1956) conceptualized it as the incorporation of the attitudes of significant others toward the self. Harter (1990) showed that both positive regard from others and perceived competence in domains of importance contribute to high self-esteem in children and adolescents.

Children's understanding of the self becomes increasingly differentiated with development (Harter, 1983, 1990). Children shift their focus from behavioral characteristics in early childhood to traitlike characteristics in middle childhood to more abstract psychological constructs during adolescence (Harter, 1986). Very young children can make judgments about the self across several domains of competence (e.g., cognitive, social, behavioral, and physical), but these judgments are not very well differentiated. Although they cannot articulate it, very young children do appear to have a sense of global self-worth. Teacher ratings of initiative taking, exploring the environment, and effective coping in young children are associated with later competence. Harter (1990) equated these behaviors with the expression of early global self-worth.

Young children (ages 4 through 7) describe themselves in terms of concrete, observable behaviors and characteristics ("I can lift this chair, so I am strong"). They reference specific skills (e.g., "I can kick the ball") rather than generalized competencies such as being athletic or smart. They do not represent higher order categories, and they tend to be globally positive about the self (Harter, 1988). Thus, in these young children it might take a more major traumatic event (Janoff-Bulman, 1992) or constant and severe negative feedback to derail them from their normal tendencies for a positive self-view.

By middle childhood (ages 8 through 12), children are developing the ability to form concepts and to make judgments about their global self-worth. According to Harter (1990), competency domains are becoming more differentiated during this time (e.g., scholastic, athletic, peer acceptance, behavioral conduct, and physical appearance). During middle childhood, children can make generalizations from specific behaviors, and they have begun to understand and use trait labels such as *smart*, *friendly*, and *popular*. Important developments during this age period are the ability to make social comparisons and the growing awareness of the evaluations of others. People's opinions of them become increasingly salient and incorporated into their self-concepts. Self-descriptions become more realistic but not necessarily more negative. Although a range of negative aspects of the self will be more possible, children with high self-esteem are more likely to minimize the importance of negative feedback because it is inconsistent with their developing self-view (Harter, 1988).

A major change in adolescence is the use of abstract concepts that include descriptions of more psychological aspects of the self (Harter, 1988). As a result of the increased differentiation that occurs during this period, adolescents may experience conflict between opposing attributes, which then can cause some distress and confusion. Adolescents with high self-esteem can identify negative aspects of the self but tend not to include them as part of the core self (Harter, 1988).

Montemayor and Eisen (1977) found that although adolescents retain the use of some physical self-descriptors, they generally describe themselves in more abstract and psychological terms than do younger children. Hart and Damon (1986) proposed that self-concept be divided into several components or self-schemes, including physical, active, social, and psychological. Hart and Damon (1986) found that all of these self-schemes are available to both the young child and the adolescent but, similar to Montemayor and Eisen (1977), they also found that development occurs along the dimensions of external to internal and concrete to abstract. For example, adolescents may refer to the physical domain in describing themselves but are more likely to consider internal attributes and to express themselves in terms of hierarchically integrated abstractions, so that "I play soccer" becomes "I'm an athlete."

It is not clear how the increasing differentiation and abstraction that is occurring over development affects children's processing of feedback from the environment and others about themselves. For example, when a parent tells a child "good boy" or "you're lazy," how is this information incorporated into the child's self-view at different ages? Because of children's differing cognitive abilities, the same parental, peer, or teacher statements might have very different meaning to children depending on their age.

Other researchers (Cooley, 1902/1956; Harter, 1986) have suggested that children learn to value themselves partially from how others regard them. Harter (1986) proposed that children's perceptions of support and acceptance from significant others substantially affect their developing self-concept. Through interpersonal interactions, children presumably acquire information about themselves and others and form expectations and beliefs about their own worth and the trustworthiness of those around them, particularly important attachment figures (Bowlby, 1973; Cummings & Cicchetti, 1990).

Very young children are able to make judgments about socioemotional support received from others, including such parental behaviors as listening to the child, reading bedtime stories, and caring about the child's feelings (Harter, 1990). How children interpret these acts potentially has important implications for their developing self-esteem. Children who feel cared for and valued probably will feel worthy themselves, whereas those who perceive rejection and criticism will more likely be self-denigrating.

Young adolescents tend to rate the support of parents and peers as being equally important to them and greater than that of close friends and teachers. Harter (1993) asked children to rate five competence domains regarding how important they believed they were to obtaining parent and peer support. Physical appearance and social and athletic competence were deemed most important for peer acceptance, whereas scholastic competence and behavioral conduct were rated most important to parental acceptance. Both types of support, in turn, were considered strong predictors of global self-worth. Thus, normatively, the acceptance and support of parents and peers affect different domains of developing competence.

By early adulthood, individuals make highly differentiated judgments about domain-specific competencies as well as continuing to articulate a separate global or overall sense of self-worth. There also is a trend in adulthood to move from the importance of general peer acceptance to competence in intimate relationships, although broader social approval continues to be more important to self-esteem than support from close friends (Harter, 1990).

In summary, significant others have a major impact on the developing self-image. Children with high self-worth report that both parents and peers accept them and hold them in high regard (Harter, 1988). In older children, adolescents, and adults, correlations between perceived support from significant others and self-worth have been found to range from .50 to .65 (Harter, 1993).

Children with high self-worth rate themselves as being competent across multiple domains. They value domains in which they perceive themselves as having the most competence and discount the importance of areas of lower competency. In contrast, individuals with low self-worth do not rate themselves as competent in all domains, and they continue to value domains in which they perceive themselves as less competent (Harter, 1988). This discrepancy between their actual and desired competency contributes to their feelings of low self-worth. The extent and valence of the feedback individuals receive from important others in their life, particularly parents and peers, contributes to their perceptions of competence in the various domains.

Attributional Style

The perception of causal connections appears to be basic to development (Corrigan, 1995; White, 1988). White (1988) suggested that "the origins of causal processing include concrete, familiar event sequences, human intended action, generative relations, and observation of regularity and covariation" (p. 36). Even infants demonstrate rudimentary causal understanding (e.g., Oakes, 1994), and toddlers can engage in social causal reasoning (Miller & Aloise, 1989). Preschoolers begin to comprehend that their own as well as others' actions may be caused by internal mental states, although they do not distinguish traits until at least age 5 or 6. After about age 8, the use of stable personality traits to explain behavior increases dramatically (Corrigan, 1995).

Preschoolers perceive themselves to be very competent when they succeed after considerable effort but less capable when their success occurs without much effort. Although young children see effort and ability as distinct, they treat them as if they were positively correlated. They infer that whoever tried hardest also had the greatest ability. In contrast, older children demonstrate an understanding that effort may compensate for low ability and high ability may compensate for low effort (Kun, 1977). Because young children do not see low ability as a stable traitlike factor, they do not perceive themselves as failures when they have a poor outcome (Friedlander, 1988), nor do they show much negative affect when they fail (Ruble, Parsons, & Ross, 1976).

There also is a tendency for young children to take more credit for success than failure. With development, however, there is an increasing trend toward internal attributions for failure (Friedlander, 1988). Nevertheless, older children and adults continue to take greater credit for success. They are more likely to accept responsibility for failure if they can attribute it to a cause over which they have some control, such as effort (Fiske & Taylor, 1991).

In a sample of 5- through 10-year-old children, Rholes, Blackwell, Jordan, and Walters (1980) examined the attributions of children given either success or failure feedback in a laboratory problem-solving task. Regardless of feedback, younger children reported exerting more effort and older children reported lower ability and worse luck. The correlation between ability and effort attributions was positive for younger children but negative for older children. That is, in older children higher effort was associated with lower ability. Finally, older children who made attributions to low ability were less persistent on the task. Taken together, these results indicate that the types of attributions children make for success and failure and the impact of attributions on behavior change with development.

There are two perspectives regarding the development of the tendency to attribute causes to internal or external sources. The Piagetian view argues that young children overestimate their ability to control events, and therefore they are more likely to attribute causality to internal factors and to perceive contingency between their actions and events when there may be none (Piaget, 1954). In contrast, others have argued that perceptions of personal or internal control increase with age, reflecting increases in actual competence and independence (Friedlander, 1988; Ruble & Rholes, 1981; Weisz & Stipek, 1982). Weisz and Stipek (1982), for example, suggested that developmental changes in perceived contingency will result in a decrease in perceived control, whereas developmental increases in actual competence will result in an increase in perceived control. That is, as young children learn that they have less control over events, their developing abilities can help compensate for it, thereby allowing them to retain some control. Perceived control, then, should remain fairly constant as competency replaces cognitive immaturity (Friedlander, 1988).

Illusory contingency appears to decline with age, although it never entirely disappears, especially in nondepressed adults (Weisz & Stipek, 1982). In a study of contingency estimates among nondepressed and depressed college students, Alloy and Abramson (1979) found that nondepressed students overestimated the degree of contingency between their responses and outcomes when noncontingent outcomes were desirable and underestimated the degree of contingency when contingent outcomes were undesirable. In contrast, depressed students accurately judged the degree of contingency regardless of its actual magnitude. Thus, an illusion of control may persist with development, although it can be altered by mood state.

Weiner and Graham (1985) distinguished between emotions associated with outcomes (e.g., being happy about success) and emotions associated with attributions (e.g., gratitude for factors leading to success), and they demonstrated that the use of attribution-linked emotions increases with age. Young children report far more outcome-linked emotions, suggesting that their causal reasoning may be less complex, and attributions for events have less impact on their emotional states than the events themselves (Weiner & Graham, 1985).

In summary, there is an increasing developmental trend toward the use of stable personality traits to explain behavior, a greater distinction between the roles of effort and ability, a greater understanding of contingency, and some increase in taking responsibility for failure. These cognitive changes affect children's developing perceptions of control, interpretations of success and failure, and attributions about the causes of positive and negative events for themselves and others (Friedlander, 1988).

Optimism–Pessimism

Optimism–pessimism or hopefulness–hopelessness involves expectations about the future and consists of both cognitive and affective components. The cognitive aspect includes time perspective, which is the concern about the future, and probabilistic thinking, which involves the probabilities associated with the future based on current and past conditions. The full concept of time and future is thought not to develop until late childhood or early adolescence, and the ability to assess probabilities is associated with the stage of formal operations, which begins around the same time (Siomopolous & Inamdar, 1979).

According to Piaget (1970; Singer & Revenson, 1996), "future" is the last time concept children learn. Preoperational children do not understand temporal continuity or the abstract concept of time, nor do they anticipate negative futures. Concrete operational children can grasp the concept of time as a constant sequence (e.g., days on a calendar) and can begin to comprehend duration of time, past, future, and infinity. By adolescence, the concept of time is fully developed. Some adolescents become preoccupied with the future and view experiences as having irrevocable effects on their future, thereby making them susceptible to hopelessness and despair (Bemporad & Wilson, 1978). Thus, because of cognitive–developmental factors, the construct of hopefulness–hopelessness is not fully developed until early adolescence, making it difficult to even assess in younger children.

Stipek, Lamb, and Zigler (1981) developed a self-report measure of children's optimism that they used with children in Grades 1 and 2. Stipek and colleagues (Stipek, 1981; Stipek et al., 1981) reported that children's optimism tended to increase over the first year of school, and they suggested that this might be due to children's increasing sense of efficacy during this important developmental period. Stipek et al. (1981) also found a significant relation between children's optimism and locus of control. They speculated that pessimism develops in children who have a sense of personal helplessness in contexts that are increasingly demanding and complex, such as the school environment. During brief exposure to failure in a laboratory setting, however, young children have been found to maintain high expectations for future performance following failure (Parsons & Ruble, 1977). It may take repeated exposure to failures in salient developmental contexts to produce negative expectations in young children.

Another factor that has been proposed as a possible precursor to hopelessness is temperament (Kashani, Soltys, Dandoy, Vaidya, & Reid, 1991; Rutter, 1987). Kashani et al. (1991) found that higher levels of hopelessness were associated with temperaments characterized as "difficult" and low in adaptability. It is possible that such children generate or have difficulty dealing with problematic circumstances, which then result in more negative outcomes for them. Thus, individuals' early experiences, which are partially a function of their temperament as well as their environment, will influence their developing sense of optimism or pessimism.

Evidence is mixed regarding age differences in hopelessness during childhood. Some studies have found greater levels of hopelessness in older compared with younger children (Garber, 1984), whereas other studies have not found age differences in self-reported hopelessness (Garber, Weiss, & Shanley, 1993; Kashani, Reid, & Rosenberg, 1989). The children in Garber's (1984) study, however, were a clinic sample between 8 and 13 years old, whereas the subjects in Garber et al.'s (1993) study were a community sample of adolescents in Grades 7 through 12. Thus, the discrepant findings across studies could be due to differences in the ages and types of samples studied.

By adulthood, most individuals report themselves as feeling relatively invulnerable and as having the expectation of a positive future (Janoff-Bulman, 1992). On the other hand, Janoff-Bulman and Hecker (1988) found that depressed college students reported that they felt less lucky, that events are more random and less controllable, and that the world is a more malevolent place than did their nondepressed peers. It is possible that for these depressed individuals, their experiences had been consistent with their negative world view, although it also is possible that their negative affect influenced their perceptions. Determining the direction of the relations among negative life events, hopelessness, and depression remains an important focus of research (Abramson et al., 1989).

In summary, children's expectations for their future are likely derived from their processing of information about their prior experiences. Their attributions about the causes of prior events and their awareness of the consequences of such events serve as foundations for their beliefs about what lies ahead. A sense of efficacy and control is likely to be associated with a more optimistic outlook, whereas feelings of inadequacy and helplessness will result in hopelessness.

ORIGINS OF THE DEPRESSIVE COGNITIVE STYLE

As noted earlier, children's concepts of self, causal inferences, and perspectives about the future develop through a variety of normal developmental processes, and these developmental processes are not necessarily the same across the different cognitions. Moreover, self-concepts, attributions, and optimism–pessimism are dimensional constructs that can range from highly negative to highly positive. What accounts for the development of the more negative patterns of thinking that characterize depressed individuals? Some theorists (Garber, 1992; Kovacs & Beck, 1978; Rose & Abramson, 1992; Seligman, Kamen, & Nolen-Hoeksema, 1988) have speculated about the causes of the depressive cognitive style and have proposed several nonmutually exclusive processes to explain the origins of depressogenic thinking that are described below.

Genetics and Personality

One conceptualization of cognitive style is that it is a personality characteristic that is heritable. There is some evidence of the heritability of mood disorders (Blehar, Weissman, Gershon, & Hirschfeld, 1988; McGuffin & Katz, 1989). One phenotypic expression of a depression genotype could be a depressive personality style that is characterized by negative cognitions.

A possible biological expression of this depression genotype could be a distinct pattern of resting brain asymmetry. Depressed persons have been found to have greater relative right-sided anterior activation of their cerebral hemispheres than nondepressed persons (Davidson, 1992). Davidson, Abramson, Tomarken, and Wheeler (1997) recently reported a significant correlation between such relative right-anterior hemispheric activation and depressogenic attributional style. It is possible that a shared genetic diathesis contributes to this covariation between these biological and psychological correlates of depression.

Evidence supporting the genetic hypothesis would come from family, twin, and adoption studies of cognitive style. Some family studies have found a significant correlation between parents' and children's depression-related cognitions (e.g., Seligman & Peterson, 1986), although such findings are consistent with either a genetic or a social learning model. In a twin study, Schulman, Keith, and Seligman (1991) compared the intraclass correlations of 115 monozygotic (MZ) versus 27 dizygotic (DZ) twins on the Attributional Style Questionnaire (Seligman, Abramson, Semmel, & von Baeyer, 1979) and found the correlations were .48 for MZ twins and 0 for DZ twins. This is an intriguing finding that needs to be replicated using more standard means of determining zygosity rather than the self-report method used by Schulman et al. (1991). Future twin studies should include other measures of cognitive style, such as self-worth, hopelessness, and dysfunctional attitudes.

It also is possible that the depressive cognitive style is really a manifestation of neuroticism, which is presumably heritable (Eysenck & Eysenck, 1985). Watson and colleagues (Watson & Clark, 1984; Watson,

Clark, & Harkness, 1994) have argued that self-report measures of depression, such as the Beck Depression Inventory (Beck, Ward, Mendelson, Mock, & Erbaugh, 1961), are really just measures of neuroticism. That is, dysfunctional cognitions and dysphoric affect all may be components of a single, more general construct—neuroticism or negative emotionality itself (Watson et al., 1994). Studies consistently find correlations between such self-report measures of depressive symptoms and measures of cognitive style (e.g., Barnett & Gotlib, 1988). This covariation could result if both depression and cognitions are either reflections of or the result of a shared personality trait such as neuroticism. Thus, if depressogenic cognitive style is a manifestation of neuroticism and neuroticism is heritable, then by inference, the origin of depressive cognitions is possibly genetic.

Finally, even if depressive cognitive style is not an inherited trait, it still might be a stable characteristic acquired over time. Kovacs and Beck (1978) suggested that depressogenic schemata are probably long-term, characteristic attitudes and problem-solving approaches that become part of the depressed patient's personality, particularly over the course of recurrent episodes. These schemata become long-term psychological templates that become part of the cognitive dimension of the depression-prone individual's personality (Kovacs & Beck, 1978). Thus, a depressive personality style might exist without necessarily being heritable.

Social Learning

Learning and development are gradual and continuous processes that occur through the dynamic interaction with others and the environment. Several specific social learning principles are likely involved in the development of the depressive cognitive style, particularly modeling and direct feedback through instruction, reinforcement, and punishment from significant others such as parents, teachers, and peers (Bandura & Walters, 1963). These processes continue over the course of development, and therefore cognitive schemata can undergo some modification as the result of living, learning, and experiencing (Kovacs & Beck, 1978).

Modeling

A simple modeling hypothesis is that children learn to think negatively about the causes of events, themselves, and their future by observing and imitating important others such as mothers, fathers, and teachers. Evidence of covariation between parents' and children's cognitive style would be consistent, although not conclusive support for this modeling perspective.

Using a community sample, Seligman and Peterson (1986) assessed attributional style in 47 mothers and their elementary school children.

They reported a correlation of .39 (p < .05) for attributions for negative events and a nonsignificant correlation of .08 for attributions for positive events. In contrast, Kaslow, Rehm, Pollack, and Siegel (1988) compared the mother–child correlations of 15 clinic depressed, 22 clinic nondepressed, and 25 nonclinic children (ages 8 through 12) but did not find a significant correlation between mothers and children on measures of either attributional style or perceived self-control.

Thus, the results are mixed with regard to the simple correlations between mothers' and children's depressive cognitions. Although it is possible that children learn to make causal inferences from observing their parents' attributional style for their (the parents') own behavior, it is probably even more likely that children learn from their parents' attributions about their (the child's) behavior. Fincham and Cain (1985; cited in Fincham & Cain, 1986) examined this hypothesis with regard to effort and ability attributions and found that in their sample of third-grade students, children's attributions correlated more closely with parents' explanations of the children's behavior than parents' explanations of their own behavior. Turk and Bry (1992) found a significant correlation between fathers' explanations of events in their adolescents' lives and adolescents' explanations about these events. Thus, children might acquire some of their beliefs about the causes of events from observing their parents' explanatory style, particularly regarding the children's behaviors.

The evidence also is mixed with regard to the relation between children's and mothers' versus fathers' cognitive styles. Seligman et al. (1984), for example, found that children's explanatory style for bad events correlated with mothers' but not fathers' attributions. Others have reported that fathers' and children's attributions about their school performance or failures were more congruent than mothers' and children's (Bird & Berman, 1985; Fincham & Cain, 1986; Turk & Bry, 1992). These disparate results across studies could be due to differences in the ages of the children and in the nature of the events about which attributions were being made. More studies are needed to identify the potentially different mechanisms through which attributional style is transmitted from mothers and fathers to their same- and different-sex children.

One important caveat about the interpretation of any parent–child correlation should be noted. If correlations are found between parents' and children's cognitive styles, this does not necessarily mean that this is the result of modeling and imitation, or that the direction of the relation is from parent to child. That is, parental cognitions could influence child cognitions or vice versa, or some shared third variable (e.g., genes, stressors) could contribute to the development of both parents' and children's cognitions. As noted earlier, familial transmission of cognitive style is consistent with a genetic view as well. Thus, although others (e.g., Kaslow et al., 1988; Seligman & Peterson, 1986) have suggested that parent–child correlations would be an indication of learning, this is only one possible mechanism of cross-generational transmission.

The finding of a significant relation between parents' and children's cognitions about the child's behavior in particular rather than in their cognition style in general (Turk & Bry, 1992) is at least more consistent with a learning than a genetic perspective. That is, if it was simply the transmission of a genetic predisposition to make internal, global, and stable attributions for negative events, then this should be true with regard to either parent- or child-focused events. Thus, it is likely that children acquire at least some of their cognitive style, particularly causal inferences, from observing their parents' explanations for their children's behaviors.

Social Feedback

Children learn about themselves and their world from direct feedback, including instruction, reinforcement, and punishment from important people in their lives such as teachers, peers, and parents. Beck and Young (1985) suggested that a "child learns to construct reality through his or her early experiences with the environment, especially with significant others. Sometimes, these early experiences lead children to accept attitudes and beliefs that will later prove maladaptive" (p. 207).

Dweck and colleagues (Dweck, 1975; Dweck & Gilliard, 1975; Dweck & Goetz, 1978; Dweck & Licht, 1980; Dweck & Reppuci, 1973) have examined the messages teachers send to girls and boys about their classroom failures and conduct. Dweck and Gilliard (1975) found that teachers tend to explain boys' failures in terms of lack of effort (e.g., "He's just being lazy"), and they give diffuse criticisms to boys that focus on nonintellectual aspects of their behavior. In contrast, teachers tend to explain girls' failures in terms of lack of ability (e.g., "She's not smart enough"). As a result, boys learn to explain their failures as being caused by their not trying—an unstable attribution—and thus the behavior and outcome can be changed. Girls, on the other hand, learn from teacher feedback that they lack ability—a stable attribute—and therefore they tend to become helpless and give up (Dweck & Licht, 1980). Thus, Dweck's program of research has shown that the foundation for children's explanatory style for performance outcomes (failure and success) and their beliefs about their academic competence are laid during the early school years, particularly as a function of the direct feedback they receive from teachers.

Peers also are an important source of feedback about the self and clearly affect children's developing sense of competence (Harter, 1986). Peer support has been linked repeatedly with adolescent well-being (e.g., Epstein, 1983; Hartup, 1983). Frequent contact with a supportive friend has been found to be associated with higher levels of self-esteem (Hirsch, Engel-Levy, DuBois, & Hardesty, 1990). In contrast, the experience of peer rejection predicts the perception of low competence in the social domain (Panak & Garber, 1992). Thus, the quality of peer relationships can substantially affect children's developing self-concept and their future expectations regarding interpersonal interactions.

Finally, and probably most important, parents constantly provide evaluative feedback to their children about the acceptability of their behavior and performance. Bowlby (1988) emphasized that children's working models of themselves are influenced by the quality of the early parental relationship reflected in what parents say to their children and how they treat them. Parents who are critical and rejecting are teaching their children that they are unworthy. Sometimes this is communicated directly by verbally abusive language such as "You are stupid and lazy." Sometimes it is communicated more indirectly by actions such as withdrawal of love and affection when the child misbehaves.

Children who are exposed to parenting characterized by repeated criticism and rejection, lack of warmth, and intrusiveness are likely to develop a highly self-critical and negative attitude toward themselves (Cole, 1990; McCranie & Bass, 1984). McCranie and Bass (1984) suggested that parental child-rearing practices involving rejection and inconsistent expressions of affection and control hinder the development of healthy self-esteem in children and thereby increase their vulnerability to depression.

Results of empirical studies examining the relation between parenting and children's cognitions about the self, particularly among offspring of depressed parents, have generally supported this view (although see Oliver & Berger, 1992, for an exception). Radke-Yarrow, Belmont, Nottelman, and Bottomly (1990) examined what very young children learn in discourse with depressed and well mothers. In a 35-minute period, mothers were observed to make over 300 comments about their child, and there were no significant differences between depressed and well mothers in this rate. However, depressed mothers were more negative, and there was a highly significant relation between mothers' negativity and child self-referent statements that included unpleasant content. Radke-Yarrow et al. suggested that such parent communications may be an early precursor to the development of a negative self-concept in children.

Jaenicke et al. (1987) found a significant association between mothers' verbal criticism of their children and their children's tendency to make self-blaming attributions for negative events. Goodman et al. (1994) revealed a significant association between negative affective statements of depressed mothers and lower perceived self-worth in their children. In a sample of young adolescents, Litovsky and Dusek (1985) reported that high self-esteem correlated positively with perceived parental acceptance and negatively with perceived parental control. Finally, Koestner, Zuroff, and Powers (1991) showed that restrictive and rejecting parenting earlier in childhood was significantly related to the development of self-criticism during adolescence. Thus, there is increasing evidence of a significant relation between parenting style and children's sense of self-worth.

In summary, through the basic social learning processes of observation and imitation, and direct feedback and instruction from teachers, mothers, fathers, and peers, children learn to make judgments about their self-worth and about the causes and consequences of their experiences. When the communications are persistently negative, children assimilate this information into a depressive cognitive schema about themselves and the world.

Exposure to Negative Life Events

It is normal to be exposed to some bad events, disappointments, losses, and failures over the course of development, and these experiences can affect a person's outlook on life. Experiences with chronically aversive life circumstances (e.g., abuse, poverty, parental discord) or a major traumatic life event (e.g., parental death, rape) are particularly likely to have an impact on individuals' sense of themselves, their world, and their future (Janoff-Bulman, 1992). When such events are uncontrollable and result in multiple and severe bad outcomes, individuals are likely to develop cognitions of universal helplessness and hopelessness (Abramson et al., 1989). Individuals who believe they were responsible for the negative events are more likely to develop a belief in personal helplessness and low self-esteem (Abramson et al., 1978).

Thus, such life experiences can provide the foundation for the development of negative beliefs. Subsequent exposure to new negative life events can reactivate and reinforce these beliefs, particularly when the conditions resemble the circumstances under which they developed (Kovacs & Beck, 1978). Through generalization, the range of these beliefs eventually will extend to stimulus conditions that are only marginally related to the original ones, and thus a negative cognitive style emerges.

For example, early loss may create cognitions of abandonment and the belief that all losses are traumatic and irreversible (Beck, 1967; Brown & Harris, 1978). Loss of one's mother at an early age has realistic and significant implications for a child's future, and it sets the stage for later losses or major difficulties to be interpreted in global, stable, and internal terms (Seligman et al., 1988). Subsequent experience with interpersonal disruptions such as rejection and conflict is likely to strengthen existing schemata about the fragility of interpersonal relationships and lead to hopelessness with respect to the social domain.

Rose and Abramson (1992) proposed a model of the development of cognitive vulnerability that emphasizes the role of negative life events. They suggested that when a negative event occurs, individuals are motivated to understand its causes, meaning, and consequences and to take action to deal with it. When the event is highly threatening or recurrent, individuals are especially motivated to engage in this epistemic activity. Through repetition of the negative event-specific cognitive process, a more general negative cognitive style is formed.

Rose and Abramson (1992) used the example of child abuse to describe how a negative cognitive style develops. Children who experience severe and repetitive abuse in the context of an important interpersonal relationship are likely to develop negative self-representations, helplessness, and hopelessness about the security of important interpersonal relationships. These children often acquire the view of themselves as unlovable and unworthy and the belief that others are rejecting, untrustworthy, and dangerous (Cummings & Cicchetti, 1990). Thus, a general cognitive style or working model of self and others develops in which they expect continued maltreatment in the future.

In a cross-sectional study, Rose, Abramson, Hodulik, Halberstadt, and Leff (1994) examined the links between certain developmental events, including early loss, parenting style, and history of sexual abuse, and depressed inpatients' levels of dysfunctional attitudes and attributional style. Rose et al. found that, controlling for severity of depression, high levels of recalled negative parenting behaviors and history of sexual abuse were significantly associated with a more negative cognitive style, whereas early loss was not. They speculated that children develop depressogenic cognitive styles in response to early negative life events, such as harsh and controlling parenting or the trauma of abuse. However, given the cross-sectional and retrospective nature of the data, the alternative explanation that individuals with a more depressive cognitive style have more negative recollections of their parents' behaviors cannot be ruled out.

Nolen-Hoeksema et al. (1992) conducted a 5-year longitudinal study of children in third grade in which they examined the relation between negative life events and attributional style. They found that in only two of seven analyses there was a small but significant effect for negative life events to predict unfavorable changes in explanatory style over time, after controlling for the child's level of depression at the time the life events were reported. Thus, although it is reasonable to speculate that exposure to traumatic or chronic negative life experiences will alter individuals' perspective about the world, themselves, and their future, more empirical studies are needed to test this hypothesis.

There are a variety of factors that might moderate whether a child develops a depressive cognitive style after exposure to aversive life events, such as the child's age at the time of the event, associated consequences of the event, social support, and the child's own coping resources. Children's age and level of cognitive development will affect their ability to process information about the causes, meaning, and consequences of the event. Brown and Harris (1978) found that depression was more common among women who had experienced loss of a mother before age 11. Loss of mother at an early age has significant global and stable implications for the future and may be particularly likely to lead to cognitions of helplessness and abandonment.

In addition, the extent of the associated consequences of the negative event will determine how much the child needs to cognitively process and deal with. For example, when the death of a parent is accompanied by additional losses of economic resources, home, friendships, and social status, this can place a tremendous burden on a child's cognitive processing capacity. The availability of social support also can influence children's understanding of life events not only by providing instrumental aid to the child but also by helping the child cognitively restructure the meaning of the event. Finally, children's own coping responses can affect their interpretation of the event. If they engage in effective coping, then they might be less likely to see themselves as helpless and may remain more hopeful about their future. Longitudinal studies are needed that examine the direct impact of negative life events on children's developing cognitive style as well as the possible moderating effects of these other factors.

THE "DEVELOPMENT OF DEPRESSION" PROJECT

The goal of the "Development of Depression" project has been to understand the processes that contribute to the development of depressive disorders among adolescents at risk for mood disorders. Elsewhere, we (Garber & Flynn, 1998) examined three of the factors described earlier to predict children's cognitive style: mothers' own cognitive style, mothers' parenting style, and negative life events. We addressed the following questions: (a) What is the relation between mothers' and children's cognitions? (b) Does parenting style predict children's cognitions? and (c) Do negative life events predict children's cognitions? The cognitions examined were derived from the cognitive models of depression (e.g., Abramson et al., 1989; Beck, 1967) and included self-worth, attributional style, and hopelessness.

Participants in the "Development of Depression" project were 240 children and their mothers. Children were first assessed when they were in sixth grade (mean age = 11.86 years, SD = 0.57). The sample of children was about 54% female, predominantly Caucasian (82%) with about 15% African American, and mostly lower middle to middle class.

The sample was obtained over 3 consecutive years by sending letters describing the study to parents of children attending the metropolitan area public schools who would be entering the sixth grade the following year. Parents were asked to complete a brief health history questionnaire about whether they had ever had any of 24 medical conditions (e.g., diabetes, heart disease, depression) or if they had ever taken any of 34 medications (e.g., Prozac, Elavil). Mothers who indicated a history of depression, use of antidepressants, or no psychiatric problems were interviewed further. The final sample consisted of 185 mothers with histories of mood disorders (e.g., major depression, dysthymia, adjustment disorder with depressed mood) with a broad range of severity and chronicity; the remaining 55 mothers were lifetime free of psychopathology.

The children were first assessed when they were in sixth grade. A different interviewer, who was unaware of the mother's psychiatric history, interviewed the mother and child about the child and administered a battery of questionnaires. Children were evaluated annually over 3 years. Children and mothers completed measures about cognitions, parenting, and life events.

The cognitive measures assessed attributional style, perceived competence, and hopelessness. Children completed the Children's Attributional Style Questionnaire (CASQ; Seligman et al., 1984) and mothers completed the Attributional Style Questionnaire (ASQ; Seligman et al., 1979), which measure attributions about the causes of positive and negative events. Mothers also completed the parent version of the Children's Attributional Style Questionnaire (CASQ-P), which measures mothers' attributions about their children's behavior.

In addition, children completed the Self-Perception Profile for Children (Harter, 1985), which assesses children's global perception of self-worth and perceived competence in five specific domains (academic, social, appearance, athletic, and behavior), and mothers completed the Self-Perception Profile for Adults (Messer & Harter, 1986). Children and mothers also completed the Children's Hopelessness Scale (Kazdin, Rodgers, & Colbus, 1986) and Hopelessness Scale for adults (Beck, Weissman, Lester, & Trexler, 1974), respectively.

Parenting was measured at the first assessment with the Children's Report of Parental Behavior Inventory (CRPBI; Schaefer, 1965; Schludermann & Schludermann, 1970), which was completed by mothers and children. The CRPBI contains 18 subscales representing three dimensions: acceptance/rejection (the extent to which the parent expresses care and affection for the child); autonomy/psychological control (the extent to which parents control their children through indirect psychological methods such as inducing guilt, instilling anxiety, and withdrawing love); and firm/lax control (the extent to which parents consistently enforce compliance by making rules or threatening punishment).

Life events were assessed at each time point using the Family Inventory of Life Events (FILE; McCubbin & Patterson, 1987). Mothers indicated which of 90 possible life events had occurred since the previous interview, which had been about 12 months earlier. The FILE includes items about such major life events as deaths, illnesses and accidents, divorce and separations, births, moves, school transitions, financial difficulties, and employment changes.

What Is the Relation Between Mothers' and Children's Cognitions?

Garber and Flynn (1998) reported significant associations between mothers' and children's global self-worth and between their perceived cognitive (scholastic) competence. The mechanisms for this covariation could be genetic, environmental, or both. Intelligence is highly heritable (Neisser et al., 1996), and therefore the mother–child correlations within the cognitive domain could reflect their similar levels of cognitive abilities. On the other hand, it also is likely that their judgments about their cognitive ability and self-worth could have been influenced by their interactions with each other and with others in the environment. For example, mothers who at times say such self-denigrating things as "I'm not very good at things" and who on other occasions say to their child, "You are just like me" are likely to influence their children's sense of self-worth and perceived competence.

Regarding attributional style, there were no significant correlations between the children's CASQ and mothers' ASQ. However, mothers' attributions about their children's behavior reported on the CASQ-P were significantly correlated with children's attributions about the same behaviors and events. Thus, although mothers' and children's general attributional style were not similar, their attributions for the same child-focused situations were significantly correlated.

These results were consistent with other studies that have found a significant association between parents' and children's attributions regarding the same child behaviors (Fincham & Cain, 1986; Kaslow et al., 1988; Turk & Bry, 1992; although see Seligman et al., 1984, for contrary findings). Thus, one possible mechanism through which children learn to explain their behavior and other important events in their life is from the attributions their parents make about these particular things. The modeling process may be more subtle than that the child simply copies what the parent says. Children might be more inclined to incorporate their parents' cognitions regarding the things that are most salient to them, their own behavior. Future studies need to examine the relation between parents' and children's cognitions particularly about those things most relevant to the child as well as any shared events.

There also is a need for studies that examine the extent to which children are aware of their parents' cognitions. How much do children actually pay attention to what their parents say and think? This could be assessed relatively easily by asking children to complete the CASQ for how they think their parents would complete it. It is possible, however, that the transmission process is quite subtle, and therefore children, particularly young ones, might not be cognizant of their parents' attributions, or, if they are aware of them, they might be unable to articulate them.

Moreover, it is likely that there will be some heterogeneity in children's awareness of their parents' cognitions. Some children pay more attention to their parents than others. This will vary by children's age, personality, and possibly gender. How much children care about what their parents think and say also will be affected by the nature of the parent–child relationship and children's developmental level. All of these factors should be examined as possible moderators of parent–child covariation in cognitive style.

Garber and Flynn (1998) found no relation between mothers' and children's hopelessness or perceived competence across most of the other domains (social, athletic, appearance, and behavior). Although this absence of parent–child covariation is potentially interesting, it must be interpreted cautiously. As Cronbach and Meehl (1955) suggested, the lack of findings could be the result of problems in measurement, research design, or theory.

In general, the cognitive measures used here have been found to be psychometrically adequate in other studies (e.g., Dobson & Breiter, 1981; Robins & Hinkley, 1989) as well as in this one. Thus, poor measurement is not likely to be the main explanation for the observed lack of relation between mothers' and children's cognitions. It is possible, however, that the cognitions measured here need to be activated by life events or primed by a mood induction (Miranda, Persons, & Byers, 1990; Riskind & Rholes, 1984). Therefore, similarities between mothers' and children's cognitions might not be apparent until the measures are completed under such activating conditions.

It also is possible that 11- to 12-year-old children might not yet have developed the kinds of perceptions of themselves or their future as assessed by these measures, although these thinking patterns might still develop as the children become more cognitively mature. Thus, mother–child correlations might become greater over time as a result of children's increasing cognitive development. Parent–child correlations also could become greater over time because of children having longer exposure to their parents, which would increase the amount of time they could be influenced by their parents' cognitive styles.

Finally, it is possible that the absence of evidence for the familial transmission of perceived competence and hopelessness is because a simple modeling or genetic theory to explain their development is insufficient. Therefore, two alternative paths to the development of depressogenic cognitions also were tested: parenting and life events.

Does Parenting Style Predict Children's Cognitions?

We (Garber & Flynn, 1998) next tested whether the three parenting subscales of the CRPBI, administered when the children were in sixth grade (Time 1), predicted child cognitions in seventh grade (Time 2). Controlling for Time 1 global self-worth, maternal acceptance and psychological control each significantly predicted Time 2 global self-worth, whereas firm control did not. That is, parenting characterized by low levels of care and acceptance and high levels of psychological control predicted low levels of global self-worth in young adolescents. These results were consistent with other studies that have found a relation between parental rejection and overcontrol and children's perceptions of low self-worth (e.g., Goodman et al., 1994; Litovsky & Dusek, 1985; McCranie & Bass, 1984). For example, Litovsky and Dusek (1985) similarly found that low self-esteem correlated negatively with perceived parental acceptance and positively with perceived parental control.

In addition, maternal psychological control contributed significant unique variance to the prediction of Time 2 attributional style, controlling for Time 1 attributional style. The construct of psychological control measures the extent to which parents influence their children's behavior through indirect psychological means, such as inducing guilt, shame, and anxiety and withdrawal of love. Children might be particularly likely to learn self-blame through such parental behaviors and thereby acquire a more internal attributional style. This is consistent with the study by Jaenicke et al. (1987), who reported a significant relation between maternal control and criticism and children's tendency to make self-blaming attributions for negative events.

These results provided further evidence that the dimensions of maternal acceptance and psychological control measure somewhat different aspects of parenting (Schaefer, 1965), and that each parenting component may separately influence the development of self-worth and attributions in young adolescents. The third parenting dimension—the extent to which mothers set firm and consistent limits—was not significantly associated with child cognitions, however. It may be that lax behavioral management strategies predict other kinds of child problems such as externalizing symptoms rather than depressive cognitive style (e.g., Barber, 1996; Loeber & Dishion, 1984; Weiss, Dodge, Bates, & Pettit, 1992).

Thus, the parent–child relationship is an important context in which cognitive vulnerabilities to depression such as low self-esteem and a depressive attributional style develop (Beck, 1967; Garber, 1992). In particular, parental child-rearing practices characterized by rejection, absence of warmth and affection, lack of autonomy, and manipulation of the love relationship will likely result in self-denigrating and self-blaming attitudes (Cole, 1990; McCranie & Bass, 1984), and thereby increase an individual's vulnerability to depression.

Studies are beginning to examine the role of child cognitions as a mediator between parenting and depression. Patterson and Capaldi (1990) suggested that the association between parental rejection and depressed mood might be mediated through low self-esteem. Stark, Schmidt, and

Joiner (1996) showed that the relation between perceived parental messages and depression were mediated by children's cognitive triad. Whisman and Kwon (1992) found a significant correlation between lower perceived parental care and higher self-reported depressive symptoms that was mediated by depressotypic attitudes and attributions. Their study, however, was based on all self-report data from college undergraduates and did not include a measure of perceived self-worth. In a cross-sectional study using multiple informants and multiple measures, Garber, Robinson, and Valentiner (1997) recently reported that the relations between low levels of parental acceptance and depression and high levels of parental psychological control and depression were mediated by perceived self-worth in young adolescents. Thus, negative cognitions, particularly about the self, might be one mechanism linking dysfunctional parenting and depression.

Do Negative Life Events Predict Children's Cognitions?

Finally, Garber and Flynn (1998) tested whether negative life events affect children's cognitions. Mothers' reports of negative life events that had occurred during the prior year significantly incremented the prediction of depressive attributional style a year later beyond attributional style measured a year earlier. These results were found when the children were in 7th grade and were replicated when they were in 8th grade. Nolen-Hoeksema et al. (1992) reported similar findings when their study participants were in Grades 5 and 6. Thus, exposure to stressors predicts unfavorable changes in explanatory style toward more internal, global, and stable attributions for negative events.

In addition, we found that negative life events significantly predicted hopelessness a year later; this finding also replicated over two timepoints. Even more interesting was that, at both timepoints, level of perceived self-worth moderated the relation between negative life events and hopelessness. That is, low self-worth significantly predicted hopelessness, particularly among children who had experienced higher levels of negative life events. Similarly, attributional style moderated the relation between life events and hopelessness in one of the two analyses. A more depressive attributional style predicted hopelessness, especially among children with high levels of negative life events.

These results were consistent with the suggestion of Stipek et al. (1981) that pessimism results from a sense of low competence in demanding circumstances. Moreover, these findings were supportive of the hopelessness theory of depression (Abramson et al., 1989) that predicts that attributional style and self-esteem are more distal predictors of depression, with hopelessness being the more proximal causal factor that mediates this relation. These data demonstrated that both attributions and self-worth predicted subsequent hopelessness. A next step will be to test this hopelessness mediation hypothesis with this sample.

Finally, it is noteworthy that negative life events did not predict self-worth. Thus, although there tends to be some relation among the different types of cognitions that are presumably vulnerabilities to depression—self-worth, attributional style, and hopelessness (Dobson & Breiter, 1981; Garber et al., 1993)—somewhat different processes might contribute to their development. Mothers' own self-worth and her level of acceptance and psychological control expressed toward her children predicted children's level of self-worth. Children's attributional style was associated with mothers' attributions about her children's behaviors, her level of psychological control expressed toward her children, and the extent of negative life events the children encounter. Finally, mothers' parenting style, per se, did not appear to influence children's hopelessness. Rather, the extent of exposure to negative life events directly affected children's hopelessness, and this was especially true for children with low self-worth.

CONCLUSION

The goal of the present chapter was to discuss the origins of the negative cognitive style that is hypothesized by cognitive models (Abramson et al., 1989; Beck, 1967) to contribute to the development of depression. A brief review of the literature testing these cognitive models revealed that there is increasing evidence of the existence of a cognitive vulnerability linked to depression. Cross-sectional studies have consistently revealed covariation between cognitive style and depression; prospective studies have found that cognitive style predicts both subsequent increases in depressive symptoms and relapse of depressive episodes; prevention studies are beginning to show that negative thinking can be changed and that this reduces the likelihood of future depressions; and children who are at risk for developing depression show evidence of a negative cognitive style prior to ever having had depression themselves. Finally, some studies have found that remitted depressed individuals continue to have negative cognitions, although the stability of the depressogenic cognitive style needs to be studied further.

The cognitive constructs most associated with depression—self-worth, attributions, and optimism–pessimism—change as a function of normal cognitive development. Several factors can influence the valence of children's developing cognitive style, including genetics and the social learning processes of modeling and feedback from significant others in their environment. In addition, experiences with negative life events and trauma can affect children's developing views of the world and future.

Results from the "Development of Depression" project reported by

Garber and Flynn (1998) indicated that children's self-worth was associated with mothers' self-worth and was predicted by low maternal acceptance and high maternal control. Children's attributional style was associated with maternal attributional style for child-focused events and was predicted by maternal psychological control as well as by negative life events. Finally, hopelessness was predicted by high levels of negative life events, particularly among children with low self-worth. Thus, somewhat different processes appear to be associated with the different cognitions. Whereas maternal cognitions and parenting style significantly predicted children's self-worth, negative life events did not. In contrast, life events predicted hopelessness, whereas maternal parenting style did not. Attributional style was associated with both parenting and life events.

Several important issues remain to be explored in the future. More studies need to examine both the mediating and moderating roles of cognitions in relation to depression. That is, what are the links among the more distal parenting processes, children's cognitive style, and subsequent depression (e.g., Garber et al., 1997)? How do these various predictors interact to predict depression? For example, how does self-worth moderate the relation between life events and depression, and to what extent is this mediated by hopelessness (e.g., Metalsky & Joiner, 1992)?

Additional developmental questions also need to be addressed. How does cognitive style change over the course of development? Does the covariation between parents' and children's cognitive styles change with development? Do the factors associated with the development of a negative cognitive style (e.g., parenting, life events) change as a function of the child's age and level of cognitive maturity (Nolen-Hoeksema et al., 1992)?

Families studies should explore the cognitive styles among various family members. For example, what are the associations between fathers' and children's as well as siblings' cognitive styles? Do these relations differ as a function of children's and parents' gender, age, and birth order?

The question of specificity also should be considered, although the specificity of the cognitive model and not simply particular cognitive variables is what needs to be tested (Garber & Hollon, 1991). That is, does the cognitive diathesis–stress model predict depression only? Are there particular kinds of cognitions and life events that predict depression rather than anxiety or other disorders? The concept of specific vulnerability has been proposed by both cognitive models (Abramson et al., 1989; Beck, 1967) and should be studied further. How these specific vulnerabilities develop is another important area for future study.

What are the implications of this work for clinical psychology in the next century? Answers to the questions outlined above would add to the body of knowledge concerning the development and etiology of depression. An important practical application of this knowledge would be the construction of interventions aimed at treating and, even more importantly, preventing depressive disorders. What should be the target of these interventions? Reducing the number and extent of negative life events children encounter would be a laudable goal, although not a very practical one. It is possible, however, to teach children ways of coping with stressors to reduce their negative impact. Given that negative life events are a risk factor for both the development of a negative cognitive style and depression, some form of coping training should be implemented with high-risk individuals.

Prevention programs aimed at altering negative cognitive styles are beginning to show some positive results (e.g., Clarke et al., 1995; Seligman, this volume). These programs need to be implemented with individuals identified as being at risk for the development of depression as a result of such factors as being offspring of depressed parents, having a negative cognitive style already, having subthreshold levels of depression, or being exposed to significant life events (e.g., divorce, deaths, abuse).

Finally, prevention programs should target families with disturbed patterns of parent–child interactions. Training aimed at helping parents to be more positive and accepting of their children and less critical and emotionally controlling might lead children to feel more confident and worthwhile. Prevention studies that provide such parent training and explicitly examine its impact on children's developing cognitive styles need to be conducted.

Preventive intervention programs with high-risk children and adolescents that target some of the presumed precursors of depression such as parenting, cognitive style, and coping with stressors are important because they can have the pragmatic effect of reducing the likelihood of the occurrence of this important mental health problem. In addition, prevention studies can provide a means of testing theory by allowing us an ethical and ecologically valid means of directly manipulating risk factors that are presumably part of the causal chain.

REFERENCES

Abramson, L. Y., Metalsky, G. I., & Alloy, L. B. (1989). Hopelessness depression: A theory-based subtype of depression. *Psychological Review, 96*, 358–372.

Abramson, L. Y., Seligman, M. E. P., & Teasdale, J. (1978). Learned helplessness in humans: Critique and reformulation. *Journal of Abnormal Psychology, 87*, 49–74.

Alloy, L. B., & Abramson, L. Y. (1979). Judgment of contingency in depressed and nondepressed students: Sadder but wiser? *Journal of Experimental Psychology: General, 108*, 441–485.

Asarnow, J. R., & Bates, S. (1988). Depression in child psychiatric inpatients:

Cognitive and attributional patterns. *Journal of Abnormal Child Psychology, 16,* 601–615.

Bandura, A., & Walters, R. H. (1963). *Social learning and personality development.* New York: McGraw-Hill.

Barber, B. K. (1996). Parental psychological control: Revisiting a neglected construct. *Child Development, 67,* 3296–3319.

Barnett, P. A., & Gotlib, I. H. (1988). Psychosocial functioning and depression: Distinguishing among antecedents, concomitants, and consequences. *Psychological Bulletin, 104,* 97–126.

Beardslee, W. R., Hoke, L., Wheelock, I., Rothberg, P. C., van de Velde, P., & Swatling, S. (1992). Initial findings on preventive intervention for families with parental affective disorders. *American Journal of Psychiatry, 149,* 1335–1340.

Beck, A. T. (1967). *Depression: Clinical, experiential, and theoretical aspects.* New York: Harper & Row.

Beck, A. T. (1976). *Cognitive therapy and the emotional disorders.* New York: International Universities Press.

Beck, A. T. (1984). Cognition and therapy. *Archives of General Psychiatry, 41,* 1112–1114.

Beck, A. T., Ward, C. H., Mendelson, M., Mock, J. E., & Erbaugh, J. K. (1961). An inventory for measuring depression. *Archives of General Psychiatry, 4,* 561–571.

Beck, A. T., Weissman, A., Lester, D., & Trexler, L. (1974). The measurement of pessimism: The Hopelessness Scale. *Journal of Consulting and Clinical Psychology, 42,* 861–865.

Beck, A. T., & Young, J. E. (1985). Depression. In D. H. Barlow (Ed.), *Clinical handbook of psychological disorders: A step-by-step treatment manual* (pp. 206–244). New York: Guilford Press.

Bemporad, J. R., & Wilson, R. (1978). A developmental approach to depression in childhood and adolescence. *Journal of the American Academy of Psychoanalysis, 6,* 325–352.

Bird, J. E., & Berman, L. S. (1985). Differing perceptions of mothers, fathers, and children concerning children's academic performance. *Journal of Psychology, 119,* 113–124.

Birmaher, B., Ryan, N. D., Williamson, D. E., Brent, D. A., & Kaufman, J. (1996). Childhood and adolescent depression: A review of the past 10 years. Part II. *Journal of the Academy of Child and Adolescent Psychiatry, 35,* 1575–1583.

Birmaher, B., Ryan, N. D., Williamson, D. E., Brent, D. A., Kaufman, J., Dahl, R., Perel, J., & Nelson, B. (1996). Childhood and adolescent depression: A review of the past 10 years. Part I. *Journal of the Academy of Child and Adolescent Psychiatry, 35,* 1427–1439.

Blackburn, I. M., Eunson, K. M., & Bishop, S. (1983). A two-year naturalistic follow-up of depressed patients treated with cognitive therapy, pharmacotherapy and a combination of both. *Journal of Affective Disorders, 10,* 67–75.

Blehar, M. C., Weissman, M. M., Gershon, E. S., & Hirschfeld, R. M. (1988). Family and genetic studies of affective disorders. *Archives of General Psychiatry, 45,* 289–293.

Bowlby, J. (1973). *Attachment and loss: Vol. 2. Separation.* New York: Basic Books.

Bowlby, J. (1988). Developmental psychiatry comes of age. *American Journal of Psychiatry, 145,* 1–10.

Brent, D. A., Perper, J. A., Moritz, G., Allman, C., Schweers, J., Roth, C., Balach, L., Canobbio, R., & Liotus, L. (1993). Psychiatric risk factors for adolescent suicide. *Journal of the American Academy of Child and Adolescent Psychiatry, 32,* 521–529.

Brown, G. W., & Harris, T. O. (1978). *Social origins of depression: A study of psychiatric disorder in women.* London: Tavistock.

Christie, K. A., Burke, J. D., Jr., Regier, D. A., Rae, D. S., Boyd, J. H., & Locke, B. Z. (1988). Epidemiologic evidence for early onset of mental disorders and higher risk of drug abuse in young adults. *American Journal of Psychiatry, 145,* 971–975.

Clarke, G. N., Hawkins, W., Murphy, M., Sheeber, L. B., Lewinsohn, P. M., & Seeley, J. R. (1995). Targeted prevention of unipolar depressive disorder in an at-risk sample of high school adolescents: A randomized trial of a group cognitive intervention. *Journal of the Academy of Child and Adolescent Psychiatry, 34,* 312–321.

Cochran, S. D., & Hammen, C. L. (1985). Perceptions of stressful life events and depression: A test of attributional models. *Journal of Personality and Social Psychology, 48,* 1562–1571.

Cole, D. A. (1990). Relation of social and academic competence to depressive symptoms in childhood. *Journal of Abnormal Psychology, 100,* 181–190.

Cooley, C. H. (1956). *Human nature and the social order.* Glencoe, IL: Free Press. (Original work published 1902)

Corrigan, R. (1995). How infants and young children understand the causes of events. In N. Eisenberg (Ed.), *Social development* (pp. 1–26). Thousand Oaks, CA: Sage.

Coyne, J. C., & Gotlib, I. H. (1983). The role of cognition in depression: A critical appraisal. *Psychological Bulletin, 94,* 472–505.

Cronbach, L. J., & Meehl, P. E. (1955). Construct validity in psychological tests. *Psychological Bulletin, 52,* 281–302.

Cummings, E. M., & Cicchetti, D. (1990). Toward a transactional model of relations between attachment and depression. In M. T. Greenberg, D. Cicchetti, and E. M. Cummings (Eds.), *Attachment in the preschool years: Theory, research and intervention* (pp. 339–372). Chicago: University of Chicago Press.

Cutrona, C. E. (1983). Causal attributions and perinatal depression. *Journal of Abnormal Psychology, 92,* 161–172.

Davidson, R. J. (1992). Anterior cerebral asymmetry and the nature of emotion. *Brain and Cognition, 20,* 125–151.

Davidson, R. J., Abramson, L. Y., Tomarken, A. J., & Wheeler, R. E. (1997).

Asymmetrical anterior temporal brain activity predicts beliefs about the causes of negative life events. Manuscript in preparation, University of Wisconsin–Madison.

Dobson, K. S., & Breiter, H. J. (1981). Cognitive assessment of depression: Reliability and validity of three measures. *Journal of Abnormal Psychology, 92,* 107–109.

Downey, G., & Coyne, J. C. (1990). Children of depressed parents: An integrative review. *Psychological Bulletin, 108,* 50–76.

Dweck, C. S. (1975). The role of expectations and attribution in the alleviation of learned helplessness. *Journal of Personality and Social Psychology, 31,* 674–685.

Dweck, C. S., & Gilliard, D. (1975). Expectancy statements as determinants of reactions to failure: Sex differences in persistence and expectancy change. *Journal of Personality and Social Psychology, 32,* 1077–1084.

Dweck, C. S., & Goetz, T. E. (1978). Attributions and learned helplessness. In J. H. Harvey, W. Ickes, & R. F. Kidd (Eds.), *New directions in attribution research* (Vol. 2, pp. 157–179). Hillsdale, NJ: Erlbaum.

Dweck, C. S., & Licht, B. (1980). Learned helplessness and intellectual achievement. In J. Garber & M. E. P. Seligman (Eds.), *Human helplessness: Theory and applications* (pp. 197–221). New York: Academic Press.

Dweck, C. S., & Reppuci, N. D. (1973). Learned helplessness and reinforcement responsibility in children. *Journal of Personality and Social Psychology, 25,* 109–116.

Eaves, G., & Rush, A. J. (1984). Cognitive patterns in symptomatic and remitted unipolar depression. *Journal of Abnormal Psychology, 93,* 31–40.

Epstein, J. L. (1983). The influence of friends on achievement and affective outcomes. In J. L. Epstein & N. Karweit (Eds.), *Friends in school: Patterns of selections and influence in secondary schools* (pp. 177–200). New York: Academic Press.

Evans, M. D., Hollon, S. D., DeRubeis, R. J., Piasecki, J., Grove, W. M., Garvey, M. J., & Tuason, V. B. (1992). Differential relapse following cognitive therapy and pharmacotherapy for depression. *Archives of General Psychiatry, 49,* 802–808.

Eysenck, H. J., & Eysenck, M. W. (1985). *Personality and individual difference: A natural science approach.* New York: Plenum Press.

Fennell, M. J. V., & Campbell, E. A. (1984). The Cognitions Questionnaire: Specific thinking errors in depression. *British Journal of Clinical Psychology, 23,* 81–92.

Fincham, F. D., & Cain, K. M. (1986). Learned helplessness in humans: A developmental analysis. *Developmental Review, 6,* 310–333.

Fiske, S., & Taylor, S. (1991). *Social cognition.* Reading, MA: Addison-Wesley.

Fleming, J. E., & Offord, D. R. (1990). Epidemiology of childhood depressive disorders. A critical review. *Journal of the American Academy of Child and Adolescent Psychiatry, 29,* 571–580.

Friedlander, S. (1988). Learned helplessness in children: Perception of control and causal attributions. In D. C. Morrison (Ed.), *Organizing early experience: Imagination and cognition in childhood* (pp. 33–53). Amityville, NY: Baywood.

Garber, J. (1984). The developmental progression of depression in female children. In D. Cicchetti & K. Schneider-Rosen (Eds.), *New directions for child development* (pp. 29–58). San Francisco: Jossey-Bass.

Garber, J. (1992). Cognitive models of depression: A developmental perspective. *Psychological Inquiry, 3,* 235–240.

Garber, J. (1995, August). *Risk for depression in adolescents.* Presented at the 103rd Annual Convention of the American Psychological Association, New York.

Garber, J., & Flynn, C. (1998). *Predictors of depressive cognitions in young adolescents.* Manuscript submitted for publication.

Garber, J., & Hilsman, R. (1992). Cognitions, stress, and depression in children and adolescents. *Child and Adolescent Psychiatric Clinics of North America, 1,* 129–167.

Garber, J., & Hollon, S. D. (1991). What can specificity designs say about causality in psychopathology research? *Psychological Bulletin, 110,* 129–136.

Garber, J., & Robinson, N. S. (1997). Cognitive vulnerability in children at risk for depression. *Cognitions and Emotions, 11,* 619–635.

Garber, J., Robinson, N. S., & Valentiner, D. (1997). The relation between parenting and adolescent depression: Self-worth as a mediator. *Journal of Adolescent Research, 12,* 12–33.

Garber, J., Weiss, B., & Shanley, N. (1993). Cognitions, depressive symptoms, and development in adolescents. *Journal of Abnormal Psychology, 102,* 47–57.

Gillham, J., Reivich, K., Jaycox, L. H., & Seligman, M. E. P. (1995). Prevention of depressive symptoms in school children: Two year follow-up. *Psychological Science, 6,* 343–351.

Goodman, S. H., Adamson, L. B., Riniti, J., & Cole, S. (1994). Mothers' expressed attitudes: Associations with maternal depression and children's self-esteem and psychopathology. *Journal of the American Academy of Child and Adolescent Psychiatry, 33,* 1265–1274.

Gotlib, I. H., Lewinsohn, P. M., Seeley, J. R., Rohde, P., & Redner, J. E. (1993). Negative cognitions and attributional style in depressed adolescents: An examination of stability and specificity. *Journal of Abnormal Psychology, 102,* 607–615.

Haaga, D., Dyck, M., & Ernst, D. (1991). Empirical status of cognitive theory of depression. *Psychological Bulletin, 110,* 215–236.

Hamilton, E. W., & Abramson, L. Y. (1983). Cognitive patterns and major depressive disorder: A longitudinal study in a hospital setting. *Journal of Abnormal Psychology, 92,* 173–184.

Harrington, R. F., Fudge, H., Rutter, M., Pickles, A., & Hill, J. (1990). Adult outcomes of childhood and adolescent depression. *Archives of General Psychiatry, 47,* 465–473.

Hart, D., & Damon, W. (1986). Developmental trends in self-understanding. *Social Cognition, 4,* 388–407.

Harter, S. (1983). Developmental perspectives on the self-system. In E. M. Hetherington (Ed.), *Handbook of child psychology: Vol. 4. Socialization, personality, and social development* (pp. 275–385). New York: Wiley.

Harter, S. (1985). *Self-perception profile for children: Revision of the perceived competence scale for children (manual).* Denver, CO: University of Denver.

Harter, S. (1986). Processes underlying the construction, maintenance, and enhancement of the self-concept in children. In J. Suls & A. Greenwald (Eds.), *Psychological perspectives on the self* (Vol. 3, pp. 137–181). Hillsdale, NJ: Erlbaum.

Harter, S. (1988). Developmental processes in the construction of the self. In T. Yawkey & J. Johnson (Eds.), *Integrative processes and socialization: Early to middle childhood* (pp. 45–78). Hillsdale, NJ: Erlbaum.

Harter, S. (1990). Causes, correlates, and the functional role of global self-worth: A life span perspective. In J. Kolligan & R. Sternberg (Eds.), *Perception of competence and incompetence across the life span* (pp. 67–98). New Haven, CT: Yale University Press.

Harter, S. (1993). Causes and consequences of low self-esteem in children and adolescents. In R. Baumeister (Ed.), *Self-esteem: The puzzle of low self-regard* (pp. 87–116). New York: Plenum Press.

Hartup, W. (1983). Peer relations. In E. M. Hetherington (Ed.), *Handbook of child psychology: Vol. 4. Socialization, personality, and social development* (pp. 103–196). New York: Wiley.

Hilsman, R., & Garber, J. (1995). A test of the cognitive diathesis–stress model in children: Academic stressors, attributional style, perceived competence and control. *Journal of Personality and Social Psychology, 69,* 370–380.

Hirsch, B. J., Engel-Levy, A., DuBois, D. L., & Hardesty, P. H. (1990). The role of social environments in social support. In B. R. Sarason, I. G. Sarason, & G. R. Pierce (Eds.), *Social support: An interactional view* (pp. 367–393). New York: Wiley.

Hollon, S. D. (1992). Cognitive models of depression from a psychobiological perspective. *Psychological Inquiry, 3,* 250–253.

Hollon, S. D., DeRubeis, R. J., & Seligman, M. E. P. (1992). Cognitive therapy and the prevention of depression. *Applied and Preventive Psychology, 1,* 89–95.

Hollon, S. D., Evans, M. D., & DeRubeis, R. J. (1990). Cognitive mediation of relapse prevention following treatment for depression: Implications of differential risk. In R. Ingram (Ed.), *Contemporary psychological approaches to depression* (pp. 117–136). New York: Plenum.

Jaenicke, C., Hammen, C., Zupan, B., Hiroto, D., Gordon, D., Adrian, C., & Burge, D. (1987). Cognitive vulnerability in children at risk for depression. *Journal of Abnormal Child Psychology, 15,* 559–572.

James, W. (1963). *Psychology.* New York: Fawcett. (Original work published 1890)

Janoff-Bulman, R. (1992). *Shattered assumptions: Towards a new psychology of trauma*. New York: Free Press.

Janoff-Bulman, R., & Hecker, B. (1988). Depression, vulnerability, and world assumptions. In L. B. Alloy (Ed.), *Cognitive processes in depression* (pp. 177–192). New York: Guilford Press.

Jaycox, L. H., Reivich, K., Gillham, J., & Seligman, M. E. P. (1994). Prevention of depressive symptoms in school children. *Behavior Research and Therapy, 32*, 801–816.

Just, N., Alloy, L. B., & Abramson, L. Y. (1998). *Remitted depression studies as tests of the cognitive vulnerability hypothesis of depression onset: A critique and conceptual analysis*. Manuscript submitted for publication.

Kandel, D. B., & Davies, M. (1986). Adult sequelae of adolescent depressive symptoms. *Archives of General Psychiatry, 43*, 255–262.

Kashani, J. H., Reid, J. C., & Rosenberg, T. K. (1989). Levels of hopelessness in children and adolescents: A developmental perspective. *Journal of Consulting and Clinical Psychology, 57*, 496–499.

Kashani, J. H., Soltys, S. M., Dandoy, A. C., Vaidya, A. F., & Reid, J. C. (1991). Correlates of hopelessness in psychiatrically hospitalized children. *Comprehensive Psychiatry, 32*, 330–337.

Kaslow, N. J., Rehm, L. P., Pollack, S. L., & Siegel, A. W. (1988). Attributional style and self-control behavior in depressed and nondepressed children and their parents. *Journal of Abnormal Child Psychology, 16*, 163–175.

Kazdin, A. E., Rodgers, A., & Colbus, D. (1986). The Hopelessness Scale for Children: Psychometric characteristics and concurrent validity. *Journal of Consulting and Clinical Psychology, 54*, 241–245.

Keller, M., Lavori, P. W., Rice, J., Coryell, W., & Hirschfeld, R. M. A. (1986). The persistent risk of chronicity in recurrent episodes of nonbipolar major depressive disorder: A prospective follow-up. *American Journal of Psychiatry, 143*, 24–28.

Koestner, R., Zuroff, D. C., & Powers, T. A. (1991). Family origins of adolescent self-criticism and its continuity into adulthood. *Journal of Abnormal Psychology, 100*, 191–197.

Kovacs, M., & Beck, A. T. (1978). Maladaptive cognitive structures in depression. *American Journal of Psychiatry, 135*, 525–533.

Kovacs, M., Feinberg, T. L., Crouse-Novak, M., Paulauskas, S. L., Pollack, M., & Finkelstein, R. (1984). Depressive disorders in childhood: II. A longitudinal study of the risk for a subsequent major depression. *Archives of General Psychiatry, 41*, 643–649.

Kun, A. (1977). Development of the magnitude-covariation and compensation schemata in ability and effort attributions of performance. *Child Development, 48*, 862–873.

Lewinsohn, P. M., Hops, H., Roberts, R. E., Seeley, J. R., & Andrew, J. A. (1993). Adolescent psychopathology: I. Prevalence and incidence of depression and other DSM-III-R disorders in high-school students. *Journal of Abnormal Psychology, 102,* 133–144.

Lewinsohn, P. M., Steinmetz, J. L., Larson, D. W., & Franklin, J. (1981). Depression related cognitions: Antecedent or consequence? *Journal of Abnormal Psychology, 91,* 213–219.

Litovsky, V. G., & Dusek, J. B. (1985). Perceptions of child rearing and self-concept development during the early adolescent years. *Journal of Youth and Adolescence, 14,* 373–387.

Loeber, R., & Dishion, T. J. (1984). Boys who fight at home and school: Family conditions influencing cross-setting consistency. *Journal of Consulting and Clinical Psychology, 52,* 759–768.

McCauley, E., Mitchell, J. R., Burke, P., & Moss, S. (1988). Cognitive attributes of depression in children and adolescents. *Journal of Consulting and Clinical Psychology, 56,* 903–908.

McCranie, E. W., & Bass, J. D. (1984). Childhood family antecedents of dependency and self-criticism: Implications for depression. *Journal of Abnormal Psychology, 93,* 3–8.

McCubbin, H. I., & Patterson, J. M. (1987). Family inventory of life events and changes. In H. I. McCubbin & J. M. Patterson (Eds.), *Family assessment inventories for research and practice* (pp. 80–108). Madison: University of Wisconsin Press.

McGuffin, P., & Katz, R. (1989). The genetics of depression and manic-depressive disorders. *British Journal of Psychiatry, 155,* 294–304.

Messer, B., & Harter, S. (1986). *Manual for the Adult Self-Perception Profile.* Unpublished manuscript, University of Denver.

Metalsky, G. I., Halberstadt, L. J., & Abramson, L. Y. (1987). Vulnerability to depressive mood reactions: Toward a more powerful test of the diathesis–stress and causal mediation components of the reformulated theory of depression. *Journal of Personality and Social Psychology, 52,* 386–393.

Metalsky, G. I., & Joiner, T. E. (1992). Vulnerability to depressive symptomatology: A prospective test of the diathesis–stress and causal mediation components of the hopelessness theory of depression. *Journal of Personality and Social Psychology, 63,* 667–675.

Metalsky, G. I., Joiner, T. E., Hardin, T. S., & Abramson, L. Y. (1993). Depressive reactions to failure in a naturalistic setting: A test of the hopelessness and self-esteem theories of depression. *Journal of Abnormal Psychology, 102,* 101–109.

Miller, P. H., & Aloise, P. A. (1989). Young children's understanding of the psychological causes of behavior: A review. *Child Development, 60,* 257–285.

Miranda, J., Persons, J. B., & Byers, C. N. (1990). Endorsement of dysfunctional beliefs depends on current mood state. *Journal of Abnormal Psychology, 99,* 237–241.

Montemayor, R., & Eisen, M. (1977). The development of self-conceptions from childhood to adolescence. *Developmental Psychology, 13,* 314–319.

Neisser, U., Boodoo, G., Bouchard, T. J., Boykin, A. W., Brody, N., Ceci, S. J., Halpern, D. F., Loehlin, J. C., Perloff, R., Sternberg, R. J., & Urbina, S. (1996). Intelligence: Knowns and unknowns. *American Psychologist, 51,* 77–101.

Nolen-Hoeksema, S., Girgus, J., & Seligman, M. E. P. (1992). Predictors and consequences of childhood depressive symptoms: A 5-year longitudinal study. *Journal of Abnormal Psychology, 101,* 405–422.

Oakes, L. M. (1994). Development of infants' use of continuity cues in their perception of causality. *Developmental Psychology, 30,* 869–879.

Oliver, J. M., & Berger, L. S. (1992). Depression, parent–offspring relationships, and cognitive vulnerability. *Journal of Social Behavior and Personality, 7,* 415–429.

Panak, W., & Garber, J. (1992). Role of aggression, rejection, and attributions in the prediction of depression in children. *Development and Psychopathology, 4,* 145–165.

Parsons, J. E., & Ruble, D. N. (1977). The development of achievement-related expectancies. *Child Development, 48,* 1075–1079.

Patterson, G. R., & Capaldi, D. M. (1990). A mediational model for boys' depressed mood. In J. Rolf, A. S. Masten, D. Cicchetti, K. H. Neuchterlin, & S. Weintraub (Eds.), *Risk and protective factors in the development of psychopathology* (pp. 141–163). New York: Cambridge University Press.

Paykel, E. S. (Ed.). (1992). *Handbook of affective disorders.* New York: Guilford Press.

Persons, J. B., & Miranda, J. (1992). Cognitive theories of vulnerability to depression: Reconciling negative evidence. *Cognitive Therapy and Research, 16,* 485–502.

Piaget, J. (1954). *The construction of reality in the child.* New York: Basic Books.

Piaget, J. (1970). *The child's conception of time.* New York: Basic Books.

Puig-Antich, J., Lukens, E., Davies, M., Goetz, D., Brennan-Quarttrock, J., & Todak, G. (1985). Psychosocial functioning in prepubertal major depressive disorders. *Archives of General Psychiatry, 42,* 500–507.

Radke-Yarrow, M., Belmont, B., Nottelman, E., & Bottomly, L. (1990). Young children's self-conceptions: Origins in the natural discourse of depressed and normal mothers and their children. In D. Cicchetti & M. Beeghly (Eds.), *The self in transition: Infancy to childhood* (pp. 345–361). Chicago: University of Chicago Press.

Rholes, W. S., Blackwell, J., Jordan, C., & Walters, C. (1980). A developmental study of learned helplessness. *Developmental Psychology, 16,* 616–624.

Riskind, J. H., & Rholes, W. S. (1984). Cognitive accessibility and the capacity of cognitions to predict future depression: A theoretical note. *Cognitive Therapy and Research, 8,* 1–12.

Robins, C. J., & Hinkley, K. (1989). Social–cognitive processing and depressive symptoms in children: A comparison of measures. *Journal of Abnormal Child Psychology, 17,* 29–36.

Robinson, N. S., Garber, J., & Hilsman, R. (1995). Cognitions and stress: Direct and moderating effects on depressive versus externalizing symptoms during the junior high school transition. *Journal of Abnormal Psychology, 104,* 453–463.

Rohde, P., Lewinsohn, P. M., & Seeley, J. R. (1990). Are people changed by the experience of having an episode of depression? A further test of the scar hypothesis. *Journal of Abnormal Psychology, 99,* 264–271.

Rohde, P., Lewinsohn, P. M., & Seeley, J. R. (1994). Are adolescents changed by an episode of major depression? *Journal of the American Academy of Child and Adolescent Psychiatry, 33,* 1289–1298.

Rose, D. T., & Abramson, L. Y. (1992). Developmental predictors of depressive cognitive style: Research and theory. In D. Cicchetti & S. L. Toth (Eds.), *Rochester symposium on developmental psychopathology* (Vol. 4, pp. 323–349). Hillsdale, NJ: Erlbaum.

Rose, D. T., Abramson, L. Y., Hodulik, C. J., Halberstadt, L., & Leff, G. (1994). Heterogeneity of cognitive style among depressed inpatients. *Journal of Abnormal Psychology, 103,* 419–429.

Ruble, D. N., Parsons, J. E., & Ross, J. (1976). Self-evaluative responses of children in an achievement setting. *Child Development, 47,* 990–997.

Ruble, D. N., & Rholes, W. S. (1981). The development of children's perceptions and attributions about their social world. In J. H. Harvey, W. Ickes, & R. F. Kidd (Eds.), *New directions in attribution research* (Vol. 3, pp. 3–36). Hillsdale, NJ: Erlbaum.

Rutter, M. (1987). The role of cognitions in child development and disorder. *British Journal of Medical Psychology, 60,* 1–16.

Schaefer, E. S. (1965). A configural analysis of children's reports of parent behavior. *Journal of Consulting Psychology, 27,* 552–557.

Schludermann, E., & Schludermann, S. (1970). Replicability of factors in children's report of parent behavior (CRPBI). *Journal of Psychology, 76,* 239–249.

Schulman, P., Keith, D., & Seligman, M. E. P. (1991). Is optimism heritable? A study of twins. *Behavior Research and Therapy, 31,* 569–574.

Segal, Z. V., & Dobson, K. S. (1992). Cognitive models of depression: Report from a Consensus Development Conference. *Psychological Inquiry, 3,* 214–224.

Seligman, M. E. P., Abramson, L. Y., Semmel, A., & von Baeyer, C. (1979). Depressive attributional style. *Journal of Abnormal Psychology, 88,* 242–247.

Seligman, M. E. P., Kamen, L. P., & Nolen-Hoeksema, S. (1988). Explanatory style across the life span. In E. M. Hetherington, R. M. Lerner, & M. Perlmutter (Eds.), *Child development in life-span perspective* (pp. 91–114). Hillsdale, NJ: Erlbaum.

Seligman, M. E. P., & Peterson, C. (1986). A learned helplessness perspective on childhood depression: Theory and research. In M. Rutter, C. E. Izard, & P. B. Read (Eds.), *Depression in young people: Developmental and clinical perspectives* (pp. 223–249). New York: Guilford Press.

Seligman, M. E. P., Peterson, C., Kaslow, N. J., Tanenbaum, R. L., Alloy, L. B.,

& Abramson, L. Y. (1984). Explanatory style and depressive symptoms among children. *Journal of Abnormal Psychology, 93,* 235–238.

Singer, D. G., & Revenson, T. A. (1996). *A Piaget primer: How a child thinks.* New York: Plume.

Siomopolous, G., & Inamdar, S. C. (1979). Developmental aspects of hopelessness. *Adolescence, 14,* 233–239.

Stark, K. D., Schmidt, K. L., & Joiner, T. E. (1996). Cognitive triad: Relationship to depressive symptoms, parents' cognitive triad, and perceived parental messages. *Journal of Abnormal Child Psychology, 24,* 615–632.

Stipek, D. J. (1981). Social–motivational development in first grade. *Contemporary Educational Psychology, 6,* 33–45.

Stipek, D. J., Lamb, M. E., & Zigler, E. F. (1981). OPTI: A measure of children's optimism. *Educational and Psychological Measurement, 41,* 131–143.

Teasdale, J. D., & Dent, J. (1987). Cognitive vulnerability to depression: An investigation of two hypotheses. *British Journal of Clinical Psychology, 26,* 113–126.

Turk, E., & Bry, B. H. (1992). Adolescents' and parents' explanatory styles and parents' causal explanations about their adolescents. *Cognitive Therapy and Research, 16,* 349–357.

Watson, D., & Clark, L. A. (1984). Negative affectivity: The disposition to experience aversive emotional states. *Psychological Bulletin, 96,* 465–490.

Watson, D., Clark, L. A., & Harkness, A. R. (1994). Structures of personality and their relevance to psychopathology. *Journal of Abnormal Psychology, 103,* 18–31.

Weiner, B., & Graham, S. (1985). An attributional approach to emotional development. In C. Izard, J. Kagan, & R. Zajonc (Eds.), *Emotions, cognition, and behavior* (pp. 167–191). New York: Cambridge University Press.

Weiss, B., Dodge, K. A., Bates, J. E., & Pettit, G. S. (1992). Some consequences of early harsh discipline: Child aggression and a maladaptive social information processing style. *Child Development, 63,* 1321–1335.

Weissman, M. M. (1987). Advances in psychiatric epidemiology: Rates and risks for major depression. *American Journal of Public Health, 77,* 445–451.

Weissman, M. M., Gammon, G., John, K., Merikangas, K., Warner, V., Prusoff, B., & Sholomskas, D. (1987). Children of depressed parents: Increased psychopathology and early onset of major depression. *Archives of General Psychiatry, 44,* 847–853.

Weissman, M. M., Klerman, G. L., Prusoff, B. A., Sholomskas, D., & Padian, N. (1981). Depressed outpatients: Results one year after treatment with drugs and/or interpersonal psychotherapy. *Archives of General Psychiatry, 38,* 51–55.

Weisz, J. R., & Stipek, D. J. (1982). Competence, contingency, and the development of perceived control. *Human Development, 25,* 250–281.

Whisman, M. A., & Kwon, P. (1992). Parental representations, cognitive distortions, and mild depression. *Cognitive Therapy and Research, 16,* 557–568.

White, P. A. (1988). Causal processing: Origins and development. *Psychological Bulletin, 104,* 36–52.

4

THE NATURE AND DEVELOPMENT OF ANXIETY AND DEPRESSION: BACK TO THE FUTURE

DAVID H. BARLOW, AMY K. BACH, AND SUSAN A. TRACEY

Neurotic disorders dominated the landscape of psychopathology for almost a century before dying a sudden and traumatic death in 1980. At that time, the publication of the *Diagnostic and Statistical Manual of Mental Disorders* (3rd ed., *DSM–III*; American Psychiatric Association, 1980) "split" neurotic disorders into a number of major classes, such as anxiety disorders, each containing its own list of more specific disorders. With its passing went the heavy theoretical baggage specifying the development and etiology of neurotic disorders. In its place by design was an atheoretical description of symptomatology.

And yet, neuroticism lives on and continues to be a serious topic for study, mostly by personality and developmental psychologists interested in traits or temperaments as possible vulnerabilities for developing anxiety and mood disorders. Constructs most readily identified in this field of study are defined slightly differently and given different labels, including harm avoidance (Cloninger, 1986), neuroticism (Eysenck, 1967), trait anxiety (Gray, 1982), behavioral inhibition (Kagan, 1994), and negative affect

(Tellegen, 1985). Nevertheless, the conceptual and empirical overlap among these constructs far outweighs any differences.

At the level of disorders, evidence for the contribution of a unitary construct to the former "neurotic" disorders includes patterns of comorbidity among and between anxiety and mood disorders (Brown, Barlow, & Liebowitz, 1994), the success of similar pharmacological and psychosocial treatments with this wide variety of disorders (e.g., Hudson & Pope, 1990; Tyrer et al., 1988), as well as evidence that comorbid diagnoses often remit after psychosocial treatment of another anxiety disorder (Brown, Antony, & Barlow, 1995; Borkovec, Abel, & Newman, 1995).

Nevertheless, anxiety and mood disorders may differ dramatically from each other on the basis of key defining features. Such phenomena as panic, perceptual derealization, psychomotor retardation, intrusive thoughts, sensitivity to social evaluation, compulsive behaviors and cognitive rituals, phobic avoidance of blood, flashbacks of trauma, worry, and agoraphobia all differ very much from one another, and yet find themselves subsumed under anxiety or mood disorders. How can one reconcile the unitary nature of *negative affectivity* (the term we will use for convenience to describe the various traits or temperaments described above) with a variety of specific features that distinguish one disorder from the other?

These and other issues regarding the nature, structure, and etiology of anxiety and mood disorders will be addressed in this chapter. The first section of the chapter presents data concerning the nature and structure of anxiety and mood disorders, including recent advances based on structural equation modeling. The second section of the chapter addresses the development of anxiety disorders, bringing together data from such diverse areas as cognition, temperament, and neurobiology.

THE STRUCTURE OF ANXIETY AND MOOD DISORDERS

Many theorists support a hierarchical model of anxiety and mood disorders, with negative affect (or generalized dysphoria) representing a higher order factor that is common to both anxiety and depression, whereas other factors may contribute to what is unique between anxiety and depression. For example, we have suggested elsewhere (Barlow, 1988, 1991; Barlow & DiNardo, 1991) that all anxiety disorders (with the possible exception of specific phobia) share a fundamental presenting characteristic, which we termed *anxious apprehension*. This term is meant to be synonymous with anxiety but highlights the notion that anxiety is a future-oriented mood state in which one is prepared to attempt to cope with upcoming negative events. Depression may be seen as differing from anxious apprehension in terms of cognitive content, or the degree of certainty with which one feels capable of coping with negative events (e.g., Alloy,

Kelly, Mineka, & Clements, 1990; Barlow, 1988). For example, for an anxious individual, there is some degree of uncertainty, but one is prepared to attempt to cope with an upcoming negative event. However, a depressed individual may give up, convinced of his or her inability to cope, resulting in cognitive and psychomotor slowing, and perhaps reduction in positive affect. Nevertheless, depression and anxiety share negative affect, common neurobiological features, and, most likely, similar diatheses, making these two constructs more alike than different. More specific lower order factors provide for further differentiation among each of the anxiety and mood disorders. Within our model, specific anxiety disorders may be differentiated on the basis of the cues that elicit anxious apprehension (i.e., the focus of anxious apprehension). For example, in panic disorder, the focus of anxious apprehension may be on internal physical sensations or loss of emotional control, whereas in generalized anxiety disorder, the focus may be on a variety of environmental cues.

The *Diagnostic and Statistical Manual of Mental Disorders* (4th ed., *DSM–IV*; American Psychiatric Association, 1994) implies a similar hierarchical model of anxiety disorders, with anxiety constituting a more general factor, and with more specific vulnerabilities and symptom development giving rise to features that distinguish one disorder from another. Recently, we conducted empirical investigations of these hierarchical models of anxiety (as well as mood disorders). In our first investigation, we examined the structure of anxiety and anxiety disorders using dimensional analyses and factor-analytic procedures to test the adequacy of these hierarchical models (Zinbarg & Barlow, 1996).

Our sample consisted of 432 patients seeking treatment at an outpatient anxiety disorder clinic (416 with a principal diagnosis of an anxiety disorder, and 16 with a principal diagnosis of a mood disorder according to *DSM–III–R* criteria; American Psychiatric Association, 1987) and 32 controls with no mental disorder. In this sample, key features of anxiety disorders were measured using a standardized battery of the following self-report questionnaires: (a) the Anxiety Sensitivity Index (Reiss, Peterson, Gursky, & McNally, 1986), (b) the Fear Survey Schedule–II (Geer, 1965), (c) the Maudsley Obsessive–Compulsive inventory (Hodgson & Rachman, 1977), (d) the Penn State Worry Questionnaire (Meyer, Miller, Metzger, & Borkovec, 1990), (e) the Self Analysis Questionnaire–Form 9 (Lovibond & Lovibond, 1991), (f) the Albany Panic and Phobia Questionnaire (Rapee, Craske, & Barlow, 1995), (g) the Social Interaction Anxiety Scale (Mattick & Clarke, 1988), and (h) the Social Phobia Scale (Mattick & Peters, 1988).

Exploratory factor analysis of these measures yielded six lower order factors: Social Anxiety, Generalized Dysphoria, Fear of Fear, Agoraphobia, Simple Fears, and Obsessions–Compulsions. We then used hierarchical confirmatory factor analysis to test the prediction that including a single higher order factor, Negative Affect (NA; L. A. Clark & Watson, 1991; Tellegen, 1985), would lead to a significant increase in goodness of fit of the model. Several indexes of overall fit, as well as a nested chi-square test, indicated that the higher order model provided a better fit to the data, when compared with a model consisting only of the six lower order factors. Thus, our data were consistent with the hierarchical structure of anxiety disorders.

Next, to examine the relationship between the seven dimensions of self-reported anxiety symptomatology and DSM diagnostic groups, we computed factor score estimates for each patient for each of the seven major factors (i.e., the six lower order factors and NA) and used discriminant function analysis to examine the factor score profiles of the different DSM anxiety disorder groups. Overall, five discriminant functions were significant in differentiating the eight diagnostic groups: (a) Social Anxiety, (b) Agoraphobia, (c) Fear of Fear, (d) Obsessions and Compulsions, and (e) Negative Affect. Mean group differences on each of the significant discriminant functions were analyzed using Fisher's protected least significant difference tests. As seen in Table 1, these results were again consistent with the hierarchical structure of anxiety. That is, the function corresponding to NA did not discriminate among anxiety disorder groups, but discriminated each anxiety disorder group from the no-mental-disorder control group. The other discriminant functions (which corresponded to four of the lower order factors) significantly discriminated among the anxiety disorder groups, as expected.

Our results suggest that NA reflects the common factor relating the

TABLE 1
Mean Scores on Varimax Rotated Discriminant Functions for Each Diagnostic Group

Group	Discriminant function				
	1	2	3	4	5
PD	-0.48_a	-0.10_a	0.68_a	-0.35_a	0.24_a
PDA	-0.21_b	1.25_b	0.38_a	-0.12_a	0.26_a
GAD	0.08_b	$-0.33_{a,c}$	-0.42_b	0.48_b	0.31_a
OCD	0.06_b	-0.68_c	$-0.47_{b,c}$	1.79_c	0.32_a
SIMP	$-0.43_{a,b}$	0.11_a	$-0.57_{b,c}$	-0.06_a	-0.31_b
MDE	0.25_b	$-0.17_{a,c}$	-1.08_c	$0.13_{a,b}$	-0.09_a
SOCP	1.76_c	-0.61_c	$-0.69_{b,c}$	-0.02_a	-0.37_b
NMD	-0.52_a	-0.81_c	-0.99_c	0.01_a	-1.45_c

Note. PD = panic disorder with no to mild agoraphobia; PDA = panic disorder with moderate to severe agoraphobia; GAD = generalized anxiety disorder; OCD = obsessive–compulsive disorder; SIMP = simple phobia; MDE = major depressive disorder and dysthymia; SOCP = social phobia; NMD = no mental disorder. Means in the same column that do not share a common subscript differ at $p < .05$ in the Fisher's protected least significant difference comparison. From "Structure of Anxiety and Anxiety Disorders: A Hierarchical Model," by R. Zinbarg and D. H. Barlow, 1996, *Journal of Abnormal Psychology, 105*, p. 189. Copyright 1996 by the American Psychological Association.

DSM anxiety disorders, but more specific lower order factors discriminate among each of the *DSM* anxiety disorders. Therefore, our results support the construct validity of the hierarchical model of anxiety disorders implicit in the *DSM*. However, elevations of the discriminant functions were not entirely specific to one diagnostic group. That is, intermediate elevations associated with some patient groups were observed, suggesting fuzzy diagnostic boundaries. For example, the generalized anxiety disorder group showed intermediate elevations on the Obsessions and Compulsions function, suggesting that, consistent with previous research (e.g., Brown, Moras, Zinbarg, & Barlow, 1993), these two disorders may be closely related.

Also of note is that the discriminant function associated with NA discriminated those with a principal diagnosis of a mood disorder from the no-mental-disorder controls as well, highlighting the relationship between anxiety and mood disorders. But the mood disorder group was not associated with a discriminant function that distinguished it from each of the other diagnostic groups (i.e., the anxiety disorders). Furthermore, in our exploratory factor analysis, generalized anxiety did not differentiate from depression, resulting in a single lower order factor, Generalized Dysphoria. This may have been due to inadequate sampling of depression items, in that only one measure of depressive content was included in our questionnaire battery, and our sample did not include those complaining only of depression.

However, these results could also reflect the high overlap among anxiety and depression, as evidenced by their high rate of co-occurrence on the syndromal level (e.g., Brown et al., 1994), as well as the considerable overlap found between dimensional measures of anxiety and depression (L. A. Clark & Watson, 1991; Kendall & Watson, 1989). Therefore our data again raise the question of whether anxiety and depression are empirically distinct phenomena.

Mixed Anxiety–Depression

Evidence from a somewhat different line of inquiry is relevant to the relationship between anxiety and depression. The literature suggests that there are many patients with anxiety and depressive symptoms who do not meet current definitional thresholds for *DSM* anxiety or mood disorders (e.g., because of insufficient frequency or duration of symptoms) but who still show substantial impairment (e.g., Barrett, Barrett, Oxman, & Gerber, 1988; L. A. Clark & Watson, 1990; Katon & Roy-Byrne, 1990).

For example, Barrett et al. (1988) assessed a large sample of patients (*N* = 1,000) from a rural primary care practice for mixed anxiety–depression (MAD) and other emotional disorders, including minor depression, chronic intermittent minor depression, labile personality, generalized anxiety disorder, a combined group consisting of panic and phobic states, and masked or suspected depression. Assessments were conducted using a structured interview based on modified Research Diagnostic Criteria. Overall, 26.5% of the sample met criteria for a disorder, with 4.1% meeting criteria for MAD. Of course, differing diagnostic convention and exclusionary criteria preclude these data from being directly relevant to *DSM–IV* categories.

Nevertheless, findings such as these prompted the *DSM–IV* task force to conduct a field trial, the results of which led to the inclusion of MAD in the *DSM–IV* appendix for proposed diagnostic categories in need of further study. In this field trial (Zinbarg et al., 1994), 666 patients from several primary care and outpatient mental health sites were administered a semistructured clinical interview. Results indicated that patients presenting with anxiety or mood symptoms that did not meet definitional thresholds for an established *DSM–III–R* anxiety or mood disorder (and who therefore received a *not-otherwise-specified* [NOS] diagnosis) were at least as common as those meeting criteria for one of these disorders. Nevertheless, these patients were experiencing significant distress or impairment associated with their symptoms, as measured by clinicians' dimensional ratings of "caseness," as well as ratings on the Global Assessment of Functioning Scale.

To compare the symptom presentation of these patients with those receiving a diagnosis of an established anxiety or mood disorder, we factor analyzed a revised version (Riskind, Beck, Brown, & Steer, 1987) of the Hamilton Anxiety (Hamilton, 1959) and Depression (Hamilton, 1960) Rating Scales, yielding four scales: Negative Affect, Depression, Anxiety, and Physiological Arousal. The group with subdefinitional threshold disorders could be significantly differentiated from patients presenting with a principal diagnosis of generalized anxiety disorder, major depressive disorder, and panic disorder with agoraphobia, in terms of scores on these scales. Profiles of individuals within the NOS group in terms of standing on the NA, Depression, and Anxiety scales were also examined (see Table 2). The modal presentation for individuals in this group was a nonspecific pattern of mixed anxious and depressive symptoms, as represented by the first three rows of Table 2.

Conceptually, the fundamental component of MAD appears to be generalized dysphoria or NA; that is, symptoms that do not cluster specifically with either anxiety or depression but are nonspecifically associated with both mood states. It has been suggested that MAD may represent the common cognitive–affective state priming the more specific features that define *DSM* anxiety and mood disorders. For example, Katon and Roy-Byrne (1990) suggested that patients presenting with mixed anxiety–depressive symptoms are at risk of developing more severe mood and anxiety disorders after experiencing stressful life events. This conceptualization of MAD, as fundamental to other disorders of emotion, is in accord with the notion of NA as a common vulnerability factor for emotional disorders

TABLE 2
Number of Patients With a Principal Diagnosis of Anxiety or
Depressive Disorder Not Otherwise Specified (N = 52) as a Function of
Standing on Scales of Negative Affect, Anxiety, and Depression

Scale standing[a]			Number of patients
Negative affect	Anxiety	Depression	
High	High	High	21
High	Low	Low	2
Low	High	High	2
High	Low	High	7
Low	Low	High	1
High	High	Low	6
Low	High	Low	4
Low	Low	Low	9

[a]High = high compared with that of group with no mental disorder; low = statistically equivalent with that of group with no mental disorder. From "The DSM–IV Field Trial for Mixed Anxiety–Depression," by R. E. Zinbarg, D. H. Barlow, M. Liebowitz, L. Street, E. Broadhead, W. Katon, P. Roy-Byrne, J. Lepine, M. Teherani, J. Richards, P. J. Brantley, & H. Kraemer, *American Journal of Psychiatry, 151*, p. 1159, 1994. Copyright 1994, the American Psychiatric Association. Reprinted by permission.

as described by L. A. Clark and Watson (1991). In fact, the four scales (NA, Depression, Anxiety, and Physiological Arousal) derived from factor analyses conducted for the MAD field trial were, for the most part, consistent with the model of anxiety and depression proposed by L. A. Clark and Watson (1991).

More specifically, L. A. Clark and Watson (1991) proposed a tripartite model of anxiety and depression, based on a comprehensive review of the literature. The authors suggested that anxiety and depression share a significant nonspecific component (general affective distress or NA) and other common symptoms, but the two constructs can be distinguished by certain unique features. Thus, the tripartite model consists of *general distress or NA*, which is a fundamental part of anxiety and depression; *physiological hyperarousal*, which is specific to anxiety; and *an absence of positive affect*, which is specific to depression. Several studies provide some empirical support for this tripartite structure (e.g., Joiner, Catanzaro, & Laurent, 1996; Watson et al., 1995).

This model may have implications for the etiology of emotional disorders in that, as suggested above, NA may represent a key vulnerability factor for the development of both anxiety and depression (L. A. Clark, Watson, & Mineka, 1994; Watson & Clark, 1984; Watson, Clark, & Harkness, 1994). Low positive affect, on the other hand, may represent a vulnerability dimension specific to depression, although presently, there is less support for this dimension as a trait vulnerability factor. Current research also suggests that autonomic arousal may not be a trait vulnerability factor of anxiety, but rather relate more specifically to the phenomena of panic as described below (L. A. Clark et al., 1994).

Structural Relationships of Dimensions of Anxiety and Mood Disorders With Tripartite Factors

These collective data begin to illustrate the relationship between anxiety and mood disorders and highlight the importance of including depression in an examination of the structure of anxiety. Therefore, we recently extended our first analysis to test the tripartite model of anxiety and depression and evaluate *DSM–IV* nosology using structural equation modeling (Brown, Chorpita, & Barlow, 1998). We extended our analysis by going beyond self-report measures (as our previous analysis may have been influenced by method variance such as response biases, item overlap, or scaling differences), including adequate sampling of mood, and by examining the additional tripartite factors, Positive Affect and Autonomic Arousal. In our sample of 350 outpatients with anxiety and mood disorders, self-report questionnaires and clinician ratings based on structured interviews were used to measure key features of selected anxiety disorders. Using these data, we repeated the confirmatory factor analysis and then evaluated structural models of the relationship among *DSM–IV* disorders and the tripartite factors.

Confirmatory factor analysis indicated that the factor structure corresponding to *DSM–IV* for the five symptom domains examined (i.e., panic disorder, generalized anxiety disorder [GAD], social phobia, obsessive–compulsive disorder, and mood disorders) provided a significantly better fit for the data than a unifactorial model in which all disorders were collapsed. This factor analysis provided a better test of the model than did the analysis of Zinbarg and Barlow (1996), because it allowed intercorrelation of the *DSM* disorder factors. The earlier factor analysis had constrained the *DSM* disorder factors to be orthogonal, although one would expect these factors to be correlated. This resulted in a poorer fit for the lower order model when compared with the higher order model, which did allow the relationship between the disorders.

Furthermore, our recent analysis enabled an examination of the relationship between the various anxiety and mood disorders. Notably, GAD was more closely associated with depression than with any other anxiety disorder; the zero-order correlation between the two disorders was .63. However, a four-factor model in which the two disorders were collapsed resulted in a significant degradation of fit of the model, suggesting that although closely related, the two disorders are distinct. These results further indicate that mood disorders may pose greater boundary problems for certain anxiety disorders than do other anxiety disorders (Brown, Marten, & Barlow, 1995; Brown, Anson, & DiBartolo, 1996). Obsessive–compulsive disorder was also strongly correlated with GAD, consistent with previous suggestions of the relationship between the two disorders.

We also compared several models of the relationship between dimen-

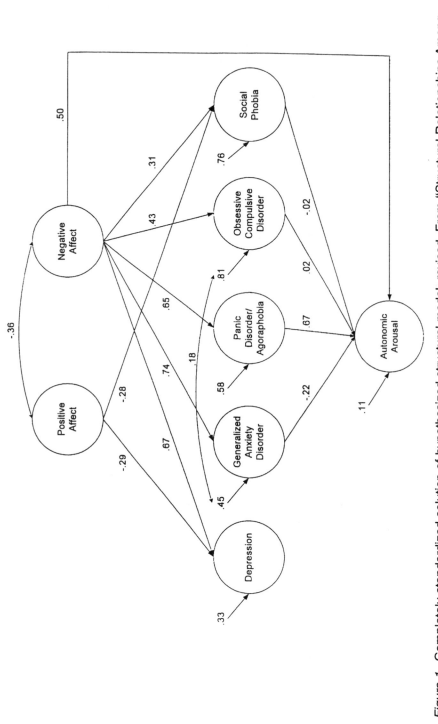

Figure 1. Completely standardized solution of hypothesized structural model, revised. From "Structural Relationships Among Dimensions of the DSM–IV Anxiety and Mood Disorders and Dimensions of Negative Affect, Positive Affect, and Autonomic Arousal," by T. A. Brown, B. F. Chorpita, and D. H. Barlow, 1998, *Journal of Abnormal Psychology, 107,* p. 187. Copyright 1998 by the American Psychological Association.

sions of key features of selected *DSM–IV* disorders and dimensions of the tripartite model of anxiety and depression. The hypothesized model (see Figure 1) entailed (a) a higher order factor, Negative Affect (NA), which influenced each of the five *DSM* disorder factors; (b) a higher order factor, Positive Affect (PA), which influenced the *DSM* mood disorder factor only; and (c) a factor, Autonomic Arousal (AA), which is influenced by the *DSM* anxiety disorder factors and NA. This model was compared with a model in which the five *DSM* disorder factors were specified as higher order factors influencing the lower order factors NA, PA, and AA, and a third model in which NA, PA, and AA were specified as higher order factors influencing the *DSM* disorders. (For clarity, the abbreviations NA, PA, and AA will only be used here to refer to latent variables in our model.)

Overall, the hypothesized model was judged to provide a better fit to the data (see Figure 1 for path coefficients). The data were in accord with the conceptualization of NA as a higher order dimension influencing both anxiety and depression. All paths from NA to the *DSM* disorders were significant, and the relative magnitude of the paths were in accord with predictions of the strength of the relationship between NA and the various disorders (D. A. Clark, Steer, & Beck, 1994). The strongest paths were from NA to GAD (.74) and NA to depression (.67). This is consistent with the notion that GAD may be the "basic" anxiety disorder because its features (e.g., chronic worry and negative affect) reflect key vulnerability dimensions of anxiety disorders.

Findings also generally indicated that PA is a higher order factor that is more specifically linked to depression. However, indexes also suggested an association between social phobia and low positive affect; PA had a stronger zero-order correlation with social phobia than with any other anxiety disorder. In fact, the path between social phobia and PA (−.28) was almost identical to the path from PA to depression (−.29), although the zero-order correlation was higher for depression. This indicates that positive affect influences depression and social phobia in a similar manner after controlling for variance in negative affect. Although this relationship was not hypothesized, previous research has also shown an association between social phobia and low positive affect (e.g., Amies, Gelder, & Shaw, 1983; Watson, Clark, & Carey, 1988).

In terms of autonomic arousal, results were supportive of hypotheses that this dimension may not represent a trait vulnerability factor for the anxiety disorders. In fact, when AA was specified as a higher order factor, degradation of fit and interpretability of the model was observed. However, a few interesting findings were noted. First, indexes suggested a strong association between panic disorder and autonomic arousal, consistent with current conceptualizations of panic disorder (Barlow, Chorpita, & Turovsky, 1996; L. A. Clark et al., 1994). Thus, AA seems to reflect the phenomena of panic as distinct from anxiety and negative affect.

In addition, results with regard to the association between GAD and AA may account for conflicting findings regarding the relationship between the two. Patients with GAD frequently endorse autonomic symptoms (Brown, Marten, & Barlow, 1995), but laboratory data suggest that they may respond to psychological stress with autonomic inflexibility (Borkovec, Lyonfields, Wiser, & Diehl, 1993; Hoehn-Saric, McCleod, & Zimmerli, 1989). Our results paralleled these findings and indicated a possible suppressor effect; the zero-order correlation (.48) between GAD and AA indicates an increase in autonomic arousal with an increase in features of GAD, whereas the path from GAD to AA ($-.22$) suggests the opposite relationship. As both GAD and AA were also strongly correlated with NA at the zero-order level, the autonomic symptoms may be due to high levels of negative affect. After accounting for variance in autonomic arousal due to NA, however, the true direct influence of features of GAD on AA may be negative. That is, key features of GAD (i.e., worry) may act to suppress autonomic arousal.

Overall, these collective data are consistent with hierarchical models of anxiety and mood disorders, as well as models of trait negative affectivity as a common vulnerability factor for anxiety and mood disorders. Nevertheless, the observed relationships among the variables may have been a result of the presence of an anxiety or mood disorder. That is, these cross-sectional investigations do not speak to the direction of causation. Therefore structural analysis of longitudinal data is needed to affirm the constructs of negative and positive affect as higher order dimensions that influence the pathogenesis, course, and treatment response of emotional disorders.

THE CAUSES OF ANXIETY DISORDERS

Animal research and investigations focusing on children have provided important insight into a psychological vulnerability for emotional disorders. Specifically, studies on the role of uncontrollable stressors in the early environment have yielded compelling data regarding the development of both depression and anxiety disorders.

Uncontrollable Stress

More than half a century ago, the results of laboratory experiments with animals implicated uncontrollable stressors in the development of emotional disorders. Pavlov (1927) wrote of a classical conditioning experiment in which it became increasingly difficult for a dog to distinguish between the stimulus used to signal the delivery of food and that used to signal the absence of food. Pavlov noted that in response to the frustrating task, the once docile dog began to bark violently and demonstrate extreme agitation. Pavlov hypothesized that the experiment had inadvertently created in the dog a condition similar to that of "neurosis" in humans. In a series of studies that followed by scientists such as W. Horsley Gantt, Jules Hymen Masserman, and Howard S. Liddell, the response labeled *experimental neurosis* was successfully reproduced.

Some years later, researchers attempted to further delineate the nature of this phenomenon. With use of operant conditioning paradigms, they were able to more specifically examine the effects of uncontrollable stressors on animals. In such studies (e.g., Overmier & Seligman, 1967; Seligman & Maier, 1967), animals that were exposed to uncontrollable stressors (i.e., electric shock) showed an impaired ability to learn contingent responses on subsequent trials. They seemed to have learned that their behavior had no effect on the termination of the electric shock and, therefore, they made no effort to control it in the future.

It is interesting to note that the findings of these studies have served primarily as the basis for animal models of depression. For example, Seligman's (1975) theory of learned helplessness is based on research with experimental neurosis. Seligman theorized that much as animals learned they were helpless when presented with aversive stimuli, so might humans perceive that they cannot control life stressors. When people develop this sense of uncontrollability, they fail to use effective coping strategies and subsequently become depressed.

In their review of studies on experimental neurosis, Mineka and Kihlstrom (1978) conclude that when faced with unpredictability and uncontrollability, animals responded in one of two ways: "Some became very agitated, with increases in general activity level and signs of high autonomic arousal (increased breathing rate, piloerection, struggling, howling, etc.). Others showed decreased activity levels and generally looked passive and withdrawn, sometimes becoming socially isolated from their conspecifics" (p. 260). As Seligman (1975) suggested, the latter response is similar to that seen in depressed humans. However, the former response has received considerably less attention. It is this response that more closely resembles anxiety and suggests a relationship between uncontrollability and the development of anxiety disorders in humans.

Uncontrollability and Anxiety

Mineka and colleagues rekindled an interest among anxiety researchers regarding the potential link between uncontrollability and the development of anxiety disorders. Questions regarding this relationship have resulted in a series of studies on the development and the effects of control in the early environment.

Mineka, Gunnar, and Champoux (1986) examined the effects of control in the socioemotional development of rhesus monkeys. Infant monkeys were assigned to one of three groups: master, yoked, and standard reared. Monkeys in the master group had control over the delivery of food, drink, and other appetitive stimuli. Monkeys in the yoked group received equal amounts of these reinforcers but did not have control over their delivery. Monkeys in the standard reared group were treated according to standard laboratory procedures. Testing began when the monkeys were approximately 7 months of age. Results showed that master monkeys engaged in significantly more exploring behavior and less clinging than did the yoked monkeys. Master monkeys also showed reduced fear to a toy robot compared with yoked monkeys. Finally, when separated from peers, master monkeys used coping strategies more effectively to reduce distress. These findings are significant in that they demonstrate the negative influence of uncontrollability in the early environment. In addition, whereas experimental neurosis paradigms suggest the importance of control over aversive stimuli, this study suggests that control over appetitive stimuli may be equally important (Chorpita & Barlow, in press).

Efforts to directly examine the role of control in humans actually date back to the work of Julian Rotter (1954). Rotter theorized that one's "locus of control" could be rated along a dimension of internal versus external causality. He suggested that a person's attribution regarding the response–stimulus relationship mediates the extent to which an event is reinforcing. Nowicki and Strickland (1973) developed the Nowicki–Strickland Locus of Control Scale, the first psychometrically sound measure of locus of control in children (Barlow et al., 1996). With use of this scale, researchers have found that an external locus of control is significantly positively correlated with both anxiety (Nunn, 1988) and depression (McCauley, Mitchell, Burke, & Moss, 1988; Siegel & Griffin, 1984) in children. These studies support the notion that a sense of being unable to control one's environment is associated with higher levels of anxiety. However, much like adult research, these findings do not provide insight into the development of uncontrollability. Research providing such information emerged only more recently through a series of studies on early environment and the role of parenting styles.

Parenting Styles and Uncontrollability

Stark, Humphrey, Crook, and Lewis (1990) assessed families in which a child was diagnosed with a mood disorder, an anxiety disorder, a mood disorder and an anxiety disorder, or neither a mood nor an anxiety disorder. Fifty-one children and their mothers completed a self-report measure assessing their perception of their family interactions. Mothers of anxious children did not differ significantly from mothers of controls in their perceptions of the family. However, children with emotional disorders rated their parents as significantly less supportive, less socially engaged, more enmeshed, and less willing to involve them in decisions being made about them and their family. These results provide insight into the familial patterns that may be associated with the onset of mood and anxiety disorders. Specifically, children who are less likely to develop a sense of autonomy and who feel they are not involved in making decisions that affect them may experience a sense of uncontrollability. Unfortunately, this study is limited by its reliance on self-report measures and the fact that children were assessed only for mood and anxiety disorders, not for other forms of psychopathology.

Siqueland, Kendall, and Steinberg (1996) examined a similar question with improved methodology. They assessed families with and without children who had an anxiety disorder to examine differences in family interactions. Participants were 17 families with a child who met DSM–IV criteria for an anxiety disorder and 27 families who served as nonclinic controls. The Anxiety Disorders Interview Schedule for Children (Silverman & Nelles, 1988) was administered to children and parents in the clinical group. This semistructured interview assesses for anxiety, mood, and externalizing disorders, as well as psychosis. All families completed self-report measures and participated in four videotaped interaction tasks in which the child and one or both parents were asked to discuss a topic about which they disagreed. Ratings of independent observers indicated that parents of children with anxiety disorders gave their children less psychological autonomy than did nonclinic parents. In addition, children with anxiety disorders rated their parents as less accepting than did nonclinic children.

In a study that yielded similar results, Dumas, LaFreniere, and Serketich (1995) evaluated the nature and frequency of control exchanges in mother–child dyads. One hundred twenty-six children were recruited from preschools and were classified as socially competent, aggressive, or anxious. The children were asked to complete a task while mothers observed and assisted. Mother–child interactions were videotaped and rated for the presence of control, coercion, and positive and aversive behavior and affect. Positive interactions included use of laughter, assistance, and affection. Aversive interactions included use of critical punishment, disapproval, or sarcasm. The authors found that, compared with mothers of aggressive or socially competent children, mothers of anxious children were more controlling and more likely to exercise control through aversive behavior or affect. In addition, mothers of anxious children were more likely to use coercive behaviors and were less likely to comply with children's efforts to assert control. Finally, anxious children complied with their mothers less often than did their aggressive and socially competent counterparts.

Taken together, these studies provide evidence that controlling parenting styles are associated with anxiety disorders in children. This is consistent with findings from a series of studies by Parker and colleagues (Parker, 1983; Parker, Tupling, & Brown, 1979; Silove, Parker, Hadzi-Pavlovic, Manicavasagar, & Blaszczynski, 1991). Parker developed an instrument for adults that retrospectively measures their perception of their mothers' and fathers' parenting styles. The Parental Bonding Instrument is a self-report scale that measures the two dimensions Parker believed underlied parental attitudes and behaviors: care and protection (Parker et al., 1979). Twelve items measure care and 13 items measure protection. Protection is measured along a dimension ranging from parental control, overprotection, and excessive contact to allowance of autonomy and independence. Care is measured along a dimension ranging from affection, emotional warmth, and empathy to indifference, emotional coldness, and rejection. Parker (1983) hypothesized that the parenting style most often associated with anxiety neurosis is a combination of high protection and low care. He referred to this parenting style as *affectionless control.*

Silove et al. (1991) administered the Parental Bonding Instrument to 80 patients seeking treatment for panic disorder or generalized anxiety disorder. This information was compared with data obtained from a matched control sample. The authors found that, overall, patients reported they had received less parental care and greater parental overprotection as children. Results of logistical regression indicated that patients with panic disorder tended to rate their parents as affectionate and overprotective, whereas patients with generalized anxiety disorder tended to rate their parents as affectionless and overprotective.

It is clear that there is evidence for a relation between high levels of anxiety in children and controlling family environments. However, at this point, the relationship must be described as correlational. Longitudinal studies focusing on very young children are needed to determine whether controlling parenting styles exist before the onset of anxiety disorders or whether this parenting style is a response to anxious behavior in children. Thus far, however, the data are at least consistent with the notion that a low sense of control contributes to high levels of anxiety. Research on exactly how and when uncontrollability might lead to the development of anxiety disorders is in the early stages. However, impressive advances in research on depression provide some preliminary answers.

Uncontrollability and Depression

As stated earlier, Seligman (1975) hypothesized that when repeatedly faced with negative life events, people develop a belief that they do not have control over their environment. Feeling helpless, they cease to act on the environment, and depression ensues. Abramson, Seligman, and Teasdale (1978) reformulated this theory. They suggest that the relationship between negative life events and learned helplessness is moderated by one's attributional style. That is, negative life events are most likely to lead to learned helplessness when a person makes internal, global, and stable attributions regarding the negative events. Abramson, Metalsky, and Alloy (1989) modified this theory and emphasized the role of hopelessness. They suggest that for many forms of depression, attributions play a causal role only when they contribute to a sense of hopelessness.

Nolen-Hoeksema, Girgus, and Seligman (1992) provided fascinating information regarding the development and subsequent effects of cognitive response styles in childhood and early adolescence. They conducted a 5-year longitudinal study that aimed to identify predictors of depression in childhood. Children were recruited from third-grade classes in suburban elementary schools. At nine assessment points over the 5-year period, children and teachers completed self-report questionnaires. The authors found that in early childhood, negative life events were the best predictors of depression. They found that the presence of depression in early childhood led to a deterioration of explanatory style. Specifically, children who experienced depression at a young age developed an increased tendency to make internal, stable, global attributions for negative life events and to make external, unstable, and specific attributions for positive events. This pessimistic explanatory style was found to predict a recurrence of depression in later childhood, with negative life events predicting the time at which relapse occurred.

The results of this study suggest that adult models of depression (e.g., Abramson et al., 1978) may apply to older children. The data indicate that by early adolescence certain cognitive response styles develop. Maladaptive cognitive response styles (which may result from childhood depression) serve as a psychological vulnerability or diathesis. Thus, when faced with negative life events, adolescents with such cognitive styles seem to be at a greater risk of developing depression.

It has been argued that the effects of negative life events, uncontrollability, and attributional style account, in part, for the preponderance of women among those with depression or anxiety disorders (Barlow, 1991; Mineka, 1985; Nolen-Hoeksema, 1987; Nolen-Hoeksema & Girgus, 1994). The notion behind this argument is that, compared with boys, girls may be subjected to a larger number of negative life events during childhood and adolescence. In addition, girls may learn that their behaviors have less impact on their environment. Both of these factors are thought to contribute to a sense of uncontrollability in girls and foster the development of pessimistic attributional styles. Maladaptive cognitive response styles then place girls at higher risk for emotional disorders. In support of this argument, there are data suggesting that girls may be more likely to experience negative life events (e.g., victimization, childhood sexual abuse) that lead to a sense of helplessness (Cutler & Nolen-Hoeksema, 1991; Nolen-Hoeksema & Girgus, 1994). Furthermore, results from a number of studies suggest that both parents and teachers respond more to the actions (positive and negative) of boys than to those of girls (see Nolen-Hoeksema, 1987, for a review). As a result, females may be more likely than males to learn from interactions with others that their behavior does not have an impact on the environment (Barlow et al., 1996; Nolen-Hoeksema, 1987).

Advances in Modeling Causes of Anxiety and Depression

A number of researchers have promoted diathesis–stress models of anxiety and depression in adults (Chorpita & Barlow, in press). In such models, negative life events moderate or act on preexisting cognitive response styles, resulting in emotional disorders. The work of Nolen-Hoeksema et al. (1992) provides preliminary support for the notion that, while moderational models may apply to depression in adults and older children, they may not apply for younger children.

Cole and Turner (1993) used structural equation modeling to further test this hypothesis. Participants were fourth- ($n = 123$), sixth- ($n = 118$), and eighth-grade ($n = 115$) boys and girls from midwestern elementary and middle schools. Participants completed self-report instruments designed to measure depressive symptoms, cognitive errors, attributional style, the frequency and valence of positive and negative events, and peers' impressions of children's competency. With use of structural equation modeling, the data were applied to both mediational and moderational models of depression. The results indicated that negative peer competency evaluations were significantly related to attributional style and the tendency to make cognitive errors. In turn, attributional style was strongly related, whereas cognitive errors were moderately related to depressive symptoms. In addition, the data suggested that the relationship between life events and depressive symptoms was partially mediated by cognitive errors. These results provide support for a mediational model of depression in childhood. There was limited support for a model in which cognitive errors moderated the relationship between positive and negative life events and depressive symptoms. Aside from this relationship, no support for a moderational model of childhood depression emerged.

As the authors themselves admonish, the results of this study are correlational and must be interpreted with caution. Nevertheless, this study represents a significant advance in the theoretical understanding of childhood depression and possibly other emotional disorders. The results suggest that the moderational model often applied to adult depression may not accurately reflect the development of depression in children. It suggests, instead, the potential fit of a mediational model, in which the influence of life events and peer competency evaluations on depressive symptoms is mediated by attributional style and cognitive errors.

In a subsequent study, Turner and Cole (1994) administered self-report instruments to fourth- ($n = 149$), sixth- ($n = 131$), and eighth-grade ($n = 129$) children. The self-report instruments were designed to measure attributional style, cognitive errors, and depressive symptoms. A modified version of the Children's Activity Inventory (Shelton & Garber, 1987) was used to measure the occurrence of pleasant and unpleasant events in three domains: sports, academics, and social. In this study, the authors specifically tested for the effects of grade, the domain of events (sports, academic, social), and cognitions associated with each domain. The results of regression analyses indicated a significant interaction of grade, event, and cognitive style for academic and social domains but not sports. The authors suggest that such an interaction may be specific to areas in which children deem success more important. Furthermore, results indicated that the interaction between cognitive style and events was significant for eighth graders but not for fourth and sixth graders. The authors concluded that a diathesis–stress model of depression would apply to older but not younger children.

Neurobiological Contributions

The findings of Nolen-Hoeksema, Cole, Turner, and their colleagues represent pioneering steps in efforts to understand how and when cognitive factors interact with the environment to lead to pathological levels of negative affect. However, careful consideration of the development of anxiety disorders cannot focus on environmental and psychological factors alone. It is also necessary to examine the relation between a sense of control and biological processes. To address this issue, it is helpful to begin by looking, once again, to the findings of animal research.

A series of studies conducted by Sapolsky (1983; Sapolsky, 1990; Sapolsky & Ray, 1989) have provided important information on the physiological effects of uncontrollability. Sapolsky examined the effects of stress on male olive baboons living on a national reserve in Kenya. He identified this group of primates as an appropriate substitute for humans because most of the stressors they face are psychological. Male olive baboons form dominance hierarchies. Dominant baboons have more access to food, comfortable resting places, and mates. Subordinate males face more intense competition for necessary resources and may be subject to more violence from other males.

In one of his earliest studies, Sapolsky (1983) found that during periods of social stability (i.e., no significant changes in the dominance hierarchy), resting levels of cortisol were lower in dominant males than they were in subordinate males. In addition, during times of stress, dominant baboons evidenced larger and faster increases in cortisol levels.

Sapolsky (1990) noted that the purpose of cortisol is to energize the body and prepare it to cope with stress. However, chronically high levels of cortisol may prove detrimental, causing problems such as hypertension, muscle atrophy, suppression of the immunological system, and impaired fertility. He concluded that the chronically high levels of cortisol in subordinate baboons result from diminished sensitivity of the pituitary gland to corticotropin-releasing factor (CRF), hypersecretion of CRF by the brain, and a failure of the brain to accurately monitor the level of cortisol in the blood. Therefore, unusually high levels of cortisol in the blood are not restricted in subordinate males. Further research from Sapolsky (1990) suggests that these differences in physiological processes of dominant and subordinate males are a result, not a cause, of the baboons' position in the hierarchy.

Sapolsky (1983, 1990; Sapolsky & Ray, 1989) came to this conclusion after conducting research during periods of instability within the social hierarchy. At such times, the dominant baboons compete for the top of the hierarchy. They temporarily face the same stressors that are routinely endured by subordinate males. Sapolsky found that the resting cortisol levels of these dominant males were excessively high, and cortisol responses were suppressed during periods of stress. In other words, during periods of social instability, cortisol levels within the dominant males did not differ from those of the subordinate males. When the hierarchy was once again stable, the group differences between hormonal levels in dominant and subordinate baboons reemerged. At that time, Sapolsky closely examined individual differences among the dominant males. He found that only dominant males with certain personality characteristics evidenced the more adaptive hormonal profile. Specifically, healthier cortisol levels were found in baboons that were best able to discriminate between threatening and nonthreatening situations and to effectively use coping strategies. He concluded that the advantage found in dominant males was not a function of status, but was rather the result of being able to predict and control environmental events.

Recent studies with humans have also suggested the significance of neurobiological processes in the development of anxiety disorders. Through a series of studies (e.g., Kagan, 1994; Reznick et al., 1986), Kagan and colleagues have assessed for differences in the physiological processes of "inhibited" and "uninhibited" children. Inhibited children are described as extremely cautious and shy, whereas uninhibited children are described as fearless and outgoing. Kagan and colleagues hypothesized that inhibited children evidence lower thresholds of reactivity in the amygdala and the hypothalamus in response to unfamiliarity or challenging situations in which coping strategies are unavailable (Kagan, 1994; Kagan, Reznick, & Snidman, 1988). Activation of these brain structures influences the pituitary–adrenal axis, the reticular activating system, and the sympathetic nervous system, thus influencing the manifestation of physiological symptoms commonly associated with anxiety (e.g., increased heart rate, muscle tension, and heightened levels of cortisol; Kagan et al., 1988).

To test this hypothesis, Kagan et al. (1988) conducted a longitudinal study of inhibited and uninhibited children. Children were assessed at 21 months, 4 years, and 5½ years of age. At each assessment point, measures of inhibited behavior and a range of physiological responses were obtained. For data obtained at 5½ years, an aggregate score of eight physiological variables was calculated. The aggregate score included measures of cortisol levels, norepinephrine levels, heart rate, pupillary dilation, and variability in voice pitch. Kagan et al. suggested that the aggregate score provides the more robust test of the relationship between physiological responses and inhibited behavior because it gives less weight to the effects of any one physiological response. In addition, this score incorporates the range of physiological responses that may accompany various forms of anxiety (Kagan, 1994). Results indicated that the aggregate score at 5½ years was significantly correlated with inhibited behavior at 21 months ($r = .70$), 4 years ($r = .66$), and 5½ years ($r = .58$). The individual physiological variable that best discriminated between inhibited and uninhibited children was cortisol levels in the laboratory. Interestingly, cortisol levels obtained at home, presumably a less stressful environment, were also significantly higher in inhibited children.

Granger, Weisz, and Kauneckis (1994) specifically examined the effects of uncontrollability on cortisol levels in children. They assessed 102 clinic-referred children and adolescents ages 7–17. Patients presented with a variety of difficulties. The assessment involved engaging in parent–child conflict. The dependent variables were cortisol levels (based on salivary samples); overcontrolled, undercontrolled, and nonspecific behavioral problems; control-related beliefs; task affect and behavior. They found that children with higher levels of neuroendocrine reactivity were more socially withdrawn and socially anxious, had more social problems, and perceived themselves as having less personal control over the outcomes of their lives. They also tended to perceive social outcomes as being less contingent on their actions in general than did low reactors. Although the findings are correlational, they suggest that children with a lower sense of control may evidence exaggerated hypothalamic–pituitary–adrenocortical reactivity in the face of stressors.

CONCLUSIONS

The work of Sapolsky, Kagan, Granger, and colleagues suggests that there may be differences in the physiological processes of those with and those without anxiety disorders. Specifically, the hypothalamic-pituitary-adrenocortical axis may have a higher threshold of reactivity in people with anxiety disorders. Although such processes most certainly play a role in the development of anxiety disorders, they do not act alone. Indeed, in this decade of the brain, it is defensible to make the bold assertion that biological contributions are more latent, nonspecific, and relatively benign in the absence of crucial environmental and psychological events.

Animal researchers documented long ago the relationship between uncontrollability and the development of "neurotic" states. More recent studies with humans suggest that certain parenting styles may foster a sense of uncontrollability in children. In fact, data from several studies suggest that smothering, overly protective parenting styles are associated with higher rates of anxiety disorders in children. Along with particular parenting styles, the depression literature indicates that negative life events may lead to a sense of uncontrollability. Research suggests that uncontrollability results in the development of a pessimistic explanatory style (i.e., a tendency to make internal, global, stable attributions for negative events) some time during adolescence. This cognitive response style has been shown to predict future episodes of depression and may very well predict the development of anxiety disorders. Structural analysis of the relationship between environmental events, uncontrollability, cognitive response styles, and anxiety disorders in children and adolescents will be extremely valuable. Such research will help to advance our understanding of the etiology of anxiety disorders and may pave the way to more effective interventions and, ultimately, prevention.

REFERENCES

Abramson, L. Y., Metalsky, G. I., & Alloy, L. B. (1989). Hopelessness depression: A theory-based subtype of depression. *Psychological Review, 96,* 358–372.

Abramson, L. Y., Seligman, M. E. P., & Teasdale, J. D. (1978). Learned helplessness in humans: Critique and reformulation. *Journal of Abnormal Psychology, 87,* 49–74.

Alloy, L. B., Kelly, K. A., Mineka, S., & Clements, C. M. (1990). Comorbidity of anxiety and depressive disorders: A helplessness–hopelessness perspective. In J. D. Maser & C. R. Cloninger (Eds.), *Comorbidity of mood and anxiety disorders* (pp. 499–543). Washington, DC: American Psychiatric Press.

American Psychiatric Association. (1980). *Diagnostic and statistical manual of mental disorders* (3rd ed.). Washington, DC: Author.

American Psychiatric Association. (1987). *Diagnostic and statistical manual of mental disorders* (3rd ed., rev.). Washington, DC: Author.

American Psychiatric Association. (1994). *Diagnostic and statistical manual of mental disorders* (4th ed.). Washington, DC: Author.

Amies, P. L., Gelder, M. G., & Shaw, P. M. (1983). Social phobia: A comparative clinical study. *British Journal of Psychiatry, 142,* 174–179.

Barlow, D. H. (1988). *Anxiety and its disorders: The nature and treatment of anxiety and panic.* New York: Guilford Press.

Barlow, D. H. (1991). Disorders of emotion. *Psychological Inquiry, 2,* 58–71.

Barlow, D. H., Chorpita, B. F., & Turovsky, J. (1996). Fear, panic, anxiety and disorders of emotion. In D. A. Hope (Ed.), *43rd Annual Nebraska Symposium on Motivation: Perspectives on anxiety, panic, and fear* (pp. 251–328). Lincoln: University of Nebraska Press.

Barlow, D. H., & DiNardo, P. A. (1991). The diagnosis of generalized anxiety disorder: Development, current status, and future directions. In R. M. Rapee & D. H. Barlow (Eds.), *Chronic anxiety: Generalized anxiety disorder and mixed anxiety–depression* (pp. 95–118). New York: Guilford Press.

Barrett, J. E., Barrett, J. A., Oxman, T. E., & Gerber, P. D. (1988). The prevalence of psychiatric disorders in a primary care practice. *Archives of General Psychiatry, 45,* 1100–1106.

Borkovec, T. D., Abel, J. L., & Newman, H. (1995). Effects of psychotherapy on comorbid conditions in generalized anxiety disorder. *Journal of Consulting and Clinical Psychology, 63,* 479–483.

Borkovec, T. D., Lyonfields, J. D., Wiser, S. L., & Diehl, L. (1993). The role of worrisome thinking in the suppression of cardiovascular response to phobic imagery. *Behaviour Research and Therapy, 31,* 321–324.

Brown, T. A., Anson, A. M., & DiBartolo, P. M. (1996). *The distinctiveness of DSM–IV generalized anxiety disorder from major depression and dysthymia.* Manuscript in preparation.

Brown, T. A., Antony, M. M., & Barlow, D. H. (1995). Diagnostic comorbidity in panic disorder: Effect on treatment outcome and course of comorbid diagnoses following treatment. *Journal of Consulting and Clinical Psychology, 63,* 408–418.

Brown, T. A., Barlow, D. H., & Liebowitz, M. R. (1994). The empirical basis of generalized anxiety disorder. *American Journal of Psychiatry, 151,* 1272–1280.

Brown, T. A., Chorpita, B. F., & Barlow, D. H. (1998). Structural relationships among dimensions of the DSM–IV anxiety and mood disorders and dimensions of negative affect, positive affect, and autonomic arousal. *Journal of Abnormal Psychology, 107,* 179–192.

Brown, T. A., Marten, P. A., & Barlow, D. H. (1995). Discriminant validity of the systems constituting the DSM–III–R and DSM–IV associated symptom criterion of generalized anxiety disorder. *Journal of Anxiety Disorders, 9,* 317–328.

Brown, T. A., Moras, K., Zinbarg, R. E., & Barlow, D. H. (1993). Diagnostic and symptom distinguishability of generalized anxiety disorder and obsessive–compulsive disorder. *Behavior Therapy, 24,* 227–240.

Chorpita, B. F., & Barlow, D. H. (in press). The development of anxiety: The role of control in the early environment. *Psychological Bulletin.*

Clark, D. A., Steer, R. A., & Beck, A. T. (1994). Common and specific dimensions of self-reported anxiety and depression: Implications for cognitive and tripartite models. *Journal of Abnormal Psychology, 103*, 645–654.

Clark, L. A., & Watson, D. (1990). *Psychometric issues relevant to a potential DSM–IV category of mixed anxiety–depression*. Unpublished manuscript, DSM–IV Subgroup on Generalized Anxiety Disorder and Mixed Anxiety–Depression.

Clark, L. A., & Watson, D. (1991). Tripartite model of anxiety and depression: Psychometric evidence and taxonomic implications. *Journal of Abnormal Psychology, 100*, 316–336.

Clark, L. A., Watson, D., & Mineka, S. (1994). Temperament, personality, and the mood and anxiety disorders. *Journal of Abnormal Psychology, 103*, 103–116.

Cloninger, C. R. (1986). A unified biosocial theory of personality and its role in the development of anxiety states. *Psychiatric Development, 3*, 167–226.

Cole, D. A., & Turner, J. E. (1993). Models of cognitive mediation and moderation in child depression. *Journal of Abnormal Psychology, 102*, 271–281.

Cutler, S. E., & Nolen-Hoeksema, S. (1991). Accounting for sex differences in depression through female victimization: Childhood sexual abuse. *Sex Roles, 24*, 425–438.

Dumas, J. E., LaFreniere, P. J., & Serketich, W. J. (1995). "Balance of power": A transactional analysis of control in mother–child dyads involving socially competent, aggressive, and anxious children. *Journal of Abnormal Psychology, 104*, 104–113.

Eysenck, H. J. (1967). *Biological bases of personality*. Springfield, IL: Charles C Thomas.

Geer, J. H. (1965). The development of a scale to measure fear. *Behaviour Research and Therapy, 3*, 45–53.

Granger, D. A., Weisz, J. R., & Kauneckis, D. (1994). Neuroendocrine reactivity, internalizing behavior problems, and control-related cognitions in clinic-referred children and adolescents. *Journal of Abnormal Psychology, 103*, 267–276.

Gray, J. A. (1982). *The neuropsychology of anxiety: An enquiry into the functions of the septo-hippocampal system*. Oxford, England: Oxford University Press.

Hamilton, M. (1959). The assessment of anxiety states by rating. *British Journal of Medical Psychology, 32*, 50–55.

Hamilton, M. (1960). A rating scale for depression. *Journal of Neurology, Neurosurgery, and Psychiatry, 23*, 56–62.

Hodgson, R. J., & Rachman, S. (1977). Obsessive–compulsive complaints. *Behaviour Research and Therapy, 15*, 389–395.

Hoehn-Saric, R., McCleod, D. R., & Zimmerli, W. D. (1989). Somatic manifestations in women with generalized anxiety disorder: Psychophysiological responses to psychological stress. *Archives of General Psychiatry, 46*, 1113–1119.

Hudson, J. I., & Pope, H. G. (1990). Affective spectrum disorder: Does antidepressant response identify a family of disorders with a common pathophysiology? *American Journal of Psychiatry, 147,* 552–564.

Joiner, T. E., Catanzaro, S. J., & Laurent, J. (1996). Tripartite structure of positive and negative affect, depression, and anxiety in child and adolescent psychiatric inpatients. *Journal of Abnormal Psychology, 105,* 401–409.

Kagan, J. (1994). *Galen's prophecy.* New York: Basic Books.

Kagan, J., Reznick, J. S., & Snidman, N. (1988). The physiology and psychology of behavioral inhibition in children. In S. Chess, A. Thomas, and M. Hertzig (Eds.), *Annual Progress in Child Psychiatry and Child Development,* 102–127.

Katon, W., & Roy-Byrne, P. (1990). Mixed anxiety and depression. *Journal of Abnormal Psychology, 100,* 337–345.

Kendall, P. C., & Watson, D. (1989). *Anxiety and depression: Distinctive and overlapping features.* San Diego, CA: Academic Press.

Lovibond, S. H., & Lovibond, P. F. (1991). *Self-report scales for the differentiation and measurement of depression, anxiety, and stress.* Unpublished manuscript.

Mattick, R. P., & Clarke, L. (1988). *Development and validation of measures of social phobia, scrutiny, fear, and social interaction anxiety.* Unpublished manuscript, University of New South Wales, Kensington, Australia.

Mattick, R. P., & Peters, L. (1988). Treatment of severe social phobia: Effects of guided exposure with and without restructuring. *Journal of Consulting and Clinical Psychology, 56,* 251–260.

McCauley, E., Mitchell, J. R., Burke, P. M., & Moss, S. J. (1988). Cognitive attributes of depression in children and adolescents. *Journal of Consulting and Clinical Psychology, 56,* 903–908.

Meyer, T. J., Miller, M. L., Metzger, R. L., & Borkovec, T. D. (1990). Development and validation of the Penn State Worry Questionnaire. *Behaviour Research and Therapy, 28,* 487–495.

Mineka, S. (1985). Animal models of anxiety-based disorders: Their usefulness and limitations. In A. H. Tuma & J. D. Maser (Eds.), *Anxiety and the anxiety disorders* (pp. 119–244). Hillsdale, NJ: Erlbaum.

Mineka, S., Gunnar, M., & Champoux, M. (1986). Control and early socioemotional development: Infant rhesus monkeys reared in controllable versus uncontrollable environments. *Child Development, 57,* 1241–1246.

Mineka, S., & Kihlstrom, J. F. (1978). Unpredictable and uncontrollable events: A new perspective on experimental neurosis. *Journal of Abnormal Psychology, 87,* 256–271.

Nolen-Hoeksema, S. (1987). Sex differences in unipolar depression: Evidence and theory. *Psychological Bulletin, 101,* 259–282.

Nolen-Hoeksema, S., & Girgus, J. S. (1994). The emergence of gender differences in depression during adolescence. *Psychological Bulletin, 115,* 424–443.

Nolen-Hoeksema, S., Girgus, J. S., & Seligman, M. E. P. (1992). Predictors and consequences of childhood depressive symptoms: A 5-year longitudinal study. *Journal of Abnormal Psychology, 101,* 405–422.

Nowicki, S., & Strickland, B. R. (1973). A Locus of Control Scale for children. *Journal of Consulting and Clinical Psychology, 40,* 148–154.

Nunn, G. D. (1988). Concurrent validity between the Nowicki–Strickland Locus of Control Scale and the State–Trait Anxiety Inventory for Children. *Educational and Psychological Measurement, 48,* 435–438.

Overmier, J. B., & Seligman, M. E. P. (1967). Effects of inescapable shock on subsequent escape and avoidance learning. *Journal of Comparative and Physiological Psychology, 63,* 28–33.

Parker, G. (1983). *Parental overprotection: A risk factor in psychosocial development.* New York: Grune & Stratton.

Parker, G., Tupling, H., & Brown, L. B. (1979). A Parental Bonding Instrument. *British Journal of Medical Psychology, 52,* 1–10.

Pavlov, I. P. (1927). *Conditioned reflexes: An investigation of the physiological activity of the cerebral cortex.* London: Oxford University Press.

Rapee, R., Craske, M., & Barlow, D. H. (1995). An assessment instrument for panic disorder that includes fear of sensation producing activities: The Albany Panic and Phobia Questionnaire. *Anxiety, 1,* 114–122.

Reiss, S., Peterson, R. A., Gursky, D. M., & McNally, R. J. (1986). Anxiety sensitivity, anxiety frequency, and the prediction of fearfulness. *Behaviour Research and Therapy, 24,* 1–8.

Reznick, J. S., Kagan, J., Snidman, N., Gersten, M., Baak, K., & Rosenberg, A. (1986). Inhibited and uninhibited behavior: A follow-up study. *Child Development, 57,* 660–680.

Riskind, J. H., Beck, A. T., Brown, G., & Steer, R. A. (1987). Taking the measure of anxiety and depression: Validity of the reconstructed Hamilton rating scales. *Journal of Nervous and Mental Disease, 175,* 474–479.

Rotter, J. (1954). *Social learning and clinical psychology.* Englewood Cliffs, NJ: Prentice Hall.

Sapolsky, R. M. (1983). Endocrine and behavioral correlates of drought in wild olive baboons. *American Journal of Primatology, 11,* 217–227.

Sapolsky, R. M. (1990). Stress in the wild. *Scientific American,* 116–123.

Sapolsky, R. M., & Ray, J. C. (1989). Styles of dominance and their endocrine correlates among wild olive baboons. *American Journal of Primatology, 18,* 1–13.

Seligman, M. E. P. (1975). *Helplessness: On depression, development, and death.* San Francisco: Freeman.

Seligman, M. E. P., & Maier, S. F. (1967). Failure to escape traumatic shock. *Journal of Experimental Psychology, 74,* 1–9.

Shelton, M. R., & Garber, J. (1987). *The Children's Activity Inventory.* Unpublished manuscript, Vanderbilt University.

Siegel, L. J., & Griffin, N. J. (1984). Correlates of depressive symptoms in adolescents. *Journal of Youth and Adolescence, 13,* 475–487.

Silove, D., Parker, G., Hadzi-Pavlovic, D., Manicavasagar, V., & Blaszczynski, A. (1991). *British Journal of Psychiatry, 159,* 835–841.

Silverman, W., & Nelles, W. B. (1988). Anxiety Disorders Interview Schedule for Children. *Journal of the American Academy of Child and Adolescent Psychiatry, 27,* 772–778.

Siqueland, L., Kendall, P. C., & Steinberg, L. (1996). Anxiety in children: Perceived family environments and observed family interaction. *Journal of Clinical Child Psychology, 25,* 225–237.

Stark, K. D., Humphrey, L. L., Crook, K., & Lewis, K. (1990). Perceived family environments of depressed and anxious children: Child's and maternal figure's perspectives. *Journal of Abnormal Child Psychology, 18,* 527–547.

Tellegen, A. (1985). Structures of mood and personality and their relevance to assessing anxiety, with an emphasis on self-report. In A. H. Tuma & J. D. Maser (Eds.), *Anxiety and the anxiety disorders* (pp. 681–706). Hillsdale, NJ: Erlbaum.

Turner, J. E., & Cole, D. A. (1994). Developmental differences in cognitive diatheses for child depression. *Journal of Abnormal Child Psychology, 22,* 15–32.

Tyrer, P., Seivewright, N., Murphy, S., Ferguson, B., Kingdon, D., Barczak, B., Brothwell, J., Darling, C., Gregory, S., & Johnson, A. L. (1988). The Nottingham study of neurotic disorder: Comparison of drug and psychological treatments. *Lancet, 2,* 235–240.

Watson, D., & Clark, L. A. (1984). Negative affectivity: The disposition to experience aversive emotional states. *Psychological Bulletin, 96,* 465–490.

Watson, D., Clark, L. A., & Carey, G. (1988). Positive and negative affectivity and their relation to the anxiety and depressive disorders. *Journal of Abnormal Psychology, 97,* 346–353.

Watson, D., Clark, L. A., & Harkness, A. R. (1994). Structures of personality and their relevance to psychopathology. *Journal of Abnormal Psychology, 103,* 18–31.

Watson, D., Clark, L. A., Weber, K., Assenheimer, J. S., Strauss, M. E., & McCormick, R. A. (1995). Testing a tripartite model: II. Exploring the symptom structure of anxiety and depression in student, adult, and patient samples. *Journal of Abnormal Psychology, 104,* 15–25.

Zinbarg, R. E., & Barlow, D. H. (1996). Structure of anxiety and anxiety disorders: A hierarchical model. *Journal of Abnormal Psychology, 105,* 181–193.

Zinbarg, R. E., Barlow, D. H., Liebowitz, M., Street, L., Broadhead, E., Katon, W., Roy-Byrne, P., Lepine, J., Teherani, M., Richards, J., Brantley, P. J., & Kraemer, H. (1994). The DSM–IV field trial for mixed anxiety–depression. *American Journal of Psychiatry, 151,* 1153–1162.

5

FAMILY LOVE AND LIFELONG HEALTH? A CHALLENGE FOR CLINICAL PSYCHOLOGY

GARY E. SCHWARTZ AND LINDA G. RUSSEK

Does love really matter? Do people's perceptions of love and caring, especially from their parents—typically the most meaningful providers of affection and support—play a role in long-term health? As Kaplan (1997, p. 150) recently phrased it, does family love provide "the ties that bind for a lifetime of health"? Or, as Dossey (1996) recently phrased the question about the relationship between social support and health, "What's love got to do with it?"

The nuclear family structure of generations past has changed dramatically as creative blends of biological, step-, and chosen members weave

This chapter is dedicated to the late Henry I. Russek, MD, who collaborated on the 35-year follow-up of the Harvard Mastery of Stress study, and to the late Stanley H. King, PhD, who conducted the original investigation. We thank Elayne Russek, who greatly facilitated this research; the Harvard men, who actively participated in the Harvard Mastery of Stress research for more than 40 years; and our students at the University of Arizona, who warmly encouraged us to address the challenge of family love and long-term health. We also thank Donald K. Routh and Robert J. DeRubeis, the editors of this volume, for their openness to include a brief introduction to dynamical energy systems theory and the systemic love hypothesis as an Appendix to this chapter.

new family configurations. The sense of safety and security that once was a hallmark of family life has been threatened as economics and changing social values reduce the quality and quantity of time that families spend together. At the same time that the safety and security of the nuclear family have been challenged in modern society, the effects of stress on long-term health and illness have been convincingly documented in the research literature.

Is there a connection between these modern challenges to family love, increased psychosocial stress, and disease? If it were found that the perceptions of family love and caring played an important role in long-term health, the social and economic implications would be substantial.

This chapter summarizes the results of a unique, prospective study of Harvard University undergraduates that uncovered a strong association between the perception of parental love and caring, measured in college in the early 1950s, and physical and psychological diseases documented 35 and 42 years later in mid-life (Russek & Schwartz, 1994, 1996b, 1997a, 1997c). The new findings from the Harvard Mastery of Stress (Funkenstein, King, & Drolette, 1957) follow-up study (Russek, King, Russek, & Russek, 1990) provide compelling confirmation for the social support literature documenting that the nature and quality of social support from various sources have a significant impact on current and future health.

The purpose of the present chapter is not to review the social support and health literature (see Berkman, 1995; Shumaker & Czajkowski, 1994; Uchino, Cacioppo, & Kiecolt-Glaser, 1996, for excellent reviews of this research) but to focus primarily on the *experience* (perception) of love and caring and the complex role that it plays in health and well-being. We use the term *caring*, in addition to the word *love*, because caring includes positive perceptions of love, understanding, empathy, and justice, as well as other positive and responsible parental role characteristics (Russek & Schwartz, 1996b).

MEASURING THE PERCEPTION OF LOVE AND CARING

Is it possible that relatively simple self-report measures of family love and caring can serve as important predictors of long-term health over 35 years or more? The concept of social support reflects loving and caring relationships in people's lives (Sarason & Sarason, 1985), and it is possible that the perception of love and caring can be assessed directly. The results of two major studies suggest that simple ratings of "feeling loved" may be as effective, if not more effective, in assessing social support than more comprehensive instruments that quantify network size, structure, and function.

In a 5-year prospective study of 10,000 Israeli men, Medalie and Goldbourt (1976) found that the question "Does your wife show you her love?" was the best predictor of the outcome measure of angina pectoris. Correspondingly, Seeman and Syme (1987) reported, in a sample of 119 men and 40 women undergoing coronary angiography, that simple ratings of "feeling loved" exerted an independent and direct effect on coronary atherosclerosis that was not confounded or mediated by any of the standard risk factors.

In the Harvard Mastery of Stress study (Funkenstein et al., 1957), 126 male subjects filled out a large battery of paper-and-pencil tests. We discovered that embedded within this large battery of instruments in different places were three different kinds of measures—numeric ratings, narrative descriptions, and multiple-choice items—that could be construed to tap perceptions of parental love and caring.

The first measure, numeric ratings, consisted of 14 pairs of terms, in which each pair was anchored with a term on the left (e.g., *loving*) and a term on the right (*rejecting*). Subjects were asked to rate their mothers and fathers separately on each of the 14 pairs of terms using the numbers 1 to 9. The 14-item scale is shown in Exhibit 1 (Russek & Schwartz, 1997c).

The second measure involved narrative descriptions. Subjects were simply asked to describe, in their own words, "What kind of person was your mother?" and "What kind of person was your father?" Many of the words they spontaneously reported could be scored as positive perceptions (such as *loving* or *warm*) or negative perceptions (such as *cold* or *intolerant*) of their parents (Russek & Schwartz, 1996b).

The third measure involved a multiple-choice question. Subjects were simply asked to select which of four answers best described their relationship with their mothers and fathers (*very close, warm and friendly, tolerant,* or *strained and cold*; Russek & Schwartz, 1997a).

In theory, each of these measures (numeric ratings, narrative descriptions, and multiple choices) address aspects of the experience of love and caring to various degrees. The question was, Could these simple measures predict health and illness 35 years later? The data were analyzed as they were discovered in the data set. The ratings data were discovered and analyzed first, the narrative descriptions were discovered after the article on ratings was written (Russek & Schwartz, 1997c) and were analyzed second, and the multiple-choice questions were discovered after the narrative descriptions article was written (Russek & Schwartz, 1996b) and were analyzed third. The publication dates reflect the different publication lags of the journals.

EXHIBIT 1
Harvard Parental Caring Scale

Ratings of Mothers

Below are a number of *descriptive terms* on which people may be judged. You are requested to *rate* your *mother* on each of these. Each term is presented in terms of two extremes, e.g., just–unjust. Use a scale of 1 to 9 to express your ratings (5 means about average). Give one rating for each term. Circle the number which expresses your rating.

Just	1	2	3	4	5	6	7	8	9	Unjust
Fair	1	2	3	4	5	6	7	8	9	Unfair
Severe	1	2	3	4	5	6	7	8	9	Mild
Stingy	1	2	3	4	5	6	7	8	9	Generous
Brutal	1	2	3	4	5	6	7	8	9	Kind
Loving	1	2	3	4	5	6	7	8	9	Rejecting
Strong	1	2	3	4	5	6	7	8	9	Weak
Clever	1	2	3	4	5	6	7	8	9	Dull
Mean to father	1	2	3	4	5	6	7	8	9	Kind to father
Nervous	1	2	3	4	5	6	7	8	9	Controlled
Hardworking	1	2	3	4	5	6	7	8	9	Lazy
Drunk	1	2	3	4	5	6	7	8	9	Sober
Poor	1	2	3	4	5	6	7	8	9	Wealthy
Punished often	1	2	3	4	5	6	7	8	9	Never punished

Ratings of Fathers

Below are a number of *descriptive terms* on which people may be judged. You are requested to *rate* your *father* on each of these. Each term is presented in terms of two extremes, e.g., just–unjust. Use a scale of 1 to 9 to express your ratings (5 means about average). Give one rating for each term. Circle the number which expresses your rating.

Just	1	2	3	4	5	6	7	8	9	Unjust
Fair	1	2	3	4	5	6	7	8	9	Unfair
Severe	1	2	3	4	5	6	7	8	9	Mild
Stingy	1	2	3	4	5	6	7	8	9	Generous
Brutal	1	2	3	4	5	6	7	8	9	Kind
Loving	1	2	3	4	5	6	7	8	9	Rejecting
Strong	1	2	3	4	5	6	7	8	9	Weak
Clever	1	2	3	4	5	6	7	8	9	Dull
Mean to mother	1	2	3	4	5	6	7	8	9	Kind to mother
Nervous	1	2	3	4	5	6	7	8	9	Controlled
Hardworking	1	2	3	4	5	6	7	8	9	Lazy
Drunk	1	2	3	4	5	6	7	8	9	Sober
Poor	1	2	3	4	5	6	7	8	9	Wealthy
Punished often	1	2	3	4	5	6	7	8	9	Never punished

THE HARVARD MASTERY OF STRESS STUDY

The Harvard Mastery of Stress study was originally designed to examine personality and family history predictors of coping with repetitive stressors in the laboratory (Funkenstein et al., 1957). The sample originally consisted of 126 randomly selected healthy male undergraduates who received physical exams and psychiatric interviews in order to be admitted into the study. The great majority were enthusiastic about the study, and much effort was spent in building a good relationship with the men. Their initial positive experience with the study helped make it possible to recruit most of the men for the follow-up study 35 years later.

The experiment included two laboratory stressors administered three times over 3 weeks: (a) tests in mental arithmetic, seemingly easy to solve but difficult when subjects are hurried and harassed by the experimenter; and (b) the use of sonic confusions produced by an instrument that delayed by 0.2 seconds the subject's hearing of his own voice as he retold a story from memory as accurately and rapidly as possible under threat of electric shock. Physiological measures were taken, including systolic and diastolic pressure, and heart rate.

Subjects were given a detailed interview after each stress test, and the subjects' style of coping with stress (severe anxiety vs. anger in/anger out) was determined (described in detail in Funkenstein et al., 1957). The subjects were encouraged to express their feelings and emotions about their experience during a session of 20 to 30 minutes carried out in as nondirective a manner as possible. Behavioral styles were noted and clinical impressions recorded, and scores were made independently by two judges. All cases in which the major emotion reported was severe anxiety regardless of any other minor emotional component constituted the severe anxiety group. Cases in which the primary emotion was anger directed at the experimenter or situation (anger out) or at himself (anger in) constituted the anger in/anger out group.

THE 35-YEAR FOLLOW-UP STUDY

In the 35-year follow-up study (Russek et al., 1990), a detailed personal and family health history was obtained in each case. All interviews were tape-recorded and subsequently evaluated by two qualified associates who had no knowledge of the identity or prior test results of any subject. Without exception, reports of all physical examinations and laboratory tests, including blood chemistry, electrocardiographic (ECG) records, chest films, and other evaluations, when available, were obtained directly from each subject's physician as yearly checkups. Diagnoses of disease were made exclusively on the basis of determinations by attending physicians and confirmed by Henry I. Russek, MD (Russek et al., 1990). Subjects were subgrouped into cardiovascular disease (coronary heart disease and/or hypertension), duodenal ulcer, alcoholism, and miscellaneous.

A diagnosis of coronary heart disease was considered established in the presence of classical symptoms, positive resting or stress-induced ECG patterns of ischemia, or history of prior confirmed myocardial infarction. Hypertension was defined as a blood pressure at or above the levels of 160 mm systolic and/or 90 mm diastolic upon repeated measurement at rest. Cardiac hypertrophy and ECG findings of left ventricular preponderance or strain served as confirmatory signs. A diagnosis of duodenal ulcer was made from the characteristic symptomatology and corroborative radiographic evidence. Chronic alcoholism was considered to be present when there was uncontrolled, habitual, and excessive use of the substance in the judgment of the physician, investigator, family, or subject himself. History of contacts with Alcoholics Anonymous, psychiatric assistance for this problem, and the need for admission to a detoxification center were noted. The diagnosis of asthma, migraine, and other illness was based on physician recognition of typical signs and symptoms of these disorders critically evaluated and treated by contemporary management. In several participants, more than one disease was found to be present, but classification was made in these cases only under the heading of the major or more serious illness.

Of the 126 male subjects in the original population (Funkenstein et al., 1957), 6 were lost to study and 4 refused participation because of the recollection of unpleasant experiences during the laboratory stress experiments. The final sample of 116 subjects (Russek et al., 1990) composed 92% of the eligible participants. Causes of death, of which there was a total of 6 in the entire sample, were determined from death certificates, alumni records, and correspondence with family and associates of the deceased.

Of the 116 subjects tested in the follow-up investigation (Russek et al., 1990), the original scoring sheets containing the three measures of perceptions of parental love and caring were available on a random sample of 77% (89) of the subjects. The mean age was 55 years (SD = 1.3).

The data were first analyzed retrospectively. Subjects were split into sick versus well subgroups (as determined by the subjects' physicians and confirmed by Henry I. Russek, MD), and differences in the three measures of perceptions of parental love and caring were examined in relation to various risk factors such as family history for disease, smoking history, and marital and divorce history of the parents and the subjects. Then, the data were analyzed prospectively to determine if perceptions of parental love and caring obtained in college could predict health in mid-life.

NUMERIC RATINGS OF PARENTAL LOVE AND CARING

Figure 1 displays the reverse-coded numeric ratings (1–9) for the 14 items, averaged across mothers and fathers, using the left-side terms to label

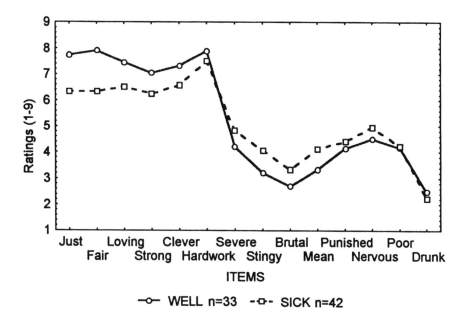

Figure 1. Ratings of parental caring by well and sick groups by item interaction, $F(13, 949) = 4.86$, $p < .000001$. From "Perceptions of Parental Caring Predict Health Status in Midlife: A 35 Year Follow-Up of the Harvard Mastery of Stress Study," by L. G. Russek and G. E. Schwartz, 1997, *Psychosomatic Medicine, 59*(2), p. 146. Copyright 1997 by Lippincott/Williams & Wilkins. Reprinted with permission.

the figure (since English is read from left to right, a subject's tendency is to read the left word first—such as *just*—and then read the right word—such as *unjust*). It can be seen that the interaction of group (sick vs. well) and item was highly significant. Words such as *just, fair,* and *loving* were rated more highly by the well subjects than by the sick subjects, and the reverse was found for words such as *severe, stingy,* and *brutal.* Because the "positive" words by themselves were highly statistically significant (*just, fair, loving, clever, hardworking,* and *strong*), whereas the "negative" words were only marginally significant, the subsequent analyses focused on the positive terms. Curves depicting the ratings of the positive words for mothers and fathers comparing the sick versus well groups are shown in Figure 2.

The results for the positive ratings were replicated across four categories of diseases (cardiovascular, ulcer, alcoholism, and mixed, see Figure 3). The results were found to hold independent of family history of disease, death and/or divorce of parents, smoking history of the subjects, and marital history of the subjects.

On the basis of these findings, subjects were split into high and low ratings scores for mothers and fathers, and the four combinations of mother and father ratings were examined as prospective predictors of long-term illness (see Figure 4). Amazingly, whereas only 25% of subjects who rated

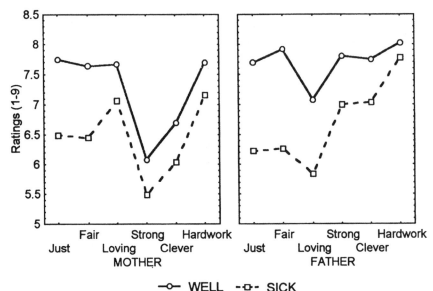

Figure 2. Positive ratings of parental caring by well and sick groups for mother and father. Main effect of well and sick groups: $F(1, 79) = 19.44$, $p < .00003$. From "Perceptions of Parental Caring Predict Health Status in Midlife: A 35 Year Follow-Up of the Harvard Mastery of Stress Study," by L. G. Russek and G. E. Schwartz, 1997, *Psychosomatic Medicine, 59*(2), p. 146. Copyright 1997 by Lippincott/Williams & Wilkins. Reprinted with permission.

both their mothers and fathers high in love and caring had diagnosed diseases in mid-life, 87% of subjects who rated both their mothers and fathers low in love and caring had diagnosed diseases in mid-life. The other two groups had moderate levels of illness in mid-life.

Ratings of parental love and caring were also independent and additive with the coping with laboratory stress measure reported in Russek et al. (1990). The association between perceptions of parental love and caring was replicated in a subset of subjects available for testing in a 42-year follow-up (Russek & Schwartz, 1994). Altogether, the ratings data strongly suggested that perceptions of parental love and caring were a powerful predictor of long-term health.

NARRATIVE DESCRIPTIONS OF PARENTAL LOVE AND CARING

Theoretically, if the selected ratings were measuring positive perceptions of parental love and caring, then the ratings should correlate with subjects' narrative descriptions of their parents. Subjects listed as few as one descriptor per parent and as many as 8 descriptors for fathers and 10 descriptors for mothers.

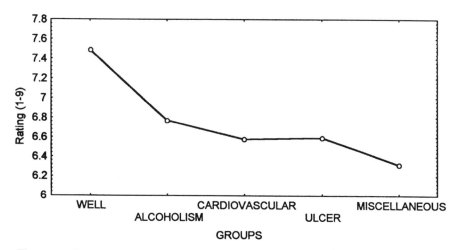

Figure 3. Positive ratings of parental caring by well and sick groups. Main effect for well and sick groups: $F(4, 76) = 4.71$, $p < .0019$. From "Perceptions of Parental Caring Predict Health Status in Midlife: A 35 Year Follow-Up of the Harvard Mastery of Stress Study," by L. G. Russek and G. E. Schwartz, 1997, *Psychosomatic Medicine, 59*(2), p. 147. Copyright 1997 by Lippincott/Williams & Wilkins. Reprinted with permission.

Subjects gave 110 different descriptors for mothers and 142 different descriptors for fathers. Each descriptor was independently evaluated by two judges as being positive, neutral, negative, or questionable. Descriptors that were evaluated by both judges as positive were termed positive. Descriptors that were evaluated by both judges as negative were termed negative. All other combinations of descriptor evaluations were simply termed other. Examples of positive descriptors generated by subjects were *loving, lovable, friendly, warm, open, understanding, kind, sympathetic, sensitive, sincere, just, fair, considerate, patient, hardworking, intelligent, discerning, respected, strong, sense of humor, cheerful,* and *secure.* Examples of negative descriptors generated by subjects were *quick-tempered, not affectionate, cold, intolerant, no self-discipline, inflexible, not overly family centered, impatient, egotistical, authoritarian,* and *opinionated.* Scores reflecting the number of positive descriptors and the number of negative descriptors per parent per subject were analyzed statistically.

The number of positive descriptors of parental love and caring for mothers was significantly correlated with the number of positive descriptors of parental love and caring for fathers ($r = .46$, $p < .0001$). In addition, higher numbers of positive descriptors in well versus sick subjects were found for both mothers and fathers. Therefore, in subsequent analyses, the number of positive descriptors for mothers and fathers were summed, creating a total positive parental descriptor score.

Positive parental descriptor scores were significantly correlated with

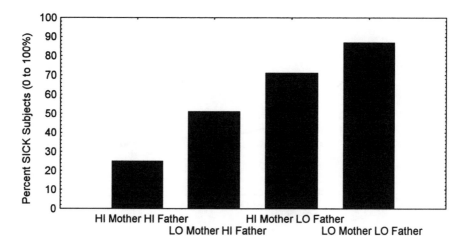

Figure 4. Percentage of sick subjects in high (HI) versus low (LO) mother ratings by high versus low father ratings subgroups. Main effect for mother, *p* < .005, and for father, *p* <. 00001. From "Perceptions of Parental Caring Predict Health Status in Midlife: A 35 Year Follow-Up of the Harvard Mastery of Stress Study," by L. G. Russek and G. E. Schwartz, 1997, *Psychosomatic Medicine, 59*(2), p. 148. Copyright 1997 by Lippincott/Williams & Wilkins. Reprinted with permission.

the ratings of individual items that were most reflective of positive parental love and caring: *loving,* $r = .29$, $p < .01$; *just,* $r = .33$, $p < .002$; *fair,* $r = .28$, $p < .01$; and *hardworking,* $r = .26$, $p < .01$. Positive parental descriptor scores were not significantly correlated with items that were less reflective of positive parental love and caring (*clever,* $r = .15$, $p < .16$; and *strong,* $r = .13$, $p < .25$). These correlations suggest that the number of positive parental descriptors may serve as a measure of the subjects' perception of positive parental love and caring.

The retrospective analyses performed on the ratings were repeated for the positive descriptors, and the findings were virtually identical. In the prospective analyses, because ratings and descriptors were only moderately positively correlated, it was possible to split subjects in four subgroups defined by high and low ratings of love and caring and high and low narrative descriptors of love and caring (see Figure 5). Whereas only 29% of subjects who gave their parents high ratings and a high number of positive descriptors had diagnosed diseases in mid-life, 95% of subjects who gave their parents low ratings and a low number of positive descriptors had diagnosed diseases in mid-life. Ratings and descriptors, combined, were more predictive than either alone.

Like the negative ratings data, the negative narrative descriptors were only marginally significant. Not surprisingly, the ratio of positive to negative descriptors, like the ratio of positive to negative ratings, was highly predictive of long-term health.

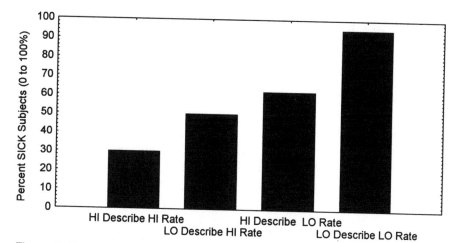

Figure 5. Percentage of sick subjects in high (HI) versus low (LO) number of positive descriptors and high versus low positive ratings subgroups. Chi-square descriptors, $p < .002$; chi-square ratings, $p < .0001$. From "Narrative Descriptions of Parental Love and Caring Predict Health Status in Midlife: A 35 Year Follow-Up of the Harvard Mastery of Stress Study," by L. G. Russek and G. E. Schwartz, 1996, *Alternative Therapies in Health and Medicine, 2*(6), p. 60. Copyright 1996 by InnoVision Communications. Reprinted with permission.

MULTIPLE-CHOICE QUESTIONS OF FEELINGS OF PARENTAL LOVE AND CARING

To further check whether the findings reflected perceptions of parental love and caring, we examined the data from multiple-choice questions. The questions simply asked, "Would you describe your relationship with your mother as: A. very close, B. warm and friendly, C. tolerant, or D. strained and cold?" (The question was repeated for fathers.)

It turned out that feelings of warmth and closeness with mothers correlated significantly with positive ratings of perceived caring from mothers ($r = .43$, $p < .001$) and number of positive descriptors of caring attributed to mothers ($r = .34$, $p < .001$). Similarly, feelings of warmth and closeness with fathers correlated significantly with positive ratings of perceived caring from fathers ($r = .25$, $p < .03$) and number of positive descriptors of caring attributed to fathers ($r = .26$, $p < .02$). It appears that feelings of warmth and closeness with parents are consistently positively associated with positive perceptions of parental caring (positive ratings and positive descriptors).

These prospective analyses generally paralleled the ratings and narrative descriptor findings. For example, the effects of feelings of warmth and closeness with mothers and fathers appeared to be additive. Whereas 47% of subjects in college who had selected feelings of warmth and closeness for mothers and fathers had diagnosed diseases in mid-life, 100% of subjects who selected feelings of tolerant and cold for mothers and fathers had diagnosed diseases in mid-life. The other two groups fell roughly in between the two extreme groups.

WHAT DO THESE FINDINGS MEAN?

Numeric ratings, narrative descriptions, and multiple-choice questions relating to perceptions of parental love and caring, obtained in college, independently predicted future health and illness 35 years later. How can such findings be explained?

There are many possible mechanisms that could contribute to the scope of the findings obtained in this sample of subjects. Possible sets of factors potentially influenced by parental love and caring include the following:

1. Nutrition, stress, and loving energy before and after birth;
2. Healthy and unhealthy behaviors developed during childhood (e.g., sleep, exercise, use of vitamins and drugs);
3. Coping styles such as anxiety, anger, hostility, depression, negative affectivity, optimism, and self-esteem;
4. Choice and stability of work, marriage, family relationships, and friendships;
5. The presence and social support of parents in one's adult life; and
6. Spiritual values and practices.

The perception of parental love and caring may be a powerful predictor of future health because parental love and caring involves and integrates so many potential mechanisms. It is possible that the relationship between the perception of parental love and caring and future health is an association rather than a reflection of a causative relationship between actual parental behavior and later outcome. This is a question for future research.

At first glance, it may seem somewhat surprising that individual differences in the perception of parental love and caring, in this particular sample, proved to be such a powerful predictor of future health and illness. Despite the fact that this unique longitudinal sample consisted of Harvard men who were, relatively speaking, economically and intellectually privileged, they were not necessarily emotionally or spiritually privileged. It is conceivable that the association between parental love and caring and health status will be even greater in samples suffering from more extreme forms of family pathology or family differences.

Because it is difficult and costly to conduct longitudinal research, especially over an extended period of time (35 and 42 years in the present study), unless existing longitudinal data sets happen to include information on love and caring (as happened to be the case in the present sample), it will be a long time before findings from new prospective studies will become available. For this reason, it makes good sense to look at these data more closely and to see whether the findings can be viewed within a larger context.

LEVELS OF LOVE AND CARING: A SYSTEMS APPROACH

The range of possible psychological processes included in the perception of love and caring is quite extensive. Using a systems approach (Schwartz, 1984, 1987), one can specify 13 categories of love and caring that directly or indirectly reflect the items originally selected by the experimenters and the descriptors spontaneously generated by the subjects, and arrange them hierarchically as levels. Table 1 lists the 13 levels.

The hypothesized *levels of love and caring* (LLC) model presumes that givers of care (be they family, friends, heath care providers, etc.) may provide different degrees of love and caring at each level, and that receivers of care will perceive different degrees of love and caring at each level. Although each level can be further divided into sublevels, this degree of detail is not essential for the present discussion. The LLC model was derived from various sources: (a) the literature on attachment (Bowlby, 1969; Parkes, Stevenson-Hinde, & Marris, 1991), love and empathy (reviewed in Hatfield & Rapson, 1993), and social support (Sarason & Sarason, 1985); (b) the spontaneous descriptors of the Harvard sample; and (c) our

TABLE 1
Thirteen Levels of Love and Caring Organized Hierarchically

Level	Category
13	Reverence and peace
12	Gratitude and forgiveness
11	Meaning and purpose
10	Inspiration and empowerment
9	Compassion and nurturance
8	Empathy and sympathy
7	Understanding and justice
6	Openness and acceptance
5	Interest and encouragement
4	Attention and awareness
3	Time and availability
2	Choice and commitment
1	Intention and energy

Note. Each higher level includes the lower levels below it. Though the precise organization can be questioned (e.g., which is "higher," understanding and justice or empathy and appreciation?), the general framework illustrates the complexity of love and caring that can be addressed in future research.

clinical and teaching experience (including an undergraduate course on the psychology of love and compassion at the University of Arizona).

The LLC model posits that the higher levels involve (encompass) the lower levels to various degrees. For example, the first level reflects the intention and energy to care, and the second level involves the choice and commitment to care. A person may have the intention and energy to care (Level 1) but not necessarily make the choice and commitment to care (Level 2). However, if a person makes the choice and commitment to care (Level 2), this person will typically have some degree of the intention and energy to care (Level 1).

As a related example, consider the third level, time and availability. A person may have the intention and energy to care (Level 1) and make a choice and commitment to care (Level 2), but not necessarily make much time to be available to provide care (Level 3). However, if a person gives significant time and is available for caring (Level 3), this person will typically have some degree of the intention and energy to care (Level 1) and will have made some choice and commitment to care (Level 2).

Levels 4, 5, and 6 reflect the shift from simple attention and awareness (Level 4), to openness and acceptance (Level 5), to genuine interest and encouragement to express one's needs, feelings, and thoughts (Level 6). Attentive people (Level 4) are not necessarily open-minded and accepting (Level 5); open-minded and accepting people (Level 5) are not necessarily encouraging (Level 6). However, people who show genuine interest and encouragement (Level 6) are often attentive (Level 4) and are open-minded and accepting (Level 5).

Levels 7, 8, and 9 reflect higher levels of complexity of caring, from understanding and justice (Level 7), to empathy and sympathy (Level 8), to compassion and kindness (Level 9). The relationship between understanding and empathy is somewhat controversial. Presumably, increased understanding improves one's ability to empathize: The greater one's ability to understand, the greater is one's ability to empathize and feel for others. Also, it is reasonable to hypothesize that a person's capacity to provide nurturance, protection, compassion, and tender support (Level 9) is influenced by her or his ability to understand others (Level 7) and empathize with others (Level 8).

From a systems perspective, Levels 10, 11, 12, and 13 reflect the highest complexity of caring. It is hypothesized that deeply caring, intelligent, and wise persons provide empowerment and inspiration for others (Level 10), they help people find meaning and purpose in their lives (Level 11), they help people develop the capacity to experience blessings and forgiveness in their lives (Level 12), and they enable people to achieve peace and reverence in their lives and the lives of their loved ones (Level 13). It is hypothesized that great teachers, therapists, spiritual leaders, parents, and friends provide these levels for the people they care about most.

A systems approach to LLC is by necessity comprehensive and inclusive. An even broader framework is to view LLC in terms of physical, behavioral, psychological, social, and spiritual levels. The 13 levels of love and caring outlined in Table 1 reflect a detailed examination of physical, behavioral, psychological, and social caring, including levels that approach "spiritual" caring (e.g., Levels 11–13) as well.

APPLICATIONS OF THE LLC MODEL TO THE HARVARD FOLLOW-UP DATA

As a preliminary first step in examining love and caring from a levels perspective, it was possible, in the Harvard data, to split the ratings of positive parental caring into two broad ranges of levels of love and caring (Russek & Schwartz, 1997b). The positive ratings contained three items reflecting higher levels of caring (*just, fair, loving*—parental interpersonal qualities that reflect some aspects of understanding, empathy, and compassion; Levels 7, 8, 9) and three items reflecting lower levels of caring (*hardworking, strong*, and *clever*—personal parental qualities that reflect some degree of the ability to provide stable caring, including the intention and commitment to care, plus time and attention; Levels 1, 2, 3, and 4). For the sake of simplicity, the higher level of caring category is termed *advanced* and the lower level of caring category is termed *basic*, assuming that each of these very broad categories actually reflects a range of multiple higher levels and multiple lower levels, respectively.

The question could then be posed: Do measures related to advanced and/or basic LLC predict future health and illness? If the general hypothesis is correct—that love and caring comprise a complex set of processes, each of which contributes to health and well-being—then ratings related to advanced levels and to basic levels should each predict health and illness. As mentioned earlier, although this dichotomy is by necessity oversimplified and is constrained by the data collected at Harvard in the early 1950s, examining these data from this perspective provides a useful first step in looking more closely at the relationship between levels of caring and health in a unique prospective investigation.

It was also possible to separate the positive descriptors generated by subjects into similar categories. Exhibit 2 lists two sets of positive words for mothers, independently rated by two judges, as reflecting higher and lower levels of love and caring. Hence it was possible to determine whether findings for spontaneous descriptors could replicate the findings for ratings.

The correlation of ratings of advanced LLC with number of advanced LLC descriptors was $r = .43$ ($n = 85$, $p < .0001$) for mothers and was $r = .36$ ($n = 83$, $p < .001$) for fathers. The correlation of ratings of basic LLC

EXHIBIT 2
Illustrative Narrative Descriptors of Parents Provided by Subjects

Mother: Higher (Advanced)	Father: Higher (Advanced)
considerate/charitable/good	considerate
courageous	friendly/good natured
fair/tolerant	generous
friend	gives good advice in handling problems
good mother/intensely inter- ested	good judge of people
handles people well	honest
loving/warm/lovable	just/fair
open	kind/helpful/thoughtful
patient	lovable
personable/sunny disposition	loving/devotion to family
practical/lots of common sense	patient self-sacrificing
self-sacrificing/devotion to family	sincere sympathetic
sensitive/understanding/sym- pathetic	understanding/tolerant
sincere/honest/loyal	
strong sense of priorities/fair	

Mother: Lower (Basic)	Father: Lower (Basic)
artistically inclined/talented	adventurous
discerning	appreciates higher education
diversity of interests	broad interests
gentle/refined/feminine	endurance/physical strength
good business sense	enjoys life/jovial/cheerful
intelligent/well read	good businessman
logical thinker	good story teller
outgoing	industrious/hardworking/ambitious
persuasive	intelligent/active mentally
popular	intense/serious/determined
respected for accomplish- ments	modest/down to earth sense of humor
secure/extraverted/confident	strong principles/forthright
strong/enduring	well informed
witty	

These descriptors are broadly classified as relatively higher (advanced) and lower (basic) in terms of levels of love and caring. The advanced descriptors include understanding/empathic/nurturing interpersonal qualities; the basic descriptors include intention/commitment/intellectual personal qualities.

with number of basic LLC descriptors was $r = .12$ ($n = 85$, $p < .268$) for mothers and was $r = .20$ ($n = 85$, $p < .064$) for fathers.

Retrospective and prospective analyses revealed that advanced and basic LLC were each associated with diagnosed diseases in mid-life in both the numeric ratings and narrative descriptors.

For the retrospective analyses, the main effect for sick versus well subjects' ratings was highly significant, $F(1, 79) = 19.43$, $p < .00003$. The well versus sick difference in ratings was somewhat greater for advanced versus basic LLC scores: two-way interaction, $F(1, 79) = 6.83$, $p < .01$. In general, mothers had somewhat larger advanced LLC scores as compared with fathers, whereas fathers had somewhat larger basic LLC scores as compared with mothers: two-way interaction, $F(1, 79) = 38.47$, $p < .000001$ (see Figure 6).

For the narrative descriptors, the main effect for sick versus well subjects' ratings was also highly significant, $F(1, 87) = 13.37$, $p < .0003$. Mothers again had somewhat larger advanced LLC scores as compared with fathers, whereas fathers had somewhat larger basic LLC scores as compared with mothers: two-way interaction, $F(1, 87) = 65.64$, $p < .000001$ (see Figure 7). The well versus sick difference in advanced versus basic LLC descriptors was not significant: two-way interaction, $F(1, 79) = 0.33$, ns.

Prospective analyses revealed that both basic and advanced LLC scores contributed to future disease for both the ratings and the narrative descriptors (Russek & Schwartz, 1997b). For example, concerning the ratings, whereas 37% of subjects who gave high ratings for both advanced and basic LLC items had diagnosed diseases in mid-life, 84% of subjects who gave low ratings for both advanced and basic LLC items had diagnosed diseases in mid-life. In both the high–low and low–high groups, 67% of subjects had diagnosed diseases in mid-life. Similar patterns were observed for the narrative descriptors (Russek & Schwartz, 1997b).

Because it is difficult and costly to conduct longitudinal research, especially over an extended period (35 and 42 years in the Harvard study), unless existing longitudinal data sets happen to include information on

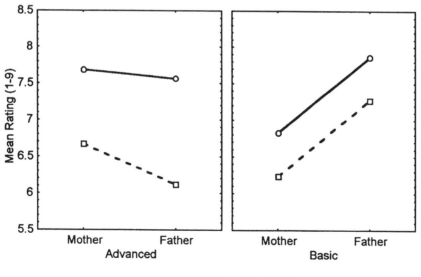

Figure 6. Mean ratings for advanced and basic levels of love and caring separately for mothers and fathers in well and sick subjects.

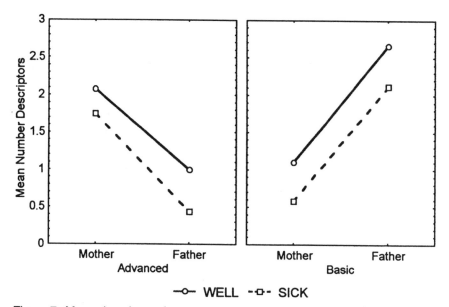

Figure 7. Mean descriptors for advanced and basic levels of love and caring separately for mothers and fathers in well and sick subjects.

love and caring (as in the Harvard sample), it will be a long time before findings from new prospective studies will become available. Systematic research is clearly needed in the future to examine the diverse levels that comprise love and caring, and then to determine the role they may play in contributing to long-term health. We highlight the need for comprehensive research in this area not only because of the sheer complexity involved in defining and measuring love and caring, but also because of the time and expense required to replicate and extend these findings from the Harvard Mastery of Stress follow-up study in future prospective research.

Toward this end, retrospective research can provide a fruitful complementary line of inquiry. For example, in a recent study of 398 undergraduates at the University of Arizona, positive ratings of parental love and caring using the Harvard Parental Caring Scale were significantly correlated with reduced reports of depression, anxiety, and somatic symptoms in both women and men (Russek, Schwartz, Bell, & Baldwin, 1997), independent of a measure of defensiveness. A new scale explicitly measuring the 13 levels of love and caring is in development.

A CHALLENGE FOR CLINICAL PSYCHOLOGY AND SOCIETY

If the findings from the 35- and 42-year follow-up to the Harvard Mastery of Stress study are correct, then it is likely that the perception of family love matters, not only emotionally and behaviorally, but biologically and economically as well. As mentioned earlier, the potential effects of family love may begin to take effect from conception, influencing the early development of a fetus biophysically and biochemically. After birth, the expression of family love, especially through parents (but not exclusively so), can shape many biological, psychosocial (including intellectual), and spiritual aspects of the child's development. Summary measures of the perception of parental love may be powerful because they tap a fundamental, overarching experience and concept that involves, directly or indirectly, most protective as well as risk factors known to influence health and illness (Russek & Schwartz, 1996b).

Although simple measures of the perception of family love seem to be powerful predictors of long-term health, the complexity of what these measures are tapping cannot be overstated. The levels of love and caring model outlined above provides one vision of such complexity and illustrates how it might be organized. However, the topic of love may require that our theories become even more complex, involving the marriage of diverse concepts and perspectives, including adding concepts from modern systems theory and physics (e.g., Russek & Schwartz, 1996a; Schwartz & Russek, 1997b, 1998) to our family of theories (see the Appendix).

In their recent review of research on the relationship of love and health, Green and Shellenberger (1996) began by noting: "That love promotes health surprises few people, yet the scientific study of love and physical health is in its infancy" (p. 46). They suggest that because love has "many facets and is manifested in many ways, it was banned from Western science, which insisted on observable and simple independent variables" (p. 46). The available research, though obviously limited, suggests that "observable and simple independent variables" of love and caring can be obtained. However, because love has "many facets and is manifested in many ways," theories of love and caring will have to become equally multifaceted as well. Systems theory can help address this challenge (see the Appendix).

FROM LOVE TO *LOVE*: A POSSIBLE HEURISTIC TOOL TO ADDRESS THE CHALLENGE

If love and caring are so complex, is it possible to teach students, therapists, and patients about this complexity and share it with the general public in a manner that is not overwhelming? The following straightforward description of love emerged in the process of our teaching an undergraduate course on the psychology of love and compassion at the University of Arizona. We warmly thank the many students who pushed us to provide them with a simple and clear heuristic tool to facilitate their understanding of our definition of love.

One way to think about love is to take the four letters "L" "O" "V" "E" and give each letter a word that captures key aspects of the meaning of the complex word *love*. We selected the words *Listening, Observing, Valuing, Empowering* from the statements provided by the Harvard sample. Together they convey core aspects of the levels of love and caring framework (Russek & Schwartz, 1997b), and present a comprehensive vision of *LOVE*.

By *Listening* is meant more than just listening with one's ears, but listening with one's "heart and whole being," so to speak, as well. It means listening as in being open, taking in, and accepting. This is a fundamental component of love in general, and family love in particular. It addresses the fundamental levels of love and caring.

By *Observing* is meant more than just seeing. It includes understanding and observing, as in celebrating (for example, as in families "observing a holiday," which is one of the definitions of the word *observing* in *Webster's Unabridged Dictionary*). Observing therefore involves understanding, celebrating, and honoring. This is a key component of love and reflects moderate levels of love and caring.

By *Valuing* is meant appreciating, taking seriously, and caring—helping a person feel important and meaningful—in a word, feeling valued. William James said shortly before he died that he wished he had emphasized feeling "appreciated" as a key component of human emotion and health. This term reflects higher levels of caring.

By *Empowering* is meant fostering, enabling, nurturing, and encouraging. When people are empowered, they learn, they grow, they soar, they achieve. This term points to the highest levels of love and caring.

Taken together, the heuristic *LOVE* provides a simple image that portrays the richness of the levels of love and caring framework derived from the Harvard Follow-Up Study (Russek & Schwartz, 1997b). The present findings and perspectives are offered with the hope that they may help us develop a more mature and meaningful vision of love in our scientific research and our service to society, complementing and extending current models of social support (Berkman, 1995; Shumaker & Czajkowski, 1994; Uchino et al., 1996) in clinical psychology.

CONCLUSION

In a recent popular book titled *Love and Survival* (Ornish, 1998), after reviewing the "increasing scientific evidence from my own research and from the studies of others that cause me to believe that love and intimacy are among the most powerful factors in health and illness," the author went on to conclude, "*I am not aware of any other factor in medicine—not diet, not smoking, not exercise, not stress, not genetics, not drugs, not surgery —that has a greater impact on our quality of life, incidence of illness, and premature death from all causes*" (pp. 2–3, italics in original). Ornish's bold conclusion, based in part on the Harvard Mastery of Stress follow-up research reported in the present chapter, deserves serious scrutiny by the science of clinical psychology. If his conclusion is supported in future research, the implications for the science and practice of clinical psychology are far-reaching.

Controversy in this area of research is likely to increase before it decreases. As the Appendix illustrates, the concept of love has deep (though not well-recognized) roots in physics, especially with regard to the concept of energy (Schwartz & Russek, 1997a). In Ornish's (1998) book, a number of investigators (the present authors included) discussed love in the context of energy. Ornish wrote:

> While allopathic medicine does not have a lot to say about how the flow and exchange of energy can affect our health—for better and for worse—this idea is a fundamental concept in most of the various forms of non-allopathic forms of medicine. Western medicine has not incorporated concepts that are now a conventional part of physics, such as Einstein's famous equation, $E = mc^2$ (energy equals mass times the speed of light squared). Paradoxically, this equation also underlies one of the most fundamental concepts of healing: In Einstein's words, "Mass [that is, matter] is merely another form of energy." According to many people, illness first begins in disturbances of energy that only later manifest in physical ways. In contrast, *one of the most profound factors that enhances the free flow of energy is love.* (p. 171, italics added)

Similarly, clinical psychology "does not have a lot to say about how the flow and exchange of energy can affect our health—for better and for worse." Although the distance between physics, psychology, and medicine may seem vast, these domains are ultimately conceptually linked by the deep concept of love. We propose that a challenge for the science of clinical psychology (and psychology in general) in the 21st century will be to approach this integration with an open mind and heart.

APPENDIX
TOWARD A MULTIFACETED VISION OF LOVE AND CARING: THE SYSTEMIC LOVE HYPOTHESIS

We have recently suggested that a dynamical energy systems approach has the potential to address much of the richness and complexity of the multifaceted nature of love and caring (Schwartz & Russek, 1997a, 1997b, 1998), bridging and integrating the biophysical, biological, psychological, and spiritual levels. Because this approach is by nature controversial, especially to clinical psychologists not trained in biophysics or energy medicine (one reviewer of a draft of this chapter described it as "bizarre" and said it was "too controversial" to be included in this volume, another reviewer described it as "science fiction" and a "lot of hooey"), we include this Appendix as a brief introduction to the challenge that unfolds when modern systems theory is integrated with modern physics and applied to clinical psychology. The interested reader should examine Russek and Schwartz (1996a) and Schwartz and Russek (1997a, 1997b, 1998) for a detailed justification to the introduction outlined below.

Interest in love and caring spans conventional medicine (e.g., family and community medicine) and alternative medicine (e.g., energy medicine and transpersonal medicine; Lawlis, 1996; Russek & Schwartz, 1996a). Similarly, interest in love and caring spans "conventional" psychology (e.g., developmental and social psychology) and "alternative" psychology (e.g., humanistic and transpersonal psychology). Whereas conventional theories view love and caring in terms of biochemical and psychosocial interactions, alternative theories add biophysical and spiritual interactions. Dynamical energy systems theory (Russek & Schwartz, 1996a; Schwartz & Russek, 1997a, 1997b, 1998) is one example of how conventional and alternative conceptual frameworks can be integrated (see Schwartz & Russek, 1997a for an extended discussion of modern integrative theoretical approaches to psychology and medicine).

For example, in everyday language, the term *love* is used to describe feelings not only for family members (including pets) and friends but also for music, science, sports, food, places, and even ideas. It is clear that the love for one's spouse and the love for smoked salmon are very different, yet the same word is used in both cases. What is clearly in common in all these examples is the experience of a strong attractive feeling (a sense of connection and union) with the object of love.

The capacity for strong, selective, attractive forces is not unique to humans; this capacity is an essential requirement for all systems to exist and function. The terms *attraction* and *affinity* exist not only in psychology but also in biology, chemistry, and physics (Russek & Schwartz, 1996a).

Love as an "attractive force" is an ancient idea. It was also an idea cherished by Sir Isaac Newton in his concept of gravity as the unifying force in nature (for Newton, gravity was an expression of his vision of God as a loving force). Modern systems theory and modern physics appreciate the need for a concept of attractive forces in nature (Kraft, 1983).

A fundamental tenet of systems theory is the idea that the whole is "greater than the sum of its parts," meaning that novel properties emerge when components join and become functional systems. The classic example is how two atoms, hydrogen and oxygen, each with their own unique properties, can create a molecular system, water, which has its own unique set of properties. It is now generally accepted that emergent properties are the rule, not the exception, in nature. The more complex the system, the more complex are the emergent properties observed. It follows that love as an attractive force may be expressed in novel and ever more complex ways as the structure and functioning of systems evolve in complexity. The level of complexity expressed in the evolution of human beings has resulted in the existence of a system that has the potential to develop loving feelings for virtually everything in nature (the passion that scholars have for virtually all known and imagined aspects of nature is clear evidence for this capacity to love). Learning how to love wisely is becoming an ever more important challenge for humankind.

Caring clearly involves more than just love. It involves the desire to nurture, protect, inspire, empower, and heal, to name a few (i.e., the higher levels in the levels of love and caring, or LLC, model). Organisms are clearly wired to care as well as to love, and humans seem to have an especially complex role in caring for their young, their friends and families, their institutions and communities, and the earth as a whole. The capacity to care may also transcend biological organisms, it may reflect a process implicit in the successful existence of systems at all levels.

All systems are composed of components that *share* matter, energy, and information. The components receive, process, and return matter, energy, and information to each other, and the returning and giving back process is a prerequisite to caring. Again, the more complex the system, the more complex may be its capacity and imperative to care.

From a dynamical energy systems perspective, the perception of family love and caring, then, could conceivably reflect a complex range of levels of love and caring, extending from implicit awareness of biophysical interactions through psychosocial and spiritual interactions. In a 42-year follow-up to the Harvard Mastery of Stress study, the capacity for biophysical energy registration was examined using the heart—the largest generator of electromagnetic signals in the body—as the stimulus (the source, in this case, from the interviewer), and the brain as the receiver (in this case, from the subject). Drawing on predictions derived from dynamical energy systems theory, it was hypothesized that, in an eyes-closed, resting baseline condition, the interviewer's electrocardiogram (ECG) could be detected in the subject's electroencephalogram (EEG), especially in subjects who had been raised in homes they perceived to be loving and caring. With the use of modern signal averaging techniques, evidence for the R spike of the interviewer's ECG was observed in the subject's EEG, primarily in those subjects who had rated their parents high in love and caring 42 years earlier when they were in college (Russek & Schwartz, 1994).

Of course, because these same men had substantially less physical disease, their history of family love and current psychobiological state could not be disentangled. However, if a person's history of love and caring is positive and leads him or her to be more open to interpersonal information, including psychophysiological information and energy (e.g., more trusting, receptive, and less defensive), predictions regarding the registration of interpersonal biophysical energy naturally follow from a systemic vision of love.

Furthermore, it is well known that the perception of interpersonal warmth is an important predictor of successful love and friendship relationships, and is also an important predictor of successful therapeutic relationships. Perception of parental warmth and closeness was also found to be a predictor of long-term health in the Harvard Mastery of stress follow-up study. The term *warmth* is clearly an energetic concept and relates to interpersonal attraction and closeness.

In summary, if love and caring translate into long-term health and well-being, as the present findings suggest, then the social and economic implications are substantial. It may literally pay to be loving and caring. Moreover, focusing on love and caring may not only help the care receiver but also help the caregiver (Dossey, 1996).

An expanded vision of love and caring (e.g., Kraft, 1983) has the potential to bring the best of religion and spirituality back into the mainstream of modern psychology and medicine (Schwartz, 1997; Schwartz & Russek, 1997a). Society will likely need to expand its vision of family, expressed not only in terms of biological family but also in terms of chosen family, and eventually the experience of global family as well. The challenge for clinical psychology and society is to embrace the concepts of love and caring in an open, mature, and integrative manner, and to give these concepts the conceptual, experimental, and practical sophistication they deserve and require.

REFERENCES

Berkman, L. F. (1995). The role of social relations in health promotion. *Psychosomatic Medicine, 57,* 245–254.

Bowlby, J. (1969). *Attachment and loss: Vol. I. Attachment.* New York: Basic Books.

Dossey, L. (1996). What's love got to do with it? *Alternative Therapies in Health and Illness, 2*(3), 8–15.

Funkenstein, D., King, S., & Drolette, M. (1957). *Mastery of stress*. Cambridge, MA: Harvard University Press.

Green, J., & Shellenberger, R. (1996). The healing energy of love. *Alternative Therapies in Health and Illness, 2*(3), 46–56.

Hatfield, E., & Rapson, R. L. (1993). *Love, sex, and intimacy: Their psychology, biology, and history*. New York: HarperCollins.

Kaplan, B. H. (1997). The ties that bind for a lifetime of health. *Psychosomatic Medicine, 59*, 150–151.

Kraft, R. W. (1983). *A reason to hope: A synthesis of Tielhard de Chardin's Vision and Systems Thinking*. Seaside, CA: Intersystems.

Lawlis, G. F. (1996). *Transpersonal medicine*. Boston: Shambala.

Medalie, J. H., & Goldbourt, U. (1976). Angina pectoris among 10,000 men: Psychosocial and other risk factors. *American Journal of Medicine, 60*, 910–921.

Ornish, D. (1998). *Love and survival: The scientific basis for the healing power of intimacy*. New York: HarperCollins.

Parkes, C. M., Stevenson-Hinde, J., & Marris, P. (Eds). (1991). *Attachment across the life cycle*. London: Tavistock/Routledge.

Russek, L. G., King, S. H., Russek, S. J., & Russek, H. I. (1990). The Harvard Mastery of Stress study 35-year follow-up: Prognostic significance of patterns of psychophysiological arousal and adaptation. *Psychosomatic Medicine, 52*, 271–285.

Russek, L. G., & Schwartz, G. E. (1994). Interpersonal heart–brain registration and the perception of parental love: A 42 year follow-up of the Harvard Mastery of Stress study. *Subtle Energies, 5*, 195–208.

Russek, L. G., & Schwartz, G. E. (1996a). The energy cardiology hypothesis: A systems approach for integrating conventional and alternative medicine. *Advances, 12*(4), 4–24.

Russek, L. G., & Schwartz, G. E. (1996b). Narrative descriptions of parental love and caring predict health status in midlife: A 35 year follow-up to the Harvard Mastery of Stress study. *Alternative Therapies in Health and Medicine, 2*(6), 55–62.

Russek, L. G., & Schwartz, G. E. (1997a). Feelings of parental caring predict health status in midlife: A 35 year follow-up to the Harvard Mastery of Stress study. *Journal of Behavioral Medicine, 20*(1), 1–13.

Russek, L. G., & Schwartz, G. E. (1997b). Perceived levels of parental love and caring predict future illness: A 35-year prospective study. *Psychosomatic Medicine, 59*, 102.

Russek, L. G., & Schwartz, G. E. (1997c). Perceptions of parental caring predict health status in midlife: A 35 year follow-up to the Harvard Mastery of Stress study. *Psychosomatic Medicine, 59*(2), 144–149.

Russek, L. G., Schwartz, G. E., Bell, I. R., & Baldwin, C. M. (1997). Perceptions of parental love and caring are associated with reduced physical, emotional and cognitive symptoms. *Psychosomatic Medicine, 59*, 85.

Sarason, I. G., & Sarason, B. R. (1985). *Social support: Theory, research and applications*. Boston: Martinus Nijhoff.

Schwartz, G. E. (1984). Psychobiology of health: A new synthesis. In B. L. Hammonds & C. J. Sheirer (Eds.), *Psychology and health: The Master Lecture Series* (Vol. 3, pp. 145–193). Washington, DC: American Psychological Association.

Schwartz, G. E. (1987). Personality and the unification of psychology and modern physics: A systems approach. In J. Aronoff, A. I. Robin, & R. A. Zucker (Eds.), *The emergence of personality*. New York: Springer.

Schwartz, G. E. (1997). Energy and information: The soul and spirit of mind–body medicine. *Advances, 13*(1), 75–77.

Schwartz, G. E., & Russek, L. G. (1997a). The challenge of one medicine: Theories of health and "eight world hypotheses." *Advances, 3*, 7–23.

Schwartz, G. E., & Russek, L. G. (1997b). Dynamical energy systems and modern physics: Fostering the science and spirit of complementary and alternative medicine. *Alternative Therapies in Health and Medicine, 3*, 46–56.

Schwartz, G. E., & Russek, L. G. (1998). Do all dynamic systems have memory? Implications of the systemic memory hypothesis for science and society. In K. H. Pribram (Ed.), *Brain and values* (pp. 249–273). Hillsdale, NJ: Erlbaum.

Seeman, T. E., & Syme, L. (1987). Social networks and coronary artery disease: A comparison of the structure and function of social relations as predictors of disease. *Psychosomatic Medicine, 49*, 341–354.

Shumaker, S. A., & Czajkowski, S. M. (Eds.). (1994). *Social support and cardiovascular disease*. New York: Plenum Press.

Uchino, B. N., Cacioppo, J. T., & Kiecolt-Glaser, J. K. (1996). The relationship between social support and physiological processes: A review with emphasis on underlying mechanisms and implications for health. *Psychological Bulletin, 119*, 488–531.

II

ASSESSMENT

6

NEW PERSONALITY MEASURES FROM OLD CLINICAL CONCEPTS: A RESEARCH AGENDA

LESTER LUBORSKY

For reasons that are mostly beyond me, my research turn of mind over the past 50-plus years has been to invent personality assessment measures that are operational measures of traditional clinical concepts. In this half century, I continually relied on some of the old concepts and they have been useful, but I naturally wanted to try to improve them.

Two newly improved measures that have met the happy fate of becoming influential worldwide are (a) the *symptom-context theme*, a measure derived from assays of the preconditions that appear before a symptom emerges, and (b) the *core conflictual relationship theme*, a measure derived

---

I have kept up my association with Dr. Lightner Witmer's Psychological Clinic, University of Pennsylvania, for the better part of the period since its founding. My very early experience in 1926 as a client at his Clinic at the University of Pennsylvania may have been a pattern-setting event: I was brought in for evaluation for reasons I never was told. I spent a few hours being tested by a very nice young woman (perhaps a graduate student) on an intelligence scale (probably an early version of the Binet Intelligence Test). At its end, Dr. Edwin Twitmeyer, Dr. Witmer's associate, talked with my mother, patted me on the head, reassured her, and predicted that I would be fine.

from the central relationship pattern (or transference pattern) within the narratives told during psychotherapy sessions.

The symptom-context theme is assessed from the patient's words before symptoms appear in psychotherapy or psychoanalytic sessions; after the many clinical–theoretical studies of the onset of symptoms (e.g., Freud, 1926/1959), it is the first time such a theme has been derived from the reliable symptom-context method (Luborsky, 1996b). The achievement of the core conflictual relationship theme measure is that it is the first time in the history of psychotherapy research that the central relationship pattern (or transference pattern) has been reliably assessed (Luborsky, 1977).

A NEW MEASURE OF THE SYMPTOM-CONTEXT THEME

I happened to stumble upon the application of the symptom-context measure at the start of my research career, just after I came to the University of Illinois in 1945. I had gone there from Duke University with Raymond Cattell to continue our collaboration on his P-technique measure for assessing a person's fluctuations in personality qualities over time. The initial aim of our joint study was to try to apply Cattell's P-technique method to a patient during psychotherapy. The data from the patient's treatment were collected in two parts: (a) from a battery of assessment procedures that I gave before each of 50 recorded psychotherapy sessions, and (b) from measures taken from the recordings of the psychotherapy sessions of the same treatment in which I was the therapist. The most up-to-date account of the findings of this 50-year-old study came out in June 1996 in my book titled *The Symptom-Context Method* (Luborsky, 1996b), published by the American Psychological Association. The book contains the first complete report of the only controlled studies of the conditions before each patient's outbreak of their recurrent symptoms during treatment sessions.

A remarkable event occurred after the start of our joint study of a patient in psychotherapy that added a special focus to my part of the research. One day, in the patient's eighth session of psychotherapy, in the midst of his talking, he stopped and said: "Right now my stomach is kicking me again." What he said at that moment set off the donné that sparked my idea for a study of the immediate context in which a recurrent symptom occurs. His stomach pain appeared to be a moment of sudden activation of a catastrophic state related to his earlier stomach ulcer. At the point of his exclamation about the pain, I realized that I could examine both the immediate context in which the stomach pain appeared in the session and the broad-based factor scores of the repeated measures for each day. The reader should examine, as examples, the following three brief contexts in which the symptom was reported; these are the first three of these occurrences (Luborsky, 1996a, 1996b).

Session 8: Stomach Pain Context
P: //the experience that this committee and these other committees will give me, and in a year, oh, perhaps a year, I can be shooting for the presidency of the YMCA. And yet, one or two main activities I'll take care of, rather than experiencing these various functions of the whole organization—[I'll be] on the tail end of the circle of authority [pause]. *Right now my stomach is kicking around.* It seems to do that every time I lie down on this couch [pause]. It seems as though it is squirting something out. I have noticed it do that before on occasions, but not very often. I just wonder why it does that. It seems to do that more when I'm hungry//

Session 14: Stomach Pain Context
P: Of course [pause]. The plan might be, have something to do with a part of my earlier plan to get myself set up, too. Pretty darned busy until this pressure gets off of it—until I get back, you might say, to normal—if I ever was normal [laughs]—normal for me. *My old stomach kicks me for one reason or another* [pause]. It seems as if there would have to be a pretty darned good reason for me to try anything like that soon [pause]. In other words, she (girlfriend) would have to show some reasonable signs of being interested before I would try it again, at least openly. I might work subversively for a while [laughs].

Session 19: Stomach Pain Context
P: I'm hoping for—I don't believe I'm hoping for too much—and then have that possibility of not winning (the girlfriend), but as long as you know you are still in the running—running in a contest for a long time just begin to wonder how the darned thing is going to work out—*there goes my stomach again*—largely seems to be a matter of sharing things—I share things with people all around me—that's one thing that people say about me—I believe it's so, might as well admit it [laughs]. Usually I add something—like in a discussion or just a social gathering//

What happens in the thoughts that are reported just before the report of pain in each of these three contexts? The patient shifts from speaking about his ambitious striving and moves instead toward a helpless deflated state. In the first example (Session 8), he begins by saying, "I can be shooting for the presidency of the YMCA," then he shifts direction downward to "I'll be on the tail end of the circle of authority." In the next example (Session 14), he first speaks optimistically of "part of my earlier plan to get myself set up," but then he shifts to the pessimistic idea "if I ever was normal." In the third example (Session 19), he speaks of "hoping" for a positive response from his girlfriend and reassures himself by the thought, "I don't believe I am hoping for too much," but then he shifts downward to "I just begin to wonder how the darn thing is going to work out." At that point, his stomach pain is activated again. So, in all three examples, he shifts before the pain from active striving to a more helpless deflated state.

The special method I worked out to analyze such symptom contexts is summarized in the diagram in Figure 1 containing the essential ingredients of the method: (a) assessment of the qualities that can be judged from the transcription of the patient's words around the moment of the immediate context of the stomach pain, versus (b) assessment of the qualities at other times when the patient was talking and no pain appeared; these nonpain samples provided comparison contexts that could serve as a baseline of comparison with the actual context of the pain experiences (Luborsky, 1996a).

The significance of the differences between ratings of the symptom segments versus nonsymptom segments was revealing. For this patient, the clinically rated qualities that were most discriminating, starting with the most, were concern about "supplies" (i.e., getting what he wanted), anxiety, helplessness, and striving and hoping for wish fulfillment. Among the other methods of assessment of significant differences were those based on precise scoring systems, for example, a helplessness manual and a dictionary of psychological words—*The General Inquirer* (Stone, Dunphy, & Smith, 1966).

The factor analysis of the daily measures provided a broad background factor that was recognized and named by Cattell (1946) as a "surgency" factor. It was when this broad factor increased that the stomach pain was most likely to appear. It was also evident that there was a parallel between the qualities in the immediate context of the symptom and those in the background context for the symptom.

The set of discriminating qualities for each patient was unique in terms of the ordering of the degree of discrimination of the real symptom context from the control nonsymptom context, and although there was considerable commonality of the qualities across patients. Over the course of the next 50 years, I was able to assemble data collected by myself and by other researchers for a series of patients with recurrent symptoms and also to examine them in the same way by the symptom-context method. These data sets served as the core data for the book on this method (Luborsky, 1996b), which has provided the field with its first and only controlled studies of the context in which recurrent symptoms appear in psychotherapy or psychoanalytic sessions.

Why did it take so long—about 100 years—for controlled studies of recurrent symptom contexts to be done? The answer became obvious after I thought it over—only occasionally is one blessed with the presence of the two necessary coconditions: (a) the appearance of an actual recurrent symptom and (b) a tape recording of the symptom event that includes the

Session timeline:

Context studied	Broad background context	Immediate context before symptom	Context during symptom	Immediate context after symptom	Broad background context
Symptom context	Whole session ratings Whole session CCRTs	Patient's and therapist's words and other behaviors	Symptom or other behavior	Patient's and therapist's words and other behaviors	Whole session ratings Whole session CCRTs
Control context	Same as above	Same as above	Control point in the same or other session in which the symptom or other behavior is *not present*	Same as above	Same as above

Figure 1. Diagram of the basic components of the symptom-context method applied to sessions before and after symptoms. CCRT = core conflictual relationship theme. Adapted from *The Symptom-Context Method: Symptoms as Opportunities in Psychotherapy*, by L. Luborsky, 1996, p. 14. Copyright 1996 by the American Psychological Association.

words before and after. So it is the necessarily slow collection of tape recordings of these instances of symptoms in their context that accounts for the slow rate of accumulation of objective studies of symptom formation by means of the symptom-context method.

After having applied the method to 7 usable cases (Luborsky, 1996b), each with a different but self-consistent recurrent symptom, I was able to summarize the qualities that discriminated the real symptom contexts from the control nonsymptom contexts. Across the 7 patients, the symptom-context qualities with the highest effect sizes (in descending order) are *hopelessness, lack of control, anxiety, feeling blocked, helplessness, concern about supplies, depression, hostility to therapist, guilt, involvement with therapist, separation concern,* and *hostility to others.*

After the array of discriminating qualities was extracted from the set of 7 patients' sessions with recurring symptoms, I thought over which theory would best explain the onset conditions of such diverse recurrent symptoms; the *symptom-context theory of symptom formation* grew slowly and unevenly until I had settled on the set of stages that leads to symptom formation in Exhibit 1.

A comparison of my new theory with the many older clinical theories showed that the symptom-context theory is consistent with vital parts of Freud's (1926/1959) theory, as well as with other classical theories of symptom formation. The similarities are greatest for the focus on helplessness,

---

EXHIBIT 1
Luborsky's Eight-Stage Symptom-Context Theory of Symptom Formation

---

1. A perception of a potential danger, with some attendant anxiety (e.g., "I will fail").
2. The danger is in relation to people, especially those with whom the person is involved (e.g., girlfriend).
3. The activation of the Core Conflictual Relationship Theme (e.g., "I want a response from girlfriend, she rejects me, I activate myself, and my stomach pains").
4. Increased cognitive disturbance (in a few patients).
5. A general increase in hopelessness and lack of control, anxiety, feeling blocked, helplessness, concern about "supplies," depression, hostility to therapist, and guilt.
6. The psychological changes are paralleled by changes on the physiological level, often involving physical symptoms (e.g., high frequency of stomach pains, high white count).
7. The background state parallels some qualities of the immediate state, especially the prominence of the core conflictual relationship theme, and may also include a cognitively disturbed state.
8. A target symptom appears with its choice based on a biopsychosocial disposition.

Examples in parentheses are from the patient with stomach ulcer pain (Luborsky, 1996a). Adapted from *The Symptom-Context Method: Symptoms as Opportunities in Psychotherapy,* by L. Luborsky, 1996, p. 395. Copyright 1996 by the Amercan Psychological Association.

hopelessness, anxiety, and related variables. But my theory differs most in (a) its emphasis on current rather than past triggers (and most of them in the moments just before the symptom); (b) its emphasis on the expected responses from other people; (c) its emphasis on the centrality of the activation of a core conflictual relationship theme (the "CCRT," described next); and (d) its emphasis on the centrality of hopelessness and helplessness, which is similar to, but even greater than in Freud (1926/1959), in Engel and Schmale (1967), and in the more exact and empirically based theory of Seligman (1975) on learned helplessness.

Finally, the new measure's most fitting applications are to personality theory and to the technique of psychotherapy (Luborsky, 1996b, 1997, 1998a). Therefore, within psychotherapy, the appearance of a recurrent symptom should be greeted as an opportunity to be seized by the therapist and by the patient as a key for unlocking the knowledge of the specific conditions contributing to its formation.

A NEW MEASURE OF THE CORE CONFLICTUAL RELATIONSHIP THEME

My second example of a new personality measure from an old concept was also the fruit of a felicitous discovery. It was first described as the CCRT method in Luborsky (1976, 1977). Its discovery came about accidentally and certainly tangentially to a different aim, as many such discoveries do. In 1975 my friend, Ed Bordin, asked me to take part in a panel at the Society for Psychotherapy Research on the nature of the therapeutic alliance. To prepare for this, I designed two novel observer-judged operational measures of the concept of the therapeutic alliance, called the *helping alliance rating method*, and a companion to it, the *helping alliance counting signs method*. The rating method only required judges to globally rate each segment of the psychotherapy session, but the counting signs method required counting and judging the intensity of each of the signs within the text that were the basis for judging the patient's experience of the alliance. As I began to use these measures, I recognized that these new alliance measures were only targeted for a specific and limited relationship pattern, that is, the one with the therapist. It was at the moment of this realization that I began to plan how to derive a measure of the *general* relationship pattern, that is, with people in general.

To move ahead on this plan, I decided to observe and track how I did the job of inferring the general relationship pattern from the sessions —the job of formulating the relationship pattern as is habitually done in dynamic psychotherapy (Luborsky, 1984). But, also I set myself the unusual component of the task: to monitor how I inferred the general relationship pattern. Self-monitoring while I was engaged in this task allowed me to recognize three aspects of the process of making such inferences:

1. I tended to derive most inferences from the relationship narratives told during sessions.
2. Within each narrative, I tended to see three components of a relationship pattern: the main wish of the patient toward other people, the response from the main other person, and the response of the self to that response of the other.
3. Across the set of narratives told by each person, I saw that there was a general relationship pattern based on the pervasiveness of the components across the narratives; it was this pattern I called the *core conflictual relationship theme*, or CCRT.

One can easily see more of how the CCRT method works by examining the example that follows. The example specifies the procedures in Figure 2 that call for scoring each narrative for each main component—the wishes, the responses from others, and the responses of the self—and then finding the most pervasive types of these components across the set of narratives (all details of method are in Luborsky, 1997, 1998c). The narratives in the example were told by an 18-year-old young man who suffered from anxiety states that appeared after certain conflicts were activated. Note, on the right side of Figure 2, the text of the narratives about three relationship episodes (RE). On the left side of the figure are the scores that were given to the text of each RE by both the tailor-made and standard categories. (Tailor-made categories are unguided, free-form individual categories; standard categories are those specified in a uniformly used list of categories designated by numbers.) For example, in the first narrative about mother, the patient says "mother says it didn't happen." The tailor-made category, "Disagrees with his view," is first given; it is then followed by standard category scores 8 (*not trustworthy*) and 14 (*unhelpful*). These standard scores are summed for the three components separately: Wishes, Responses from Other, and Responses of Self. Across the relationship episodes, the most pervasive content is expressed as the most frequent types of components; these are combined to form this patient's CCRT: (Wish) I want to be close; (Response from Other) the person rejects me; (Responses of Self) I become tense, anxious, discouraged, and unresponsive. The main symptom of recurrent anxiety states appears in the Response of Self. In essence, then, the CCRT is a composite of the most often repeated types of each of the three components across the relationship narratives. The rationale for this measure was that the repetition across narratives reflects the operation of a relationship schema that serves to guide the conduct of the person's relationships.

After much more experience with this CCRT measure by me and by

RE #1: *Mother*

NRO: Disagrees with his view (8, 14)

W: To get sexual information (8?, 11?)

(W): To get close to M. (11?, 8)

PRO: (past) Explains (11, 13)

NRO: Rejects (4, 12)

NRS: Frustration (21, 20?)

NRS: Upset, shame (26, 25)

//This might have been a dream. //$_{RO}$ Mother says it didn't happen.// $_{W,(W)}$ Up until we moved, when I had questions about sex,//$_{RO}$ mother would explain. //When we moved to _____, one day I asked and//$_{RO}$ she said, sorry we can't talk about that. You're getting to that age. //$_{RS}$ Bothered me 'cause my young sister, age 9 or 10, laughed.//

RE #2: *Mother*

NRO: Disagrees with his view (8, 14)

PRO: (past) Closeness (11?, 13?)

(W): To be physically close (11, 8?)

NRO: Rejection: chooses someone else (4, 12)

//$_{RO}$ Another incident Mother said never happened. //$_{RO,(W)}$ We, brother and I before sister was born—when it was really cold, would sleep with parents. //$_{RO}$ Parents took my brother in bed with them and they wouldn't take me.

RE #3: *Therapist*

NRS: Unresponsive, distant (8, 16?)

NRS: Headache (31?, --)

NRS: Tense (27, 19?)

NRS: Lack of response on his part (8, 16?)

NRO: No rapport (12, 14?)

NRS: Lack of response on his part (8, 16?)

T: What's happening now?

P: // $_{RS}$ I feel generally unresponsive. // $_{RS}$ I'm getting a headache//

// $_{RS}$ tense//$_{RS}$ thinking all week about relating all this stuff to what I was 10 years ago [sigh] and not getting any, I mean, nothing comes out//

//. . . like groups of guys who have embarrassing moments of silence. // $_{RO}$ It proves no perfect rapport exists. // $_{RS}$ I feel blank.

Figure 2. Sample of text and core conflictual relationship theme (CCRT) scoring for Mr. Howard (Session 3). All designations are given in Luborsky (1998c). RE = Relationship Episode; PRO = Positive Responses from Others; W = Wish; (W) = Wish Inferred; NRS = Negative Response of Self; PRS = Positive Response from Self; RO = Response from Others; RS = Response from Self. Adapted from *Understanding Transference: The Core Conflictual Relationship Theme Method* (2nd ed.), by L. Luborsky and P. Crits-Christoph, 1998, pp. 81–83. Copyright 1998 by the American Psychological Association.

others, much evidence was found that supported its reliability: For eight studies, the mean weighted kappa for wishes was .61, for responses from others .67, and for responses of self .71 (Luborsky & Diguer, 1998).

This general measure of the central relationship pattern, the CCRT, was also discovered to be a good candidate as a reliable measure of Freud's (1912/1958) original clinical concept of the transference template that had never before been objectively measured. I first addressed this in Luborsky (1977) and most recently in Luborsky (1997; Luborsky & Crits-Christoph, 1990, 1998). To show the degree of similarity of the old clinical concept of the transference template with the evidence from the new CCRT measure, I went back to Freud's manifold descriptions of his transference concept and identified 23 facets of Freud's observations (Luborsky, 1998b). For each of them, I brought together the related evidence that came from the CCRT. In 18 of these comparisons, evidence was found for the similarity of the clinical concept of transference with each facet of the quantitatively measured version of the CCRT. For the other 5 facets, a study has not yet been done.

Recently, I found evidence for another kind of bridge across the measures of the two concepts: The symptom-context theme turns out to be similar to the CCRT (Luborsky, 1996b). Because each of these two measures is broad-based and complex, I was drawn inevitably to examine the degree of commonality between them. In the *Symptom-Context Method* book (Luborsky 1996b), considerable correspondence was found in all of the 7 cases of recurring symptoms that could be examined in detail. I concluded with the principle that what leads up to the appearance of a recurrent symptom has much in common with the pattern of conflictual elements across narratives about relationships.

CONCLUSIONS

Principles for Translating Useful Old Clinical Concepts Into Useful New Clinical–Quantitative Measures

I have given accounts of the construction of two very satisfying new clinical–quantitative measures that were derived from very satisfying old clinical concepts. For each of these two measures, it has turned out to be a worthwhile side trip to examine the translation steps that were taken to arrive at the operational measures. For each of these journeys, at least three steps had to be taken:

Step 1: Formulating the clinical concept while engaged in paying close attention to monitoring how the clinician is doing the inference process —just as I did with the illuminating single cases described in this chapter.

Step 2: Translating each of the introspectively recognized aspects of the inference process into tangible, quantifiable operations—just as was done in making a formulation of the central relationship pattern, by abstracting the relationship narratives from the session, by applying scoring categories to the three components of each narrative, and then by looking to see which types of each of the three components were most pervasive across the narratives and thus formed the CCRT measure.

Step 3: Examining the reliability and validity of the measure—just as was done so successfully with each of the two exemplified measures, the symptom-context theme and the CCRT.

The Inevitable Gap Between a Clinical Concept and Its Operational Measures

Yet, even though the identified quantifiable operations came out very well as scorable procedures, it is inevitable that there will remain some gap between the clinical formulation of a concept and the clinical–quantitative measures of that concept, as I illustrate again and again in the cases in the *Symptom-Context Method* book (Luborsky, 1996b). It is in part the richness and in part the vagueness of the clinical concepts that make it impossible for a quantitative measure to capture all of their complexities. But, over the years, despite this limit, these two clinical–quantitative measures, which are translations of clinical concepts, have captured enough of what is central in their cognate clinical concepts to have made valuable contributions both to personality theory and to the clinical practice of psychotherapy (as summarized in Luborsky, 1996b, 1998c).

A Successful Operational Measure Warrants a Celebration

Finally, it must be remembered that when some parts of clinical concepts can be reliably and validly captured through a clinical–quantitative measure, a celebration is in order. When we as psychologists are able to take such an important step, it means that we can profit from translation principles that yield the improved measures that guide independent judges to be able to agree. It should also be remembered that advances in knowledge typically cluster around prior advances in method (Boring, 1942, p. 609), and ultimately the field of clinical psychology will then be able to make further significant scientific advances with the help of these new measures.

REFERENCES

Boring, E. G. (1942). *Sensation and perception in the history of experimental psychology*. New York: Appleton-Century.

Cattell, R. B. (1946). *The description and measurement of personality.* New York: World Book.

Engel, G., & Schmale, A. (1967). Psychoanalytic theory of somatic disorders: Conversion, specificity and the disease onset situation. *Journal of the American Psychoanalytic Association, 15,* 344–365.

Freud, S. (1958). The dynamics of the transference. In J. Strachey (Ed. and Trans.), *The standard edition of the complete psychological works of Sigmund Freud* (Vol. 12, pp. 99–108). London: Hogarth Press. (Original work published 1912)

Freud, S. (1959). Inhibitions, symptoms and anxiety. In J. Strachey (Ed. and Trans.), *The standard edition of the complete psychological works of Sigmund Freud* (Vol. 20, pp. 87–174). London: Hogarth Press. (Original work published 1926)

Luborsky, L. (1976). Helping alliances in psychotherapy: The groundwork for a study of their relationship to its outcome. In J. L. Claghorn (Ed.), *Successful psychotherapy* (pp. 92–116). New York: Brunner/Mazel.

Luborsky, L. (1977). Measuring a pervasive psychic structure in psychotherapy: The core conflictual relationship theme. In N. Freedman & S. Grand (Eds.), *Communicative structures and psychic structures* (pp. 367–395). New York: Plenum Press.

Luborsky, L. (1984). *Principles of psychoanalytic psychotherapy: A manual for supportive–expressive (SE) treatment.* New York: Basic Books.

Luborsky, L. (1996a). The context for stomach ulcer pains. In L. Luborsky (Ed.), *The symptom-context method—Symptoms as opportunities in psychotherapy* (pp. 177–199). Washington, DC: American Psychological Association.

Luborsky, L. (1996b). *The symptom-context method: Symptoms as opportunities in psychotherapy.* Washington, DC: American Psychological Association.

Luborsky, L. (1997). The Core Conflictual Relationship Theme (CCRT): A basic case formulation method. In T. Eells (Ed.), *Handbook of psychotherapy case formulation* (pp. 58–83). New York: Guilford Press.

Luborsky, L. (1998a). *The conditions for the onset of symptoms in psychotherapy and psychoanalysis.* Manuscript in preparation.

Luborsky, L. (1998b). The convergence of Freud's observations about transference with the CCRT evidence. In L. Luborsky & P. Crits-Christoph (Eds.), *Understanding transference: The Core Conflictual Relationship Theme method* (2nd ed.; pp. 307–325). Washington, DC: American Psychological Association.

Luborsky, L. (1998c). A guide to the CCRT method. In L. Luborsky & P. Crits-Christoph (Eds.), *Understanding transference: The Core Conflictual Relationship Theme method* (2nd ed.; pp. 15–42). Washington, DC: American Psychological Association.

Luborsky, L., & Crits-Christoph, P. (1990). *Understanding transference: The CCRT method (The Core Conflictual Relationship Theme).* New York: Basic Books.

Luborsky, L., & Crits-Christoph, P. (Eds.). (1998). *Understanding transference: The Core Conflictual Relationship Theme method* (2nd ed.). Washington, DC: American Psychological Association.

Luborsky, L., & Diguer, L. (1998). The reliability of the CCRT measure: Results from eight samples. In L. Luborsky & P. Crits-Christoph (Eds.), *Understanding transference: The Core Conflictual Relationship Theme method* (2nd ed.; pp. 97–107). Washington, DC: American Psychological Association.

Seligman, M. (1975). *Helplessness: On depression, development and death.* San Francisco: Freeman.

Stone, P. J., Dunphy, D. C., & Smith, M. S. (1966). *The General Inquirer: A computer approach to content analysis.* Cambridge, MA: MIT Press.

7

CONTEMPORARY COGNITIVE APPROACHES TO STUDYING CLINICAL PROBLEMS

RICHARD M. McFALL, TERESA A. TREAT, AND RICHARD J. VIKEN

As clinical psychology celebrates its centennial, the field of psychology finds itself in the throes of a so-called cognitive revolution. This zeitgeist is reflected in some of the chapters in this centennial collection, for example. Perhaps it is fitting, therefore, to use this historic occasion to examine the cognitive revolution more closely, particularly in relation to clinical psychology, and to consider its implications for the next century of clinical science.

We begin by raising what may seem an impertinent question: What is so new or revolutionary about psychologists studying cognition? Exhibit 1 traces the roots of psychology, prior to Witmer's founding of clinical psychology, as commonly summarized in introductory textbooks. We can see that from its very inception psychology has been studying human cognition. In fact, many of today's cognitive constructs—for example, sensation, perception, consciousness, intelligence, learning, categorization, memory, recall, identification, recognition, association, imagery, and problem solving—can be traced to the pioneering work of Witmer's 19th-century predecessors.

EXHIBIT 1
Historical "Roots" of Psychology

Maskelyne and Kinnebrook (1795); Bessel (1816, 1822): observation, "error," and the "personal equation."

Müller (1840): founder of physiology in Bonn, Germany; studied what happened in the nerves with "feeling"; law of specific nerve energies; mentor of Hermann von Helmholtz.

Helmholtz (1858): studies of sound (pitch, timbre, loudness); physiological mechanisms of the inner ear; and discrimination and identification of stimuli (instruments, voices).

Fechner (1860): *Elements of Psychophysics*; extended Gaussian theory of error to the comparison of sensations.

Wundt (1879): First psychology laboratory in Leipzig, Germany; conducted reaction time experiments aimed at studying indirectly the structure of consciousness.

J. McK. Cattell (1883–1886): Wundt's lab assistant; interested in consistent individual differences in reaction times across stimulus modalities.

Galton (1885): First mental testing center, London (J. McK. Cattell coined term *mental test* in 1890).

Münsterberg (1891): created 14 "mental abilities" tests of complex functions in children (e.g., reading, classification, mathematical operations).

Kraepelin (early 1890s): created tests of complex mental functions (e.g., memory, attention).

Breuer and Freud (1895): published *Studies in Hysteria*.

Binet (1895–1896): Began developing tests of complex mental abilities (e.g., spatial judgment, motor skill, memory, comprehension, attention).

Witmer (1896): After doctorate with Wundt in Leipzig (1892), established first psychological clinic at the University of Pennsylvania; methods aimed at discriminating mental abilities and defects.

So, if cognition has been central to psychology for well over 100 years, what *is* revolutionary about today's cognitive revolution? Obviously, it is not the basic subject matter. What is revolutionary are the powerful new conceptual and methodological tools that contemporary cognitive scientists and neural scientists have developed for studying cognition—tools that have enhanced significantly the research leverage, thereby yielding clear advances in one's understanding of human cognition. As Burke (1996) and others have argued, scientific advances often are the unexpected by-products of new conceptual frameworks and methodological tools. This certainly has been true of the current "revolution" in cognitive and neural psychology. We believe that the new cognitive concepts and tools hold great promise for the next century of clinical science.

Not all psychologists would characterize psychology's cognitive revolution as we have here. Clinical psychologists from the cognitive–behavioral school, for example, probably would be more inclined to describe the cognitive revolution in terms of the burgeoning use of cognitive–behavioral techniques in psychotherapy, and the increased efficacy of these techniques for treating such clinical problems as depression, obsessive–compulsive disorder, and panic disorder. Other psychologists would be more inclined to describe the revolution in terms of the increased prominence of social–cognition constructs in many contemporary theories of social and personality psychology. There simply is no universally accepted definition of the cognitive revolution; instead, the revolution seems to be open to multiple interpretations, with the particular choice depending largely on the interests of the psychologist offering the definition.

And therein lies the problem. Although cognition clearly is central to many areas of psychology, on closer examination it becomes apparent that these different areas are using similar terms in different ways to refer to quite different things. Thus, psychologists' shared enthusiasm for cognition is more illusory than real—an artifact of ambiguous, inconsistent, and even competing interpretations of this construct, each carrying different assumptions and implications. This kind of conceptual fuzziness, and the confusion it creates, is a serious impediment to scientific progress (Meehl, 1978; Popper, 1962). The differing views of cognition are not likely to be equally valid and useful; therefore, the first step in examining the cognitive revolution is to sharpen, rather than blur, the differences among the competing views. Only then can we consider the cognitive revolution's implications for the next century of clinical science.

With this in mind, we have identified (McFall, Treat, & Viken, 1997) at least three general ways in which psychologists have conceptualized cognition: (a) as a *thing*; (b) as an *experiential event*[1]; and (c) as a *process*. Key distinctions among these views are as follows.

Cognition as a thing: Here cognition is treated as a noun. Cognitions are reified as things "in the head" that one has or holds; they are viewed as internal, unobservable determinants of behavior. Sometimes they are depicted almost as though they "had minds of their own," or as influences that individuals may struggle to control or avoid. One role of psychotherapy, from this perspective, is to eliminate, counter, or restructure the patient's deviant, distorted, or disruptive cognitions. This perspective assumes that because a person's cognitions are internal and unobservable, they are accessible primarily through introspective, self-report methods of assessment, although sometimes they may be inferred from behavioral indicators. Examples of constructs fitting this category are *attitudes, attributions, beliefs, goals, ideas, schemata,* and *thoughts.*

Cognition as an experience: Here cognition is treated either as a verb or as a verb–adjective combination. Cognitions are mental experiences (verb form) or experiential affective states (adjective form, linked to the verb "to feel"). In both forms, cognitive experiences are phenomenological, subjective, and usually transient. Therapies based on this view of cognition

---

[1]In an earlier paper (McFall, Treat, & Viken, 1997), we characterized this second type of cognition as an *event* and then proceeded to describe it in experiential terms, much as we have done here. We renamed it slightly in this chapter simply to emphasize the experiential aspect and to help clarify the distinctions among the three concepts of cognition.

typically attempt to alter patients' cognitive experiences by providing new, corrective experiences. For instance, therapists might treat disruptive cognitions by instructing patients to relive traumatic experiences, or, paradoxically, they might expose patients to the very cognitive experiences that previously had been so disruptive. Again, because they are subjective and experiential, these cognitions are assumed to be accessible primarily through introspective assessment methods, although sometimes they also may be inferred from behavior. Examples of cognitive experiential verbs are *to attribute*, *to believe*, *to expect*, and *to think*. Examples of verb–adjective affective states are (to feel) *anxious*, *depressed*, *frightened*, *stressed*, and *worried*.

Cognition as a process: Here cognition is treated as a noun, but in this case it is not reified or given ontological or substantive status. Rather, this noun form is used to identify particular complex and dynamic patterns that characterize the information-processing activities or operations of persons in general. Thus far, this view of cognition has not led to any widely recognized therapeutic techniques, although its clinical implications are intriguing and ripe for development. In contrast to the first two views of cognition, this view assumes that persons usually do not have accurate knowledge of their own cognitive processing. Thus, such processing must be assessed through systematic, quantifiable, direct observations of actual cognitive performance in specific tasks under controlled conditions. Examples of such cognitive processes are *categorization*, *classification*, *feature detection*, *memory*, *perception*, *recall*, and *recognition*.

TWO COGNITIVE REVOLUTIONS

These competing conceptions of cognition suggest that there are two (at least) cognitive revolutions in psychology! These revolutions seem to have developed in parallel, with little influence on one another, and with surprisingly little in common aside from their superficially (and misleadingly) similar terminology. Not surprisingly, these two revolutions are closely allied with the "two worlds" of psychology first described by Cronbach (1957) and can be differentiated on the basis of their participants, concepts, methodologies, and problem focus.

Generally speaking, the main participants in one of the revolutions tend to be clinical, social, and personality psychologists, whose cognitive constructs fit the more subjective, introspective traditions, in which cognitions are treated as things, experiences, or some blend of the two. These psychologists tend to rely on correlational, quasiexperimental, and idiographic methods to study individual differences in cognition. The focus of their theory and research is the prediction, explanation, and control of socially relevant behaviors, such as aggression, depression, or anxiety. Clinical psychologists, in particular, seek to identify individual differences associated with deviance, and to develop interventions that will prevent or ameliorate such deviance. Because of their focus on applied problems, psychologists in this first group give high priority to ecological validity and clinical significance in their choice of theoretical constructs and research methods.

In contrast, the leading participants in the other revolution tend to be cognitive and neural scientists, most of whom long ago rejected an introspective perspective, and who now treat cognition as the dynamic, observable patterns of information processing. These psychologists rely on highly controlled laboratory experiments and mathematical modeling techniques to build nomothetic models of cognitive processes and the conditions that underlie their systematic variability. Individual differences typically are regarded as "error" to be minimized in the search for general laws. Because of their focus on basic scientific questions, psychologists in this second group emphasize experimental control, careful scaling of stimuli and responses, and quantitative modeling in their theory and methods (see Townsend, 1990; Townsend & Ashby, 1984).

Of course, the notion that there are two cognitive revolutions, linked to the two worlds of psychology, is an abstract heuristic. Clearly, there are exceptions and limitations to such a generalization. For example, a few clinical, personality, and social psychologists have advocated process models of cognition (e.g., Kelly, 1955; Lang, 1995; Lang & Cuthbert, 1984; McFall & Dodge, 1982; Mischel & Shoda, 1995; Neufeld & Williamson, 1996), and others have argued for the use of constructs, measures, and research methods consistent with such models (e.g., Kihlstrom & Nasby, 1981; Meehl, 1973; Nasby & Kihlstrom, 1986).

It is not always easy to classify cognitive theories according to this two-world scheme. Theorists often do not provide sufficiently clear and explicit statements of their underlying cognitive assumptions and constructs to allow classification. Other theorists lack coherence; for instance, they may treat cognition as a process in their formal theoretical statements but betray quite a different conception of cognition in their choice of research methods, data analyses, or discussion of results and implications. Even the most conscientious scientists sometimes are inconsistent, slipping between formal and casual language systems without sensing the conflict. Nevertheless, we believe that the conceptual differences between these two worlds of cognition are not trivial, and that attention to such differences will lead to advances in clinical science.

The chasm separating these two worlds of cognition in psychology is neither inevitable nor unbridgeable. Our list of pioneering 19th-century psychologists (see Exhibit 1), for example, includes several experimenters who studied individual differences even as they searched for general laws: Bessel (1816, 1822) took a nomothetic approach to studying individual differences in the "personal equation"; James McKeen Cattell (1883–1886), working as an assistant in Wundt's lab, studied individual differences in reaction times across stimulus modalities; and Binet (1895–1896) studied general developmental patterns of mental functioning at the same time that he assessed individual differences in such patterns and made differential predictions of school performance in children (see Boring, 1957; Gould, 1996b; McFall & McDonel, 1986). Other sciences also provide examples of the potentially productive interplay between investigations of patterns of variability in probability distributions, on the one hand, and measures of central tendencies, on the other hand (e.g., Burke, 1996; Feynman, 1985; Gould, 1996a; Swets, 1996).

Thus, in principle, there is no reason why psychologists could not bridge the gap that currently separates their two worlds of cognition. It is our contention that the effort required to build such a bridge would be a good investment. Specifically, we are encouraged by the prospects of a hybrid psychology, combining the best concepts and methods from cognitive and neural science with the special contributions from clinical, personality, and social psychology—specifically, a focus on important substantive problems, a concern for ecological validity, and an attention to patterns of variability both between and within individuals across time and situation. This hybrid should advance the interests of the entire field of psychology. Clinical, personality, and social psychology will benefit from the increased rigor and precision. Cognitive and neural psychology will benefit, in return, from the challenges posed to their idealized models by expanding the scope of the testing and application of such models. Indeed, one of the primary aims of the present chapter is to illustrate the promise of such a hybrid approach for psychology by describing specific examples from our own research—a collaboration involving clinical scientists (the present authors and A. Michele Lease), cognitive scientists (Robert M. Nosofsky and James T. Townsend), and neural scientists (Donald B. Katz and Joseph E. Steinmetz).

TOWARD A HYBRID MODEL

The first step in building a hybrid cognitive model is to make explicit one's choices from among the competing assumptions, concepts, and methods. In this section, we outline the major choices we have made in our own work and explain the rationales for these choices. The aim of outlining our assumptive structure is to be as clear and coherent as possible. We do not presume that our choices are the only ones that reasonable scientists might make. However, we do invite readers to adopt our structure provisionally, and then to take a guided tour of our research to see what this particular hybrid approach has to offer.

What Is Cognition?

Consistent with contemporary theories in cognitive and neural science, as summarized above, we conceptualize cognition as the dynamic information-processing activities, or operations, of human organisms. Forty years ago, Paul Meehl (Meehl, Klann, Schmieding, Breimeier, & Schroeder-Slomann, 1958) offered an analysis of *mind* that still seems germane (simply substitute the terms *cognitive* and *cognition* for the earlier, but now less-fashionable terms *mental* and *mind*, and translate *events* into *processes* rather than *experiences*):

> the mental processes of man are conceived by the psychologist, first of all, as *events*, (i.e., not *things*); and secondly, the "things" which participate in these events . . . (note, not "produce" or "underlie," but *constitute*) the mental events, are material entities. . . . thought, passion, love, guilt, etc., are not produced by the body . . . rather they are all literally *activities* of living tissue. Thinking and willing are actions by the human machine. . . . if you ask . . . "Where does the mind go when the body dies?" this question cannot make any sense. . . . Such a question is like asking, "Where does the timekeeping go when a watch is smashed?" Answer: Nowhere, because timekeeping is not a thing but an event, and in this smashed watch, events of that kind no longer take place. . . . The *word* "mind" is, grammatically, a noun, but it refers to acts and dispositions. The monistic view can be succinctly expressed by the analogical equation Mind:Brain::Timekeeping:Watch::Function:Structure::Event:Thing. (pp. 159–160)

Our view of cognition, like Meehl's, is monistic. Quite simply, the processing of internal and external information is an essential, ongoing activity of living organisms. The aim of contemporary cognitive scientists is to build theoretical models (a) that provide accurate descriptive representations of these activities, (b) that reduce uncertainty about these activities by increasing one's ability to predict and control them, and (c) that allow us to use measures of cognitive activity to predict other significant events, such as clinically relevant behaviors. To the extent that our theoretical models do these three things, we can conclude that they are valid and, hence, that we know something about cognition (see Polya, 1957; Popper, 1962).

How Are Brain and Cognition Related?

Our view of cognition is *not* reductionistic; on the contrary, we view the organism as a single, unified entity. But the scientific study of humans is analytic; that is, it involves building and testing simplified models that represent only selected aspects of whole persons. The number of potential theoretical models is almost limitless, and models may be developed across the entire spectrum of abstraction—from the most molecular to the most molar. In this wealth of possibilities, no level of abstraction has a greater prior claim to "truth" than any other. Theories at the molecular level, for example, are not inherently better at capturing "reality" than theories at a more molar level. Nor does a model at one level of description necessarily provide causal explanations for models at any other level. For instance, changes in brain chemistry cannot be said to cause specific cognitive activities, such as specific patterns of perception or recall. Rather, different levels of description for the ongoing activities of the organism are simply that—different ways of representing different facets of the same, unified, dynamically changing organism. Ultimately, the relative "truth value" of models at different levels of description, at different scales, is determined by the relative utility of the competing models for answering specific questions. Every model is created with a particular problem focus and with a limited range of convenience; thus, a model that proves useful for addressing questions in one area may have little or no utility for addressing questions in other areas. Each model's truth value, therefore, is evaluated only with respect to how well it serves its specific purposes, in relation to alternative models.

There is no question about it: Without a brain, little cognitive activity of interest takes place. However, there is little theoretical connection between models of the electrochemical activity of the brain, on one level, and models of cognitive processing activity, on another level. Models that describe either the brain or cognitive processing, respectively, simply represent different levels of analysis of the dynamic, complex, and integrated activities of a whole organism. Perhaps there may come a time when some meta-theory will allow us to translate back and forth between the constructs at these two different levels, but we have no such conceptual bridge now. The best we can do currently, if we wish to relate brain activity to cognitive processing, is to note patterns of correspondence between these two separate descriptive systems (e.g., observing the correlation between brain-scan patterns and performance on cognitive tasks). But we must avoid the logical fallacy of interpreting such correlations as evidence of causation.

One last point about this relationship: Because neuroscience models and cognitive science models represent two different descriptive systems for the same organism, there need not be a *physical isomorphism* between brain architecture, as modeled in neuroscience, and cognitive architecture, as modeled in cognitive science. The only required correspondence between the two systems is a *logical isomorphism*. That is, they may not yield logically contradictory or incompatible predictions; if they do, then at least one of the two systems must be wrong. By the same token, the principle of logical isomorphism makes it possible for us to use what is known in one system to inform model development in the other system by setting logical constraints on the plausible theoretical options.

How Are Cognitive Processes to Be Measured?

Nasby and Kihlstrom (1986) criticized the cognitive theories and interventions of clinical psychologists for being focused on cognitive *products* (conscious thoughts) to the neglect of cognitive *processes*. To make matters worse, many psychologists "do not even assess what a person thinks, but what a person reports thinking, or, more often, reports having thought" (p. 218). Given the well-known limitations of introspective, self-report measures (e.g., Nisbett & Wilson, 1977), psychologists' continued reliance on them is puzzling. Perhaps they simply see no alternatives. Whatever the reason, Nasby and Kihlstrom (1986) concluded that improvements in cognitive theories and interventions will require not only improved integrative models but also improved methods and techniques of cognitive assessment.

Clinical psychologists could improve their cognitive assessments by attending to recent theoretical and methodological advances in cognitive and neural psychology. Most clinical psychologists no doubt are familiar with the use of some "cognitive" tasks in psychopathology research, such as the Stroop task (e.g., Cooper & Fairburn, 1992), the card sort task (e.g., Persons & Foa, 1984), and the dichotic listening task (e.g., Bruder et al., 1997). Clinical psychologists probably have used these three non-self-report cognitive tasks more often than any others to assess differences between preselected groups of subjects (e.g., normal vs. anxious, compulsive, depressed, or eating disordered). Although these are appropriate assessment tasks for some purposes, they do not begin to exhaust the possibilities provided by the newer generation of more focused, sensitive, and informative tools now available for assessing cognitive processes and for testing theoretical models. As we said at the outset, the newer cognitive assessment tools are the defining feature of the cognitive revolution and have the potential to spur dramatic advances in clinical psychology. Thus, when building our own hybrid model, we borrowed freely from the toolboxes of our cognitive science colleagues, adapting the most promising methods to our particular research questions.

The cognitive scientist's toolbox differs from the typical clinician's toolbox in several important ways. First it seldom contains all-purpose, off-the-shelf, standardized tests of individual differences on "cognitive" personality trait dimensions. Instead, it contains methods designed to sample the pattern of subjects' performance on specific information-processing tasks assessing processes of theoretical interest. To sample *categorization*, for instance, cognitive scientists instruct subjects to sort the items from a standard stimulus set into an implicit or explicit category structure. Similarly, to sample *feature detection* or *recognition memory*, they require subjects to identify the "targets" in a stimulus set containing both "signal" and "noise" items. For each cognitive process, one or more corresponding assessment paradigms have been developed. Interestingly, these cognitive paradigms are consistent with McClelland's (1973) recommendations for improving clinical assessment; that is, they sample subjects' optimal performance on standard tasks under controlled conditions, rather than sampling subjects' self-reports of typical performance. This strategy not only avoids validity problems, such as response biases and deception, but also does not require troublesome assumptions about subjects' knowledge of their own cognitive processes.

A second major strength of the cognitive scientist's tools is that they often are designed to provide tests of the fit between observed performance and quantitative models of expected performance—as derived from theories of cognitive processing, its architecture, its dynamics, and its relation to other behaviors. To the extent that these mathematical modeling techniques require quantitative predictions stated before data collection, they represent "riskier," more informative tests of theories than do the more traditional null-hypothesis significance tests (Cohen, 1994; Loftus, 1997). Thus, they also yield stronger theoretical inferences (Meehl, 1978; Platt, 1964). Of course, specifying theoretical expectations with quantitative precision requires that stimuli and responses be selected carefully and scaled to represent the dimensions of theoretical interest; that the underlying probability distributions of stimuli and responses be known in advance, if not actually controlled; and that the shapes of the statistical functions underlying the theoretical relationships be anticipated (e.g., linear vs. nonlinear; Townsend, 1990).

A third strength of the cognitive scientist's tools is that they include a number of powerful, well-developed, quantitative models that are relatively content free. Prominent examples of such general quantitative models are signal detection theory (SDT; Macmillan & Creelman, 1991); choice theory (Luce, 1963); and general recognition theory (Ashby & Townsend, 1986). SDT, for instance, has been applied successfully to a range of problems, from medical diagnosis to weather forecasting to library information retrieval systems (Swets, 1996). This suggests that SDT and other similar content-free quantitative models of cognitive processing may prove useful in the study of clinically relevant problems as well (McFall & Treat, in press).

Of course, the ultimate test of any tool is how well it allows us to do things that we could not have done without it. Perhaps the greatest strength of the cognitive scientist's tools is their proven explanatory power and predictive utility. Over the past two decades, mathematical modeling techniques have contributed significantly to psychology's understanding of the architecture of human information processing, and the roles that cognitive processes play in human behavior more generally. A prime example of such methodologically driven theoretical advances is Nosofsky's (1992) use of multidimensional scaling (MDS) techniques to build and test an exemplar-based theoretical model that has resolved previous puzzles in classification, identification, recognition memory, and category learning. Because Nosofsky's work has been influential in our own thinking, we preface the tour of our research with a brief summary of his seminal work and an explanation of its potential relevance to clinical science.

MAPPING THE MULTIDIMENSIONAL ORGANIZATION OF PERCEPTUAL PROCESSING

Basic Cognitive Research

We need to define four key cognitive processes: (a) *classification*, assigning distinct items in a stimulus set to groups without feedback; (b) *identification*, assigning a unique response to each item; (c) *recognition memory*, judging whether each item is "old" or "new" (i.e., previously seen or not); and (d) *category learning*, learning to place distinct items into particular categories with feedback. Because these presumably are related cognitive processes, it should be possible to predict performance on one task from performance on the others. Over the years, however, cognitive scientists have found it surprisingly difficult to account for the observed relations among performances on these four tasks. To help solve this classic problem (Medin & Schaffer, 1978; Shepard, 1957, 1958a, 1958b), Nosofsky (1984, 1986, 1992) proposed an exemplar-based approach.

According to this approach, each unique stimulus (or exemplar) is stored in memory, and task-dependent similarities among exemplars are responsible for differential performance on classification, identification, recognition memory, and learning tasks. Thus, a stimulus should be classified into the category that contains the most similar exemplars; a stimulus should be misidentified as another stimulus as a function of its similarity to that stimulus; a "new" stimulus should be remembered as "old" the more similar it is to "old" stimuli; and a category structure should be learned more quickly if the stimuli in each to-be-learned category are perceived as more similar to one another than to members of a different category.

Deterministic MDS techniques are used to represent relevant exemplars as points in a multidimensional perceptual space (which may or may not be the same as the physical space in which the stimuli lie); the similarity of each stimulus pair then is a decreasing function of distance between the two stimuli in this perceptual space (Davison, 1983; Kruskal & Wish, 1978; Nosofsky, 1992; Schiffman, Reynolds, & Young, 1981). The similarity of the stimuli can be modified as a function of subjects' "attention to" each of the dimensions of perceptual space. Increasing attention to a dimension "stretches" the length of that dimension in perceptual space, such that the stimuli are more dissimilar along that dimension, whereas decreasing attention to a dimension "shrinks" the length of that dimension in perceptual space, such that the stimuli are more similar along that dimension. Thus, as shown in the top of Figure 1, the distances among exemplars along the shape (triangle–circle), size (large–small), and color (black–white) dimensions indicate equal attention strengths for these dimensions (from Nosofsky, 1986). In the bottom of Figure 1, however, the distances among exemplars along the color dimension have been stretched, illustrating an increased attention strength for the color dimension.

To interrelate performance on identification, classification, and recognition memory tasks, Nosofsky (1986) allowed these attention strengths to vary across tasks, so that performance can be optimized. For example, whereas attending to one dimension may be critical for correct identification of stimuli, attending to a different dimension may be necessary for accurate recognition memory performance. Kruschke and colleagues (Kruschke, 1992; Nosofsky, Kruschke, & McKinley, 1992) have generalized No-

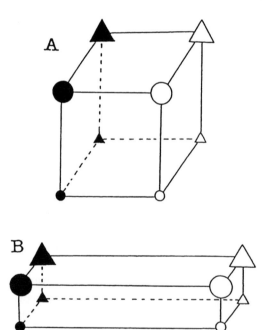

Figure 1. Schematic illustration of the role of selective attention in modifying similarities among exemplars: (A) equal distances on dimensions of shape (triangle–circle), size (large–small), and color (black–white) indicate equal attention strengths; (B) the greater distance among exemplars on the color dimension indicates greater relative attention strength for this dimension. From "Attention, Similarity, and the Identification–Categorization Relationship," by R. M. Nosofsky, 1986, *Journal of Experimental Psychology: General, 115*, p. 42. Copyright 1986 by the American Psychological Association. Reprinted with permission of the author.

sofsky's approach to account for performance on category-learning tasks, by modeling learning as a function of increasing attention to the relevant dimensions of the category structure and decreasing attention to the irrelevant dimensions of the category structure. Thus, MDS techniques are capable of not only mapping efficiently the perceived similarities among items in a large stimulus set, but also providing excellent predictions of performances on identification, classification, recognition memory, and learning tasks.

Clinical Implications of Tools for Mapping Perceptual Organization

Theories linking perceptual organization to behavior have been prominent in clinical psychology for many years (e.g., Bruner, Goodnow, & Austin, 1956; Kelly, 1955; Rotter, 1954; Sarbin, Taft, & Bailey, 1960). Despite their intuitive appeal, however, such theories have suffered from inadequate methodologies for assessing both individual differences in perceptual organization and contextual contributions to systematic variability in perceptual organization. As a consequence, their theoretical contributions have been largely metaphorical. MDS methods of modeling perceptual organization, as used by Nosofsky (1992), may offer quantitative solutions to the methodological limitations of such theories (see Jones, 1983; Rudy & Merluzzi, 1984).

Consider, for instance, George A. Kelly's (1955) theory, *The Psychology of Personal Constructs*, a clinical–personality theory consistent with many of the views expressed in this chapter.[2] According to the theory's fundamental postulate, "A person's processes are psychologically channelized by the ways in which he anticipates events" (p. 46). "A person anticipates events by construing their replications" (p. 50). To "construe" is to filter events, attending to some aspects while ignoring others; to place interpretations on the selected events; and to structure the implicative relations among these interpretations. The construal process is inherently

[2]George Kelly vigorously and steadfastly resisted everyone's efforts (as he used to say) "to pigeonhole" his theory, typically as "phenomenological" or "cognitive." His resistance was principled. First, he had strong objections—philosophical, logical, conceptual, and methodological—to many of the theories with which he found himself being lumped, particularly the "softer," introspective theories. But, second, he also was a "sharpener" who was at least as interested in how things differed as in how they were similar. He was concerned that his theory's unique strengths were obscured by the "leveling" effects of pigeonholing. To him, labeling was a form of stereotyping, allowing people to believe that they "knew" a theory without really having to study it in depth or judge its merits. His was an unconventional theory, not easily grasped at first, making it a tempting target for simplifying labels. Above all, however, Kelly's fascination with the implications of different ways of construing the world (what he called *constructive alternativism*) led him to resist pigeonholing, even when done in a respectful and scholarly way. In 1964–1965, for example, his former student, Walter Mischel, suggested during a colloquium at Ohio State University that Kelly really should be considered "one of the first behaviorists." With impish wit, Kelly declined this sympathetic portrait. If Kelly were alive today, he undoubtedly would be quick to highlight, with incisive humor, the limits of the parallels we see between his theory and contemporary cognitive theories.

dimensional, implying both similarities and contrasts among events. Much of the process is preverbal or nonverbal—embraced in the realm of physiology—making it inaccessible to introspection and ordinary verbal self-report. The fact that persons may construe events differently lays the foundation for a psychology of individual differences; yet, to the extent that individuals construe events similarly, their psychological processes—construct systems and context-dependent behaviors—will be more similar, laying the foundation for a psychology of social interaction and community.

Assessing this construal process involves mapping the content, organization, and implications of each individual's personal construct system. To do this, Kelly (1955) developed the *repertoire grid technique*, or Rep Test, a precocious tool quite unlike most traditional psychological tests. However, despite attempts to refine, systematize, and extend the Rep Test over the years (e.g., Kihlstrom & Cunningham, 1991), the measure's value has been limited by a number of inherent problems. First, the test lacks standardization; each subject is asked to create a unique stimulus set consisting of the persons who fill specific roles in the subject's life. Because no two subjects are considering the same stimuli, it is difficult to compare construct systems across individuals. Second, the test is too "verbal"; the subject is instructed to consider the "significant others" in groups of three, assigning verbal labels to the bipolar construct dimension that best captures how the subject sees two of these people as "alike" and "different" from the third. Finally, the test lacks adequate methods of quantitative scoring, analysis, and interpretation; lacking good norms and scales, it does not yield actuarial interpretations and predictions. Despite these serious limitations, the Rep Test in many ways was a conceptual precursor of the MDS methodology, because it was an attempt to measure individual differences in perceptual organization.

In summary, then, clinical meta-theories, such as Kelly's (1955), have much in common with modern cognitive theories of human information processing, but until now have been hampered by a lack of rigorous methodologies and assessment techniques. We believe that MDS techniques, such as those used by Nosofsky (1992), may offer clinicians a promising approach to the assessment of perceptual organization. Such tools may allow clinicians to map individual differences in cognitive processing, and then to use these maps to predict clinically relevant behavior. We will illustrate this use of MDS with examples from our own research.

INDIVIDUAL DIFFERENCES IN MEN'S PERCEPTION OF WOMEN: DOES COGNITIVE STRUCTURE INFLUENCE CATEGORY LEARNING?

Clinical research has suggested that sexually coercive behavior may be related to individual differences in men's perceptual sensitivity to women's affect cues. For example, a study comparing heterosexual cue-reading accuracy in three groups of incarcerated men—rapists, violent nonrapists, and nonviolent nonrapists—revealed that rapists were less accurate than control subjects at reading women's affect cues in an identification task (Lipton, McDonel, & McFall, 1987). A related pattern also was found among college men (McDonel & McFall, 1991). What accounts for such differences (cf. Malamuth & Brown, 1994)? Do sexually coercive men perform poorly because they simply care less about doing well on the task? Or does their performance reflect something more theoretically interesting, such as underlying differences in perceptual organization, which might help explain some instances of sexually coercive behavior? What do cognitive meta-theories suggest?

Both Nosofsky's (1992) and Kelly's (1955) models suggest that between-subjects variability in performance on identification tasks may be related to individual differences in the cognitive structures that subjects impose on stimulus arrays. The hypothesized relationship between structure and performance is neither simple nor absolute. A subject's task performance is expected to vary as a function of the "fit," or congruence, between the task structure, on the one hand, and the perceptual structure imposed on task stimuli by the subject, on the other hand. Where task performance depends on attention to women's affect, for example, men who allocate relatively greater attention to affect should perform better, on average, than men who allocate greater attention to some other dimension, such as degree of physical exposure. In tasks favoring attention to physical exposure, however, the relative performance levels of these two subject groups should be reversed.

A direct test of this congruence hypothesis requires some method of systematically mapping the multidimensional structure of subjects' perceptual processing of task stimuli. Until recently, because no adequate method was available, investigators were forced to resort to indirect tests—either comparing "known groups" assumed to use different cognitive structures or randomly assigning subjects to different experimental conditions on the assumption that the experimental manipulations produced the intended effect on subjects' cognitive structures. By using MDS techniques, however, it now may be possible to assess perceptual structures more directly, thereby allowing a more rigorous test of the congruence hypothesis.

We explored this possibility in a two-part study (Viken, Treat, & McFall, 1997). In the first part, we used MDS techniques to map the structure of men's perception of women. In the second part, we used these maps to make differential predictions—consistent with the congruity hypothesis—concerning subjects' likely patterns of performance in three category-learning tasks. Subjects were 74 undergraduate men. They first rated the "similarity" of all possible pairs of 14 photographs of women (a total of 91 pairs) on a 10-point scale (0 = *very different*; 9 = *very similar*).

We did not say what we meant by "similarity"; each subject was free to base his ratings on his own definition. The 14 photos were part of a 26-photo stimulus set that had been selected from a larger collection of photos clipped from newsstand magazines and catalogs. Male pilot subjects had rated the larger collection on 14 bipolar dimensions (e.g., attractiveness, activity level, affect, physical exposure, approachability, etc.). On the basis of these normative pilot data, the final stimulus set of 26 photos had been selected to represent the entire two-dimensional space of *affect* (positive–negative) and *exposure* (from modest to revealing clothing). Fourteen of these photos were used in the MDS similarity-rating task. All 26 were used in the three category-learning tasks.

The object of the three category-learning tasks was the same: Subjects were shown individual photos of 26 women and were instructed to guess whether the woman in each photo *did* or *did not* have an unnamed characteristic. On the basis of feedback from the experimenter, subjects were supposed to "learn" the underlying category structure. Each learning task consisted of four blocks of 26 trials each; the order of the 26 photos varied across blocks. The tasks differed, however, in critical ways that allowed us to assess learning performance under different conditions.

In the first learning task, all subjects received massed, random feedback. That is, they received oral feedback (number "correct" out of 26 guesses) only at the end of each completed block of 26 trials; all subjects received the same feedback regardless of their guesses, so category learning was not expected. This first task was designed to provide a baseline assessment of each subject's classification behavior before the influence of response-contingent feedback. Category learning was assessed in the second and third learning tasks, in which all subjects received immediate, accurate feedback following each guess. The only difference between the second and third learning tasks was the particular category structure that subjects were supposed to learn. For half of the subjects in the second learning task, the underlying category structure centered on *affect*: All women with positive affect were included; all women with negative affect were excluded. For the other half of the subjects, the underlying category structure focused on *exposure*: All women whose bodies were "exposed" were included; all women whose bodies were "covered" were excluded. In the third learning task, these target attributes were switched; subjects who previously received feedback based on the affect category structure now received feedback based on the exposure category structure, and vice versa. Equal numbers of subjects were assigned randomly to these two orders.

After completing the three learning tasks, subjects also completed two self-report measures, one assessing subjects' history of sexually coercive behavior (Rapaport & Burkhart, 1984), the other assessing their judgment about the justifiability of a hypothetical man continuing to make sexual advances following various negative reactions from his female partner

(McDonel & McFall, 1991). These measures allowed us to explore associations between cognitive structures, learning, and self-reports of coercion and heterosocial judgment.

To map individual differences in subjects' perceptual structures, we analyzed photo similarity-rating data using ALSCAL (SPSS Inc., 1992). A separate nonmetric Euclidean MDS model was fit to each subject's similarity ratings. On the basis of the fit indexes of S-stress (a measure of badness of fit, ranging from 0 to 1, with low values being best) and R^2 (the percentage of variance in subjects' ratings explained by the MDS solution), we used three-dimensional MDS solutions in all subsequent analyses (mean S-stress = .11; mean R^2 = .88). Thus, each dimension of each subject's MDS solution contained stimulus coordinates for each of the 14 photo stimuli used in the rating task. Next, we completed two separate multiple regression analyses on each subject's MDS solution, in which the stimulus coordinates for the three MDS dimensions were regressed on the normative ratings for affect and exposure. This allowed us to estimate the relative importance of affect and exposure to each subject's similarity ratings. Multiple Rs for affect ranged from .14 to .92 (M = .58); multiple Rs for exposure ranged from .15 to .98 (M = .78). A ratio of the multiple Rs for affect and exposure was computed for each subject. This ratio served as our primary index of individual differences in subjects' perceptual processing of women. Subjects with ratio scores in the top third of the sample (i.e., with high relative attention to exposure) were classified as *exposure oriented* (EO); subjects with ratio scores in the bottom third were classified as *affect oriented* (AO).

Learning data were analyzed by computing choice theory (Luce, 1963) indexes for sensitivity (the inverse of the similarity index) and bias from each subject's hits, misses, false alarms, and correct rejections for each block of 26 learning trials. Log transformations of these indexes (Macmillan & Creelman, 1991) yielded scale values similar to the more familiar SDT measures of sensitivity and bias. Sensitivity scores of zero indicated random responding; positive scores indicated increased sensitivity. Bias scores of zero indicated a bias toward saying "she does" have the attribute; bias scores below zero indicated a bias toward saying "she does not."

At last, we were in a position to test the congruity hypothesis. We predicted that subjects would perform better (i.e., would have higher sensitivity scores) when the category structure to be learned was congruent with the perceptual organization subjects brought into the tasks. Specifically, AO subjects should perform best when the category-learning task focused on the affect dimension of women's photos; EO subjects should perform best when the learning task focused on the exposure dimension. Figure 2 summarizes the results for AO and EO subjects across the first three blocks of trials in the affect and exposure learning conditions. (Results for the fourth block were consistent with these, but analyses were

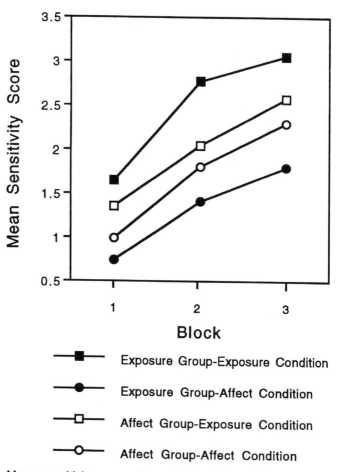

Figure 2. Mean sensitivity across three blocks of the affect and exposure category-learning tasks for the affect-oriented and exposure-oriented groups of men (from Viken, Treat, & McFall, 1997).

more complicated because of asymptotic performance.) Our predictions clearly were supported. Note that there was a main effect for learning task, with all subjects showing greater sensitivity in the exposure learning task than in the affect learning task. As predicted, however, AO subjects earned higher sensitivity scores than EO subjects within the affect condition, whereas EO subjects earned higher sensitivity scores than AO subjects within the exposure condition. EO subjects also showed the greatest within-group disparity in sensitivity scores across learning conditions, suggesting that they had more difficulty shifting perceptual dimensions. These findings may have implications for understanding how perceptual structures contribute to the likelihood of sexual coercion.

Not surprisingly, few relationships were found between the two self-report measures and subjects' group classification (AO vs. EO) or subjects' performance on the learning tasks. Indeed, it would be paradoxical to expect subjects who are relatively insensitive to women's affect, for example, to have enough sensitivity to report accurately on how coercive their own behavior has been. As might be expected, however, the AO group's ratings of the justifiability of the hypothetical man's continued sexual advances were more dependent on the degree of negative reaction from the woman partner than were the ratings of the EO group.

Three aspects of this study deserve highlighting. First, at no time were the words *exposure* or *affect* mentioned to subjects. Subjects were sorted into the AO and EO groups entirely on the basis of our MDS mapping of the perceptual organization underlying their similarity ratings of paired photographs of women. Thus, our assessment of perceptual structure did not rely on self-report but was based on samples of perceptual processing of our stimulus set. Second, the stimulus set was constructed with care to represent the two-dimensional space of interest. Knowing the normative values of these stimuli allowed us to use regression methods to assess the relationship between subjects' perceptual structures and the predetermined stimulus dimensions of theoretical interest. Using MDS in this way is very different from using it to "discover" structural dimensions in subjects' perceptions. The distinction is analogous to the difference between confirmatory and exploratory factor analysis—one being a form of deductive hypothesis testing, the other being essentially an inductive fishing expedition. Finally, MDS methods are not tied to specific content, but potentially have utility for assessing cognitive structures across a broad range of content. To illustrate their generality, we describe our use of these same MDS methods to study an entirely different clinical problem.

COGNITIVE STRUCTURE AND BULIMIA: WOMEN'S DIFFERENTIAL PERCEPTION OF AFFECT AND BODY SIZE

Many clinical theories of bulimia nervosa assign an etiological role to women's cognitive processing of body-size information. For methodological reasons, however, it has been difficult to test these theories without relying on indirect, self-report measures of perceptions. By using MDS methods, it now should be possible to sample the structure of women's perception more directly, thereby permitting more stringent tests of cognitive theories of bulimia. We should expect not only to see a pattern of congruence between perceptual structure and performance on basic cognitive processing tasks, as in the preceding study, but also to find meaningful connections between cognitive structure and clinical symptoms, such as bulimic behaviors. This was the focus of our next study (Viken, Treat, Nosofsky, McFall, & Palmeri, 1997).

First, we needed to develop a standard stimulus set with theoretically relevant content and well-defined properties. We photographed a sample of volunteer undergraduate women with widely varying body sizes. Photos were taken under standard conditions: lighting, distance, and background were controlled; the women had their hair pulled back, wore no make-up, and were dressed in black tights and white T-shirts. Each woman was photographed with both happy and sad facial expressions. All photos then were rated by a new sample of undergraduate women on the dimensions of *affect* and *body size*. On the basis of these normative ratings, a final stimulus set of 24 photos was selected, representing the full two-dimensional space of happy–sad and heavy–light.

In the next step, 355 undergraduate women from introductory psychology classes were screened with the Bulimia Test (Smith & Thelen, 1984). Twenty volunteers with scores of 88 or above were recruited as bulimic subjects; another 21 volunteers with scores below 45 were recruited as controls. (The group labels indicated the relative presence or absence of symptomatic behaviors, not *Diagnostic and Statistical Manual of Mental Disorders*, or DSM, diagnoses.) The experimental session involved three tasks: (a) MDS *photo-rating task*, in which subjects rated the "similarity" of all possible pairs of women in the 24 photos of our standard stimulus set (a total of 276 ratings), using a 10-point scale and defining "similarity" for themselves; (b) *prototype classification task*, which is described below; and (c) *self-estimates task*, in which subjects estimated on a 100-point scale the importance of several attributes (e.g., body size, affect, attractiveness) to their similarity ratings.

In the prototype classification task, subjects were shown two photos from the standard stimulus set; the women in these photos were selected to represent diagonal corners of the two-dimensional space (i.e., Woman A = happy and heavy; Woman B = sad and light). Subjects were told that these were prototypical of two "types" of women. Subjects then viewed the remaining photos in the stimulus set one at a time and classified each woman as either Type A or Type B. Next, subjects were shown a different pair of prototypes; the women in these photos represented the other two diagonal corners of the two-dimensional space (i.e., Woman X = sad and heavy; Woman Y = happy and light). Subjects again classified each of the remaining stimulus photos as either Type X or Type Y. Order of classification tasks was counterbalanced across subjects, and photo order varied across the two classification sequences.

In contrast to our strategy in the first study, subjects were classified as bulimic or control, based on their Bulimia Test scores. Thus, instead of sorting subjects into groups based on MDS attention weights for affect and body size, we were able to compare the attention weights of our predefined groups.

Our MDS analyses of subjects' similarity ratings on the photo-rating task proceeded along somewhat different lines than in the previous study.

We used the normative ratings of the photos to "fix" their stimulus coordinates for affect and body size in the MDS analysis; then we estimated each subject's attention weights for these two fixed dimensions (Davison, 1983; Schiffman et al., 1981). Conceptually, the attention weights obtained from this simpler procedure are comparable with the multiple Rs derived from individual MDS analyses in the first study.

Subjects' responses to the prototype classification task were analyzed twice—both times using signal detection theory (SDT) methods—yielding two separate sensitivity and bias scores. In the first analysis, subjects' responses were classified as hits, misses, false alarms, and correct rejections as though the "correct" dimension in the prototype classification task had been affect. In the second analysis, the same responses were rescored as though body size had been the "correct" dimension. In this way, we could assess the relative degree to which each subject's classification responses reflected sensitivity to each of the two dimensions.

We predicted a congruence between group membership and cognitive structure, as mapped by the MDS solution. That is, we expected bulimic subjects to show greater attention to body size than control subjects, and expected control subjects to show greater attention to affect than bulimic subjects. As can be seen in Figure 3, the MDS analysis of subjects' perceptual structures clearly confirmed our predictions.

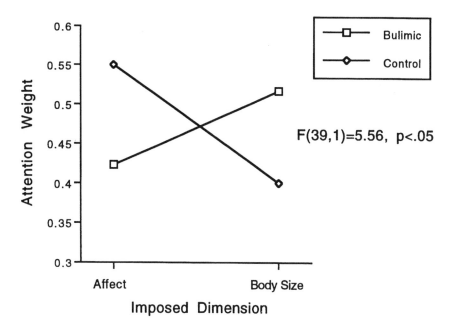

$F(39,1)=5.56$, $p<.05$

Figure 3. Mean attention weights from a weighted multidimensional scaling solution of bulimic and control subjects for the dimensions of affect and body size in their paired similarity ratings of women's photos (from Viken, Treat, Nosofsky, McFall, & Palmeri, 1997).

We also predicted a congruence between group membership and sensitivity scores on the classification task, with bulimic subjects earning higher sensitivity scores for body size than control subjects; with control subjects earning higher sensitivity scores for affect than bulimics; and with bulimics showing a greater disparity between their two sensitivity scores than control subjects. These predictions also received strong support, as shown in Figure 4.

Finally, we predicted a congruence between cognitive structure and sensitivity scores, as in Nosofsky's work on the relationship between perceptual organization and classification. As expected, subjects' sensitivities to affect and body size correlated strongly with subjects' relative attention to affect and body size on the first classification, $r(39) = .77$ and $-.82$, respectively, $ps < .01$.

Group membership did not predict subjects' self-estimates of the importance of affect and body size (natural log ratio of estimates), $t(39) = 0.46$, ns. Subjects' relative self-estimates also were unrelated either to subjects' relative attention to affect and body size, $r(39) = .21$, ns, or to subjects' sensitivities to affect and body size on the first classification, $r(39) = .14$ and $-.22$, ns. These findings demonstrate the incremental utility of assessing subjects' actual cognitive processing, rather than relying on subjects' introspective self-reports.

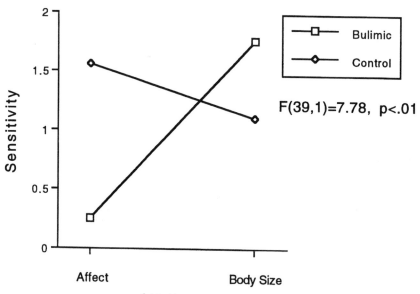

Figure 4. Mean sensitivity scores of bulimic and control subjects for attributes of affect and body size in classification task (from Viken, Treat, Nosofsky, McFall, & Palmeri, 1997).

STABILITY OF INDIVIDUAL DIFFERENCES IN PERCEPTUAL STRUCTURES

For perceptual structures to play an influential role in the development of psychological symptoms, the structures would need to show a reasonable degree of temporal stability—at least when assessed under similar circumstances. Viken, Vazques, and Treat (1996) assessed the stability of attention weights in 30 undergraduate women, who were paid $5 for each of two 1-hour sessions, scheduled approximately 1 week apart. In each session, subjects completed the MDS photo rating task described in the previous study; they rated all possible pairs of 24 photos (a total of 276 ratings per session) in the stimulus set of women representing the two-dimensional space of affect (happy–sad) and body size (heavy–light).

Test–retest correlations for attention weights on the affect and body size dimensions, respectively, were $r(29) = .81$, $p < .001$, and $r(29) = .75$, $p < .001$. The mean attention weight for affect was .53 ($SD = .18$) in Session 1 and .54 ($SD = .20$) in Session 2. The mean attention weight for body size was .33 ($SD = .13$) in Session 1 and .35 ($SD = .12$) in Session 2. Thus, the MDS solutions were reasonably stable over a 1-week period, and the mean attention weights for the two stimulus dimensions were similar to the values yielded by control subjects in the preceding study.

Perceptual structures should be fairly stable when assessed repeatedly over short periods under similar conditions, as demonstrated in this study, but it would be a mistake to expect them to be stable when assessed under different circumstances or over extended periods. They are not fixed things, but are dynamic, emergent properties of the activity of information processing in humans. These perceptual structures should vary systematically in relation to changes in learning histories and contextual factors. For example, we might expect different blood alcohol levels to influence the structure of men's perception of women, or the ingestion of a high-fat drink to influence women's perception of women. In both cases, we might expect to see predictable patterns of dynamic change in subjects' perceptual organization. For example, alcohol might decrease men's attention to women's affect; a high-fat drink might increase women's attention to body size. It would be a serious error if clinical psychologists started to treat subjects' perceptual structures as stable personality traits.

COGNITIVE INFLUENCES ON CLASSICAL EYE-BLINK CONDITIONING: IMPLICATIONS FOR COGNITION AND BRAIN FUNCTIONS

At what "level" of the cognitive system do the perceptual structures that we have been mapping with MDS techniques exert their influence on information processing? Kelly (1955, p. 51) suggested that much of the construal process is "embraced in the realm of physiology," making it preverbal or nonverbal, hence inaccessible to ordinary introspection. Kelly's view is consistent with many contemporary theories in cognitive and neural science, but it is at odds with many clinical theories of cognition, which continue to rely on subjects' introspective self-reports of cognitive processes. Our next experiment (Treat, Katz, McFall, Viken, & Steinmetz, 1997) capitalized on the principle of *logical isomorphism*, as discussed earlier in this chapter, to shed light on this "level" question. Specifically, our design included a classical eye-blink conditioning procedure (Sears, Finn, & Steinmetz, 1994); this allowed us to invoke what we already know about the brain systems involved in eye-blink conditioning to make logical inferences about the level at which perceptual processes operate.

Subjects were volunteer undergraduate women. First, they completed our MDS photo rating task, rating the similarity of all possible pairs of women in the 24 photos of our standard stimulus set, representing the two-dimensional space of affect and body size. Then they participated in a modified version of a classical eye-blink conditioning procedure. An air puff was delivered to the subject's eye 500 ms following the presentation of a conditioned stimulus (CS+; high tone). No air puff was presented following a CS− (low tone). Conditioning consisted of 100 trials in 10 blocks of 10, with a variable intertrial interval (mean of 20 s), and with a randomized and balanced order of CS+ and CS− across blocks. We added a new wrinkle to this standard eye-blink conditioning procedure; namely, we introduced a background contextual manipulation. In each trial, one of our standard set of 24 photos of women was displayed on a monitor in front of the subject. This photo remained on the screen throughout the conditioning trial, then a different photo was displayed at the beginning of the next trial. For half of the subjects, these background photos were paired randomly with the CS+/US (unconditioned stimulus) and CS−. For the other half of the subjects, the stimulus dimension of body size in the photo was correlated with the CS+/US (heavy body) and CS− (light body). Subjects were told nothing about the reasons for the photos on the monitor. Conditioning was assessed by recording blink amplitude and timing by means of electrodes placed near the eye. After completing the conditioning procedure, subjects were asked to describe any relationship they observed between the characteristics of the photos displayed on the monitor and the pattern of tones and air puffs.

Conditioning typically is reflected in two indexes over trials. First, subjects' eye-blink responses become differentiated, with an increased probability of blinking following a CS+ and a decreased probability of blinking following a CS−. Second, the eye-blink response following the CS+ gradually becomes intricately timed, achieving maximal closure 500 ms after the CS+, so that it coincides with the presentation of the US air puff.

We know that eye-blink conditioning depends on subcortical neural systems operating outside of awareness and beyond conscious control (Steinmetz & Thompson, 1994). We also know that conscious efforts to control this blink response actually interfere with both the discrimination and timing aspects of the conditioned response. Therefore, if eye-blink conditioning is facilitated by the presentation of background photos in which women's body size is correlated with the CS–US presentation, then this suggests that subjects probably are processing the body size information in the photos at a subcortical level.

As shown in Figure 5, the background photos facilitated conditioning when body size was correlated with the conditioning stimuli, but not when the photos were paired randomly with the conditioning stimuli. By the 9th and 10th blocks of trials, subjects in the body-size condition were blinking significantly more often following the CS+ than after the CS−, whereas subjects in the random condition showed no evidence of differential responding. Moreover, as illustrated in Figure 6, by the 9th and 10th blocks of trials, the conditioned eye-blink responses of subjects in the body-size condition were becoming well timed to avoid the air puff, occurring 500 ms after the CS+. Subjects in the random condition showed no such timing; if anything, their eye blinks were becoming less well timed over blocks. Interestingly, after the conditioning procedure was completed, many subjects could not provide a clear verbal account of the actual relationship

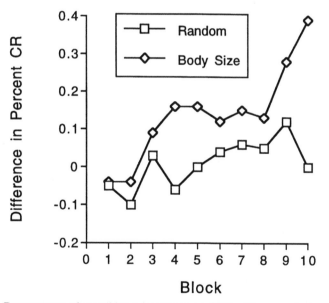

Figure 5. Percentage of conditioned responses (CR; difference between eye-blink responses to CS+ and CS−) for subjects in the random and body-size background photo conditions (from Treat, Katz, McFall, Viken, & Steinmetz, 1997). CS = conditioned stimulus.

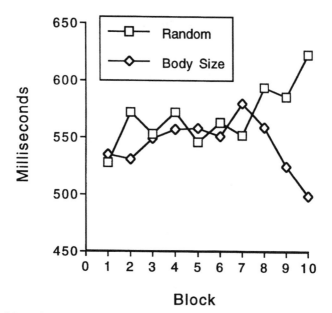

Figure 6. Mean latency (milliseconds) to peak eye-blink response following CS+ for subjects in the random and body size background photo conditions (from Treat, Katz, McFall, Viken, & Steinmetz, 1997). CS = conditioned stimulus.

between the background photos and either the CS or the US. All of these results support the view that the perceptual structures exert at least part of their influence at a preverbal, subcortical level.

CHILDREN'S PERCEPTION OF THEIR OWN PEER GROUPS

In all of the studies presented thus far, MDS methods have been used to capture the structures imposed by adult subjects on standard stimulus sets consisting of normatively defined photos representing two-dimensional spaces selected for their theoretical and clinical interest. It would be a mistake, however, to leave the impression that MDS methods are limited to these populations, paradigms, or theoretical questions. To illustrate the wide range of potential applications, we conclude our research tour with a study in which MDS methods were used to map children's perception of their own peer-group structures.

The impetus for this study was the skepticism of our colleague, A. Michele Lease, about the utility of conventional approaches for analyzing the structure of children's social relationships. Typically, researchers interested in children's social relationships have imposed their own preconceptions on these relationships and have asked research questions designed to verify these preconceptions. For example, it now is customary for researchers to classify children into one of five status categories of "social acceptance" based on peer-nomination data (i.e., popular, rejected, neglected, controversial, or average). Lease, McFall, Treat, and Viken (1997) took a different approach, using MDS methods to examine the structure of children's social relationships as seen through the eyes of the children themselves. The results generated by this new method then were compared with the results obtained by conventional methods. Although space limitations prevent a detailed summary of this research, a synopsis may give readers the flavor of the work and convey some of its promise.

Participants were 36 fifth graders and 37 sixth graders from four classrooms in two midwestern elementary schools (47% female, 53% male; all Caucasian; 71% mean classroom participation rate). They completed three tasks in a fixed order, with no apparent difficulty.

1. *MDS similarity ratings*: They rated the "similarity" of all possible pairs of same-sex classmates on a 7-point scale (total number of ratings ranged from 21 to 55), defining "similarity" for themselves.
2. *Behavioral ratings*: They rated each same-sex classmate on a list of 12 behaviors, using a 5-point scale to indicate how well each behavior described each classmate. (The behavioral data will not be discussed here.)
3. *Sociometric nominations*: Each child nominated three same-sex peers in each of two categories ("play with the most" and "play with the least" during free time).

These nomination data were standardized within groups (class and sex), and traditional indexes of *social preference* ("like most" minus "like least"; LM − LL) and *social impact* (LM + LL) were derived. In addition, these nomination data were used to generate a new pairwise social variable, called *mutual liking*. Each pair of classmates was given a score on a 4-point scale (1 = *reciprocal LL nominations*; 2 = *one child nominated the other as LL*; 3 = *one child nominated the other as LM*; 4 = *reciprocal LM nominations*; no score was entered when neither child nominated the other as LL or LM, or when one child was nominated for LL whereas the other was nominated for LM).

Two-dimensional MDS solutions provided remarkably good fits to the similarity-rating data for each of the eight peer groups (median badness-of-fit was .15 for boys, .17 for girls). Figures 7 and 8 display the MDS results for two groups of girls (with fictitious names). Superimposed on the MDS similarity-rating configuration are lines summarizing the mutual-liking data (solid lines connect pairs with reciprocal LM nominations; dashed lines connect pairs with reciprocal LL nominations). To interpret these figures, recall that the distance between girls reflects their degree of similarity as perceived by their peers—the closer, the more similar. As

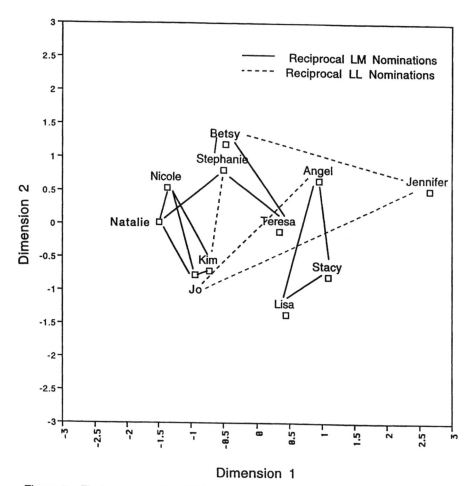

Figure 7. First example of multidimensional scaling configuration (with fabricated names) of peer-group structure, based on pairwise similarity ratings of the peer group, with an overlay of mutual-liking pattern for the same group, showing pairs with reciprocated like-most or like-least nominations (from Lease, McFall, Treat, & Viken, 1997). LM = like most; LL = like least.

these figures illustrate, there was a striking correspondence between the MDS similarity-rating configuration and the mutual liking variable. In fact, MDS analyses of the pairwise mutual-liking data accounted for 20% to 50% of the variability (R^2) in seven of the eight MDS similarity-rating configurations. In comparison, traditional social preference and social impact indexes showed little correspondence with the MDS configuration. One advantage of the mutual-liking variable over the traditional indexes is that it summarizes each child's pairwise social status within the context of the entire peer group.

Qualitative analyses of the MDS configurations suggested that they provided meaningful, interpretable snapshots of same-sex peer-group struc-

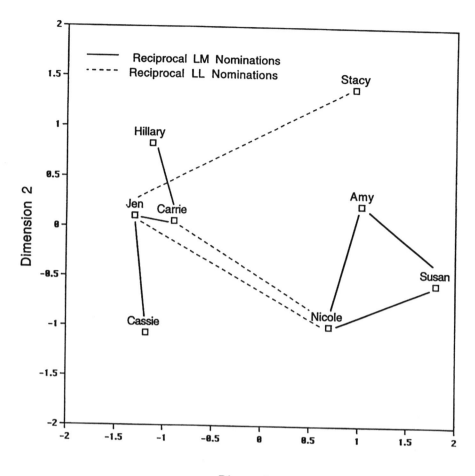

Figure 8. Second example of multidimensional scaling configuration (with fabricated names) of peer-group structure, based on pairwise similarity ratings of the peer group, with an overlay of mutual-liking pattern for the same group, showing pairs with reciprocated like-most or like-least nominations (from Lease, McFall, Treat, & Viken, 1997). LM = like most; LL = like least.

tures within these classrooms. Structural differences across classrooms are interesting, for example. Note that the configuration in Figure 7 is spaced much more closely and uniformly than is the configuration in Figure 8, in which two distinct social groups emerge. Both figures reveal the presence of an isolated outlier (Jennifer, Stacy). MDS outliers are not necessarily the same individuals who would have been detected as "at risk" by traditional methods that classify children as "neglected" or "rejected." Overall, the graphic portraits of classroom social structures yielded by MDS solutions for the similarity ratings and mutual-liking variable seem promising. Our enthusiasm was bolstered by the remarkably consistent pattern of results we obtained in a replication study involving 92 fifth graders from five more classrooms.

CONCLUSION

These examples from our own research illustrate how we have borrowed three tools from cognitive science (MDS, prototype classification task, category learning task) and one tool from neuroscience (classical eyeblink conditioning paradigm) in an effort to advance our understanding of three clinical problems (men's sexually coercive behavior; eating disorders among women; and children's peer-group relations). Our purpose in describing this research was not to provide a "how-to" guide on specific methods. When describing MDS, for instance, we glossed over many details and complications, such as computational issues, and the factors involved in choosing among different models, assumptions, and statistical methods.

Nor was it our purpose to promote these specific methods alone. The particular methods we used in our research certainly are not the only possibilities and may not be the most powerful for all circumstances. We chose them because they were well-suited to our specific research questions; other methods may be better-suited to other questions. To illustrate the range of possible methods and the importance of matching methods to questions, we point to two additional examples involving research into two different clinical problems: schizophrenia and emotion.

Neufeld and his colleagues (see Neufeld & Williamson, 1996, for a review) have used a variety of cognitive science methods to map the neurophysiological underpinnings of schizophrenia. Among other things, they have used MDS to compare perceptions of verbal information between individuals with schizophrenia and normal individuals; have used template matching in a memory-search task to compare encoding of information between paranoid and nonparanoid schizophrenics; have used recall of categorical word lists to assess mnemonic organization in schizophrenics; have used a visual recognition task in which information is presented tachistoscopically to each eye in order to assess lateralization abnormalities in schizophrenia; and have used performance indexes, such as response latencies and the variance of response times, to test quantitative models of information-processing deficits specific to paranoid schizophrenia.

Lang and his colleagues (see Lang, 1995, for a review) have used a different combination of physiological and cognitive methods to build and test a theory of human emotion focused on fear and anxiety. The theory is formulated explicitly within an information-processing framework, while being grounded firmly in the underlying neurophysiology. Emotions are hypothesized to be response dispositions (states of readiness or vigilance) driven by two motivational systems (appetitive and aversive). To test specific predictions derived from the theory, Lang and his colleagues used a "startle probe" paradigm to sample response dispositions under varying emotional conditions. Specifically, they assessed subjects' startle responses (electromyograph amplitude and latency of the early eye-blink reflex) to acoustic and visual stimulus probes presented while the subjects were viewing photos with predefined affective valence and level of arousal. Psychophysiological measures (e.g., heart-rate acceleration; blood-pressure level; and electrodermal reactivity) were gathered concomitantly.

Our purpose in describing our own research, as well as these additional examples, has been to highlight the potential benefits of bringing clinical science into closer alignment with the contemporary theories and methods of cognitive and neural science. We believe that these examples illustrate the potential power of hybrid clinical–cognitive–neuroscience models.

Finally, we believe that some clinical theories of cognitive processing, such as Kelly's (1955) *Psychology of Personal Constructs*, may achieve their full promise at last, thanks to the emerging cognitive methodologies that make it possible to put important theoretical ideas to the rigorous experimental tests they deserve. Clinical psychologists should welcome this challenge, adopting only the most powerful theories and methods, whatever their source, and following the path carved by the empirical, experimental evidence, wherever it may lead. As clinical psychology begins its second century, the time is ripe for this kind of hybrid "cognitive revolution."

REFERENCES

Ashby, F. G., & Townsend, J. T. (1986). Varieties of perceptual independence. *Psychological Review, 93,* 154–179.

Boring, E. G. (1957). *A history of experimental psychology* (2nd ed.). New York: Appleton-Century-Crofts.

Breuer, J., & Freud, S. (1895). *Studies on hysteria.* Leipzig, Germany: Franz Deuticke.

Bruder, G. E., Stewart, J. W., Mercier, M. A., Agosti, V., Leite, P., Donovan, S., & Quitkin, F. M. (1997). Outcome of cognitive–behavioral therapy for depression: Relation to hemispheric dominance for verbal processing. *Journal of Abnormal Psychology, 106,* 138–144.

Bruner, J. S., Goodnow, J. J., & Austin, G. A. (1956). *A study of thinking.* New York: Wiley.

Burke, J. (1996). *The pinball effect: How renaissance water gardens made the carburetor possible—and other journeys through knowledge.* Boston: Little, Brown.

Cohen, J. (1994). The earth is round ($p < .05$). *American Psychologist, 49,* 997–1003.

Cooper, M. J., & Fairburn, C. G. (1992). Selective processing of eating, weight and shape related words in patients with eating disorders and dieters. *British Journal of Clinical Psychology, 31*, 363–365.

Cronbach, L. J. (1957). The two disciplines of scientific psychology. *American Psychologist, 12*, 671–684.

Davison, M. L. (1983). *Multidimensional scaling.* New York: Wiley.

Fechner, G. T. (1860). *Elements of psychophysics* (Vol. I). Leipzig, Germany: Breit-kopf & Härtel.

Feynman, R. P. (1985). *QED: The strange theory of light and matter.* Princeton, NJ: Princeton University Press.

Gould, S. J. (1996a). *Full house: The spread of excellence from Plato to Darwin.* New York: Harmony Books.

Gould, S. J. (1996b). *The mismeasure of man* (Rev. ed.). New York: Norton.

Jones, L. E. (1983). Multidimensional models of social perception, cognition, and behavior. *Applied Psychological Measurement, 7*, 451–472.

Kelly, G. A. (1955). *The psychology of personal constructs* (2 vols.). New York: Norton.

Kihlstrom, J. F., & Cunningham, R. L. (1991). Mapping interpersonal space. In M. J. Horowitz (Ed.), *Person schemas and maladaptive interpersonal patterns* (pp. 311–336). Chicago: University of Chicago Press.

Kihlstrom, J. F., & Nasby, W. (1981). Cognitive tasks in clinical assessment: An exercise in applied psychology. In P. C. Kendall & S. D. Hollon (Eds.), *Assessment strategies for cognitive–behavioral interventions* (pp. 287–317). New York: Academic Press.

Kruschke, J. K. (1992). ALCOVE: An exemplar-based connectionist model of category learning. *Psychological Review, 99*, 22–44.

Kruskal, J. B., & Wish, M. (1978). *Quantitative applications in the social sciences: Multidimensional scaling* (Vol. 11). Newbury Park, CA: Sage.

Lang, P. J. (1995). The emotion probe: Studies of motivation and attention. *American Psychologist, 50*, 372–385.

Lang, P. J., & Cuthbert, B. N. (1984). Affective information processing and the assessment of anxiety. *Journal of Behavioral Assessment, 6*, 369–395.

Lease, A. M., McFall, R. M., Treat, T. A., & Viken, R. J. (1997). *Children's perception of their own peer groups: A view from the inside.* Unpublished manuscript, Indiana University, Department of Psychology, Bloomington, IN.

Lipton, D. N., McDonel, E. C., & McFall, R. M. (1987). Heterosocial perception in rapists. *Journal of Consulting and Clinical Psychology, 55*, 17–21.

Loftus, G. R. (1997). Psychology will be a much better science when we change the way we analyze data. *Current Directions in Psychological Science, 5*, 161–171.

Luce, R. D. (1963). Detection and recognition. In R. D. Luce, R. R. Bush, & E. Galanter (Eds.), *Handbook of mathematical psychology* (Vol. 1, pp. 103–189). New York: Wiley.

Macmillan, N. A., & Creelman, C. D. (1991). *Detection theory: A user's guide.* Cambridge, England: Cambridge University Press.

Malamuth, N. M., & Brown, L. M. (1994). Sexually aggressive men's perceptions of women's communications: Testing three explanations. *Journal of Personality and Social Psychology, 67,* 699–712.

McClelland, D. C. (1973). Testing for competence rather than for "intelligence." *American Psychologist, 28,* 1–14.

McDonel, E. C., & McFall, R. M. (1991). Construct validity of two heterosocial perception skill measures for assessing rape proclivity. *Violence and Victims, 6,* 17–30.

McFall, R. M., & Dodge, K. A. (1982). Self-management and interpersonal skills learning. In P. Karoly & F. Kanfer (Eds.), *Self-management and behavior change: From theory to practice* (pp. 353–392). New York: Pergamon Press.

McFall, R. M., & McDonel, E. C. (1986). The continuing search for units of analysis in psychology: Beyond persons, situations, and their interactions. In R. O. Nelson & S. C. Hayes (Eds.), *Conceptual foundations of behavioral assessment* (pp. 201—241). New York: Guilford Press.

McFall, R. M., & Treat, T. A. (in press). Quantifying the information value of clinical assessments with signal detection theory. *Annual Review of Psychology, 50.*

McFall, R. M., Treat, T. A., & Viken, R. J. (1997). Contributions of cognitive theory to new behavioral treatments. *Psychological Science, 8,* 174–176.

Medin, D. L., & Schaffer, M. M. (1978). Context theory of classification learning. *Psychological Review, 85,* 207–238.

Meehl, P. E. (1973). *Psychodiagnosis: Selected papers.* Minneapolis: University of Minnesota Press.

Meehl, P. E. (1978). Theoretical risks and tabular asterisks. Sir Karl, Sir Ronald, and the slow progress of soft psychology. *Journal of Consulting and Clinical Psychology, 46,* 806–834.

Meehl, P. E., Klann, R., Schmieding, A., Breimeier, K., & Schroeder-Slomann, S. (1958). *"What, then, is man?"* St. Louis, MO: Concordia.

Mischel, W., & Shoda, Y. (1995). A cognitive–affective system theory of personality: Reconceptualizing situations, dispositions, dynamics, and invariance in personality structure. *Psychological Review, 102,* 246–268.

Nasby, W., & Kihlstrom, J. F. (1986). Cognitive assessment of personality and psychopathology. In R. E. Ingram (Ed.), *Information processing approaches to clinical psychology* (pp. 217–239). Orlando, FL: Academic Press.

Neufeld, R. W. J., & Williamson, P. C. (1996). Neuropsychological correlates of positive symptoms: Delusions and hallucinations. In C. Pantelis, H. E. Nelson, & T. R. E. Barnes (Eds.), *Schizophrenia: A neuropsychological perspective* (pp. 205–235). New York: Wiley.

Nisbett, R. E., & Wilson, T. D. (1977). Telling more than we can know: Verbal reports on mental processes. *Psychological Review, 84,* 231–259.

Nosofsky, R. M. (1984). Choice, similarity, and the context theory of classification.

Journal of Experimental Psychology: Learning, Memory, and Cognition, 10, 104–114.

Nosofsky, R. M. (1986). Attention, similarity, and the identification–categorization relationship. *Journal of Experimental Psychology: General, 115,* 39–57.

Nosofsky, R. M. (1992). Similarity scaling and cognitive process models. *Annual Review of Psychology, 43,* 25–53.

Nosofsky, R. M., Kruschke, J. K., & McKinley, S. C. (1992). Combining exemplar-based category representations and connectionist learning rules. *Journal of Experimental Psychology: Learning, Memory, and Cognition, 18,* 211–233.

Persons, J. B., & Foa, E. B. (1984). Processing of fearful and neutral information by obsessive–compulsives. *Behaviour Research and Therapy, 22,* 259–265.

Platt, J. R. (1964). Strong inference. *Science, 146,* 347–353.

Polya, G. (1957). *How to solve it: A new aspect of mathematical method* (2nd ed.). Princeton, NJ: Princeton University Press.

Popper, K. (1962). *Conjectures and refutations.* New York: Basic Books.

Rapaport, K., & Burkhart, B. R. (1984). Personality and attitudinal characteristics of sexually coercive college males. *Journal of Abnormal Psychology, 93,* 216–221.

Rotter, J. B. (1954). *Social learning and clinical psychology.* Englewood Cliffs, NJ: Prentice Hall.

Rudy, T. E., & Merluzzi, T. V. (1984). Recovering social–cognitive schemata: Descriptions and applications of multidimensional scaling for clinical research. *Advances in Cognitive–Behavioral Research and Therapy, 3,* 61–102.

Sarbin, T. R., Taft, R., & Bailey, D. E. (1960). *Clinical inference and cognitive theory.* New York: Holt, Rinehart & Winston.

Schiffman, S. S., Reynolds, M. L., & Young, F. W. (1981). *Introduction to multidimensional scaling: Theory, methods, and applications.* Orlando, FL: Academic Press.

Sears, L. L., Finn, P. R., & Steinmetz, J. E. (1994). Abnormal classical eye-blink conditioning in autism. *Journal of Autism and Developmental Disorders, 24,* 737–751.

Shepard, R. N. (1957). Stimulus and response generalization: A stochastic model relating generalization to distance in psychological space. *Psychometrika, 22,* 325–345.

Shepard, R. N. (1958a). Stimulus and response generalization: Deduction of the generalization gradient from a trace model. *Psychological Review, 65,* 242–256.

Shepard, R. N. (1958b). Stimulus and response generalization: Tests of a model relating generalization to distance in psychological space. *Journal of Experimental Psychology, 55,* 509–523.

Smith, M. C., & Thelen, M. H. (1984). Development and validation of a test for bulimia. *Journal of Consulting and Clinical Psychology, 52,* 863–872.

SPSS, Inc. (1992). *SPSS for Windows professional statistics.* Chicago: Author.

Steinmetz, J. E., & Thompson, R. F. (1994). Brain substrates of aversive classical conditioning. In J. Madden, IV (Ed.), *Neurobiology of learning, emotion, and affect* (pp. 97–120). New York: Raven Press.

Swets, J. A. (1996). *Signal detection theory and ROC analysis in psychology and diagnostics: Collected papers.* Mahwah, NJ: Erlbaum.

Townsend, J. T. (1990). Truth and consequences of ordinal differences in statistical distributions: Toward a theory of hierarchical inference. *Psychological Bulletin, 108,* 551–567.

Townsend, J. T., & Ashby, F. G. (1984). Measurement scales and statistics: The misconception misconceived. *Psychological Bulletin, 96,* 394–401.

Treat, T. A., Katz, D. B., McFall, R. M., Viken, R. J., & Steinmetz, J. E. (1997). *Cognitive influences on classical eye-blink conditioning: Implications for cognition and brain functions.* Unpublished research, Indiana University, Department of Psychology, Bloomington, IN.

Viken, R. J., Treat, T. A., & McFall, R. M. (1997). *Individual differences in men's perception of women: Does cognitive structure influence category learning?* Unpublished manuscript, Indiana University, Department of Psychology, Bloomington, IN.

Viken, R. J., Treat, T. A., Nosofsky, R. M., McFall, R. M., & Palmeri, T. (1997). *Cognitive structure and bulimia: Women's differential perception of affect and body size.* Unpublished manuscript, Indiana University, Department of Psychology, Bloomington, IN.

Viken, R. J., Vazques, H. A., & Treat, T. A. (1996). *Reliability of individual differences in women's perception of body size and affect.* Unpublished manuscript, Indiana University, Department of Psychology, Bloomington, IN.

III

INTERVENTIONS

8

THE PREDICTION AND PREVENTION OF DEPRESSION

MARTIN E. P. SELIGMAN

In this chapter, I will first explore the relationship of optimism and pessimism to depression. Then I will examine what I take to be an "epidemic of depression" in the United States, taking a speculative detour to ask the question of why there is so much depression today, particularly among young people. Finally, I will discuss the possibility of preventing depression in young adults and in children.

The background to my present work begins with an embarrassing fact that kept recurring in my previous learned helplessness experiments: After inescapable shock, one third of subjects—whether they were dogs, rats, or humans—did not become helpless, another one tenth on average were helpless just to begin. About 20 years ago, Lyn Abramson, Lauren Alloy, and Judy Garber tried to convince me that what modulated whether or not a human being became helpless was the personality trait of optimism or pessimism. This trait became the notion of explanatory style (Buchanan & Seligman, 1995).

This work is supported by National Institute of Mental Health Grants MH19604 and MH52270. Part of the discussion of self-esteem was adapted from *The Optimistic Child* (Seligman, Reivich, Jaycox, & Gillham, 1995).

EXPLANATORY STYLE

There are three dimensions to explanatory style. The first, unfortunately the easiest to remember but the least important for the theory, is *internal/external*, the extent to which you blame factors having to do with yourself as opposed to blaming factors having to do with other people or circumstances. The theory says if you chronically blame yourself for what happens, then when you fail, your self-esteem will go down, and you will feel guilty and worthless. On the other hand, if you chronically blame other people or circumstances, your self-esteem and self-worth will not go down when you fail; rather, you get angry. So if you do not get the job you want, you might think, "I'm stupid" (internal), or on the other hand, you might think, "There's a recession going on in the world" (external). So internal style for bad events produces low self-esteem in the face of bad events, whereas an external style leaves self-esteem intact, but produces anger.

The next dimension of the theory—*stable/unstable*—is the much more important question of whether or not you chronically find permanent, unchangeable factors that cause your failures, or whether you find changeable, temporary ones. So you might think, "I'm stupid" if you do not get the job. Stupidity abides; it is stable and apt to be around the next time you try; on the other hand, you might think, "I didn't try hard" or "I was in a bad mood" or "I had a hangover." These latter explanations are all changeable, temporary factors. According to this theory, if you chronically blame stable factors, then when you fail, you will show depression and helplessness for a long period of time. On the other hand, if you chronically find temporary factors, you will be resilient from depression and helplessness.

The final dimension of the theory is whether or not the factor you invoke is usually *pervasive* and *global* or whether it is *local* and *specific*. So if you do not get the job you want, you might think, "I'm stupid." Stupidity is going to hurt you in many circumstances (global), or you might think, "I have no talent at selling" (specific). The theory says if you chronically find global factors, then you are going to do badly across several domains when you fail. For example, if your marriage is going badly, and you think you are a stupid and unlikable person, then you are going to do badly at work. On the other hand, if you can usually find specific factors, then when you are doing badly at work, you will still be able to do well in your love life.

If you put all of those considerations together, pessimists, from the point of view of this theory, are people who chronically say to themselves, "It's me," "It's going to last forever," and "It's going to undermine everything I do."

That was the theory that my colleagues and I advanced about 20 years ago (Abramson, Seligman, & Teasdale, 1978). We then devised a questionnaire to measure explanatory style and developed a content-analytic method to derive explanatory style from verbatim utterances (Peterson, Luborsky, & Seligman, 1983; Peterson et al., 1982). When we first formulated the theory, we began to look at different populations of depressed adults and found that, indeed, pessimistic explanatory style correlated reasonably well with depression of various kinds. But a simple correlation was not very exciting, because the theory says that pessimism is more than a correlate of depression (it is of course a primary *symptom* of depression), but it is a risk factor just like cigarette smoking is a risk factor for later lung cancer. We then conducted a series of experiments when students arrived at class for the fall semester several years in a row. We measured their explanatory style and their depression, and 6 weeks later, we asked the students what would count as a failure for them on the mid-term exam. The mean response was B plus, which was very good because it meant that almost everyone was going to be a subject in this experiment. A week later they got their mid-term exam, which was very hard, and a week later they got back their grades along with the copy of a depression inventory.

Who got markedly more depressed after doing badly in their own eyes in the mid-term? Thirty percent of the students who scored as pessimists on the explanatory style questionnaire became markedly more depressed. Thirty percent of the students who failed the mid-term in their own eyes became markedly more depressed; but 70% of the students who were both pessimists to begin with and then failed their mid-term became markedly more depressed (Metalsky, Abramson, Seligman, Semmel, & Peterson, 1982). There are currently a rather large number of studies that have looked longitudinally at depression with parallel findings (Buchanan & Seligman, 1995). Among University of Pennsylvania (UP) undergraduates, if you score in the bottom quartile of pessimism, you have two to eight times the risk of encountering moderate to severe depressive symptoms over the next 3 years.

PESSIMISM AND THERAPY

Rob DeRubeis and Steve Hollon (DeRubeis et al., 1990) have been asking the question, What are the active ingredients in different kinds of therapies? There are basically four kinds of treatments that all work moderately well—60% to 70% of the time in moderate and severe depression. They are antidepressant medications, electroconvulsive shock, interpersonal therapy, and cognitive therapy (CT), which Aaron Beck and Albert Ellis invented about 20 years ago (Beck, Rush, Shaw, & Emery, 1979; Ellis, 1962). CT is the most relevant to the alleviation of pessimism in depression. There are three things to be said about CT and pessimism: First, by looking at different psychological changes during CT and later changes in depression, we can ask, What are the active ingredients? The change from pessimism to optimism is a substantial active ingredient (DeRubeis et al., 1990). The second fact is that disputing pessimistic thoughts, a basic skill of CT, is a "sticky" skill, because when you become a good disputer, it maintains itself: The change from pessimism to optimism that is learned in CT for depression is stable and lasting (Seligman et al., 1988). Third, if you try to predict who relapses from depression (and depression is a recurring disorder), it is the people who do not change from pessimism to optimism who tend to relapse (Seligman et al., 1988).

EPIDEMIOLOGY OF DEPRESSION

In the course of working on depression over the past 30 years, two remarkable changes have happened: First, there is roughly 10 times as much of it now as there was between 30 and 40 years ago. Because this is the only order of magnitude effect that I know in the social sciences, let me say something about why people think this is the case. In the late 1970s, the National Institute of Mental Health decided to try to find out how many of the different mental illnesses there were in the United States (Robins et al., 1984). For the first time, a huge sample, 10,000 representative Americans, were investigated to discover the lifetime prevalence of these major mental illnesses. The sample was so large that the prevalence changes across the century could be charted. The subjects ranged in age from young people to people in their 90s, and they were asked about each of the symptoms of depression (which avoids the problem of a change in the meaning of the label "depressed" over time): for example, Was there ever a time in your life when you try to kill yourself? Was there ever a time in your life when you lost 20 lb in a month without trying or dieting? and so on.

Because such a large number of adults of different ages were interviewed, the study gave the first picture ever of mental illness over many years and made it possible to trace the changes that had taken place over the course of the 20th century. The single most surprising change was in the lifetime prevalence of depression. The lifetime prevalence of a disorder is the percentage of the population that has had it at least once in their lifetime. When the statisticians looked at these findings, they saw something very odd. The findings showed that the people born around 1925— who, because they were old had more chance to develop the disorder— had not suffered from depression much at all. Only 4% of them ever had severe depression by the time they were well into middle age. And when the statisticians looked at the findings for people born even earlier—before World War I—they found something even more surprising. Again, the lifetime prevalence had not climbed, as one would have thought; only a mere 1% had depression by the time they were in old age. But of people born around 1955, who had the least opportunity to develop depression, 7% already had been severely depressed by their early 20s.

So there has been at least a tenfold increase in depression over roughly 50 years. But not only is severe depression much more common now, it also attacks its victims much younger. If you were born in the 1930s and later had a depressed relative, your own first depression, if you had one, struck on average between the ages of 30 and 35. If you were born in 1956, your first depression struck on average between ages 20 and 25—10 years sooner.

This trend is still accelerating—more depression, beginning younger and younger. Peter Lewinsohn, an eminent West Coast depression researcher, and his colleagues gave diagnostic interviews to 1,710 randomly selected western Oregon adolescents. By age 14, 7.2% of the youngest adolescents born in 1972–1974 had a severe depression; in contrast, 4.5% of the older adolescents, born in 1968–1971, had a severe depression (Lewinsohn, Rohde, Seeley, & Fischer, 1993). "Severe" means marked symptoms of low mood, cognitive impairment, passivity, and bodily changes. In another study that measured the prevalence of full-blown depressive disorder in 3,000 youths 12–14 years old in the southeastern United States, 9% had experienced a major depressive disorder (Garrison, Addy, Jackson, et al., 1992). Numbers this large are unprecedented.

To those of us who work with depression, this high a percentage of youths suffering severe depression and depressive disorder at such a young age is nothing short of astonishing and dismaying. Because severe depression recurs in about half of those who have had it once, the extra years of depression when it occurs 10 or 20 years early add up to an ocean of tears.

WHY AN EPIDEMIC OF DEPRESSION?

Why should it be, in a nation in which the hands on the nuclear clock are far away from midnight, in a nation that has more money, more power, more records, more books, more education, and on and on and on, that depression should be so much more prevalent than it was when the nation was younger, when it was less prosperous and less powerful?

I want to speculate about three things, and I want to emphasize the third one because it is the one you may find the least congenial. The first factor is that, in general, depression is a disorder of the "I," failing in your own eyes relative to your goals. In a society in which individualism is becoming more rampant, I think the "I" is bigger than it has ever been. People who believe that they are the only thing in the world are more set up for depression than people who have a large "we," which is the second factor. When our grandparents failed, they had comfortable spiritual furniture that they could sit in. Most of them had their relationship with God, their relationship with a nation they believed in (patriotism), their relationship with a community, and a large extended family. Faith in God, community, nation, and the large extended family has eroded in the past 40 years. So the second factor is that the spiritual furniture that we used to sit in, which has traditionally buffered us against the problems of depression, has fallen into disuse.

SPECULATIONS ON THE SELF-ESTEEM MOVEMENT

But it is the third factor, the self-esteem movement, that I want to emphasize. I have five children who range from 4 to 27 years of age, so I have had the privilege of reading children's books every night for a whole generation, and there has been a sea change in children's books in the past 25 years. Twenty-five years ago (during the Great Depression), the emblematic children's book was *The Little Engine That Could*. It is about doing well in the world, about overcoming obstacles. Now the emblematic children's books are about feeling good, having high self-esteem, and exuding confidence.

There is something called the self-esteem movement which started, not surprisingly, in California in the 1960s. The California legislature in 1989 sponsored a report that suggested that self-esteem be taught in every classroom (*Toward a State of Esteem*, 1990). This is a movement with teeth; this is the movement underlying the demise of IQ testing. This is the movement underlying the end of tracking in public schools, lest children on lower tracks feel bad about themselves. This is the movement that has made competition a dirty word. This is a movement that has led to less plain old hard work. Shirley MacLaine suggested to President Clinton that he create a cabinet-level secretary of self-esteem.

I believe that self-esteem is just a meter, an epiphenomenon that reads out the state of the system. Basically, when you are doing well in school, when you are doing well with the people you love, when you are doing well in sports, it registers high. When you are doing badly, it registers low. I scoured the self-esteem literature looking for the causality as opposed to correlation, looking for any evidence that high self-esteem *causes* better grades, more popularity, less teenage pregnancy, less dependence on welfare, as is claimed in California. There is a simple experimental design that perfectly separates cause from correlation: Take a group of children in September, all the B students, for instance; measure their self-esteem, and come back in June. If self-esteem causes grade change, the B students with high self-esteem will tend to go up to As, and the B students with low self-esteem will go down toward Cs. There is nothing of this causal sort to be found in the literature.

In the campaign to feel good and to enjoy high self-esteem, Americans began to believe that we should strive to avoid dysphoria—anger, sadness, and anxiety. These were deemed inconveniences to be banished altogether if possible, and certainly to be minimized. The self-esteem movement may destroy self-esteem because, in attempting to cushion bad feeling, it also minimizes the three good uses of feeling bad.

Anxiety, depression, and anger all scream out for you to terminate them. This is indeed their reason for being: They galvanize you into action to change yourself or your world, and by doing so, to terminate the negative emotion. It is natural to want to avoid feeling bad, and when it comes to our children, we instinctively rush in to protect them from negative feelings. The feel-good society legitimizes this impulse.

GOOD USES OF FEELING BAD

But feeling bad has three crucial uses, and all of them are needed for learning optimism and for escaping helplessness. Dysphoria—principally, anxiety, depression, and anger—has a long history in evolutionary theory. These states are not mere inconveniences. Each bears a message for you. Anxiety warns you that danger is around. Sadness informs you that a loss threatens. Anger alerts you to the possibility of trespass. All these messages of necessity carry pain, and it is this very pain that makes it impossible to ignore what is going wrong and goads you to act to remove the threat.

The first good use of feeling bad is that dysphoria bears a message. Bad feeling is far from being a flawless system. Many, perhaps most of its messages are false alarms—your wife is not having an affair, your boss is not thinking of firing you, the paper boy did not intend to humiliate you by throwing the paper under the sprinkler. A worse flaw is that when the feelings become chronic and paralyzing, and when they set off too many false alarms, we call this state "emotional illness," and we try to dampen it with drugs or correct it with psychotherapy. But dysphoria's primary virtue is that most of the time, the system is your first line of defense against danger, loss, and trespass.

The second good use of feeling bad concerns flow (Csikszentmihalyi, 1990). When does time stop for you? When do you feel truly at home, wanting to be nowhere else? Playing touch football, listening to Bruce Springsteen, speaking to a group, painting a fence or a picture, making love, writing a letter to the editor, or engaging in conversation about psychology? This state is called *flow*, and it is one of the highest states of positive emotion. It is a state that makes life worth living. Researchers have been studying it—who has it, when does it come, what impedes it— for two decades. Flow occurs when your skills are used to their utmost—

matched against a challenge just barely within your grasp. Too little challenge produces boredom. Too much challenge or too little skill produces helplessness and depression. Flow cannot be achieved without frustration. Success after success, unbroken by failure, regrouping, and trying again will not produce flow. Rewards alone, high self-esteem, confidence, and good cheer do not produce flow. The cushioning of frustration, the premature alleviation of anxiety, and learning to avoid the highest challenges all impede flow. A life without anxiety, frustration, competition, and challenge is not the good life; it is a life devoid of flow.

The third good use of bad feeling concerns the persistence needed to overcome helplessness. Any complicated task your child might undertake consists of several steps, each of which is more or less easy to fail at. If he fails at any step, tries again, and then succeeds at that step, he gets to go on to the next step. If the steps are not too numerous, and no one of them insurmountable, he will succeed—but only if he keeps trying after each subfailure. If he stops trying after any particular subfailure, he will fail at the whole task.

Every subfailure, as well as every big failure, produces bad feeling—some admixture of anxiety, sadness, and anger. These emotions, when moderate, are galvanizing, but they are also daunting. Your child has one of only two tactics available when he feels bad. He can stay in the situation and act, trying to terminate the emotion by changing the situation, or he can give up and leave the situation. This tactic also terminates the emotion by removing the situation altogether. The first tactic I call mastery, the second I call learned helplessness.

In order for your child to experience mastery, it is necessary for him to fail, to feel bad, and to try again repeatedly until success occurs. None of these steps can be circumvented. Failure and feeling bad are necessary building blocks for ultimate success and feeling good.

Almost all of life's most challenging tasks abound with subfailure. If they did not, someone else would have gotten there first—high-jumped 8 feet, won the big account, or made friends with the aloof boy who turns out to be the perfect lover. On rare occasions, having extraordinary talent or sheer good luck will shortcut many of the subfailures. But for most children, most of the time, little worth doing is accomplished without persistence.

Children need to fail. They need to feel sad, anxious, and angry. When we impulsively protect our children from failure, we deprive them of learning persistence skills. When they encounter obstacles, if we leap in to bolster self-esteem, to soften the blows, and to distract them with congratulatory ebullience, we make it harder for them to achieve mastery. And if we deprive them of mastery, we weaken self-esteem just as certainly as if we had belittled, humiliated, and physically thwarted them at every turn.

So it is no accident that the self-esteem movement in particular, and the feel-good ethic in general, had the untoward consequence of producing low self-esteem on a massive scale. By overcushioning feeling bad, it has made it that much harder for our children to feel good, to experience flow. By circumventing feelings of failure, it made it that much more difficult for our children to feel mastery. By blunting warranted sadness and anxiety, it created children at high risk for unwarranted depression. By encouraging cheap success, it produced a generation of very expensive failures.

Until January of 1996, I believed that self-esteem was merely a meter with little if any causal efficacy. The lead article in the journal *Psychological Review* convinced me that I was wrong and that self-esteem is causal: Roy Baumeister (1996) reviewed the literature on genocidal killers, on hit-men, on gang leaders, on violent criminals and argued that these perpetrators have high self-esteem, and that high self-esteem causes violence. His work suggests that if you teach unwarrantedly high self-esteem to children, a subgroup of these children will also have a mean streak in them. When these children confront the real world with this inflated self-esteem, and it tells them they are not as great as they have learned to believe, they will lash out with violence. So it is possible that the twin epidemics among young people in the United States today, depression and violence, both come from this misbegotten concern: valuing how our young people of today feel about themselves more highly than how we value how well they are doing in the world.

PREVENTION OF DEPRESSION

What can be done about the epidemic of depression? I will discuss two sets of projects both done at the University of Pennsylvania: one with young adults, UP freshmen, and the second with children right before puberty.

I preface this with a plea. The field of prevention in psychological work is impoverished, both intellectually and financially, and this impoverishment has a fascinating history. Something quite double-edged happened to all of applied psychology after World War II. The traditional mission of applied psychology is, I believe, threefold. One mission consists of taking disordered people and making them less disordered. The second mission consists of taking normal people and making their lives more fulfilling and productive. The third mission consists of nurturing genius and high talent. In 1946, the Veteran's Administration system began to fund clinical psychologists, and applied psychologists in the United States found they could make a good living curing mental disorders. In 1947, the national institute of mental illness, called the National Institute of Mental Health (NIMH), was founded, and academics found that they could get grants by pitching in with research relevant to the cure of mental disorders. Much of scientific and human value has been accomplished as a result, but psychology lost much of its concern for the normal person and for the very talented person. Psychology became a subject about repairing weakness and not a subject about building human strength. It is no accident that the American public regards psychologists as victimologists and as the pathologizers of American life, as the discipline that tries to excuse the Menendez brothers, and as the discipline that looks for child sexual abuse under every adult emotional problem.

It is also part of the reason that work on prevention of mental illness is impoverished. Thinking about notions of human strength rather than human weakness leads, I believe, more readily to effective strategies of prevention. I will hazard the guess that the prevention of the major mental illnesses will come to fruition when we understand how to build courage, persistence, interpersonal skills, honesty, optimism, hope, and resilience— when we understand the building of human strength. One of my central goals as president of the American Psychological Association is to remind the profession that psychology must concern itself with building human strength as well as with repairing weakness.

The prevention research that I now summarize is in line with this theme. The people who did the work with University of Pennsylvania undergraduates are Peter Shulman, Rob DeRubeis, Steve Hollon, Art Freeman, and Karen Reivich. This work has been supported by the (all-too-small) Prevention Research Branch of the National Institute of Mental Health.

Our logic is to take young people at risk for depression, teach them the skills of CT before they are depressed, and ask if we can thereby prevent depressive and anxiety disorders. Our study of UP freshmen at risk for depression started about 5 years ago. When students were admitted to the university and sent back their letter of acceptance, they then received a letter from me by return mail. It said, "Please take this questionnaire" (the Attributional Style Questionnaire); it turned out that 100% of the students sent the questionnaire back. We scored it, and students in the bottom quartile of pessimism received another letter from me saying that when they arrived in September, we were going to be running workshops about how to cope with this unfamiliar new environment; if they were willing, they would be randomized either into a control group or into one of these workshops. So for the past several years, the most pessimistic quartile of UP's freshman class has been in these workshops or has been in our assessment-only control group.

We teach two sets of skills in the workshop, which is conducted in groups of 10 by UP clinical graduate students. We teach people to be disputers of catastrophic thoughts and we teach them a set of behavioral skills, such as assertiveness training, graded task assignment, and stress management.

After 18 months of follow-up, I can report partial results, with 119 students in the control group and 106 students taking the 16-hour workshop. Every 6 months, each student has a complete diagnostic interview, and we look primarily at moderate and severe episodes of depression and anxiety. Thirty-two percent of the students in the control group have had a moderate to severe episode of depression in contrast to 22% of the group that was in the workshop ($p < .04$, one-tailed). Similar results obtained for generalized anxiety disorder (moderate only, because there were no severe episodes). Fifteen percent of the controls and only 7% of students who took the workshop had an episode of generalized anxiety disorder ($p < .02$, one-tailed). Mediation analyses found a significant mediator in the change from pessimism to optimism.

Finally, I turn to prevention among school children. The people who actually worked on this project are Karen Reivich, Jane Gillham, Rob DeRubeis, Lisa Jaycox, Steve Hollon, Andrew Shatte, and Peter Schulman, and we are supported by the NIMH Prevention Research Branch. We have done five studies in which we take 10- to 12-year-old children and teach them the parallel cognitive and behavioral antidepression skills before depression strikes. In these studies, we select children for two risk factors: mild symptoms of depression and parental fighting. We have found that each of these predicts depression in young children; so if a child scores high on a z score for these two, he or she is eligible for our training program. We teach these skills in "child" form, in groups of 10 after school, using skits, cartoons, role playing, and lots of refreshments.

I will only report one study here, the one with a 2-year term follow-up, done in Abington Township, near Philadelphia (Gillham, Reivich, Jaycox, & Seligman, 1995; Jaycox, Reivich, Gillham, & Seligman, 1994). Karen Reivich has done a parallel study in the inner city of Philadelphia, and Jane Gillham has done the study with parents and with children, teaching both the parents and the children the antidepression skills, as well as teaching the parents how to coach their children. Karen Reivich, Jane Gillham, and Andrew Shatte have taught teachers in the public schools to deliver the workshop and compared them with clinically trained psychology graduate students. These data are incomplete and will be presented in future papers.

Here are the results of the Abington study:

1. Over the 2-year follow-up, the percentage of children who show symptoms in the moderate to severe range of depression is shockingly high (between 20% and 45%).
2. The children who took the workshop have only about half the rate of moderate or severe depressive symptoms as the control group.

3. Immediately after the workshop, the untreated group has significantly more depressive symptoms than the group that took the workshop.

4. This difference gets bigger and bigger over time; that is, as the children in the control group go through puberty, get their first social and sexual rejections, move from top dog in middle school to the bottom of the heap in high school, they get more and more depressed. At 24 months, 44% of them are showing moderate to severe depressive symptoms, whereas only 22% of the workshop group have moderate or severe symptoms (Group $\times$ Time, $p < .05$).

We believe that this indicates that teaching children cognitive and behavioral antidepression skills before puberty, but late enough in childhood so that they are meta-cognitive (capable of thinking about thinking), is a fruitful strategy. We believe that when they use these skills to cope with the first rejections of puberty, they get better and better at using these skills, and the mediation analysis shows that the change from pessimism to optimism is a partial mediator of the prevention of depressive symptoms.

CONCLUSION

I believe that there is an epidemic of depression among young people in the United States today. Depression is not just about mental suffering; it is also about lower productivity and worse physical health. If this epidemic were to continue, I believe that the nation's place in the world would be in jeopardy. I believe that the United States will lose its economic place to less pessimistic nations, and it will sap our will to bring about social justice in this country. I therefore think it is urgent to end this epidemic.

This epidemic will not be ended by Prozac. We are not going to give antidepressant drugs to an entire generation of young Americans for two reasons. First, antidepressant drugs do not seem to be effective before puberty (Fisher & Fisher, 1997). Second, there are grave moral dangers to make an entire generation dependent on drugs for their mood and their productivity. We are also not going to do therapy with an entire generation. There are simply not enough good therapists to go around. But what I believe we can do is to take the skills that work effectively in psychotherapy, translate them into an educative mode, and, in the schools and homes of America, teach them to all children at risk for depression.

REFERENCES

Abramson, L. Y., Seligman, M. E. P., & Teasdale, I. (1978). Learned helplessness in humans: Critique and reformulation. *Journal of Abnormal Psychology, 87,* 49–59.

Baumeister, R. (1996). Relation of threatened egotism to violence and aggression: The dark side of high self-esteem. *Psychological Review, 103, 5–33.*

Beck, A. T., Rush, A. J., Shaw, B. F., & Emery, G. (1979). *Cognitive therapy of depression: A treatment manual.* New York: Guilford Press.

Buchanan, G. M., & Seligman, M. (Eds.). (1995). *Explanatory style.* Hillsdale, NJ: Erlbaum.

Csikszentmihalyi, M. (1990). *Flow.* New York: Harper.

DeRubeis, R., Evans, M., Hollon, S., Garvey, M., Grove, W., & Tuason, V. (1990). How does cognitive therapy work? A systematic investigation of cognitive and interpersonal therapy. *Journal of Consulting and Clinical Psychology, 50,* 862–869.

Ellis, A. (1962). *Reason and emotion in psychotherapy.* New York: Lyle Stuart.

Fisher, R. L., & Fisher, S. (1997). Are we justified in treating children with psychotropic drugs? In S. Fisher & R. P. Greenberg (Eds.), *From placebo to panacea: Putting psychiatric drugs to the test* (pp. 307–322). New York: Wiley.

Garrison, C., Addy, C., Jackson, K., et al. (1992). Major depressive disorder and dysthymia in young adolescents. *American Journal of Epidemiology, 135,* 792–802.

Gillham, J., Reivich, K., Jaycox, L., & Seligman, M. E. P. (1995). Prevention of depressive symptoms in school children: Two year follow up. *Psychological Science, 6, 343–351.*

Jaycox, L., Reivich, K., Gillham, J., & Seligman, M. E. P. (1994). Prevention of depressive symptoms in school children. *Behaviour Research and Therapy, 32,* 801–816.

Lewinsohn, P., Rohde, P., Seeley, J., & Fischer, S. (1993). Age–cohort changes in the lifetime occurrence of depression and other mental disorders. *Journal of Abnormal Psychology, 102,* 110–120.

Metalsky, G. I., Abramson, L. Y., Seligman, M. E. P., Semmel, A., & Peterson, C. (1982). Attributional styles and life events in the classroom: Vulnerability and invulnerability to depressive mood reactions. *Journal of Personality and Social Psychology, 43, 612–617.*

Peterson, C., Luborsky, L., & Seligman, M. E. P. (1983). Attributions and depressive mood shifts: A case study using the symptom-context method. *Journal of Abnormal Psychology, 92, 96–103.*

Peterson, C., Semmel, A., von Baeyer, C., Abramson, L. T., Metalsky, G. I., & Seligman, M. E. P. (1982). The attributional style questionnaire. *Cognitive Therapy and Research, 6, 287–300.*

Robins, L., Helzer, J., Weissman, M., Orvaschel, H., Gruenberg, E., Burke, J., &

Regier, D. (1984). Lifetime prevalence of specific psychiatric disorders in three sites. *Archives of General Psychiatry, 41*, 949–958.

Seligman, M. E. P., Castellon, C., Cacciola, J., Schulman, P., Luborsky, L., Ollove, M., & Downing, R. (1988). Explanatory style change during cognitive therapy for unipolar depression. *Journal of Abnormal Psychology, 97*, 1–6.

Seligman, M., Reivich, K., Jaycox, L., & Gillham, J. (1995). *The optimistic child.* Boston: Houghton Mifflin.

Toward a state of esteem. (1990). Sacramento: California Department of Education.

9

EXPECTATIONS FOR AND EVALUATIONS OF PSYCHOSOCIAL TREATMENT OF YOUTHS WITH ANXIETY DISORDERS

PHILIP C. KENDALL

My research, for over two decades, has had a dual focus on (a) the nature of childhood and adolescent disorders and (b) how this basic research knowledge contributes to successful interventions. Relatedly, my work concerns evaluations of the efficacy and effectiveness (Hoagwood, Hibbs, Brent, & Jensen, 1995) of psychosocial treatments for child and adolescent disorders. Several trends in recent history were concurrent with my work, including the following three: (a) The Institute of Medicine (1989) convened a board that documented the need and set forth a plan for the study of effective interventions for youths; (b) there has been an increase in the number of studies addressing issues pertinent to the nature of and interventions for childhood disorders; and (c) the National Institute of Mental Health has arranged a separate review panel for research pro-

Research reported in this chapter was supported or facilitated by several grants from the National Institute of Mental Health (MH44042)

posals addressing the treatment of child and adolescent disorders. It is my belief that the next century of clinical psychology will, consistent with Witmer's (1897) initial step, move forward in developing, evaluating, and disseminating programs of intervention for specific psychopathologies of youths.

Two childhood disorders have been central to my work: (a) impulsivity and (b) anxiety. At first, I was primarily involved in addressing questions such as "What are the features of the cognitive problems in impulsive children and how do we best treat them?" (Kendall & Braswell, 1985, 1993). But impulsivity as a topic for psychologists declined and was rapidly replaced by attention deficit disorder (ADD), ADD replaced by attention deficit hyperactivity disorder (ADHD), and the eventual widespread increase in the number of youths accurately and inaccurately receiving this diagnosis. In part, the rapid endorsement of ADHD as a primary concern for child clinical psychology is linked to the widespread prescription of medications. Relatedly, I have witnessed the increasing inaccuracy in the use of this diagnostic category. It struck me that the field was being pushed by outside forces to treat the children who bothered adults. Parents or teachers would say "I can't deal with this child," and mental health professionals would be asked to provide a remedy. Children with ADHD often bother others, and the adults they bother then refer them for professional assistance. These sociopolitical events, and the fact that our treatment modified impulsivity (e.g., Kendall & Braswell, 1982) but had limitations when applied for ADHD, detracted from my continued interest in impulsivity.

There are nevertheless numerous other children with severe emotional distress—youths who are not disruptive to class and do not tire and frustrate parents. Often, these youths keep their distress to themselves, suffer internally, and typically go without professional assistance. Anxious youths do not self-refer. To the extent youths with an anxiety disorder are developing misinformation about their world, expecting dire consequences from their actions, misperceiving excessive demands in the environment, and underestimating their ability to be productive, they are taking their unwanted anxious distress with them into their adolescent and early adult years. With enthusiasm, my research focus turned away from impulsivity and toward addressing the needs of the youths whose "silent scream" was going unheard.

The nature of cognitive dysfunction in the anxiety disorders and how best to provide the optimal treatment for anxious youths soon dominated my research and writing (e.g., Kendall et al., 1992; Kendall, Howard, & Epps, 1988). Anxiety disorders in childhood, although not as dramatic in presentation as externalizing disorders, represent a serious mental health problem for youths and their families.

My work[1] has addressed (a) the assessment of anxiety in youths and (b) the development and evaluation of treatments for anxiety-disordered youths. The assessment work addressed psychometric analyses of existing self-report measures and, noting the absence of measures needed to assess two important constructs (children's self-talk and coping ability), my colleagues and I developed and published measures to assess these constructs: the Negative Affectivity Self-Statement Questionnaire (Ronan, Kendall, & Rowe, 1994) and the Coping Questionnaire (Kendall & Marrs-Garcia, 1997). Structured diagnostic interview procedures are essential to clinical assessment, yet the *Diagnostic and Statistical Manual of Mental Disorders* (DSM) criteria change! Do these DSM changes influence the children who are or are not receiving diagnoses? Our research indicated that, for the third revised edition (*DSM–III–R*; American Psychiatric Association, 1987) and the fourth edition (*DSM–IV*; American Psychiatric Association, 1994), there is consistency in the children identified across DSM criteria (Kendall & Warman, 1996). Emerging from this and other assessment research, a reasonable battery of instruments for the measurement of anxiety disorders in youths has been recommended (Kendall & Ronan, 1990; Kendall & Treadwell, 1996; Ronan, 1996).

The bulk of work conducted by my colleagues and I has (a) been guided by an integrative theory and (b) addressed the development and evaluation of psychosocial treatments. Specifically, there is a dramatic need for the development and evaluation of psychosocial treatments for anxiety-disordered youth—a task that has taken much longer than I originally thought, and has yet to reach full conclusion. It is to a description of theory and our program of treatment research that I turn.

GUIDING THEORY

The integrationist perspective often labeled *cognitive–behavioral* incorporates and emphasizes behavior, cognition, affect, and social factors. Accordingly, cognitive–behavioral treatment strategies with children and adolescents use enactive, performance-based procedures as well as cognitive interventions to produce changes in thinking, feeling, and behavior (Kendall, 1991, 1993). The model places the greatest emphasis on the learning process and the influence of contingencies and models in the environment, while underscoring the centrality of the individual's information-processing style (Kendall, 1985).

The cognitive–behavioral therapist plays three important roles to fa-

---

[1]My research could not have been accomplished without the involvement of many colleagues. Although I cannot be certain that I have mentioned all of them in this chapter, most of their names appear among the citations to specific projects described herein and listed among the references.

cilitate improvement in the areas of cognition, behavior, and affect: consultant, diagnostician, and educator. Through a collaborative process, the therapist, as a consultant, strives to develop client skills such as independent thinking and decision making. The therapist is not the expert who provides a specific solution to child problems but a collaborator who encourages the child to generate possible options and evaluate the consequences of each option to determine the best solution(s) for that child. As a diagnostician, the therapist gathers information from multiple sources (teacher, parent, and child) and evaluates the data in relation to knowledge of psychopathology and normal development. This information is used to identify the nature of the problem and to create an optimal treatment plan. As an educator, the therapist provides affective education, teaches cognitive and behavioral skills (e.g., healthy self-talk), and shapes coping skills. The therapist encourages the child to recognize individual strengths and to use them as coping skills. The therapist collaborates in problem solving, integrates and evaluates diagnostic information, and educates the child in coping skills.

One of the essential features of cognitive–behavioral therapy is identifying dysfunctional thinking and its impact on the child's adjustment. Children with psychological problems may experience either of two types of cognitive dysfunction: distortions or deficiencies (Kendall, 1993; Kendall & MacDonald, 1993). *Cognitive deficiencies* describe a lack of or insufficient amount of information processing, leading to a tendency to act without thinking or planning. Children who are impulsive often exhibit this type of dysfunctional cognitive processing. In contrast, cognitive distortions involve active information processing that is faulty or misguided, resulting in misperceptions of oneself or the environment. Aggressive children tend to demonstrate both distortions (e.g., Dodge, 1985) and deficiencies (see Kendall, Ronan, & Epps, 1991; Southam-Gerow & Kendall, 1997). Cognitive distortions are a part of the psychology of children with internalizing difficulties, for example, depression, dysphoria, and the anxiety disorders seen in youths. Accordingly, treatments need to address any distorted information-processing styles that contribute to unwanted anxious arousal.

Therapists following a cognitive–behavioral model work to modify the child's cognitive processing and develop a new schema or "coping template" (Kendall, 1993). Therapists teach and facilitate new skills, provide new experiences to "test out" dysfunctional notions (often out of the office), and assist the child in a healthy processing of these experiences. The therapist guides the child's processing of multiple experiences and helps build a new cognitive structure through which the child can identify and solve problems. The new coping template is then applied in new exposure experiences.

PROGRAM OF RESEARCH

The Child and Adolescent Anxiety Disorders Clinic (CAADC) was established to (a) provide clinical services and (b) conduct basic and applied investigations within a clinic and with genuine clinical cases. Over the past decade, CAADC has undertaken studies of the nature of anxiety disorders in children, conducted multiple baselines and randomized clinical trials to evaluate treatment outcomes, and described issues and recommendations for enhanced practice. The child-focused treatment manual (Kendall, Kane, Howard, & Siqueland, 1990) has been modified for use in groups (Flannery-Schroeder & Kendall, 1996) and as family therapy (Howard & Kendall, 1996a, 1996b). Following a brief description of the CAADC and the treatment procedures, I will present and discuss the outcomes of our studies of the cognitive, social, and familial factors associated with anxious distress in youths.

THE CHILD AND ADOLESCENT ANXIETY DISORDERS CLINIC

The CAADC is an outpatient clinic now serving 8–14-year-old children with a primary diagnosis of an anxiety disorder. The clinic is housed within the Division of Clinical Psychology at Temple University. The majority of participants are referred from multiple community sources ranging from school guidance counselors to local mental health clinics. Some clients' parents learned about the CAADC through newspaper and magazine articles and television and radio programs that have discussed our work. The children treated at CAADC received a primary *DSM* diagnosis of generalized anxiety disorder (formerly overanxious disorder, or OAD, in *DSM–III–R*), separation anxiety disorder (SAD), or social phobia (formerly avoidant disorder, or AD, in *DSM–III–R*). Children are excluded from participation if they meet one of the following conditions: psychotic symptoms, a disabling physical condition, current use of antianxiety medication, or participation in an alternative treatment.

Following referral and a brief telephone screening process, parents and children each complete the Anxiety Disorders Interview Schedule (Silverman & Albano, 1996) and questionnaires during an intake evaluation by a staff diagnostician. Diagnosticians are trained to achieve an interrater reliability of at least .85 for all diagnoses. A multimethod battery of assessment measures is administered to parents, child, and teacher. The assessment measures include standardized instruments as well as questionnaires designed for specific studies. In addition, behavioral observations are obtained when the child is asked to talk about himself or herself in front of a video camera for 5 minutes. This battery of measures is administered pre-, mid-, post-, and 1 year following treatment.

Once a child has been diagnosed with an anxiety disorder, randomization is used in both the assignment of clients to treatment conditions and the assignment of clients to therapists. Waitlist cases are assessed before and after the wait period, and all cases are assessed pre-, mid-, post-, and 1 year following treatment. Weekly group supervision provides an area to strategize and discuss concerns.

PSYCHOSOCIAL TREATMENT: COGNITIVE–BEHAVIORAL THERAPY

The 16–20 session treatment (Kendall et al., 1990) has two segments and is presented in a workbook titled the *Coping Cat* (Kendall, 1992). The first segment (8 sessions) is educational in nature; children learn the following four steps for coping with anxiety: (a) recognizing the physiological symptoms of anxiety; (b) challenging and modifying anxious self-talk; (c) developing a plan to help cope with the situation (i.e., generating coping thoughts and actions); and (d) evaluating performance and using self-reinforcement. To help the children remember these steps, we implemented the acronym FEAR as a mnemonic: **F**eeling frightened? **E**xpecting bad things to happen? **A**ctions and attitudes that can help, and **R**esults and rewards. The second segment of treatment involves the application of newly learned skills in real-world exposure situations tailored to the child's specific anxieties. These exposure tasks require "hard work" from the children.

Behavioral training strategies such as modeling, in vivo exposure, role play, relaxation training, and contingent reinforcement are used in the treatment. Throughout the sessions, therapists use social reinforcement to encourage and reward the children, and the children are taught to reinforce their own successful coping. In addition, children practice using these coping skills in anxiety-provoking situations that arise at home or in school.

EVALUATING THE OUTCOMES OF TREATMENT

At CAADC, we endorse an empirical approach to the evaluation of treatment. Evaluations have used multiple-baseline designs and randomized clinical trials, with multimethod assessment and blind procedures with clinical evaluators. In this section, I describe the outcomes of these evaluations.

Participants in the initial multiple-baseline evaluation (Kane & Kendall, 1989) were 4 children diagnosed with overanxious disorder (2 also met criteria for simple phobia). Treatment was initiated after baseline assessment periods of 1, 2, or 3 weeks. Results indicated meaningful improvements for all 4 cases. On the basis of parent, teacher, and child reports at posttreatment, the target problem behaviors were treated successfully, and a variety of anxiety-related behaviors fell within the normative range. According to both parent and child report at 3- to 6-month follow-up, 2 of the children maintained complete treatment gains and, based on child report, the other 2 children's anxious behavior also remained in the normative range. For 1 child in particular, for whom there was a familial distress, parent report indicated some return of emotional problems.

The multiple-baseline evaluation was sufficiently positive that we moved forward with a randomized clinical trial. In this study (Kendall, 1994), the effects of treatment for children diagnosed with one of three primary anxiety disorders (i.e., OAD, SAD, AD) were examined and reported. There were 47 participants; 27 children were treated immediately and 20 were controls who received treatment after an 8-week waitlist period. Although a 16-week waitlist would have been methodologically preferred, it was determined to be too lengthy a wait for clinically distressed child participants.

At pretreatment, nonsignificant differences on assessment measures were found between the children in the treatment and waitlist conditions. At posttreatment, parent and child reports showed statistically significant reductions in the child's distress and anxiety. These scores often fell within the normative range, suggesting not only statistical significance but also clinical significance (Kendall & Grove, 1988). On the basis of parent diagnostic interview data, 64% of the treated cases no longer met diagnostic criteria for an anxiety disorder as compared with 5% of the waitlist condition (i.e., 1 participant). Follow-up data gathered 1 year after the completion of treatment suggested that the treatment gains were maintained. A study of long-term follow-up (Kendall & Southam-Gerow, 1996) located and examined 36 participants who had completed treatment 3.35 years (on average) earlier (2 refused to participate, others could not be located). Participants were reassessed using checklists and a structured diagnostic interview with a parent. In addition, the children completed self-report measures and a recall interview. During the child's interview, open-ended questions were asked to elicit their memories of the experience of treatment (e.g., What was most *important* for you about the program?). The interview also inquired regarding specific questions about the features of the treatment considered theoretically salient (e.g., Do you remember the FEAR steps?). The open-ended questions measured the child's perceived factors, and the specific questions assessed theoretical factors.

Results indicated that the treatment gains reported at posttreatment and 1-year follow-up were maintained at the long-term follow-up with no significant diminishment: The percentage of cases no longer meeting diagnostic criteria were consistent! It should also be noted that the duration of time from the end of therapy to long-term follow-up was nonsignificantly correlated with maintenance. Regarding factors of theoretical interest, a significant relationship was found between improvement and recall of the FEAR steps (e.g., significantly related to positive changes before treatment to long-term follow-up on parent and child measures of improvement). Recall of relaxation techniques was also meaningfully associated with changes on self-report measures of anxiety and depression.

The worthwhile and lasting effects of the cognitive–behavioral treatment for children were supported by the research outcomes. It is important to note that, because excessive childhood anxiety may foreshadow related problems in adulthood (adults diagnosed with agoraphobia and generalized anxiety disorder reported experiencing symptoms of separation anxiety and generalized anxiety during childhood; Last, Phillips, & Statfield, 1987), the present results have implications for interventions designed to prevent adult anxiety disorders.

Despite these supportive results, might treatment impact be affected by child characteristics such as ethnicity and gender? Because the children treated at the CAADC were heterogeneous with respect to gender and ethnicity, it permitted the investigation of both differential treatment effects and the number and content of excessive fears across gender and ethnicity. Participants were 81 children treated at the CAADC (participants were from other reports of treatment outcomes): 41% were girls and 59% were boys; 89% were Caucasian and 11% were African American (Treadwell, Flannery-Schroeder, & Kendall, 1995). Results indicated no treatment–outcome differences as a function of gender or ethnicity. Also, the types of anxieties and fears children self-reported did not differ as a function of gender. Nine of the 10 most frequently cited fears were the same for both sexes; however, girls reported a greater number of excessive fears compared with boys. No differences in self-reported anxiety or number of excessive fears were found between African Americans and Caucasians, and no significant differences were found in the content of their fears. Although somewhat preliminary and in need of additional study (see also Neal & Kinsley, 1995), these results indicated that boys and girls, and African American and Caucasian youths, are equally likely to experience clinical levels of anxiety and fear and that the cognitive–behavioral intervention is useful for 9–13-year-old clinically anxious youths of various ethnicity.

A second and more elaborate randomized clinical trial was undertaken. In this project, 94 anxiety-disordered youths (age 9–13 years) participated. On the basis of multiple-method measurement (e.g., parent ratings, self-reports, diagnosis, behavioral observations, and teacher reports), the outcomes again provided support for the efficacy of the cognitive–behavioral treatment in the reduction of dysfunctional anxiety (Kendall et al., 1997). In terms of the children's diagnoses using the parent diagnostic interview, 71% of the treated children no longer had their primary diagnosis as primary at the end of treatment, and 53% no longer met diagnostic criteria for their primary anxiety disorder at all. Evaluations of 1-year follow-up data supported the maintenance of the treatment-produced gains.

The child-focused intervention can be considered to have been supported by the empirical evaluations, but the question of the involvement of parents in the treatment and in the maintenance of gains needs further consideration. Although parents were a part of the child-focused intervention, a family treatment would actually include parents in the sessions with the anxiety disordered youth, with the possibility that parents would themselves learn some beneficial coping skills, would see the gains in their child and be guided to respond to the child in an improved manner, and would be invested in maintaining the gains after treatment was completed. Of course, the possibility also exists that the presence of the parents could interfere with child disclosure, the child's development of a working relationship with the therapist, and the therapist's ability to engage the child in the content of the program and the exposure activities.

The initial examination of the family treatment (cognitive–behavioral family therapy; Howard & Kendall, 1996a) involved 6 children (age 9 to 13 years) who were diagnosed with a childhood anxiety disorder and treated with an 18-session, family-based therapy. The evaluation used assessments from multiple sources and a multiple-baseline (2, 4, and 6 weeks) across-cases design. Changes in diagnostic status, standardized parent- and teacher-report measures, and parent and child reports on specific measures of coping indicated meaningful treatment-related gains. Gains were considered clinically significant and were, in general, maintained at 4-month follow-up. Although measured features of the family (i.e., overt and covert conflict and family members' perceptions of their family) did not reflect change, the results of measures of the child's functioning suggested the utility of a family-based treatment for childhood anxiety disorders.

In Australia, clinical researchers have also examined strategies for the treatment of anxious youths (e.g., Barrett, Dadds, & Rapee, 1996). The *Coping Cat* was modified to the *Coping Koala*, and the outcomes by the investigators were quite similar to the treatment-produced changes reported from the CAADC. For example, Barrett et al. (1996) found that 70% of cases at posttreatment no longer met diagnostic criteria for their anxiety disorder.

The collective set of outcomes to date are supportive of the efficacy of the treatment: two multiple baseline evaluations and two randomized clinical trials conducted at CAADC and an independent international replication of the randomized clinical trial. Using criteria recommended for the identification of empirically supported psychological therapies (e.g., Chambless & Hollon, 1998), one can reasonably conclude that the treatment is efficacious for children with an anxiety disorder. However, evidence supporting the efficacy of the treatment does not equate with a total solution to the problem. Questions remain, and additional research is required.

CURRENT AND CONTINUING CONCERNS

The field of clinical psychology is appropriately concerned with four questions: (a) the empirical evaluation of treatment, (b) the identification of moderators of the effects of treatment, (c) the unearthing of those forces that mediate treatment outcome, and (d) the clinical significance of outcomes.

Empirically Supported Psychological Therapies

Not only are insurance companies looking to the evidence to make decisions about the management of psychological care, so too are members of our field asking questions about what works under what circumstances, and for whom (Kiesler, 1966). Criteria have been developed and proposed to be used in the determination of those treatments that are empirically supported (American Psychological Association Task Force, 1995; Chambless & Hollon, 1998), and a special section of the *Journal of Consulting and Clinical Psychology* provided a series of reviews of the literature as well as commentaries that addressed the merits and demerits of this approach (Kendall, 1998). As the criteria are applied to our work, both by myself and by other reviewers of the field (e.g., Kazdin & Weisz, 1998), we find that two multiple-baseline evaluations, two separate randomized clinical trials conducted in Philadelphia, a randomized clinical trial undertaken in Queensland, Australia, and a preliminary prevention intervention also conducted in Australia can be applied to consideration of efficacy. From reviews of these studies, the treatment can be said to be efficacious. This conclusion is favorable for the anxiety-disordered youth who will likely receive improved services as a result of this work, but there is the need for additional randomized clinical trials to compare the treatment program with other forms of intervention. It remains to be determined if the treatment efficacy is specific to anxiety disorders and if there are other treatments equally or more efficacious.

In addition to questions of efficacy, it is important to address concerns associated with effectiveness. A treatment that is efficacious—successful for those who complete it—may not be as favorable viewed in terms of effectiveness if there are problems with clients not completing the program. A large percentage of cases dropping out of treatment, for example, may render an efficacious treatment to the status of limited effectiveness. Does attrition affect the conclusions about the efficacy and effectiveness of the cognitive–behavioral treatment of youths with anxiety disorders? In our work, attrition has been low (18%) compared with other published studies, with much of the attrition coming from the waitlist condition (dropping out from treatment is less than half the total attrition rate; Kendall & Sugarman, 1997). Nevertheless, we must ask if the efficacy of the treatment for those who completed treatment is applicable to the intent-to-treat sample—all participants who initially were involved at the time of randomization to conditions. Analyses related to this issue indicate that the gains from treatment can be generalized to the intent-to-treat sample. Although added research will be needed for a firm conclusion, the low attrition and the already-published favorable effects for the intent-to-treat sample combine to suggest that the treatment is not only efficacious but also of reasonable effectiveness.

Moderators of Outcomes

A moderator variable specifies the conditions under which a given effect occurs, as well as the conditions under which the direction or strength of an effect vary (see Holmbeck, 1997). A moderator variable affects the relationship between two variables such that the nature of the impact of the predictor on the criterion varies depending on the level of the moderator. Moderator variables provide the scientific basis for answers to questions that begin with "It depends." If A is expected to be related to C, but only under certain conditions of B, then B is a moderator. There are two constructs that deserve consideration and further research attention.

In our diagnostic experience, we have observed children who do not disclose anxious symptoms and, despite parental report of distress, also present as nonanxious on self-report measures. The observation of differential disclosure of emotional distress led to hypotheses regarding potential corresponding variations in treatment outcome (Panichelli-Mindel, Flannery-Schroeder, Callahan, & Kendall, 1997). To test this notion, we identified children who had completed treatment (and were included in earlier reports of outcome) as disclosers or nondisclosers on the basis of agreement between the child and parent diagnostic interviews. A nondisclosing child was identified when the parent interview about the child produced a diagnosis but the child interview resulted in the absence of an anxiety-disorder diagnosis. Analyses of changes produced by treatment indicated that the treatment was successful for both groups, but that the beneficial gains were, to a degree, moderated by discloser or nondiscloser status: The disclosers evidenced larger treatment-produced effect sizes than did nondisclosers.

Why are disclosers more responsive to treatment? At first blush, disclosers may simply be open and willing to discuss their distress and hence benefit more from treatment. If disclosers openly acknowledge and describe their distressing situations, then a therapist is better able to construct treatment experiences. On the other hand, when working with nondisclosers, the therapist may have less treatment time because of the need for additional effort to establish rapport and facilitate involvement.

The results of the initial study of a family-based treatment for child anxiety are encouraging (Howard & Kendall, 1996a) and indicate the need for continued evaluations. However, the experience of one family suggested that family issues and stress can influence (moderate) the outcomes of a family-focused treatment. The stress of separation and divorce seemed to undermine the treatment. It seems important for future research to assess the functioning of the family (e.g., stress level) and family members before implementing treatment and to examine the potential moderating influences on child adjustment. Characteristics of the child and characteristics of the child's family are illustrative sources, but not exhaustive resources, for the potential identification of moderators of outcome. Other factors deserve attention: cognitive developmental issues, length of treatment, treatment components, and therapist factors.

Mediators of Outcomes

A mediator specifies how a given effect occurs—the mechanism by which an effect occurs. With treatment outcome research, the treatment variable influences the mediator that then influences the outcome. If A influences B and B influences C, B is a mediating variable between A and C.

The role of self-talk as a mediator of change was examined by Treadwell and Kendall (1996). The "power of nonnegative thinking," a concept I introduced in 1984, guided our work. We considered both positive self-talk and negative self-talk, and we examined the correlations to determine if either or both were mediators of therapy-produced changes. The findings evidenced that, consistent across child self-report measures, reductions in negative thinking mediated treatment gains. However, positive self-talk was not a mediator of treatment gains. Taken together, these results document the potency of reduced negative thinking and support the "power of nonnegative thinking."

Other mediators are worthy of consideration and research examination. Heightened self-efficacy, for example, is a potentially promising variable. Changes on the Coping Questionnaire (CQ; Kendall & Marrs-Garcia, 1997) are said to reflect changes in the child's self-perceived efficacy in handling stressful, anxiety-producing situations. Treatment has produced marked and significant CQ changes, and these could reflect the fact that changes in self-efficacy are mediating the changes reported on other variables. Also, given the child clients' recall of the "FEAR steps" and "talking about problems" (Kendall & Southam-Gerow, 1996, p. 729) at the long-term follow-up, these factors, too, could be contributing mediational forces.

Clinical Significance

What is the future for outcome evaluation methodology? In addition to the various methodological niceties used in modern outcome evaluations, normative comparisons are a way to examine clinical significance (Kendall, 1997). *Normative comparisons* are a useful but stringent procedure for evaluating the potency of interventions (Kendall & Grove, 1988). Normative comparisons consist of comparing the behavior of treated subjects, when appropriate, to that of nondisturbed subjects. Statistical comparisons are required before normative comparisons, so the examination of clinical significance is not a replacement for statistical significance. When norms are used for these purposes, and children are the target sample, then the reference norms must be age appropriate. Analyses of clinical significance, using normative comparisons, have indicated that a meaningful percentage of those cases outside the normative range are returned to within the normative range at posttreatment.

PLANS AND PRIORITIES FOR THE FUTURE

Several topics guide plans for the future. The following themes direct our research energies.

1. The presence of social anxiety in childhood and adolescence has been found to be associated with later problems with substance use and abuse. Also, untreated anxiety disorders in youths seem to persist across the life span. Clearly, there is the need for preventive interventions. One approach would be to identify behaviorally inhibited youths (Kagan & Snidman, 1991) and provide a preventive program to reduce the number of these youths who later develop an anxiety disorder. Another approach would use a paper-and-pencil screen to identify at-risk youths in middle schools. In both, the goal would be to not only reduce later anxiety disorders but also to have a beneficial effect on their sequelae (e.g., excessive substance use). We are currently, along with colleagues at two other sites, evaluating a school-based prevention program.

2. Anxiety disorders in youths do not occur in isolation. Rather, comorbidity rules. As additional data are gathered, it will be important to examine further the potential role of comorbid conditions on the outcomes of psychosocial interventions. Although the evidence of favorable treatment outcome available to date is based on highly comorbid cases and comorbid status did not uniformly have a negative impact on outcome, continued research is warranted.

3. The role of self-talk in anxiety disorders in youths has begun to be examined. For example, we know that successful treatment is mediated by a reduction in negative self-talk (Treadwell & Kendall, 1996). However,

much more work is needed to assess and evaluate the functional role of self-talk in children's social appraisals, interpersonal relations, emotional reactions, and behavioral responses. Moreover, reduction of negative self-talk is only one mediational explanation, and several other possibilities deserve evaluation as well.

4. Positive changes in coping have been identified, as measured by the child and parent versions of the CQ. Additional studies of the psychometric properties of the CQ are needed, as are studies of the potential mediational role of self-perceived coping efficacy. Relatedly, treatments would benefit from additional knowledge about the coping styles and processes that are effective and ineffective for children with anxiety disorders.

5. Although the treatment has application with several anxiety disorders, there are others (e.g., posttraumatic stress disorder, obsessive–compulsive disorders) for which modified if not alternate versions of treatment need to be developed. Additional treatment development, manual preparation, and research evaluations are needed to enhance the treatment of related, but different, child anxiety disorders.

6. As reviewed earlier, research suggests that a cognitive–behavioral treatment for anxiety disorders in youths is efficacious. Given that this research-clinic treatment can be considered efficacious, the question of whether or not it will be comparably effective in other service clinic settings (i.e., any nonresearch based setting) remains to be examined. Can the positive effects of treatments be transported to community service clinics? Although difficulties inherent in this process of "transportability" (Kendall & Southam-Gerow, 1995) may explain the dearth of research, at least one study with adult panic sufferers (Wade, Treat, & Stuart, 1998) supports the transportability of manualized or researched treatments, and a similar evaluation of the child anxiety program is presently under way. Potential barriers exist from the research process to the practice clinic. Nevertheless, the future may best be served by the transport of efficacious and well-established treatments into the practice world, as well as the systematic study of the factors that impede and facilitate this process.

7. The treatment is guided by a therapist manual. Therapist supervision often addresses the application of the manualized strategies to the specific cases. To what extent does the manual permit flexible application? Does flexibility influence the efficacy of the program? In an initial investigation, Kendall and Chu (in press) found that the therapists who provided the treatment in the randomized clinical trial (Kendall et al., 1997) self-reported varying degrees of flexibility in applying components of the manual-based therapy and that this variation in therapist flexibility was not meaningfully associated with indexes of treatment outcome.

8. When a psychosocial intervention is implemented for a child in a child-focused therapy, are there "spillover effects" for members of the child's family? Do parents who have difficulties with anxiety benefit from

their indirect exposure to the treatment applied with their children? What are the spillover effects on family interactions of children who have been treated successfully? This question guides our current thinking and research on the outcomes associated with psychosocial treatments for youths with anxiety disorders.

NO-CURE CRITICISM

Despite the accomplishments made in the field of child therapy research, and the likely additional gains that will accrue to clients, young clients receiving treatments that have been found to be effective do not automatically display gains, do not always generalize their gains, and do not always maintain gains throughout the rest of their lives. Psychological therapy does not cure psychological disorders. Cure refers to remedial healing that rids one of an illness or bad habit. Cure is not the same as care, which refers to looking after someone with a difficulty that will not be cured. Do we as psychologists expect that psychotherapy will uniformly produce gains that are maintained over time and generalized to new situations? If the answer is yes, then we expect a cure. Our evidence suggests that, instead, psychological therapy is not a cure. We provide reasoned and integrative programs for the treatment of psychological disorders but we do not cure anything. We teach skills for the *management* of psychological distress. Anxiety is not cured: Youths with anxiety disorders learn skills to manage their arousal and discomfort. For example, cognitive self-talk or physiological cues linked to anxious arousal do not totally disappear. Rather, the client learns to recognize these cues, to use them to trigger management strategies, and to engage in the ongoing process of managing the unwanted arousal. Efficacious psychosocial intervention, such as the one described here, provides skills for children to use in their successful management of their psychopathology.

CONCLUSION

The pediatric dentist and the child therapist: surprising similarities!

Given the statement above, it is reasonable for one to ask, "What does pediatric dentistry have to do with the treatment of anxiety disorders in youths?" Consider the following.

The pediatric dentist is an intentionally stark contrast to the prototype for the child psychotherapist, whose on-the-street moniker would be closer to a warm and supportive hand-holder than to the stressful and discomforting, yet required, dentist. In reality, however, the dentist and the effective child therapist are not that different. For the child therapist to be effective, there is the need for difficult work to be done: challenging ways of thinking, testing distorted notions, and exposing the child to the experiences that are emotionally distressing. The psychological treatment of anxiety in children is not free of emotional distress but is built on experiencing distress and overcoming it. And, even after treatment outcomes are accomplished, the work remains—just as brushing, flossing, and twice-a-year check-ups supplement dental treatments. Effective psychological treatment requires continued effort to prevent avoidance, to entertain rational expectations, and to practice coping.

Like painless dentists, we too put forth effort to reduce patient distress. We have play activities, rewards for participation, and other incentives to maintain child interest and involvement. However, effective treatments for anxiety do not coddle, overnurture, or overprotect anxious clients. Anxious youths, with guidance, can handle more challenges than we might first think, and their confidence in handling difficulty is enhanced by the confidence that is communicated to them as we require them to do those very things that they were once felt incompetent to undertake. Painless, yes, but for treatment to be effective, it is itself not without distress.

REFERENCES

American Psychiatric Association. (1987). *Diagnostic and statistical manual of mental disorders* (3rd ed., rev.). Washington, DC: Author.

American Psychiatric Association. (1994). Diagnostic and statistical manual of mental disorders (4th ed.). Washington, DC: Author.

American Psychological Association Task Force on Psychological Intervention Guidelines. (1995). *Template for developing guidelines: Interventions for mental disorders and psychological aspects of physical disorders.* Washington, DC: American Psychological Association.

Barrett, P. M., Dadds, M., & Rapee, R. (1996). Family treatment of childhood anxiety: A controlled trial. *Journal of Consulting and Clinical Psychology, 64,* 333–342.

Chambless, D., & Hollon, S. (1998). Defining empirically supported therapies. *Journal of Consulting and Clinical Psychology, 66,* 7–18.

Dodge, K. A. (1985). Attributional bias in aggressive children. In P. C. Kendall (Ed.), *Advances in cognitive–behavioral research and therapy* (Vol. 4, pp. 75–111). San Diego, CA: Academic Press.

Flannery-Schroeder, E., & Kendall, P. C. (1996). *Cognitive–behavioral therapy for anxious children: Therapist manual for group treatment.* Ardmore, PA: Workbook Publishing.

Hoagwood, K., Hibbs, E., Brent, D., & Jensen, P. (1995). Introduction to the special section: Efficacy and effectiveness in studies of child and adolescent psychotherapy. *Journal of Consulting and Clinical Psychology, 63,* 683–687.

Holmbeck, G. (1997). Toward terminological, conceptual, and statistical clarity in the study of mediators and moderators: Examples from the child-clinical and pediatric psychology literatures. *Journal of Consulting and Clinical Psychology, 65*, 599–610.

Howard, B., & Kendall, P. C. (1996a). Cognitive–behavioral family therapy for anxiety-disordered children: A multiple-baseline evaluation. *Cognitive Therapy and Research, 20*, 423–444.

Howard, B., & Kendall, P. C. (1996b). *Cognitive–behavioral family therapy for anxious children: Therapist manual.* Ardmore, PA: Workbook Publishing.

Institute of Medicine. (1989). *Research on children and adolescents with mental, behavioral, and developmental disorders* (Report No. IOM 8907). Washington, DC: National Academy Press.

Kagan, J., & Snidman, N. (1991). Infant predictors of inhibited and uninhibited profiles. *Psychological Science, 2*, 40–44.

Kane, M. T., & Kendall, P. C. (1989). Anxiety disorders in children: A multiple-baseline evaluation of a cognitive–behavioral treatment. *Behavior Therapy, 20*, 499–508.

Kazdin, A. E., & Weisz, J. (1998). Identifying and developing empirically supported child and adolescent treatments. *Journal of Consulting and Clinical Psychology, 66*, 19–36.

Kendall, P. C. (1985). Toward a cognitive–behavioral model of child psychopathology and a critique of related interventions. *Journal of Abnormal Child Psychology, 13*, 357–372.

Kendall, P. C. (1991). Guiding theory for treating children and adolescents. In P. C. Kendall (Ed.), *Child and adolescent therapy: Cognitive–behavioral procedures* (pp. 3–24). New York: Guilford Press.

Kendall, P. C. (1992). *Coping cat workbook.* Ardmore, PA: Workbook Publishing.

Kendall, P. C. (1993). Cognitive–behavioral therapies with youth: Guiding theory, current status, and emerging developments. *Journal of Consulting and Clinical Psychology, 61*, 235–247.

Kendall, P. C. (1994). Treating anxiety disorders in youth: Results of a randomized clinical trial. *Journal of Consulting and Clinical Psychology, 62*, 100–110.

Kendall, P. C. (1997). Editorial. *Journal of Consulting and Clinical Psychology, 65*, 1–4.

Kendall, P. C. (1998). Empirically supported psychological therapies. *Journal of Consulting and Clinical Psychology, 66*, 1–6.

Kendall, P. C., & Braswell, L. (1982). Cognitive–behavioral self-control therapy for children: A components analysis. *Journal of Consulting and Clinical Psychology, 50*, 672–689.

Kendall, P. C., & Braswell, L. (1985). *Cognitive–behavioral therapy for impulsive children.* New York: Guilford Press.

Kendall, P. C., & Braswell, L. (1993). *Cognitive–behavioral therapy for impulsive children* (2nd ed.). New York: Guilford Press.

Kendall, P. C., Chansky, T. E., Kane, M. T., Kim, R., Kortlander, E., Ronan, K. R., Sessa, F. M., & Siqueland, L. (1992). *Anxiety disorders in youth: Cognitive–behavioral interventions.* Needham, MA: Allyn & Bacon.

Kendall, P. C., & Chu, B. (in press). Retrospective self-reports of therapist flexibility in a manual-based treatment for youths with anxiety disorders. *Journal of Clinical Child Psychology.*

Kendall, P. C., Flannery-Schroeder, E., Panichelli-Mindel, S., Southam-Gerow, M., Henin, A., & Warman, M. (1997). Therapy for anxiety-disordered youth: A second randomized clinical trial. *Journal of Consulting and Clinical Psychology, 65,* 366–380.

Kendall, P. C., & Grove, W. (1988). Normative comparisons in therapy outcome. *Behavioral Assessment, 10,* 147–158.

Kendall, P. C., Howard, B. L., & Epps, J. (1988). The anxious child: Cognitive–behavioral treatment strategies. *Behavior Modification, 12,* 281–310.

Kendall, P. C., Kane, M., Howard, B., & Siqueland, L. (1990). *Cognitive–behavioral therapy for anxious children: Treatment manual.* Ardmore, PA: Workbook Publishing.

Kendall, P. C., & MacDonald, J. P. (1993). Cognition in the psychopathology of youth, and implications for treatment. In K. S. Dobson & P. C. Kendall (Eds.), *Psychopathology and cognition* (pp. 387–432). San Diego: Academic Press.

Kendall, P. C., & Marrs-Garcia, A. L. (1997). *Psychometric analyses of a therapy-sensitive measure of children's coping: The Coping Questionnaire (CQ).* Manuscript submitted for publication.

Kendall, P. C., & Ronan, K. R. (1990). Assessment of children's anxieties, fears, and phobias: Cognitive–behavioral models and methods. In C. R. Reynolds & R. W. Kamphaus (Eds.), *Handbook of psychological and educational assessment of children* (pp. 223–244). New York: Guilford Press.

Kendall, P. C., Ronan, K. R., & Epps, J. (1991). Aggression in children/adolescents: Cognitive–behavioral treatment perspectives. In D. Popler & K. Rubin (Eds.), *Development and treatment of childhood aggression* (pp. 341–360). Hillsdale, NJ: Erlbaum.

Kendall, P. C., & Southam-Gerow, M. A. (1995). Issues in the transportability of treatment: The case of anxiety disorders in youths. *Journal of Consulting and Clinical Psychology, 63,* 702–708.

Kendall, P. C., & Southam-Gerow, M. A. (1996). Long-term follow-up of a cognitive–behavioral therapy for anxiety-disordered youth. *Journal of Consulting and Clinical Psychology, 64,* 724–730.

Kendall, P. C., & Sugarman, A. (1997). Attrition in the treatment of childhood anxiety disorders. *Journal of Consulting and Clinical Psychology, 65,* 883–888.

Kendall, P. C., & Treadwell, K. R. H. (1996). Cognitive–behavioral treatment for childhood anxiety disorders. In E. D. Hibbs & P. S. Jensen (Eds.), *Psychosocial treatments for child and adolescent disorders: Empirically based strategies for clinical practice* (pp. 23–41). Washington, DC: American Psychological Association.

Kendall, P. C., & Warman, M. J. (1996). Anxiety disorders in youth: Diagnostic consistency across DSM–III–R and DSM–IV. *Journal of Anxiety Disorders, 10*, 453–463.

Kiesler, D. (1966). Some myths of psychotherapy research and the search for a paradigm. *Psychological Bulletin, 65*, 110–136.

Last, C., Phillips, J., & Statfield, A. (1987). Childhood anxiety disorders in mothers and their children. *Child Psychiatry and Human Development, 18*, 103–117.

Neal, A. M., & Kinsley, H. (1995). What are African-American children afraid of? II. A twelve-month follow-up. *Journal of Anxiety Disorders, 9*, 151–161.

Panichelli-Mindel, S., Flannery-Schroeder, E., Callahan, S., & Kendall, P. C. (1997). *Disclosure and nondisclosure among anxiety disordered youth: Participant characteristics and treatment outcomes*. Manuscript submitted for publication.

Ronan, K. R. (1996). Bridging the gap in childhood anxiety assessment: A practitioner's resource guide. *Cognitive and Behavioral Practice, 3*, 63–90.

Ronan, K., Kendall, P. C., & Rowe, M. (1994). Negative affectivity in children: Development and validation of a self-statement questionnaire. *Cognitive Therapy and Research, 18*, 509–528.

Silverman, W. K., & Albano, A. M. (1996). *The Anxiety Disorders Interview Schedule for DSM–IV: Child and parent versions*. Albany, NY: Graywind.

Southam-Gerow, M. A., & Kendall, P. C. (1997). Parent-focused and cognitive–behavioral treatments of antisocial youth. In D. Stoff, J. Breiling, & J. D. Maser (Eds.), *Handbook of antisocial behavior* (pp. 384–394). New York: Wiley.

Treadwell, K. R. H., Flannery-Schroeder, E. C., & Kendall, P. C. (1995). Ethnicity and gender in relation to adaptive functioning, diagnostic status, and treatment outcome in children from an anxiety clinic. *Journal of Anxiety Disorders, 9*, 373–384.

Treadwell, K. R. H., & Kendall, P. C. (1996). Self-talk in anxiety-disordered youth: States-of-mind, content specificity, and treatment outcome. *Journal of Consulting and Clinical Psychology, 64*, 941–950.

Wade, W., Treat, T., & Stuart, G. (1998). Transporting an empirically supported treatment for panic disorder to a service clinic setting: A benchmarking strategy. *Journal of Consulting and Clinical Psychology, 66*, 231–239.

Witmer, L. (1897). The organization of practical work in psychology. *Psychological Review, 4*, 116.

10

COGNITIVE–BEHAVIORAL TREATMENT OF OBSESSIVE–COMPULSIVE DISORDER

EDNA B. FOA AND MARTIN E. FRANKLIN

As the 21st century approaches, economic pressures such as managed care and increased competition for limited research funding have spawned serious questions about the future of clinical psychology. In the future arena of mental health, perhaps clinical psychologists will find their niche in the development and validation of psychological treatments. The leading position that clinical psychologists have assumed in the development of cognitive–behavioral interventions can be seen as a clear precedent in this direction. Indeed, much of the cognitive–behavioral outcome research on obsessive–compulsive disorder (OCD) in the last three decades was spearheaded by clinical psychologists. And the therapies eventuating from these efforts have greatly improved the prognosis for OCD sufferers.

In this chapter, we examine the phenomenology and treatment of OCD. We begin with a discussion of diagnostic issues and cognitive–behavioral conceptualizations of OCD. Next, we review the treatment out-

This chapter was supported in part by National Institute of Mental Health Grants MH45404 and MH55126 awarded to Edna B. Foa.

235

come literature on exposure and ritual prevention (EX/RP), which is widely considered the psychological treatment of choice for adult sufferers of OCD. Finally, we examine the available literature on pediatric OCD treatment, which, despite some recent advances, continues to lag behind the adult literature in outcome studies.

OCD DIAGNOSIS AND RELATED ISSUES

DSM–IV Definition

The *Diagnostic and Statistical Manual of Mental Disorders* (4th ed.; *DSM–IV*; American Psychiatric Association, 1994) defines OCD by the presence of recurrent obsessions and/or compulsions that interfere significantly with daily functioning. Obsessions are "persistent ideas, thoughts, impulses, or images that are experienced as intrusive and inappropriate and cause marked anxiety or distress" (p. 418). Compulsions are "repetitive behaviors ... or mental acts ... the goal of which is to prevent or reduce anxiety or distress" (p. 418). Although most OCD patients present with both obsessions and compulsions, both are not required to make a diagnosis.

The *DSM–IV* definition includes several significant modifications of the third revised edition (*DSM–III–R*; American Psychiatric Association, 1987) of OCD. Obsessions and compulsions are defined in *DSM–IV* as functionally linked: Obsessions are defined as thoughts, images, or impulses that *cause* marked anxiety or distress, and compulsions are defined as overt (behavioral) or covert (mental) actions that are performed in order to *reduce* the distress brought on by obsessions or according to rigid rules. This modification is supported by data from the *DSM–IV* field study on OCD, in which over 90% of participants reported that their compulsions were functionally related to their obsessions (Foa et al., 1995).

The traditional view that obsessions are mental events and compulsions are behavioral events was also revised in *DSM–IV*. Behavioral rituals are equivalent to mental rituals in their functional relationship to obsessions, in that both are attempts to reduce obsessional distress, prevent feared harm, or restore safety. Thus, whereas all obsessions are mental events, compulsions are now defined as either behavioral (e.g., handwashing) or mental (e.g., silently repeating special prayers).

Changes were also made with respect to the requirement for insight in diagnosing OCD. It has been argued that a continuum of "insight" or "strength of belief" more accurately depicts the clinical picture of OCD than the previously prevailing view that *all* obsessive–compulsives recognize the senselessness of their obsessions and compulsions (Kozak & Foa, 1994). The growing consensus about this issue (Foa et al., 1995; Insel &

Akiskal, 1986; Lelliott, Noshirvani, Basoglu, Marks, & Monteiro, 1988) led to the inclusion in *DSM–IV* of an OCD subtype "with poor insight" that includes individuals who indeed have obsessions and compulsions but do not view them as senseless.

Prevalence and Course

OCD was once thought to be quite rare, but recent epidemiological studies estimate that about 2.5% of the adult population in the United States has clinically significant OCD (Karno, Golding, Sorenson, & Burnam, 1988). Recent studies with children and adolescents suggest lifetime prevalence rates of approximately 1% (e.g., Flament et al., 1988; Valleni-Basile et al., 1994). There is a slight predominance of women suffering from OCD in adulthood (Rasmussen & Tsuang, 1986), whereas a 2:1 male-to-female ratio has been observed in several pediatric clinical samples (e.g., Swedo, Rapoport, Leonard, Lenane, & Cheslow, 1989). Age of onset typically ranges from early adolescence to young adulthood, with earlier onset in males; modal onset in males is 13–15 years old, and in females, 20–24 years old (Rasmussen & Eisen, 1990). Although the more typical presentation of OCD occurs during or following adolescence, cases of OCD have been reported in children as young as age 2 (Rapoport, Swedo, & Leonard, 1992). OCD usually develops gradually, but acute onset has been documented in some cases. Chronic waxing and waning of symptoms is typical, but episodic and deteriorating courses are characteristic of about 10% of patients (Rasmussen & Eisen, 1989). OCD is frequently associated with disruption of gainful employment (Leon, Portera, & Weissman, 1995), with marital and other interpersonal relationship problems (Emmelkamp, de Haan, & Hoogduin, 1990; Riggs, Hiss, & Foa, 1992), and with impairment in other areas of functioning. An adolescent sample identified as having OCD (Flament et al., 1988) later reported social withdrawal to prevent contamination and to conserve energy for obsessive–compulsive behaviors (Flament et al., 1990).

Associated Disorders

OCD frequently co-occurs with other Axis I disorders, including other anxiety disorders. In one study, Rasmussen and Tsuang (1986) reported lifetime incidence of simple phobia of 30%, social phobia of 20%, and panic disorder of 15%. Major depression has also been found to co-occur with OCD in approximately 30% of OCD sufferers in an epidemiological study (Karno et al., 1988) and may be even more common in clinical samples (e.g., Foa, Kozak, Steketee, & McCarthy, 1992). Other disorders that co-occur with OCD at rates higher than expected in the general population include Tourette's syndrome (Rasmussen & Eisen,

1989), anorexia nervosa (Kasvikis, Tsakiris, Marks, Basoglu, & Noshirvani, 1986), and bulimia (Hudson, Pope, Yurgelun-Todd, Jonas, & Frankenburg, 1987).

Many studies have found a wide range of comorbid Axis II disorders in OCD patients (e.g., Pfohl, Black, Noyes, Coryell, & Barrash, 1991), with some studies indicating that comorbid personality disorder diagnosis predicted poor outcome of behavioral treatment (AuBuchon & Malatesta, 1994; Fals-Stewart & Lucente, 1993), and that schizotypal personality disorder in particular predicted poor response to behavior therapy (Minichello, Baer, & Jenike, 1987).

Differential Diagnosis

The similarity between the criteria for OCD and other *DSM–IV* disorders can pose diagnostic difficulties. Below we review some of the more common diagnostic issues likely to arise with OCD, and we suggest ways to differentiate between OCD and other symptoms.

Obsessions Versus Ruminations

Depressive ruminations and obsessions can be difficult to differentiate, especially in patients who experience both types of thoughts. The distinction rests primarily on the content of the thoughts and on whether or not the patient reported resistance to such thoughts. Unlike obsessions, ruminations are generally pessimistic ideas about the self or the world, and the content of ruminations shifts frequently. In addition, depressive ruminators tend not to suppress their ruminations the way that individuals with OCD attempt to suppress obsessions. In cases in which depression and OCD co-occur, both phenomena may be present but only obsessions should be addressed by means of exposure exercises.

Other Anxiety Disorders

Although OCD does co-occur with other anxiety disorders and diagnostic criteria are sometimes similar among anxiety disorders, the symptoms associated with each can usually be distinguished. For example, contamination-related OCD and specific phobia can both result in persistent avoidance of insects. However, unlike an individual with OCD, an insect phobic can usually avoid insects successfully (e.g., refusing to walk on grass where insects might be present) or reduce anxiety quickly by escaping insects when avoidance is not possible (e.g., running away from encountered insects). In contrast, the individual with OCD who is obsessed with germs carried by insects often continues to feel contaminated even after the insect is gone. This distress often prompts subsequent avoidance behaviors (e.g., discarding clothing that might have been touched by insects) not typically observed in specific phobias.

It can also be difficult to distinguish the excessive worries characteristic of generalized anxiety disorder (GAD) from obsessions. In differentiating the two, consider that the worries of GAD patients are excessive concerns about real-life circumstances and are typically experienced as appropriate (ego syntonic). In contrast, obsessive thinking is more likely to be unrealistic or magical, and obsessions are usually experienced as inappropriate (ego dystonic). There are exceptions to this general rule of thumb: OCD patients also report everyday worries such as their children becoming ill. However, parents with GAD may focus their concern on unrealistic long-term consequences of the illness (e.g., falling behind in school, failure to achieve future career goals), whereas parents suffering from OCD may focus on the contamination aspect of illness (e.g, their child's skin being covered with "infectious bacteria").

Tourette's Syndrome and Tic Disorders

Differentiating the stereotyped motor behaviors that characterize Tourette's syndrome and tic disorders from compulsions hinges on the functional relationship between these behaviors and any obsessive thoughts. Motor tics are generally experienced as involuntary and are not aimed at neutralizing distress brought about by obsessions. There is no conventional way of differentiating them from compulsions without obsessions, but OCD with "pure" compulsions is extremely rare (Foa et al., 1995). There appears to be a high rate of comorbidity between OCD and tic disorders (e.g., Pauls, Towbin, Leckman, Zahner, & Cohen, 1986), thus both disorders may be present in a given patient. In such cases, differentiating among tics and compulsions is especially important, as they are treated using different methods.

Hypochondriasis and Body Dysmorphic Disorder

The health concerns that characterize hypochondriasis and the preoccupation with imagined physical defects of body dysmorphic disorder (BDD) are both formally similar to the obsessions of OCD. To differentiate these disorders from OCD, the assessing clinician should examine for content specificity of the fear-provoking thoughts. Most individuals with hypochondriasis or BDD are singly obsessed, whereas most individuals with OCD have multiple obsessional themes.

Delusional Disorder and Schizophrenia

Approximately 5% of OCD patients report complete conviction that their obsessions and compulsions are realistic, with an additional 20% reporting strong but not fixed conviction. Therefore, it is important to consider the diagnosis of OCD "with poor insight" even if the patient denies the senselessness of their obsessions and compulsions. Delusional disorder can best be differentiated from OCD on the basis of the presence of compulsions in OCD (Eisen, Beer, Pato, Venditto, & Rasmussen, 1997), as obsessions even of delusional intensity are usually accompanied by compulsions.

As in the delusions of schizophrenia, the content of obsessions in OCD can be quite bizarre. However, bizarreness in and of itself does not preclude an OCD diagnosis. For example, one OCD patient treated at our center was fearful that people he interacted with would "steal his mind" unless he performed compulsions. Other symptoms of formal thought disorder must also be present to diagnose schizophrenia, such as loose associations, hallucinations, flat or grossly inappropriate affect, and thought insertion or projection. When an individual meets criteria for both OCD and schizophrenia, both diagnoses should be given.

COGNITIVE–BEHAVIORAL THEORIES OF OCD

Several cognitive–behavioral theories have been advanced to account for the etiology and maintenance of OCD. The earliest account was proposed by Dollard and Miller (1950), who adopted Mowrer's (1939, 1960) two-stage theory of fear acquisition. According to this theory, through the pairing of a neutral event with an innately aversive event, the former takes on the aversive properties of the latter, thus producing fear responses. In a second stage, after fear to the neutral event has been established, escape or avoidance behavior (i.e., compulsions) evolves to reduce that fear. Such avoidance is maintained by the negative reinforcement associated with its ability to attenuate fear. Although Mowrer's theory may not adequately explain fear acquisition (Rachman & Wilson, 1980), it is congruous with clinical and experimental observations: obsessions evoke anxiety or distress and compulsions reduce it (e.g., Roper & Rachman, 1976; Roper, Rachman, & Hodgson, 1973).

Some cognitive theorists have suggested that OCD arises from exaggeration of negative consequences (e.g., Carr, 1974). However, clinical observations suggest that exaggerated evaluation of danger is typical of all anxiety disorders and thus does not explain the distinguishing characteristics of OCD psychopathology. A more elaborate cognitive account for OCD was proposed by Salkovskis (1985), who proposed that five assumptions are specifically characteristic of OCD: (a) Thinking of an action is analogous to actually doing it; (b) failure to try to prevent harm to self or others is morally akin to causing the harm; (c) responsibility for harm is not diminished by extenuating circumstances; (d) failure to perform rituals in response to harm-related thoughts is the same as a real intention to harm; and (e) one should exercise control over one's thoughts.

Salkovskis's (1985) theory inspired interest in studying the role of responsibility in the psychopathology of OCD (e.g., Rachman, Throdarson, Shafran, & Woody, 1995). Most of these investigations were conducted on nonclinical samples using individuals with high scores on self-report measures of OCD. One study by Lopatka and Rachman (1995) used patients who met *DSM–III–R* criteria (American Psychiatric Association, 1987) for OCD. In this study, degree of perceived responsibility was manipulated with the hypothesis that increased responsibility would amplify the urge to check, the amount of discomfort experienced, and the estimated probabilities of bad outcome. The hypothesis was only partially supported by the data. Whereas low responsibility did decrease discomfort, estimates of the probability of anticipated harm, and urges to perform checking rituals, high responsibility did not produce changes in these variables.

To further examine the role of responsibility in OCD, Foa, Amir, Bogert, and Molnar (1998) developed the Obsessive Compulsive Responsibility Scale, which includes high-risk, low-risk, and OC-relevant scenarios. For each scenario, OCD and nonpatient participants were asked to estimate the degree of urge to rectify the situation, distress upon leaving the situation unrectified, and personal responsibility for harm to others if the unrectified situation were to result in harm. Results indicated that in low-risk and OC-relevant situations, individuals with OCD reported greater urge, distress, and responsibility than did nonpatients. However, no group differences were detected on the high-risk situations: Both groups indicated by far the highest values for this type of situation. These results seem to indicate that nonpatients better differentiate situations that merit attention and corrective action from situations in which the risk is too low to merit concern. Although individuals with OCD can also make such discriminations, they tend to display inflated responsibility for low-risk situations.

Clinical observations have led some investigators to hypothesize that memory deficits for actions underlie compulsive checking (e.g., Sher, Frost, & Otto, 1983). However, the empirical findings on this issue are equivocal. Some support for an action-memory deficit was found in nonclinical checkers (e.g., Rubenstein, Peynirgioglu, Chambless, & Pigott, 1993; Sher et al., 1983). In contrast, a study using a clinical sample found that compared with nonpatients, checkers *better* recalled their fear-relevant actions (e.g., plugging in an iron, unsheathing a knife) but not their fear-irrelevant actions (e.g., putting paperclips in a box; Constans, Foa, Franklin, & Mathews, 1995).

Foa and Kozak (1985) construed anxiety disorders as representing distinct pathological cognitive structures that involve pathological or mistaken representations of threat. They further hypothesized that several types of fear structures occur in obsessive–compulsives. Associations between the stimuli (e.g., public toilet seats) and meaning (e.g., a high probability of contracting AIDS) are evident in the patient with unrealistic fears of public bathrooms. For other obsessive–compulsives, certain harmless stimuli are strongly associated with distress, without regard to harm. For example, some patients reduce distress about disarray by rearranging objects, but do not anticipate any harmful consequences of the disorganization, except that it "just doesn't feel right."

Foa and Kozak (1985) also suggested that obsessive–compulsives often assume that, in the absence of clear evidence for safety, a situation must be dangerous; conversely, they fail to conclude that in the absence of clear evidence for danger, a situation must be safe. For example, to feel safe, an OCD sufferer may want to have a guarantee that the doorknob is clean before touching it, whereas a person without OCD would assume that the doorknob is safe and would not hesitate touching it unless there were clear danger cues. Because such guarantees are not possible in everyday life, rituals that are performed to reduce the likelihood of harm can never really provide the level of desired safety and must be repeated.

Although exposure therapy for pathological anxiety originated from a learning theory perspective, from the start, exposure and ritual prevention has been construed as a program for modifying mistaken beliefs (Meyer, 1966). In the same vein, to explain the efficacy of exposure therapy with anxiety disorders, Foa and Kozak (1986) proposed that exposure exercises are successful to the extent that they include information that corrects the pathological elements of the specific cognitive structure of the patient. To address the hypothesized need for OCD patients to search for complete safety, clinical psychologists present therapy as an opportunity to learn to tolerate ambiguity about safety.

COGNITIVE–BEHAVIORAL TREATMENT OF ADULT OCD

Exposure and Ritual Prevention

The prognostic picture for OCD has improved dramatically since Meyer (1966) reported on two patients who responded well to a treatment that included prolonged exposure to obsessional cues and strict prevention of rituals. This procedure, known at the time as *exposure and response prevention* (EX/RP), was later found to be extremely successful in 10 of 15 cases and partly effective in the remainder. Patients treated with this regimen also appeared to maintain their treatment gains: At a 5-year follow-up, only 2 of 15 patients had relapsed (Meyer & Levy, 1973; Meyer, Levy, & Schnurer, 1974).

As was the case with Meyer's (1966) program, EX/RP treatments conducted today typically include both prolonged exposure to obsessional cues and procedures aimed at blocking rituals. Exposure exercises are often done in real-life settings (in vivo), such as by asking the patient who fears accidentally causing a house fire by leaving the stove on to leave the house without checking the burners. When patients report specific feared consequences if they refrain from rituals, these fears can also be addressed through imaginal exposure. In fact, in vivo and imaginal exposure exercises are designed specifically to prompt obsessional distress. It is believed that repeated, prolonged exposure to feared thoughts and situations provides information that disconfirms mistaken associations and evaluations held by the patients and thereby promotes habituation (Foa & Kozak, 1986). Exposure is usually done gradually, with situations provoking moderate distress confronted before more upsetting ones. Exposure homeworks are routinely assigned between sessions, and patients are also asked to refrain from rituals.

Since Meyer's (1966) initial positive report of the efficacy of EX/RP, many subsequent studies of EX/RP have indicated that most EX/RP treatment completers make and maintain clinically significant gains. Foa and Kozak's (1996) review of 12 outcome studies ($N = 330$) reporting number of treatment responders revealed that ar average of 83% of treatment completers were classified as responders at posttreatment. In 16 studies reporting long-term outcome ($N = 376$; mean follow-up interval of 29 months), 76% were responders.

In general, EX/RP has been found quite effective in ameliorating OCD symptoms and has produced great durability of gains following treatment discontinuation. In our review of the literature, it also was clear that there are many variants of EX/RP treatment, some that are relevant for outcome and some that do not appear to be so. We review the literature on the relative efficacy of the ingredients that comprise EX/RP to help clinicians decide which EX/RP components are most essential.

EX/RP Treatment Variables

Exposure Versus Ritual Prevention Versus EX/RP

To separate the effects of exposure and ritual prevention on OCD symptoms, Foa, Steketee, Grayson, Turner, and Latimer (1984) randomly assigned patients with washing rituals to treatment by exposure only (EX), ritual prevention only (RP), or their combination (EX/RP). Each treatment was conducted intensively (15 daily 2-hr sessions conducted over 3 weeks) and was followed by a home visit. Patients in each condition were found to be improved at both posttreatment and follow-up, but EX/RP was superior to the single-component treatments on almost every symptom measure at both assessment points. In comparing EX with RP, patients who received EX reported lower anxiety when confronting feared contaminants than patients who had received RP, whereas the RP group reported greater decreases in urge to ritualize than did the EX patients. Thus, it appeared that EX and RP affect different OCD symptoms. The findings from this study clearly suggest that exposure and ritual prevention should be implemented concurrently; treatments that do not include both components yield inferior outcome.

Implementation of Ritual Prevention

Promoting abstinence from rituals during treatment is thought to be essential for successful treatment outcome, but the preferred method of ritual prevention has changed over the years. In Meyer's (1966) EX/RP treatment program, hospital staff physically prevented patients from performing rituals (e.g., turning off water supply in patient's room). However, physical intervention by staff or family members to prevent patients from ritualizing is no longer typical or recommended. It is believed that such prevention techniques are too coercive to be an accepted practice today. Moreover, physical prevention by others may actually limit generalizability to nontherapy situations in which others are not present to intercede. Instead, instructions and encouragement to refrain from ritualizing and avoidance are now recommended (see Kozak & Foa, 1996, for a detailed review of these instructions). As noted above, although exposure can reduce obsessional distress, in itself, it is not so effective in reducing compulsions. To maximize treatment effects, the patient needs to voluntarily refrain from ritualizing while engaging in systematic exposure exercises. The therapist should strongly emphasize the importance of refraining from rituals and should help the patient with this difficult task by providing support, encouragement, and suggestions about alternatives to ritualizing.

Use of Imaginal Exposure

Treatment involving imaginal exposure plus in vivo exposure and ritual prevention was found superior at follow-up to an in vivo exposure plus ritual prevention program that did not include imaginal exposure (Foa, Steketee, Turner, & Fischer, 1980; Steketee, Foa, & Grayson, 1982). However, a second study did not find that the addition of imaginal exposure enhanced long-term efficacy compared with in vivo exposure only (de Araujo, Ito, Marks, & Deale, 1995). However, the treatment program in the former study differed from that of de Araujo et al.'s on several parameters (e.g., 90-minute vs. 30-minute imaginal exposures, respectively), and thus the source of these studies' inconsistencies cannot be identified.

In our clinical work, we have found imaginal exposure to be helpful for patients who report that disastrous consequences will result if they refrain from rituals. Because many of these consequences cannot be readily translated into in vivo exposure exercises (e.g., burning in hell), imaginal exposure allows the patient an opportunity to confront these feared thoughts. Also, the addition of imagery to in vivo exposure may circumvent the cognitive avoidance strategies used by patients who try intentionally not to consider the consequences of exposure while confronting feared situations in vivo. In summary, although imaginal exposure does not appear essential for immediate outcome, it may enhance long-term maintenance and can be used as an adjunct to in vivo exercises for patients with disastrous consequences. For patients who only report extreme distress as a consequence to not ritualizing, imaginal exposure may not be needed.

Duration of Exposure

Duration of exposure is also thought to be important for outcome: Prolonged continuous exposure is more effective than short interrupted exposure (Rabavilas, Boulougouris, & Stefanis, 1976). Indeed, reduction in anxiety (habituation) within the exposure session to the most distressing item and reduction in the peak anxiety across sessions were associated with improvement following EX/RP treatment (Kozak, Foa, & Steketee, 1988). Studies have indicated that continuous exposure of approximately 90 minutes duration is needed for anxiety reduction (Foa & Chambless, 1978) and for decrease in urges to ritualize (Rachman, de Silva, & Roper, 1976). While a useful guideline, exposure should sometimes be continued beyond 90 minutes if the patient has not experienced anxiety reduction within that time, or terminated if the patient reports substantial reduction in obsessional distress sooner.

Gradual Versus Abrupt Exposures

No differences in OCD symptom reduction were detected in a study comparing patients who confronted the most distressing situations from the start of therapy with those who confronted less distressing situations first, yet patients preferred the more gradual approach (Hodgson, Rachman, & Marks, 1972). Because patient motivation and agreement with treatment goals is a key element of successful EX/RP, situations of moderate difficulty are usually confronted first, followed by several intermediate steps before the most distressing exposures are accomplished. However, it is important to confront the highest item on the treatment hierarchy within the first week of intensive treatment (daily 2-hr sessions conducted over 3 weeks) to allow for sufficient time to repeat these difficult exposures over the latter 2 weeks.

Frequency of Exposure Sessions

Optimal frequency of exposure sessions has yet to be established. Intensive exposure therapy programs that have achieved excellent results (see

Foa et al., 1992) typically involve daily sessions over the course of approximately 1 month, but quite favorable outcomes have also been achieved with more widely spaced sessions (e.g., de Araujo et al., 1995). Clinically, we have found that weekly sessions may be sufficient for highly motivated patients with mild OCD symptoms who readily understand the importance of daily exposure homeworks. Patients with more severe symptoms or those who for various reasons cannot readily comply with EX/RP tasks are more likely to require intensive treatment.

Therapist-Assisted Versus Self-Exposure

Evaluations of the presence of a therapist during exposure have yielded inconsistent results. In one study, OCD patients receiving therapist-assisted exposure were more improved immediately posttreatment than were those receiving clomipramine and self-exposure, but this difference was not evident at follow-up (Marks et al., 1988). However, these results are difficult to interpret in light of the study's complex design. A second study using OCD patients also indicated that therapist-assisted treatment was not superior to self-exposure at posttreatment or at follow-up (Emmelkamp & van Kraanen, 1977), but the number of patients in each condition was too small to render these findings conclusive.

In contrast to the negative findings of Marks et al. (1988) and Emmelkamp and van Kraanen (1977), therapist presence yielded superior outcome of a single 3-hour exposure session compared with self-exposure for persons with specific phobia (Ost, 1989). Because specific phobias are on the whole less disabling and easier to treat than OCD, one could surmise that therapist presence should also influence treatment outcome with OCD. Moreover, using meta-analytic procedures, Abramowitz (1996) found that therapist-controlled exposure was associated with greater improvement in OCD and general anxiety symptoms compared with self-controlled procedures. In light of the inconsistent findings reported above, no clear answer is available on the role of therapist assistance with exposure tasks in OCD treatment.

EX/RP Versus Other Treatment Approaches

In this section, we review the literature on the efficacy of standard individual EX/RP treatment versus other approaches, including family-based EX/RP treatment, group treatment, cognitive therapy, and pharmacotherapy.

Family Involvement Versus Standard EX/RP Treatment

Emmelkamp et al. (1990) examined whether family involvement in treatment would enhance the efficacy of EX/RP for OCD. Patients who were married or living with a romantic partner were randomly assigned to receive EX/RP either with or without partner involvement in treatment. Each treatment lasted 5 weeks and consisted of eight 45–60-minute sessions with the therapist; exposures were not practiced in session. Results indicated that OCD symptoms were significantly lowered following treatment for both groups. No differences between the treatment emerged, and initial marital distress did not predict outcome. However, the reduction in anxiety or distress reported for the sample as a whole was modest (33%), which could have resulted from the relatively short treatment sessions and absence of in vivo exposure exercises in treatment sessions.

Mehta (1990) also examined the effect of family involvement on EX/RP treatment outcome. To adapt the treatment to serve the large numbers of young unmarried people seeking OCD treatment and the "joint family system" prevalent in India, Mehta used a family-based rather than spouse-based treatment approach. Patients who did not respond to previous pharmacotherapy were randomly assigned to receive treatment by systematic desensitization and EX/RP either with or without family assistance. Sessions in both conditions were held twice per week for 12 weeks; response prevention was described as "gradual." In the family condition, a designated family member (parent, spouse, or adult child) assisted with homework assignments, supervised relaxation therapy, participated in response prevention, and was instructed to be supportive. On self-reported OCD symptoms, a greater improvement was found for the family-based intervention at posttreatment and 6-month follow-up. Although the study had methodological problems that complicate interpretation of findings (e.g., use of self-report OCD measures only, unclear description of treatment procedures), it offers evidence that family involvement may be helpful in OCD treatment.

Individual Versus Group EX/RP

Intensive individual EX/RP, although effective, can pose practical obstacles such as high cost for treatment and scheduling problems. In addition, because experts in EX/RP treatment are few and far between, patients may need to wait for long periods of time, or travel substantial distances, in order to be treated.

To examine the relative efficacy of group therapy for OCD, Fals-Stewart, Marks, and Schafer (1993) conducted a controlled study. OCD patients were randomly assigned to individual EX/RP, group EX/RP, or a psychosocial control condition (relaxation). Each of the active treatments was 12 weeks long, with sessions held twice weekly, and included daily exposure homeworks. Significant improvement in OCD symptoms was evidenced in both active treatments, with no differences detected between individual and group EX/RP immediately posttreatment or at 6-month follow-up. Profile analysis of OCD symptom ratings collected throughout treatment did indicate a faster reduction in symptoms for patients receiving individual treatment.

These results offer evidence for the efficacy of group treatment. However, because patients were excluded from this study if they were diagnosed with any personality disorder or with comorbid depression based on Beck Depression Inventory (BDI) scores (Beck, Ward, Mendelson, Mock, & Erbaugh, 1961) greater than 22, it may be that the sample was somewhat atypical. In addition, none of the participants had received previous OCD treatment, which is also unusual for this population and suggestive of a less severe sample. Thus, inferences about the broader population of OCD patients merit caution until these results are replicated.

EX/RP Versus Cognitive Therapies

Increased interest in cognitive therapy (e.g., Beck, 1976; Ellis, 1962) coupled with dissatisfaction with formulations of treatment as mediated by processes such as extinction (Stampfl & Levis, 1967) or habituation (Watts, 1973) prompted examination of the efficacy of cognitive procedures for anxiety disorders in general and for OCD in particular. In the first of these studies, Emmelkamp, van der Helm, van Zanten, and Plochg (1980) compared Self-Instructional Training (SIT; Meichenbaum, 1975) plus EX/RP with EX/RP alone. Following two sessions of relaxation training for both groups, the SIT and EX/RP treatments were conducted twice weekly for 5 weeks; sessions were of 2-hour duration. Both groups improved on all outcome measures; on assessor-rated avoidance associated with main compulsion, a superiority of EX/RP alone emerged. Thus, self-instructional training may have slightly hindered, rather than enhanced, efficacy.

Emmelkamp, Visser, and Hoekstra (1988) then examined the efficacy of Rational Emotive Therapy (RET), a cognitive therapy program that focuses on irrational beliefs. Patients were randomly assigned to receive EX/RP or RET. Treatment consisted of 10 sessions (60 minutes each) conducted over 8 weeks. In the EX/RP condition, patients were assigned exposure exercises from their treatment hierarchy to perform at home twice per week for at least 90 minutes; no exposure within session was conducted. RET involved determining the irrational thoughts that mediated negative feelings, confronting these thoughts with cognitive techniques, and modifying them with the aim of reducing anxiety and thereby decreasing the need to ritualize. Irrational beliefs were challenged Socratically by the therapist during sessions; patients were instructed to challenge their irrational thinking between sessions. Patients receiving RET were not instructed to expose themselves to feared situations, nor were they explicitly instructed to refrain from such exposure. Results indicated that both groups were improved at posttreatment with no between-groups differences. Because a large percentage of the sample received additional treatment during the follow-up period, long-term comparisons were difficult to interpret.

Emmelkamp and Beens (1991) examined whether a combined package of cognitive therapy plus EX/RP would enhance the effects of EX/RP. They compared a program that included 6 sessions of RET alone followed by 6 sessions of RET plus self-controlled EX/RP with a program that included 12 sessions of self-controlled EX/RP. In both programs, the first 6 sessions were followed by 4 weeks of no treatment, after which the additional 6 sessions were delivered. As in Emmelkamp et al.'s (1988) study, treatment sessions were conducted approximately once per week, and lasted for 60 minutes each. EX/RP sessions did not include therapist-assisted exposure, and patients were assigned twice-weekly exposure homework exercises. The first 6 sessions of the RET program were equivalent to that used in the Emmelkamp et al. (1988) study and did not include exposure homework or antiexposure instructions. When self-controlled EX/RP was introduced following the first 6 RET-only sessions, the latter was focused on irrational thoughts that emerged during exposure homeworks. Mean reduction of anxiety associated with main OC problem was 25% for RET and 23% for EX/RP following 6 sessions. Following 6 more sessions (RET + EX/RP in one condition and EX/RP only in the other), both groups continued to improve on most measures compared with pretreatment; no significant group differences emerged. About 30% of the sample dropped out during treatment, which is relatively high and a limitation to the generalizability of the findings.

Van Oppen et al. (1995) compared self-controlled EX/RP with an OCD-specific cognitive intervention. Patients were randomly assigned to receive 6 sessions (45-minute duration) of cognitive therapy or EX/RP followed by 10 sessions of treatment that include components from both. To examine the effects of "purer" versions of cognitive therapy and EX/RP, the therapist did not introduce behavioral experiments (exposures) into the cognitive treatment until after Session 6. Conversely, in the first 6 EX/RP sessions, care was taken by the therapist to specifically avoid any discussion of disastrous consequences. Results indicated that cognitive therapy without behavioral experiments and EX/RP without discussion of disastrous consequences led to OCD symptom reductions of 20% and 23%, respectively. After the second phase (10 additional sessions), both groups continued to improve.

Hiss, Foa, and Kozak (1994) investigated whether formal relapse prevention techniques following intensive EX/RP enhanced maintenance of gains. All discussions about cognitive factors typically included during the core treatment (e.g., discussion of lapse vs. relapse, posttreatment exposure instructions, themes of guilt and personal responsibility, and feared consequences) were removed. Patients received this modified EX/RP, followed by either a relapse prevention treatment or a psychosocial control treatment (associative therapy). All patients in both conditions were classified as responders at posttreatment (defined as 50% or greater reduction in OCD symptoms), with treatment gains better maintained in the relapse prevention group than in the associative therapy condition at 6-month follow-up. The percentage of responders at follow-up was 75% in the relapse prevention condition and 33% in associative therapy.

The results of studies examining the relative and combined efficacy of EX/RP and cognitive interventions have been mixed. In general, the EX/RP treatments used in these studies involved shorter sessions, fewer sessions, and absence of therapist-assisted exposure. These factors may have attenuated outcome compared with programs that used intensive regimens with therapist-assisted exposure in session (e.g., 80% reduction on assessors' ratings of rituals in Foa et al., 1992; 60% and 66% Yale-Brown Obsessive Compulsive Scale reduction in Hiss et al., 1994). Thus, the issue of whether the cognitive therapies described above are comparable or preferable to intensive EX/RP, including therapist-aided exposure, has yet to be determined.

The issue of whether or not cognitive therapy improves the efficacy of EX/RP may have practical implications but little theoretical interest, because both exposure therapy and cognitive therapy intend to modify mistaken cognitions. Indeed, Foa and Kozak (1986) argued that the disconfirmation of erroneous associations and beliefs is a crucial mechanism underlying the efficacy of exposure treatments. For example, a patient and therapist sitting on the bathroom floor in a public restroom conducting an exposure to contaminated surfaces routinely discuss risk assessment, probability overestimation, and so on as the therapist helps the patient achieve the cognitive modification necessary for improvement. The practical issue of interest is how to maximize efficacy: Is informal discussion of cognitive distortions during the exposure exercises sufficient, or should the therapist engage in formal Socratic questioning of hypothesized distortions such as inflated responsibility? Investigations that compare amputated versions of exposure and cognitive therapy (e.g, van Oppen et al., 1995) cannot provide an answer to this question.

EX/RP Versus Pharmacotherapy

Many controlled studies have indicated that serotonergic antidepressants (e.g., clomipramine, fluoxetine) are superior to placebo in ameliorating OCD symptoms (for a review, see Greist, Jefferson, Kobak, Katzelnick, & Serlin, 1995). However, only a few controlled studies have examined the relative or combined efficacy of antidepressant medications and EX/RP. These studies are reviewed below.

Using a rather complex experimental design, Marks, Stern, Mawson, Cobb, and McDonald (1980) randomly assigned 40 patients to initially receive either clomipramine or pill placebo (PBO) for 4 weeks. Six weeks of inpatient psychological treatment (daily 45-minute sessions) followed for both groups. During the first 3 weeks of this phase, 10 patients from each medication condition received EX/RP whereas the other 10 received relaxation. At Week 7, those patients who had received relaxation were switched to EX/RP and the remaining continued to receive EX/RP. At the end of the 6-week psychosocial treatment period, patients were discharged from the hospital but remained on medication until Week 36, when a 4-week taper period commenced. Patients were followed for another year upon drug discontinuation. Results suggested that, compared with PBO, clomipramine produced significant improvements in mood and rituals only in those patients who were initially depressed. Compared with relaxation at Week 7, EX/RP was associated with greater reductions in rituals, but not with improvements in mood.

Several methodological issues, including the overly complex experimental design, complicated interpretation of findings. In particular, the inpatient behavior therapy condition, consisting of 45-minute long daily sessions for 3–6 weeks (depending on treatment condition), may have used insufficiently strict response prevention instructions (after exposure [in session], patients were asked not to carry out rituals for the rest of the session and to resist ritualizing for a specified time thereafter). Length of treatment session may also have been problematic, as is the lack of information regarding what patients did on the inpatient unit for 6 weeks when they were not in session. Weaknesses in the experimental design led to underestimation of changes attributable to the behavioral treatment at Week 7 (EX/RP vs. relaxation comparison), and the design did not allow for a direct comparison of clomipramine and exposure alone across the same time period. Moreover, the drug-only period was too short (4 weeks) to allow optimal assessment of the efficacy of clomipramine alone.

The efficacy of clomipramine (CMI) and EX/RP was examined again by Marks et al. (1988). Forty-nine patients were randomized to one of four treatment conditions, three of which included CMI for approximately 6 months and one of which included PBO. One of the CMI groups received antiexposure instructions for 23 weeks, the second group had self-controlled exposure for 23 weeks, and the third group received self-controlled exposure for 8 weeks followed by therapist-aided exposure from Week 8 until Week 23; the PBO group also received self-controlled exposure for 8 weeks followed by therapist-aided exposure from Week 8 until Week 23. Inspection of the means in the PBO group at the different treatment stages indicated that therapist-aided exposure was superior to self exposure: Mean reduction after 8 weeks of self-exposure was 20% for rituals and 23% for OCD-related discomfort, whereas mean reduction after an additional nine sessions of therapist-aided exposure was 71% and 68%, respectively. However, in the absence of a placebo group that received therapist-aided exposure first, it remains possible that order effects mediated the superiority of therapist-aided exposure. Because of confounds introduced by the complicated design, it is not possible to directly compare the effects of CMI with that of EX/RP. An additional issue is that evaluators were able to guess accurately 90% of the time whether patients received CMI or PBO, indicating problems with the blinding procedure.

With the growing awareness of the severe side effects associated with CMI, Cottraux et al. (1990) compared the efficacy of a more serotonergically selective medication, fluvoxamine (FLU), with that of EX/RP. Patients were assigned to one of three conditions: FLU with antiexposure instructions, FLU + EX/RP, and PBO with EX/RP. In the antiexposure condition, patients were specifically instructed to avoid feared situations or stimuli. Treatment continued for 24 weeks, after which EX/RP was stopped and medication was tapered over 4 weeks. EX/RP treatment was provided in weekly sessions and consisted of two distinct treatment phases: self-controlled exposure between sessions and imaginal exposure during sessions for the first 8 weeks, followed by 16 weeks of therapist-guided exposure and ritual prevention. Other psychosocial interventions (e.g., couples therapy, cognitive restructuring, assertiveness training) were also provided as deemed necessary. Assessment included evaluators' ratings by blind procedures and self-report measures. At posttreatment (Week 24), reduction in assessor-rated duration of rituals per day were FLU + antiexposure 42%, FLU + EX/RP 46%, and PBO + EX/RP 25%. At 6-month follow-up, reductions in assessor-rated duration of rituals per day were FLX + antiexposure 42%, FLX + EX/RP 45%, and PBO + EX/RP 35%. Although FLX + EX/RP produced slightly greater improvement in depression at posttreatment than did PBO + EX/RP, the superiority of the combined treatment for depression was not evident at follow-up. Interestingly, the majority of the FLX + antiexposure patients reported engaging in exposure on their own, thus invalidating the comparison between exposure and antiexposure with fluvoxamine.

To examine whether antidepressant medication reduces OCD symptoms only through reduction of depression, Foa et al. (1992) divided OCD patients into highly depressed (BDI $\geq$ 21) and mildly depressed (BDI $\leq$ 20) groups and then randomly assigned patients in both groups to receive either 6 weeks of treatment by imipramine or PBO. Upon completion of the medication-only phase, all patients received 3-week (15 session) intensive EX/RP followed by 12 weekly supportive sessions. Contrary to hypothesis, although imipramine reduced depression in the depressed patients, it did not significantly reduce OCD symptoms in either depressed or nondepressed patients at Week 6: Mean reductions in assessor-rated fear of 13% and 26% were observed in depressed and nondepressed imipramine patients, respectively, as were reductions of 17% and 34% on assessor-rated compulsive behavior. Moreover, imipramine did not enhance immediate or long-term outcome of EX/RP: OCD and depressive symptoms were both significantly reduced in each of the four groups following EX/RP, even in the depressed group who initially received placebo. Mean percentage reductions in assessor ratings of obsessions and compulsions at posttreatment (Week 10) were as follows: 58% and 82% for the depressed imipramine group, 42% and 85% for the depressed PBO group, 51% and 82% for the nondepressed imipramine group, and 64% and 84% for the nondepressed PBO group.

The relative and combined efficacy of CMI and intensive EX/RP is being examined in a multicenter study in progress at Allegheny University of the Health Sciences and Columbia University (Kozak, Liebowitz, & Foa, in press). An EX/RP program that includes an intensive phase (fifteen 2-hour sessions conducted over 3 weeks) and follow-up phase (6 brief sessions delivered over 8 weeks) is compared with CMI, EX/RP + CMI, and PBO. Preliminary findings with treatment completer data as well as intent-to-treat data suggest that the active treatments appear superior to placebo, EX/RP appears superior to CMI, and the combination of the two treatments does not appear superior to EX/RP alone. However, the design used in the Allegheny–Columbia study may not optimally promote an additive effect of CMI because the intensive portion of the EX/RP program was largely completed before patients reached their maximum dose of CMI.

In summary, although there is clear evidence that both pharmaceutical treatment with serotonergic medications and EX/RP treatments are effective for OCD, information about their relative and combined efficacy remains scarce because most of the studies that examined these issues have been methodologically limited. Nevertheless, no study has found clear long-term superiority for combined pharmacotherapy plus EX/RP over EX/RP alone. The absence of conclusive findings notwithstanding, many experts continue to advocate combined procedures as the treatment of choice for OCD (e.g., Greist, 1992). In clinical practice, it is common to see patients for EX/RP treatment who are taking SRIs concurrently.

SUMMARY

The review in this chapter indicates clearly that much is already known about cognitive–behavioral treatment (CBT) and pharmacotherapy for OCD. Our clinical practice with adults has been strongly influenced by the findings of these investigations, although not all of the decisions we make in our clinical practice are unequivocally supported by empirical studies. For instance, no controlled direct comparison study has indicated that intensive CBT is better than less intensive treatment, yet we typically provide intensive treatment to adult patients with at least moderately severe OCD. Although our clinical experience suggests that weekly CBT sessions are probably insufficient to produce meaningful gains in most adult OCD patients, it has yet to be established whether twice or thrice weekly sessions would be comparable with daily sessions in both immediate and long-term outcome. Future research should examine this important issue to establish a "dose-response" curve for CBT. In addition, more empirical study of predictors of CBT treatment entry and response are needed to allow us to identify the optimal treatment course to pursue with any particular patient.

We are confident on empirical and clinical grounds that CBT for OCD must involve both exposure and strict ritual prevention instructions, and that avoidance of the most anxiety-evoking exposures on the part of the patient is likely to compromise outcome. With respect to the therapist-assisted versus self-exposure issue, we routinely choose therapist-assisted exposure in our clinical practice. Future studies of this issue must be conducted carefully and with sufficient sample sizes, as we believe that reducing therapist assistance with exposure exercises would be premature at this time given the data and clinical observations. With respect to the role of cognitive interventions, we consider our EX/RP program a "cognitive–behavioral" treatment in that we target cognitions and behaviors for change; however, we do not typically include formal cognitive restructuring exercises to bring about that change. Future research should be directed at delineating which cognitive and behavioral procedures are most effective for correcting particular pathological emotions, rather than at running horse races where each participant is not operating at full strength (e.g., cognitive therapy without experiments, behavior therapy without discussion of feared consequences). Consistent with the empirical research conducted so far, we believe that although antidepressant medications for OCD are unlikely to interfere with the efficacy of CBT, combination treatment is not necessarily more effective than CBT alone. However, the partial symptom reduction typical of pharmacotherapy for OCD may make some patients more willing to tolerate the distress associated with CBT, and thus premedication may be helpful in such cases.

With respect to the question as to what factors might enhance long-term effectiveness of CBT for OCD, we have observed that OCD patients who show great improvement immediately after CBT are more likely to retain their gains at follow-up than those who make only moderate post-treatment gains. Thus, emphasis on the procedures likely to lead to maximal short-term efficacy will also serve the patient well in the long run. In our clinical experience, thorough understanding of the treatment rationale, active engagement in exposure exercises, strict adherence to ritual prevention instructions, willingness to design and implement exposure exercises between sessions, and willingness to confront even the most difficult times on the fear hierarchy are all factors associated with positive treatment outcome. Thus, verbal reinforcement of patients when they accomplish these things and reinstruction when they do not are important in promoting lasting change. In addition, relapse prevention techniques designed specifically for OCD have been found effective in promoting maintenance of gains at follow-up (Hiss et al., 1994). In clinical practice, we begin alluding to relapse prevention procedures long before the active treatment is completed, and we focus on maintaining gains in the last few active treatment sessions. Some continuing contact with the treating clinician is also thought to be of benefit; thus, brief follow-up sessions are held in the first few months after the active treatment is completed, with contacts as needed following the formal follow-up phase. As part of relapse prevention, we often ask our patients to plan exposure and ritual prevention exercises for hypothetical obsessions they may encounter in the future (e.g., "If you became obsessed in 6 months that touching tree bark would result in your contracting a terrible illness, what exercises should you do?") to encourage patients to problem-solve around OCD issues for themselves, rather than relying on the therapist's direct instruction. We also emphasize to patients that the occasional occurrence of an obsession is probably beyond their control and not a cause for great alarm provided that they implement exposure and response prevention to combat these recurring obsessions and urges to ritualize. The patients who are most accepting of this reality are often the ones most able to apply what they learned in treatment, and this process enables them to keep their OCD symptoms under good control long after active treatment has terminated. Our emphasis to patients is that the road to relapse is paved with rituals and avoidance rather than with occasional obsessive intrusions, and that compulsive activity is actually more likely to increase the frequency and intensity of obsessions in the long run even if it reduces anxiety temporarily.

TREATMENT OF PEDIATRIC OCD

As is the case with adults, there is evidence for the efficacy of CMI compared with placebo in pediatric OCD (e.g., DeVeaugh-Geiss et al., 1992), as well for the selective serotonin reuptake inhibitors (SRIs) (e.g., fluoxetine; Riddle et al., 1992). Results of these and other studies suggest partial treatment response and high rates of relapse upon drug discontinuation (e.g, Leonard et al., 1991). In light of these findings, treatment researchers have begun to examine the effectiveness of CBT involving EX/RP for pediatric OCD. At present, no controlled studies of this treatment have been published. There is, however, a growing literature of case reports and case series suggesting that EX/RP may be helpful in ameliorating pediatric OCD symptoms. We will review two recent case series that involved similar EX/RP treatment programs, and will then introduce the design of a controlled study that has recently been funded by the National Institute of Mental Health (NIMH). We will conclude with some recommendations about how to modify EX/RP treatments used with adults to better serve the needs of pediatric patients and their families.

March, Mulle, and Herbel (1994) treated 15 children and adolescents with OCD using a manualized behavioral treatment package that included psychoeducation, EX/RP, and anxiety management training (AMT). Results indicated a mean OCD symptom reduction of 50% at posttreatment, with 12 of 15 patients classified as responders. Moreover, treatment gains were maintained at follow-up. Because all but one child was also receiving pharmacotherapy with SRIs, the separate effects of behavior therapy cannot be determined. However, the degree of improvement and long-term maintenance of gains were greater than what has been typically reported in studies of pharmacotherapy alone, suggesting a significant contribution of behavior therapy.

At Allegheny University, the effectiveness of EX/RP without AMT for pediatric OCD was examined in a case series (Franklin et al., 1998). In this uncontrolled study, 14 children and adolescents received EX/RP; 8 of the 14 received concurrent pharmacotherapy with SRIs. Results indicated a mean reduction of 67% in OCD symptoms at posttreatment and 62% at follow-up (mean time to follow-up = 9 months). Similar to March et al.'s (1994) study, 12 of 14 patients were classified as responders. Patients who received EX/RP alone responded similarly to those receiving combined treatment, although these results must be interpreted with caution in light of nonrandom assignment to condition and low statistical power to detect differences. On the whole, these results converge with those of March et al. in suggesting that EX/RP may be an effective treatment for pediatric OCD. In addition, it appears from the Franklin et al. study that AMT procedures may not be necessary in conducting EX/RP.

The clinical presentation of OCD appears similar in adults and children (Swedo et al., 1989), but there are important differences among these groups that influence how the treatment is conducted with children. Less intensive treatment (e.g., weekly instead of daily) is usually scheduled to avoid taxing children's attentional resources, although in our clinic children with severe OCD are usually seen intensively. Children also have more difficulty with abstract reasoning, which can be overcome by using analogies readily understood by children such as those suggested by March and Mulle (1993). Great care must be taken to help children and their families "externalize" OCD rather than engage in blaming the child for the disruptions caused by the illness. Another adjustment typically made in treatment of pediatric OCD is that children are given greater latitude to select exposure exercises than are adults. This is done to promote the spirit of mutual collaboration, or "team spirit" in combating OCD, instead of imposing rules on children who may generally be less amenable to following adult instructions without involvement in the process. Family members are routinely involved in implementing exposure homeworks in pediatric treatment, whereas this is less typical with adult patients. Especially with the youngest children, parents can be enlisted to serve as "co-therapists" directly involved in treatment planning and implementation. However, the clinician must also be ready to minimize parents' direct involvement in treatment sessions if their involvement leads to conflict and other processes that take away from time available for implementing EX/RP procedures. Also with young children, reinforcement schedules can be utilized to increase investment in completing exposure exercises, self-monitoring, and so on. One patient seen in our clinic would have his hard work in session reinforced by allotting time at the end of session to "surf the Net" with the therapist on a clinic computer.

The absence of controlled studies examining the relative and combined efficacy of EX/RP and SRIs prevents us from drawing strong conclusions about these treatments in pediatric OCD samples. To address this important issue, a multicenter collaborative study recently sponsored by the NIMH has begun at Allegheny University of the Health Sciences and Duke University Medical Center (E. B. Foa & J. S. March, principal investigators). In this study, children and adolescents with OCD will be randomly assigned to receive one of five treatments: (a) EX/RP; (b) Sertraline (SER); (c) EX/RP + SER; (d) a psychosocial control treatment called Coping With Stress; or (e) pill placebo. This study will provide more definitive conclusions about pediatric OCD treatment and may also serve to promote similar research efforts in the field.

CONCLUSION

It is clear from our review of the literature that an enormous amount of progress has been made within the past three decades in the development of effective psychosocial and pharmacologic treatments for OCD. Along with professionals from several other disciplines, clinical psychologists have been in the vanguard of applied research designed to alleviate the suffering of patients once thought to be beyond our help. At the same time, there is still much that remains to be discovered, because not all patients who receive the available treatments experience substantial OCD symptom relief in the long run. Undoubtedly, the expertise of clinical psychologists will be needed in designing future OCD treatment outcome and experimental psychopathology studies; implementing these studies; developing new psychosocial treatments; providing clinical services as part of treatment outcome trials; and then analyzing, interpreting, publishing, and disseminating research findings. Yet despite the encouraging findings for EX/RP, the impact of this therapy will be limited if clinicians working in the mental health facilities where most OCD patients receive care are not exposed to information about EX/RP's potential usefulness for their OCD clients. Thus, in addition to fulfilling our varied roles in OCD treatment research, it is incumbent upon us to assume responsibility for teaching frontline clinicians in need of education, training, and supervision in the state-of-the-art therapies for OCD.

REFERENCES

Abramowitz, J. S. (1996). Variants of exposure and response prevention in the treatment of obsessive–compulsive disorder: A meta-analysis. *Behavior Therapy, 27,* 583–600.

American Psychiatric Association. (1987). *Diagnostic and statistical manual of mental disorders.* (3rd ed., rev.). Washington, DC: Author.

American Psychiatric Association. (1994). *Diagnostic and statistical manual of mental disorders.* (4th ed.). Washington, DC: Author.

AuBuchon, P. G., & Malatesta, V. J. (1994). Obsessive compulsive patients with comorbid personality disorder: Associated problems and response to a comprehensive behavior therapy. *Journal of Clinical Psychiatry, 55,* 448–453.

Beck, A. T. (1976). *Cognitive therapy and the emotional disorders.* New York: International Universities Press.

Beck, A. T., Ward, C. H., Mendelson, M., Mock, J., & Erbaugh, J. (1961). An inventory for measuring depression. *Archives of General Psychiatry, 4,* 561–571.

Carr, A. T. (1974). Compulsive neurosis: A review of the literature. *Psychological Bulletin, 81,* 311–318.

Constans, J. I., Foa, E. B., Franklin, M. E., & Mathews, A. (1995). Memory for actions in obsessive compulsives with checking rituals. *Behaviour Research and Therapy, 33,* 665–671.

Cottraux, J., Mollard, E., Bouvard, M., Marks, I., Sluys, M., Nury, A. M., Douge, R., & Ciadella, P. (1990). A controlled study of fluvoxamine and exposure in obsessive–compulsive disorder. *International Clinical Psychopharmacology, 5,* 17–30.

de Araujo, L. A., Ito, L. M., Marks, I. M., & Deale, A. (1995). Does imagined exposure to the consequences of not ritualising enhance live exposure for OCD? A controlled study: I. Main outcome. *British Journal of Psychiatry, 167,* 65–70.

DeVeaugh-Geiss, J., Moroz, G., Biederman, J., Cantwell, D., Fontaine, R., Greist, J. H., Reichler, R., Katz, R., & Landau, P. (1992). Clomipramine hydrochloride in childhood and adolescent obsessive–compulsive disorder: A multicenter trial. *Journal of the American Academy of Child and Adolescent Psychiatry, 31,* 45–49.

Dollard, J., & Miller, N. E. (1950). *Personality and psychotherapy: An analysis in terms of learning, thinking and culture.* New York: McGraw-Hill.

Eisen, J. L., Beer, D. A., Pato, M. T., Venditto, T. A., & Rasmussen, S. A. (1997). Obsessive–compulsive disorder in patients with schizophrenia or schizoaffective disorder. *American Journal of Psychiatry, 154,* 271–273.

Ellis, A. (1962). *Reason and emotion in psychotherapy.* New York: Lyle Stuart.

Emmelkamp, P. M. G., & Beens, H. (1991). Cognitive therapy with obsessive–compulsive disorder: A comparative evaluation. *Behaviour Research and Therapy, 29,* 293–300.

Emmelkamp, P. M. G., de Haan, E., & Hoogduin, C. A. L. (1990). Marital adjustment and obsessive–compulsive disorder. *British Journal of Psychiatry, 156,* 55–60.

Emmelkamp, P. M. G., van der Helm, M., van Zanten, B. L., & Plochg, I. (1980). Treatment of obsessive compulsive patients: The contribution of self-instructional training to the effectiveness of exposure. *Behaviour Research and Therapy, 18,* 61–66.

Emmelkamp, P. M. G., & van Kraanen, J. (1977). Therapist-controlled exposure in vivo: A comparison with obsessive–compulsive patients. *Behaviour Research and Therapy, 15,* 491–495.

Emmelkamp, P. M. G., Visser, S., & Hoekstra, R. J. (1988). Cognitive therapy vs. exposure in vivo in the treatment of obsessive compulsives. *Cognitive Therapy and Research, 12,* 103–114.

Fals-Stewart, W., & Lucente, S. (1993). An MCMI cluster typology of obsessive–compulsives: A measure of personality characteristics and its relationship to treatment participation, compliance and outcome in behavior therapy. *Journal of Psychiatric Research, 27,* 139–154.

Fals-Stewart, W., Marks, A., & Schafer, J. (1993). A comparison of behavioral group therapy and individual behavior therapy in treating obsessive–compulsive disorder. *Journal of Nervous and Mental Disease, 181,* 189–193.

Flament, M. F., Koby, E., Rapoport, J. L., Berg, C. Z., Zahn, T., Cox, C., Denckla, M., & Lenane, M. (1990). Childhood obsessive–compulsive disorder: A prospective follow-up study. *Journal of Child Psychology and Psychiatry and Allied Disciplines, 31,* 363–380.

Flament, M. F., Whitaker, A., Rapoport, J. L., Davies, M., Berg, C. Z., Kalikow, K., Sceery, W., & Shaffer, D. (1988). Obsessive compulsive disorder in adolescence: An epidemiological study. *Journal of the American Academy of Child and Adolescent Psychiatry, 27,* 764–771.

Foa, E. B., Amir, N., Bogert, K., & Molnar, C. (1998). *Inflated perception of responsibility for harm in obsessive–compulsive disorder.* Manuscript submitted for publication.

Foa, E. B., & Chambless, D. L. (1978). Habituation of subjective anxiety during flooding in imagery. *Behaviour Research and Therapy, 16,* 391–399.

Foa, E. B., & Kozak, M. J. (1985). Treatment of anxiety disorders: Implications for psychopathology. In A. H. Tuma & J. D. Maser (Eds.), *Anxiety and the anxiety disorders* (pp. 421–452). Hillsdale, NJ: Erlbaum.

Foa, E. B., & Kozak, M. J. (1986). Emotional processing of fear: Exposure to corrective information. *Psychological Bulletin, 99*, 20–35.

Foa, E. B., & Kozak, M. J. (1996). Obsessive compulsive disorder: Long-term outcome of psychological treatment. In M. Mavissakalian & R. F. Prien (Eds.), *Long-term treatments of anxiety disorders* (pp. 285–309). Washington, DC: American Psychiatric Press.

Foa, E. B., Kozak, M. J., Goodman, W. K., Hollander, E., Jenike, M., & Rasmussen, S. (1995). DSM–IV field trial: Obsessive–compulsive disorder. *American Journal of Psychiatry, 152*, 90–96.

Foa, E. B., Kozak, M. J., Steketee, G. S., & McCarthy, P. R. (1992). Treatment of depressive and obsessive–compulsive symptoms in OCD by imipramine and behavior therapy. *British Journal of Clinical Psychology, 31*, 279–292.

Foa, E. B., Steketee, G. S., Grayson, J. B., Turner, R. M., & Latimer, P. (1984). Deliberate exposure and blocking of obsessive–compulsive rituals: Immediate and long-term effects. *Behavior Therapy, 15*, 450–472.

Foa, E. B., Steketee, G. S., Turner, R. M., & Fischer, S. C. (1980). Effects of imaginal exposure to feared disasters in obsessive–compulsive checkers. *Behaviour Research and Therapy, 18*, 449–455.

Franklin, M. E., Kozak, M. J., Cashman, L., Coles, M., Rheingold, A., & Foa, E. B. (1998). Cognitive–behavioral treatment of obsessive compulsive disorder: An open clinical trial. *Journal of the American Academy of Child and Adolescent Psychiatry, 37*, 412–419.

Greist, J. H. (1992). An integrated approach to treatment of obsessive compulsive disorder. *Journal of Clinical Psychiatry, 53*, 38–41.

Greist, J. H., Jefferson, J., Kobak, K. A., Katzelnick, D. J., & Serlin, R. C. (1995). Efficacy and tolerability of serotonin transport inhibitors in obsessive compulsive disorder: A meta-analysis. *Archives of General Psychiatry, 52*, 53–60.

Hiss, H., Foa, E. B., & Kozak, M. J. (1994). Relapse prevention program for treatment of obsessive–compulsive disorder. *Journal of Consulting and Clinical Psychology, 62*, 801–808.

Hodgson, R. J., Rachman, S., & Marks, I. M. (1972). The treatment of chronic obsessive–compulsive neurosis: Follow-up and further findings. *Behaviour Research and Therapy, 10*, 181–189.

Hudson, J. I., Pope, H. G., Yurgelun-Todd, D., Jonas, J. M., & Frankenburg, F. R. (1987). A controlled study of anorexia nervosa and obsessive nervosa. *British Journal of Psychiatry, 27*, 57–60.

Insel, T. R., & Akiskal, H. S. (1986). Obsessive–compulsive disorder with psychotic features: A phenomenologic analysis. *American Journal of Psychiatry, 143*, 1527–1533.

Karno, M., Golding, J. M., Sorenson, S. B., & Burnam, A. (1988). The epidemiology of obsessive–compulsive disorder in five U.S. communities. *Archives of General Psychiatry, 45*, 1094–1099.

Kasvikis, Y. G., Tsakiris, R., Marks, I. M., Basoglu, M., & Noshirvani, H. F.

(1986). Past history of anorexia nervosa in women with obsessive–compulsive disorder. *International Journal of Eating Disorders, 5,* 1069–1075.

Kozak, M. J., & Foa, E. B. (1994). Obsessions, overvalued ideas, and delusions in obsessive–compulsive disorder. *Behaviour Research and Therapy, 32,* 343–353.

Kozak, M. J., & Foa, E. B. (1996). Behavior therapy for obsessive compulsive disorder. In V. B. Van Hasselt & M. Hersen (Eds.), *Sourcebook of psychological treatment manuals for adult disorders* (pp. 65–122). New York: Plenum Press.

Kozak, M. J., Foa, E. B., & Steketee, G. S. (1988). Process and outcome of exposure treatment with obsessive–compulsives: Psychophysiological indicators of emotional processing. *Behavior Therapy, 19,* 157–169.

Kozak, M. J., Liebowitz, M. L., & Foa, E. B. (in press). Cognitive behavior therapy and pharmacotherapy for OCD: The NIMH-sponsored collaborative study. In W. Goodman, M. Rudorfer, & J. Maser (Eds.), *Treatment refractory obsessive compulsive disorder.* Mahwah, NJ: Erlbaum.

Lelliott, P. T., Noshirvani, H. F., Basoglu, M., Marks, I. M., & Monteiro, W. O. (1988). Obsessive–compulsive beliefs and treatment outcome. *Psychological Medicine, 18,* 697–702.

Leon, A. C., Portera, L., & Weissman, M. M. (1995). The social costs of anxiety disorders. *British Journal of Psychiatry, 166(Suppl. 27),* 19–22.

Leonard, H. L., Swedo, S. E., Lenane, M. C., Rettew, D. C., Cheslow, D. L., Hamburger, S. D., & Rapoport, J. L. (1991). A double-blind desipramine substitution during long-term clomipramine treatment in children and adolescents with obsessive–compulsive disorder. *Archives of General Psychiatry, 48,* 922–927.

Lopatka, C., & Rachman, S. (1995). Perceived responsibility and compulsive checking: An experimental analysis. *Behaviour Research and Therapy, 33,* 673–684.

March, J. S., & Mulle, K. (1993). *"How I ran OCD off my land": A cognitive behavioral program for the treatment of obsessive–compulsive disorder in children and adolescents.* Unpublished manuscript.

March, J. S., Mulle, K., & Herbel, B. (1994). Behavioral psychotherapy for children and adolescents with obsessive–compulsive disorder: An open trial of a new protocol-driven treatment package. *Journal of the American Academy of Child and Adolescent Psychiatry, 33,* 333–341.

Marks, I. M., Lelliott, P., Basoglu, M., Noshirvani, H., Monteiro, W., Cohen, D., & Kasvikis, Y. (1988). Clomipramine, self-exposure, and therapist-assisted exposure for obsessive compulsive rituals. *British Journal of Psychiatry, 152,* 522–534.

Marks, I. M., Stern, R. S., Mawson, D., Cobb, J. & McDonald, R. (1980). Clomipramine and exposure for obsessive compulsive rituals: I. *British Journal of Psychiatry, 136,* 1–25.

Mehta, M. (1990). A comparative study of family-based and patients-based behavioural management in obsessive–compulsive disorder. *British Journal of Psychiatry, 157,* 133–135.

Meichenbaum, D. (1975). Self-instructional methods. In F. H. Kanfer & A. P. Goldstein (Eds.), *Helping people change* (pp. 357–392). New York: Pergamon Press.

Meyer, V. (1966). Modification of expectations in cases with obsessional rituals. *Behaviour Research and Therapy, 4,* 273–280.

Meyer, V., & Levy, R. (1973). Modification of behavior in obsessive–compulsive disorders. In H. E. Adams & P. Unikel (Eds.), *Issues and trends in behavior therapy* (pp. 77–136). Springfield, IL: Charles C Thomas.

Meyer, V., Levy, R., & Schnurer, A. (1974). The behavioural treatment of obsessive–compulsive disorders. In H. R. Beech (Ed.), *Obsessional states* (pp. 233–258). London: Methuen.

Minichello, W. E., Baer, L., & Jenike, M. A. (1987). Schizotypal personality disorder: A poor prognostic indicator for behavior therapy in the treatment of obsessive–compulsive disorder. *Journal of Anxiety Disorders, 1,* 273–276.

Mowrer, O. A. (1939). A stimulus–response analysis of anxiety and its role as a reinforcing agent. *Psychological Review, 46,* 553–565.

Mowrer, O. A. (1960). *Learning theory and behavior.* New York: Wiley.

Ost, L.-G. (1989). One-session treatment for specific phobias. *Behaviour Research and Therapy, 27,* 1–7.

Pauls, D. L., Towbin, K. E., Leckman, J. F., Zahner, G. E., & Cohen, D. J. (1986). Gilles de la Tourette's syndrome and obsessive–compulsive disorder: Evidence supporting a genetic relationship. *Archives of General Psychiatry, 43,* 1180–1182.

Pfohl, B., Black, D. W., Noyes, R., Coryell, W. H., & Barrash, J. (1991). Axis I and Axis II comorbidity findings: Implications for validity. In J. M. Oldham (Ed.), *Progress in Psychiatry: No. 20. Personality disorders: New perspectives on diagnostic validity* (pp. 147–161). Washington, DC: American Psychiatric Press.

Rabavilas, A. D., Boulougouris, J. C., & Stefanis, C. (1976). Duration of flooding sessions in the treatment of obsessive–compulsive patients. *Behaviour Research and Therapy, 14,* 349–355.

Rachman, S., de Silva, P., & Roper, G. (1976). The spontaneous decay of compulsive urges. *Behaviour Research and Therapy, 14,* 445–453.

Rachman, S., Throdarson, D. S., Shafran, R., & Woody, S. R. (1995). Perceived responsibility: Structure and significance. *Behaviour Research and Therapy, 33,* 779–784.

Rachman, S. J., & Wilson, G. T. (1980). *The effects of psychological therapy.* Oxford, England: Pergamon Press.

Rapoport, J. L., Swedo, S. E., & Leonard, H. L. (1992). Childhood obsessive compulsive disorder. *Journal of Clinical Psychiatry, 51*(2, Suppl.), 10–13.

Rasmussen, S. A., & Eisen, J. L. (1989). Clinical features and phenomenology of obsessive–compulsive disorder. *Psychiatric Annals, 19,* 67–73.

Rasmussen, S. A., & Eisen, J. L. (1990). Epidemiology of obsessive compulsive disorder. *Journal of Clinical Psychiatry, 51,* 10–14.

Rasmussen, S. A., & Tsuang, M. T. (1986). Clinical characteristics and family history in DSM–III obsessive–compulsive disorder. *American Journal of Psychiatry, 143*, 317–382.

Riddle, M. A., Scahill, L., King, R. A., Hardin, M. T., Anderson, G. M., Ort, S. I., Smith, J. C., Leckman, J. F., & Cohen, D. J. (1992). Double-blind, crossover trial of fluoxetine and placebo in children and adolescents with obsessive–compulsive disorder. *Journal of the American Academy of Child and Adolescent Psychiatry, 31*, 1062–1069.

Riggs, D. S., Hiss, H., & Foa, E. B. (1992). Marital distress and the treatment of obsessive–compulsive disorder. *Behavior Therapy, 23*, 585–597.

Roper, G., & Rachman, S. (1976). Obsessional–compulsive checking: Experimental replication and development. *Behaviour Research and Therapy, 14*, 25–32.

Roper, G., Rachman, S., & Hodgson, R. (1973). An experiment of obsessional checking. *Behaviour Research and Therapy, 11*, 271–277.

Rubenstein, C. S., Peynirgioglu, Z. F., Chambless, D. L., & Pigott, T. A. (1993). Memory in sub-clinical obsessive–compulsive checkers. *Behaviour Research and Therapy, 31*, 759–765.

Salkovskis, P. M. (1985). Obsessional compulsive problems: A cognitive behavioral analysis. *Behaviour Research and Therapy, 23*, 571–583.

Sher, K. J., Frost, R. O., & Otto, R. (1983). Cognitive deficits in compulsive checkers: An exploratory study. *Behaviour Research and Therapy, 21*, 357–364.

Stampfl, T. G., & Levis, D. J. (1967). Essential of implosive therapy: A learning-theory-based psychodynamic behavioral therapy. *Journal of Abnormal Psychology, 72*, 496–503.

Steketee, G. S., Foa, E. B., & Grayson, J. B. (1982). Recent advances in the treatment of obsessive–compulsives. *Archives of General Psychiatry, 39*, 1365–1371.

Swedo, S. E., Rapoport, J. L., Leonard, H., Lenane, M., & Cheslow, D. (1989). Obsessive–compulsive disorder in children and adolescents: Clinical phenomenology of 70 consecutive cases. *Archives of General Psychiatry, 46*, 335–341.

Valleni-Basile, L. A., Garrison, C. Z., Jackson, K. L., Waller, J. L., McKeown, R. E., Addy, C. L., & Cuffe, S. P. (1994). Frequency of obsessive–compulsive disorder in a community sample of young adolescents. *Journal of the American Academy of Child and Adolescent Psychiatry, 33*, 782–791.

van Oppen, P., de Haan, E., van Balkom, A. J. L. M., Spinhoven, P., Hoogduin, K., & van Dyck, R. (1995). Cognitive therapy and exposure in vivo in the treatment of obsessive compulsive disorder. *Behaviour Research and Therapy, 33*, 379–390.

Watts, F. (1973). Desensitization as an habituation phenomenon: II. Studies of interstimulus interval length. *Psychological Reports, 33*, 715–718.

11

USING BASIC RESEARCH TO CRAFT EFFECTIVE INTERVENTIONS FOR MARITAL DYSFUNCTION

THOMAS N. BRADBURY, MATTHEW D. JOHNSON,
ERIKA E. LAWRENCE, AND RONALD D. ROGGE

About 90% of all adults marry at some time in their life (U.S. Bureau of the Census, 1992), and although the divorce rate in the United States is beginning to stabilize (De Vita, 1996), it is doing so at a very high level—about half of all first marriages are projected to end in separation or divorce (Bumpass, 1990). Moreover, about half of all children will experience the breakup of their parents' marriage (Bumpass, 1984), and those who do will perform more poorly in school, display more maladaptive behavior, and have poorer relationships with parents and peers (Amato & Keith, 1991). It comes as little surprise that marital and family problems are the primary reasons why people seek professional assistance in the United States (Veroff, Kulka, & Douvan, 1981).

The argument we will make in this chapter is that the response of the mental health profession to problems involving marital discord is in-

Preparation of this chapter was supported by Grant R29-MH48674 from the National Institute of Mental Health. We thank Benjamin Karney for his assistance with this chapter, and we thank two reviewers for numerous helpful comments and observations.

complete. The field has made rapid progress in understanding how to treat distressed marriages, but, as psychologists, we are also learning about the severe constraints we impose on ourselves when we wait until marriages are already distressed before we intervene. In this chapter, we will make the case that *prevention strategies* have been underutilized in efforts to address this problem. The more important point we will develop is that focusing on prevention may enable us to forge stronger links between basic research on how marriages succeed and fail and the interventions that are needed to help couples who want to have more satisfying and durable marriages and families. Prevention is emphasized here, not because it is the next best thing to try, but because it puts us in a position to conduct basic research that can directly inform our interventions. As outlined below, this link between research and intervention has not been fully realized in the domain of marital therapy.

THE EFFECTS OF MARITAL THERAPY: A QUICK SYNOPSIS

Jacobson and Addis (1993, p. 86) provided a useful summary of the marital therapy outcome literature. They focus on Behavioral Couples Therapy (BCT), the most extensively studied form of marital therapy, and they ask,

> What percentage of treated couples are happily married by the end of treatment? Most tested treatments report no better than 50% success. There is remarkable uniformity both across studies and across treatment modalities in this success rate.... What about long-term outcomes? Little is known about these long-term outcomes, because few researchers have followed their couples beyond a few years after treatment termination.... One 2-year follow-up found that 30% of those couples who recovered during the course of therapy had relapsed (Jacobson, Schmaling, & Holtzworth-Munroe, 1987). In another study, a 4-year follow-up revealed a 38% divorce rate, which was based on the entire sample of couples who received treatment (Snyder, Wills, & Grady-Fletcher, 1991). Thus, at least two studies have found substantial relapse in Behavioral Couples Therapy at the time of a long-term follow-up.[1]

Turning to nonexperimental data, Seligman's (1995) analysis of the *Consumer Reports* study shows that of the people receiving less than 6 months of treatment by marriage counselors, 22% report that treatment "made things a lot better"; 37% of the people receiving more than 6 months of

---

[1]A meta-analysis by Shadish et al. (1993) and a review by Whisman and Snyder (1997) offer somewhat more favorable perspectives on the marital therapy outcome literature, perhaps because they focus less than Jacobson and Addis (1993) on the results of long-term follow-up analyses.

treatment were helped to this same degree. When asked about the extent to which treatment affected their ability to relate to others, productivity at work, and coping with everyday stress, just 9% of those receiving less than 6 months of treatment said it "made things a lot better"; this figure rose to 16% for those receiving more than 6 months of treatment. In a related study conducted in Germany, Hahlweg and Klann (1997) examined the outcomes of marital therapy in a field study of 84 counselors and 495 of their marital therapy cases. Although couples tended to be very satisfied with the treatment, effect sizes comparing marital functioning before and after treatment were low: "About 30% of the clients could be regarded as reliably improved at postassessment, leaving substantial numbers of couples unchanged or still distressed by the end of therapy" (p. 419). Taken together, these studies indicate that there is considerable room for improvement in helping couples to overcome their relationship problems.

In summary, there is good reason to believe that a lot of people are suffering from marital distress and that this suffering is not being alleviated consistently by prevailing forms of couples therapy. To a large degree, this may be due to a tendency among many distressed couples to wait until their relationship is irrevocably damaged before taking steps to change it—a case of too little too late. Of course, at this juncture there can be no guarantee that prevention programs will prevent marital dysfunction for most couples (see Bradbury, Cohan, & Karney, in press), or that prevention programs will prevent distress among those couples for whom available marital therapies are ineffective. Nor does it follow that efforts to improve marital therapies should be in any way discouraged or dismissed. Nevertheless, the results obtained with marital therapies to date are sufficiently disappointing to warrant reevaluating them beginning with their most basic assumptions (e.g., see Jacobson & Christensen, 1996) and, in keeping with the theme of this chapter, to justify strong consideration of preventive approaches.

THE LINK BETWEEN BASIC RESEARCH AND MARITAL THERAPY

When couples experience significant levels of distress in their relationships, we as therapists have to contend not only with the factors that might have given rise to that distress but also with the repercussions that distress may have caused for the couple and for the individual spouses. This includes arguing, avoidance, outbursts of contempt and violence, and a lot of hurt, pain, and isolation. By analogy, we are less like an emergency room physician who is called upon to set a fracture that happened a few hours ago and more like a general practitioner who is asked to treat a patient

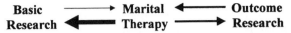

Figure 1. Marital therapy has reciprocal links with basic research and outcome research; in principle, marital therapy can inform, and can be informed by, both forms of research. In practice, marital therapy is more likely to inform, than be informed by, basic research on marriage.

who broke his or her leg several months ago and then continued to hobble around on it; we have to attend not only to the broken bone but also to the swelling and bruising, the sore hip and foot, and the infection that ensued. More important, the responses to marital distress are often idiosyncratic to each marriage and fluctuate over short periods of time. When coupled with the fact that most basic research on marital functioning addresses factors that differentiate distressed couples, as a group, from nondistressed couples, one can see that this research is not particularly informative as we set out to improve marital therapies. The clinical presentation of marital dysfunction tends to be unique to each couple, and basic research does not—and perhaps cannot—fully address this complexity in a meaningful way.

Figure 1 depicts the notion that marital therapies can be improved through reciprocal links with basic research and outcome research, but the link from basic research to marital therapy tends to be weak. Instead, what we tend to see is that phenomena observed in clinical settings have had a great deal of impact on the nature of basic research on marriage that gets conducted; the link from marital therapy to basic research is relatively strong. This is evident, for example, in the research on the attributions made by satisfied and dissatisfied married couples. Clinical observation with distressed couples suggested the need to conduct basic research to understand the attributional inferences spouses were making, and as a consequence a great deal is known about the attributions spouses make, and their associations with observable behavior and changes in marital satisfaction (e.g., Bradbury, Beach, Fincham, & Nelson, 1996; Fincham & Bradbury, 1993). However, this research has had little direct bearing on the form of cognitive–behavioral marital therapy.[2]

A link from marital therapy to basic research is no doubt desirable, but it does mean that the extreme and salient phenomena observed among clinically distressed couples may be unduly influential in models of marital success and failure. Our view of marital functioning is heavily filtered through a clinical lens, which may well give us a distorted sense of how marriages normally operate. For example, the study of marital conflict

---

[2]We are not arguing here that cognitive–behavioral marital therapy is poorly conceived; in fact quite the opposite is the case (e.g., Baucom & Epstein, 1990). Our point is that basic questions about the contribution of cognitive variables in general, and attributions in particular, to the onset and course of marital dysfunction were unresolved when cognitive–behavioral models of marital therapy were formalized.

emerged from clinical observations of behaviorally oriented practitioners (e.g., Stuart, 1969), and clarification of conflict and problem-solving patterns served as the foundation for social learning models of marriage (e.g., Jacobson & Margolin, 1979). Nevertheless, the link between marital conflict behavior and marital outcomes is not unambiguous: (a) Effect sizes from longitudinal studies tend to be weak (see Karney & Bradbury, 1995b), (b) higher levels of negative behavior early in marriage are related to a more favorable longitudinal course of the relationship (Karney & Bradbury, 1997; also see Bradbury, 1998), and (c) modification of negative behavior around the time of marriage leads to enduring behavioral changes over the ensuing 5 years without concomitant changes in self-reported marital satisfaction (Hahlweg, 1996).

The more general point here is that the imbalance in the degree of influence from marital therapy to basic research, versus the degree of influence from basic research to marital therapy, is a problem because our interventions for marital problems tend to be cut off from basic research about marriage. We believe it is important that our interventions for marital problems be firmly grounded in an understanding of how marriages operate and, for whatever reason, this is not occurring at present. This represents a lost opportunity for developing marital therapies that derive from basic research on marriage and, of course, it highlights the need to conduct research that will be relevant and informative in the clinical context. Outlining the characteristics of such research, particularly so that it can overcome the heterogeneity in how couples respond to their marital distress, is beyond the scope of this chapter (cf. Whisman & Snyder, 1997). Instead, we direct our attention to interventions designed to prevent marital dysfunction, as they may hold greater promise for linking basic research and treatment.

STRENGTHENING THE LINK BETWEEN BASIC RESEARCH AND INTERVENTION: MAKING A CASE FOR PREVENTION

When we work with young couples around the time of marriage, we can largely sidestep the idiosyncratic and harmful consequences that come along with marital discord. In principle, this means that our interventions can be somewhat more uniform across couples. And, more important, those interventions can be based on basic research addressing the mechanisms by which marriages succeed and fail. If we can clarify key features of these mechanisms—that is, if we can clarify how young couples, who are almost uniformly very satisfied with their marriages, achieve different outcomes— then we can design our interventions to modify these mechanisms, and we should be able to alter the longitudinal course of otherwise at-risk mar-

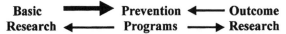

Figure 2. In contrast to marital therapy, programs designed to prevent marital dysfunction are in a very good position to be informed by basic research on marital success and failure.

riages.[3] As depicted in Figure 2, when we shift our focus from marital therapies to prevention programs, we are in a much better position to bring basic research back into our interventions. As Floyd, Markman, Kelly, Blumberg, and Stanley (1995, p. 221) noted, "perhaps the best way to improve interventions is to conduct more basic research to discover more of the pathways to marital success used by different couples."

Here it is useful to take stock of existing prevention programs. These programs can take any number of forms (e.g., weekend workshops, seminars, and religious programs), but the program that comes closest to taking full advantage of basic research and outcome research is Markman and colleagues' Prevention and Relationship Enhancement Program (PREP; see Floyd et al., 1995). The premise of this program is to teach premarital couples the skills they need to handle conflict and negative emotion, and it has yielded some noteworthy effects 5 years following intervention. Specifically, in comparison with a no-treatment control group, couples participating in PREP maintain their early levels of marital quality over 36 months (Markman, Floyd, Stanley, & Storaasli, 1988) and, at least for husbands, over 60 months (Markman, Renick, Floyd, Stanley, & Clements, 1993). At the same time, it is important to recognize that PREP has not yet been shown to be effective among couples who come from families of divorce (Van Widenfelt, Hosman, Schaap, & van der Staak, 1996), nor has it been shown to prevent divorce among couples who go on to marry (Markman et al., 1993).

Thus, although the PREP approach is obviously a step in the right direction, a lot of additional work is needed before we can reliably prevent marital dysfunction (see Bradbury & Fincham, 1990). With regard to outcome research, there is a need to test existing programs using random assignment of couples to groups and attention-only control groups, particularly with relatively large, representative samples, and there is a need to determine whether these interventions work with couples who are at risk

---

[3]Several studies now document the high rates of aggression that occur among newlywed marriages. For example, O'Leary et al. (1989) report that 31% of the men and 44% of the women in their newlywed sample reported aggressing against their partners in the year prior to marriage. Although this might suggest that these couples would be unhappy as newlyweds, this apparently is not the case; Lawrence and Bradbury (1997) found that even severely aggressive newlywed couples are functioning, on average, in the satisfied range on standard measures of marital satisfaction shortly after marriage. While it does not follow that prevention programs for aggressive couples should be identical to those for nonaggressive couples, the vast majority of newlywed spouses do report satisfactory marriages.

for eventual marital problems (see Sullivan & Bradbury, 1997). With regard to basic research, a great deal of work remains to be done in identifying fundamental mechanisms involved in marital failure. The scope of this task is outlined in the next section.

A GLIMPSE TOWARD BASIC RESEARCH ON THE CAUSES OF MARITAL DYSFUNCTION

To find out how much work remains to be done in understanding the mechanisms underlying marital dysfunction, Karney and Bradbury (1995b) conducted a meta-analysis of all 115 known longitudinal studies of marriage, involving about 45,000 marriages. This analysis identified seven key problems that constrain the contribution that basic research can make to preventing marital dysfunction. The purpose of this section is to outline these problems and to suggest some strategies that can be undertaken to avoid them in future research.

First, many studies are conducted with samples that include couples varying widely in the duration and quality of their marriage; newlywed couples are studied along with well-established couples without regard for how they might be different. As a result, these studies do not permit investigation of the initial *onset* of marital distress in a way that is distinct from the *continuing course* of marital distress. To be maximally effective, prevention programs need to modify factors that contribute to the onset of distress rather than those that merely correspond with marital distress in deteriorating relationships. The resolution to this problem is to study the longitudinal course of relatively homogeneous groups of couples, and particularly newlyweds, because the first few years of marriage are the highest risk period for marital dysfunction (National Center for Health Statistics, 1990).

Second, the dependent variable in most longitudinal studies of marriage is often crude. Despite the severe constraints that arise in attempting to use just two waves of data to understand longitudinal change in marriage, the vast majority of studies do just this. This yields an incomplete portrayal of how marriages develop and change, and efforts to link key independent variables to these limited dependent variables make it difficult to determine why marriages evolve from being satisfied to being dissatisfied to ending in permanent separation or divorce. Investigators with numerous waves of data have also resorted to analyses using only two data points to quantify the course of marriage, largely because statistical procedures for simultaneously studying these data have not been well established.

A valuable alternative to this approach is to conduct repeated assessments of spouses to determine their marital quality, and to then analyze those data using growth curve modeling (e.g., Bryk & Raudenbush, 1992).

With growth curve modeling, each individual's data points are used to generate three parameters reflecting the trajectory of their marital satisfaction: (a) the intercept, or the initial level of marital satisfaction; (b) the slope, or the rate at which marital satisfaction changes over the assessment interval; and (c) the residual, or the extent to which the observed data points deviate from the best-fitting line (see Karney & Bradbury, 1995a). Figure 3 shows these three parameters for two husbands who participated in a 4-year longitudinal study of marriage beginning shortly after their wedding. Both husbands are quite high in their initial level of satisfaction, and the intercepts, which are extrapolated from the best-fitting line for their data, reflect this fact. As is common, marital quality declined for both husbands, though more so for Husband B; this is reflected in the slope values. And finally, the data points for Husband B are more widely dispersed around his best-fitting line than are those for Husband A; this is reflected in the residual values. By quantifying the longitudinal trajectory of marriage in terms of these three parameters, general questions about the effects of an independent variable on the longitudinal course of marriage can be made quite specific, as the effect can be localized as relating to any one of these three parameters.

The tendency to collect data from only one spouse is a third factor that constrains the relevance of basic longitudinal research on marriage for understanding marital failure and, in turn, for preventing marital dysfunction. Only about half of the longitudinal studies reviewed by Karney and Bradbury (1995b) involve data collected from both spouses. Although data from individual spouses can be useful for examining intrapersonal perceptions of marriage, data from both spouses are needed for investigating the interpersonal aspects of marriage that contribute to marital dysfunction.

High rates of attrition are a fourth problem that arises in longitudinal studies of marriage. On average, about 31% of each sample is lost to attrition, which sharply reduces the investigator's power to detect effects. A fifth and closely related problem is that attrition is not random; younger, poorer, less-educated, and minority participants are often lost from the initial samples. One important consequence of this nonrandom attrition is that research findings might be used to develop prevention programs for couples of diverse sociodemographic backgrounds, when in fact the research findings themselves were developed on an older, better educated, Caucasian sample; the effectiveness of the programs might be compromised as a consequence. Large-scale studies of diverse populations with aggressive retention strategies (e.g., high rates of reimbursement, ethnically diverse research teams that permit matching between investigators' and participants' ethnic diversity) are needed to overcome this problem.

A sixth concern evident in longitudinal studies of marriage is that unstable couples—that is, couples marked by separation or divorce—are typically excluded from analyses. This is either because they have declined

Four-year trajectories for two husbands

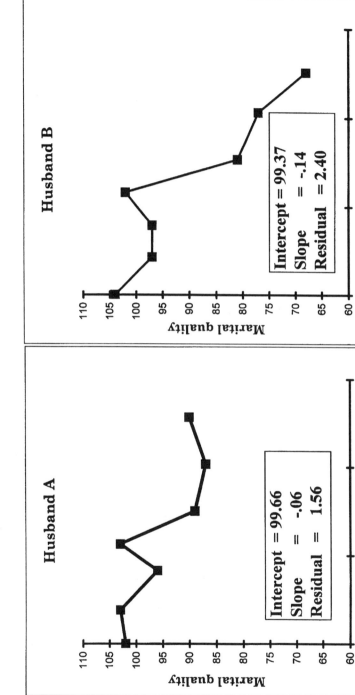

Figure 3. Marital quality as a function of time for two husbands. Repeated assessments of marital quality can be used to quantify the trajectory of a marriage, in terms of the intercept, or the initial level of satisfaction; the slope, or the rate at which marital satisfaction changes; and the residual, or the degree to which observed data points deviate from a best-fitting line. Husband A and Husband B have similar intercepts, but Husband B's marital satisfaction is declining at a more rapid rate than that of Husband A. Husband B's residual term is also greater than that of Husband A.

to continue their participation in the study or because there are too few unstable couples to analyze separately. As a result, conclusions drawn from longitudinal studies of marriage may not clarify factors that distinguish couples who will divorce from those who remain in intact marriages. To the extent that prevention programs are seeking to prevent divorce, the loss of unstable couples from basic longitudinal studies represents a significant limitation. Although it could be argued that the loss of unstable couples might simply underrepresent the effects of particular variables on the longitudinal course of marriage (i.e., the range of marital outcomes is being restricted, thereby reducing any validity correlations involving those outcomes), this overlooks the emerging possibility that the factors that give rise to marital instability are different from those that give rise to satisfaction in intact marriages (see Rogge & Bradbury, in press).

A final limitation in existing longitudinal studies of marriage is that emphasis is placed on null model tests rather than tests of competing models. That is, when the effects of independent variables are investigated, they are investigated with reference to whether or not they are significantly associated with marital outcomes. This can be informative, but a more powerful strategy for refining models of marital dysfunction is to investigate the relative contributions of independent variables and how they might combine to account for variation in marital success and failure.

Karney and Bradbury (1997) provided an example of the competing models approach. They observed that the two most reliable predictors of marital outcomes reflected either a personality-based or intrapersonal model, represented most consistently by negative affectivity or neuroticism, or an interpersonal model, represented primarily by observed problem-solving behavior. Although there has been some speculation that behavior mediates the association between negative affectivity and marital outcomes (e.g., Kelly & Conley, 1987), this possibility had not been tested, and these two models had never been compared. Karney and Bradbury examined these two factors simultaneously in relation to trajectories of marital satisfaction and found that behavior did not mediate the personality–marital outcome link. Instead, negative affectivity was related to initial levels of marital satisfaction (i.e., the intercept parameter) but not the rate at which satisfaction changed, whereas marital conflict behavior was related to the rate at which satisfaction changed (i.e., the slope parameter) but not the intercept.[4] Lower intercepts were also related to more rapid declines in satisfaction. This study helps to rule out an otherwise viable candidate that might account for the rate at which marriages change, and it underscores

---

[4]Karney and Bradbury (1997) originally hypothesized that negative affectivity would be associated with the residual term, such that individuals high in negative affectivity would be more reactive or variable in their satisfaction ratings across time. This hypothesis could not be tested because there was insufficient samplewide variation in the residual term, probably owing to the relatively infrequent rate (i.e., semiannually) at which marital satisfaction was sampled.

the importance of prevention programs that target behavioral skills as a means of preventing declines in marital satisfaction. This study also demonstrates how a traitlike variable could be used to identify couples at risk for marital difficulties (and thus identify couples who could maximally benefit from intervention), whereas a variable that may give rise to change in marital satisfaction could serve as the basis for any subsequent intervention these couples might receive.

CONCLUSION

In this chapter we have argued that linking interventions to basic research on marital functioning is essential for the refinement of existing treatments. We also argued that marital therapies have not had a strong foundation in basic research; basic research appears more likely to draw from marital therapy than vice versa. Indeed, a central supposition in this chapter is that the link from basic research to intervention is stronger in the case of prevention programs than in the case of marital therapies. One basis for this supposition is the view that distressed couples respond in idiosyncratic ways to the marital difficulties they are encountering, so that therapies need to address not only the factors that have given rise to the original difficulties but also to the pain, hurt, depression, frustration, and isolation that have ensued. Most basic research on marital distress is not well-suited for distinguishing between these types of problems, and, because it tends to focus on distressed couples in a relatively undifferentiated manner, this research also reveals little about the unique ways that distressed couples experience and respond to their distress. For these reasons, basic research on marriage has had relatively little direct influence on the nature of marital therapy. Couples who are just entering marriage, in contrast, tend to be very satisfied with their relationship, and most have not had to contend with serious difficulties. In principle, it should be possible to identify mechanisms that increase the likelihood of marital distress and disruption for all couples, and to then devise preventive interventions that will hinder the operation of these mechanisms. Thus, in this sense the link from basic research to preventive interventions should be strong, and stronger than in the case of marital therapies.

The utility of this perspective will hinge on whether marital distress can be prevented with relatively uniform programs for all young couples, or whether some significant degree of individual tailoring of programs to couples is necessary for bringing about good marital outcomes. Data are not yet available to distinguish between these two possibilities, and until they are it will be most parsimonious to assume that, in the absence of relationship distress, relatively uniform programs can be effective. However, to the extent that individual tailoring is necessary, then we may need to acknowledge that (a) basic research on marriage may play only a limited role in the development and refinement of preventive interventions, along with therapeutic interventions or that (b) a different genre of research is needed that can provide more information about different types of couples and the interventions that will be effective for each of them.

We emphasized that continued efforts should be made toward developing effective marital therapies, but we also adopted the view that prevention programs warrant special attention because they might benefit more directly from basic research about how marriages succeed and fail. A review of the longitudinal literature on marriage showed, however, that a new generation of longitudinal research on marriage is needed before key questions about marital success and failure can be answered. We outlined several important limitations in the longitudinal literature and offered suggestions for how this next generation of research might proceed.

Much has been learned from efforts made to understand and alter the longitudinal course of marriage. This task is as demanding as it is complex, however, and it will be important to conduct basic research and outcome research that will directly facilitate the development of interventions for couples experiencing or likely to encounter distress in their marriage.

REFERENCES

Amato, P. R., & Keith, B. (1991). Parental divorce and the well-being of children: A meta-analysis. *Psychological Bulletin, 110,* 26–46.

Baucom, D. H., & Epstein, N. (1990). *Cognitive–behavioral marital therapy.* New York: Brunner/Mazel.

Bradbury, T. N. (Ed.). (1998). *The developmental course of marital dysfunction.* New York: Cambridge University Press.

Bradbury, T. N., Beach, S. R. H., Fincham, F. D., & Nelson, G. (1996). Attributions and behavior in functional and dysfunctional marriages. *Journal of Consulting and Clinical Psychology, 64,* 569–576.

Bradbury, T. N., Cohan, C. L., & Karney, B. R. (in press). Optimizing longitudinal research for understanding and preventing marital dysfunction. In T. N. Bradbury (Ed.), *The developmental course of marital dysfunction.* New York: Cambridge University Press.

Bradbury, T. N., & Fincham, F. D. (1990). Preventing marital dysfunction: Review and analysis. In F. D. Fincham & T. N. Bradbury (Eds.), *The psychology of marriage: Basic issues and applications* (pp. 375–401). New York: Guilford Press.

Bryk, A. S., & Raudenbush, S. W. (1992). *Hierarchical linear models: Applications and data analysis methods.* Newbury Park, CA: Sage.

Bumpass, L. L. (1984). Children and marital disruption: A replication and update. *Demography, 21,* 71–82.

Bumpass, L. L. (1990). What's happening to the family? Interactions between demographic and institutional change. *Demography, 27,* 483–498.

De Vita, C. J. (1996). The United States at mid-decade. *Population Bulletin, 50,* 1–44.

Fincham, F. D., & Bradbury, T. N. (1993). Marital satisfaction, depression, and attributions: A longitudinal analysis. *Journal of Personality and Social Psychology, 64,* 442–452.

Floyd, F. J., Markman, H. J., Kelly, S., Blumberg, S. L., & Stanley, S. M. (1995). Preventive intervention and relationship enhancement. In N. S. Jacobson & A. S. Gurman (Eds.), *Clinical handbook of couple therapy* (pp. 212–226). New York: Guilford Press.

Hahlweg, K. (1996, December). Prevention of marital distress: Results of a German 5-year study. In K. Hahlweg (Chair), *Prediction and Prevention of Marital Distress.* Conference sponsored by the Federal Department for the Family, Seniors, Women, and Youth, Heidelberg, Germany.

Hahlweg, K., & Klann, N. (1997). The effectiveness of marital counseling in Germany: A contribution to health services research. *Journal of Family Psychology, 11,* 410–421.

Jacobson, N. S., & Addis, M. E. (1993). Research on couples and couple therapy: What do we know? Where are we going? *Journal of Consulting and Clinical Psychology, 61,* 85–93.

Jacobson, N. S., & Christensen, A. (1996). *Integrative couple therapy.* New York: Norton.

Jacobson, N. S., & Margolin, G. (1979). *Marital therapy: Strategies based on social learning and behavior exchange principles.* New York: Brunner/Mazel.

Jacobson, N. S., Schmaling, K. B., & Holtzworth-Munroe, A. (1987). Component analysis of behavioral marital therapy: 2-year follow-up and prediction of relapse. *Journal of Marriage and Family Therapy, 13,* 187–195.

Karney, B. R., & Bradbury, T. N. (1995a). Assessing longitudinal change in marriage: An introduction to the analysis of growth curves. *Journal of Marriage and the Family, 57,* 1091–1108.

Karney, B. R., & Bradbury, T. N. (1995b). The longitudinal course of marriage and marital instability: A review of theory, method, and research. *Psychological Bulletin, 118,* 3–34.

Karney, B. R., & Bradbury, T. N. (1997). Neuroticism, marital interaction, and the trajectory of marital satisfaction. *Journal of Personality and Social Psychology, 72,* 1075–1092.

Kelly, E. L., & Conley, J. J. (1987). Personality and compatibility: A prospective analysis of marital stability and satisfaction. *Journal of Personality and Social Psychology, 52,* 27–40.

Lawrence, E., & Bradbury, T. N. (1997). *Interspousal aggression and marital dysfunction: A longitudinal analysis.* Manuscript submitted for publication.

Markman, H. J., Floyd, F. J., Stanley, S. M., & Storaasli, R. D. (1988). Prevention of marital distress: A longitudinal investigation. *Journal of Consulting and Clinical Psychology, 56,* 210–217.

Markman, H. J., Renick, M. J., Floyd, F. J., Stanley, S. M., & Clements, M. (1993). Preventing marital distress through communication and conflict management training: A 4- and 5-year follow-up. *Journal of Consulting and Clinical Psychology, 61,* 70–77.

National Center for Health Statistics. (1990). Advance final report of final marriage statistics. *Monthly Vital Statistics Report, 38*(Suppl.).

O'Leary, K. D., Barling, J., Arias, I., Rosenbaum, A., Malone, J., & Tyree, A. (1989). Prevalence and stability of marital aggression between spouses: A longitudinal analysis. *Journal of Consulting and Clinical Psychology, 57,* 263–268.

Rog͟e, R. D., & Bradbury, T. N. (in press). Recent advances in the prediction of marital outcomes. In R. Berger & M. T. Hannah (Eds.), *Handbook of preventive approaches to couples therapy.* New York: Brunner/Mazel.

Seligman, M. E. P. (1995). The effectiveness of therapy: The *Consumer Reports* study. *American Psychologist, 50,* 965–974.

Shadish, W. R., Montgomery, L. M., Wilson, P., Wilson, M. R., Bright, I., & Okwumabua, T. (1993). Effects of family and marital psychotherapies: A meta-analysis. *Journal of Consulting and Clinical Psychology, 61,* 992–1002.

Snyder, D. K., Wills, R. M., & Grady-Fletcher, A. (1991). Long-term effectiveness of behavioral versus insight-oriented marital therapy. *Journal of Consulting and Clinical Psychology, 59,* 138–141.

Stuart, R. B. (1969). Operant-interpersonal treatment for marital discord. *Journal of Consulting and Clinical Psychology, 33,* 675–682.

Sullivan, K. T., & Bradbury, T. N. (1997). Are premarital prevention programs reaching couples at risk for marital dysfunction? *Journal of Consulting and Clinical Psychology, 65,* 24–30.

U.S. Bureau of the Census. (1992, October). Marriage, divorce, and remarriage in the 1990s. *Current Population Reports, P23*(No. 180), 4.

Van Widenfelt, B., Hosman, C., Schaap, C., & van der Staak, C. (1996). The prevention of relationship distress for couples at risk: A controlled evaluation with nine-month and two-year follow-ups. *Family Relations, 45,* 156–165.

Veroff, J., Kulka, R. A., & Douvan, E. (1981). *Mental health in America.* New York: Basic Books.

Whisman, M. A., & Snyder, D. K. (1997). Evaluating and improving the efficacy of conjoint couple therapy. In W. K. Halford & H. J. Markman (Eds.), *Clinical handbook of marriage and couples intervention* (pp. 679–693). New York: Wiley.

IV

SERVICE DELIVERY

12

INTEGRATING SCIENCE AND PRACTICE IN AN ENVIRONMENT OF MANAGED CARE

JOHN F. KIHLSTROM AND LUCY CANTER KIHLSTROM

The relations between science and practice within psychology are currently strained, but they were not always so, and they need not be so in the future. This is because, for clinical psychology at least, there is no conflict between science and practice. In this chapter, we begin by reviewing the history and origins of clinical psychology and the Boulder model of the scientist–practitioner. Given recent developments within the field, and the emerging pressures from the larger environment, we then suggest a redefinition of the scientist–practitioner—a redefinition that may be required because of external threats to the past practices of clinical psychology. Clinical psychology is uniquely positioned to respond to these

An earlier version of this chapter was presented at the 103rd Annual Convention of the American Psychological Association, New York, in August 1995, as part of a Presidential Panel, "Healing the Science–Practice Wars," cosponsored by Divisions 42, 12, and 29. This chapter is based in part on research supported by Training Grant MH15783 and Research Grant MH35856 from the National Institute of Mental Health. We thank the Internet subscribers to the Society for a Science of Clinical Psychology and MANAGED-BEHAVIOURAL HEALTHCARE lists for preliminary discussions of some of these issues.

threats and to take an active role in shaping the management of mental health treatment and practice in this country.

To that end, several overarching strategies are suggested. The strategies presented are overarching because this chapter is not intended to be a "cookbook" or a "how-to" manual. Rather, its purpose is to raise issues that are, and will be, important to the survival of clinical psychology, and its intent is to foster thought, dialogue, and action. The specific mechanisms that may be selected should be left to groups in various regions of the country because the intensity of and emphasis on issues may vary widely by geographic location.

CLINICAL PSYCHOLOGY FROM BOULDER TO GAINESVILLE

At the beginning of clinical psychology, 100 years ago, science and practice were thoroughly intertwined. When Witmer established the first psychological clinic, in 1896 at the University of Pennsylvania (Witmer, 1907/1996; see also Benjamin, 1996; Fagan, 1996; McReynolds, 1996; Routh, 1996), William James (1890/1980) had already published his seminal *Principles of Psychology*, making extensive use of clinical material in his chapters on consciousness and the self. And even before Ebbinghaus (1885) made the nonsense syllable famous, Theodule Ribot (1882) had published *Diseases of Memory*, attempting to derive basic psychological principles from observations of clinical cases of amnesia.

The modern field of clinical psychology had its origin in the years just after World War II, with the emergence of the Veterans Administration (VA) and the National Institute of Mental Health (Routh, 1994, 1997; for summary histories, see Hilgard, 1987; Humphreys, 1996; for enlightening personal histories, see Maher, 1992; Shakow, 1969). The framework for the new profession was provided by the 1949 "Boulder model" of the scientist–practitioner. In the early VA system, psychologists were mostly supervised by psychiatrists who had little research training and whose viewpoint was essentially psychoanalytic. According to the Boulder model, which dominated clinical training for at least the next two decades, competence in general psychology, and in research methods and statistics, was essential to the training of clinical practitioners.

In the Boulder model, the whole point of clinical psychology was to put psychotherapy, psychological assessment, and ancillary procedures on a firm scientific base and to make sure that the scientists who were creating this base had contact with the living material of the field. Clinical practice was to be part of a dialectical enterprise, both responding to and contributing to advances in knowledge of basic psychological processes (Davison & Lazarus, 1995). Practitioners were supposed to be active researchers using the best techniques at hand but also actively engaged in improving these techniques. All practitioners were to be scientists, and although not all scientists were to be practitioners, at least there was a sense that scientists and practitioners were engaged in a common enterprise. As a result, training in clinical psychology culminated in the award of a scholarly degree, the PhD. Reinforcing the sense of common purpose, most clinical psychologists were employed in academic departments of psychology, medical schools, and state and VA hospitals, instead of in private practice.

All this began to change in the late 1960s and the early 1970s, as the Community Mental Health Centers Act of 1963 expanded the opportunities for the employment of psychologists. The rise of community mental health centers, and the prospects of national health insurance, raised the further question of whether clinical psychology should declare its independence of psychiatry. When this question was answered in the affirmative, clinical psychologists began to move into private practice in large numbers, and clinical psychology began a slow but inexorable shift away from the Boulder model.

The departure from the Boulder model has been exacerbated by recent shortages in academic positions, the further closing of inpatient facilities, and retrenchment in the medical schools that together have made the private practice of clinical psychology even more attractive as a career option. Moreover, the scientific community must bear some of the responsibility for this state of affairs: All too often, basic researchers have treated their clinical colleagues with benign neglect, to the point at which, in many of our best departments, either clinical training does not occur at all or it has been effectively segregated from the rest of the organizational unit (Beutler, Williams, Wakefield, & Entwistle, 1995). Either way, the effect has been to reduce the opportunities for interaction between scientists and practitioners, to the detriment of each.

The idea of the scientist–practitioner has not been abandoned, but it is increasingly being challenged. Whereas, in the years immediately following 1949, there was only one model for clinical training and practice, the 1990 Gainesville conference set out a number of alternatives to the Boulder model, some amounting to a pure practitioner model that emphasizes the acquisition of competence in specific clinical techniques, and the ingenuity of the individual practitioner in addressing the problems presented by the individual patient or client. In the pure practitioner model, research skills are deemphasized because most clinical psychologists do not have the time or opportunity, or perhaps the inclination, to engage in research. But to say that practitioners need not themselves be scholars is not to say that science is irrelevant to practice or that clinical practitioners can safely avoid training in general psychology, research methods, and statistics. The fact is that clinical psychology derives much of its status, including its independence from psychiatry and its claim to third-party payments for services rendered, from the assumption that its practices are firmly based on scientifically validated principles and techniques. Thus, *there can be* no conflict between science and practice, so long as clinical psychology wishes to retain its identity, autonomy, and status as a profession (McFall, 1991, 1996).

REDEFINING THE SCIENTIST–PRACTITIONER

The previous discussion should not be misinterpreted: There is room for creative practitioners to go beyond established knowledge in constructing innovations. Systematic desensitization may have sprung from Hullian learning theory, but cognitive therapy had its origins in the creativity of practitioners (Beck, 1967; Ellis, 1962) who did not know anything about cognitive psychology—not least because at the time they were making their innovations there was so little cognitive psychology to know. Clinical innovation need not slavishly follow developments in basic research and theory; sometimes, it stimulates these very developments, so that science follows the lead of practice and not vice versa (Davison & Lazarus, 1995). Even so, the innovative scientist–practitioner adopts an essentially scientific stance in which enthusiasm for technique is tempered by a self-critical attitude, especially about pronouncements that appear unsupported by or incompatible with well-established scientific principles and in which case reports are followed quickly by properly designed and controlled studies of outcome or validity.

Much has been said and written about clinical practice as an art, in which the individual practitioner uses intuition and creativity to address the needs of the particular individuals who arrive at the clinic. This image, which derives from the notion of a "medical art," is accurate in some sense: It takes intuition and creativity to fill in the gaps between the general principles adduced by scientific research and the particular circumstances of the individual case at hand. But this intuition and creativity is not unconstrained: It is grounded in principles uncovered by empirical science. To be explicit: Clinical psychology is an applied science, like engineering; to the extent that it is an art, it is an art like architecture. Engineers put scientific knowledge to practical use: In order to build a bridge that stays up and carries traffic properly, the engineer relies on principles of physics and geology. As Maher (1966) noted:

> In order to build a bridge over a certain river, we must know the details of the soil mechanics, water flow, prevailing winds, topography, traffic usage, availability of labor and materials, and so on. When we consider all these, the total picture might not be like any other bridge that has ever been built. Nevertheless, none of the principles or assumptions that go into the final decisions could be made in contradiction to the laws of physics, economics, and the like. (p. 112)

Similarly, architects exercise a great deal of creativity and ingenuity in designing buildings and fitting them to their sites, but in the final analysis the test of whether the architect has done his or her job is whether the building stands up and is livable.

Like engineers and architects, then, clinical psychologists practice their art within the confines of what is sanctioned by scientific knowledge. To give examples that are perhaps closer to home for clinical psychologists, consider radiologists, who depend on the principles of anatomy and physics to locate and destroy tumors in cancer patients. Similarly, anesthesiologists rely on principles of chemistry and physiology to make sure that their patients feel no pain during surgery.

THE THREAT TO CLINICAL PSYCHOLOGY

Thus, clinical practice is based on, and constrained by, scientific knowledge. If that is really the case, then why has so much attention been given to the idea of a "science–practice *war*"? There is definitely a conflict between science and practice within psychology, but this is only a small part of a wider conflict: Psychotherapy in general, and clinical psychology in particular, are institutions under attack.

To refer to psychotherapy or clinical psychology as institutions may seem somewhat odd, but that is what they are. From a theoretical perspective, *institutions* are socially constructed, ordered, routine-reproduced, programs, rule systems, or patterns of behavior. Marriage, sexism, academic tenure, the handshake, the army, and insurance are all institutions (Jepperson, 1991). They have rules that have often been constructed and implicitly, if not explicitly, accepted by their members; they operate as relative fixtures in their respective environmental contexts; and they are accompanied by taken-for-granted accounts (Jepperson, 1991, p. 149).

Clinical psychology, and even psychotherapy, can be considered institutions because people believe that they require some level of formal education and training and that they should be guided by accepted methods of operation. For example, professional organizations like the American Psychological Association (APA) have constructed formal rules about who may practice clinical psychology, what kind of training is required, what types of settings may provide such training, and the appropriate professional conduct of individual practitioners. Not everyone may agree with the established rules that guide clinical training programs or that govern the practice of clinical psychology. However, few individuals who seek to engage in the practice, or organizations who train or employ such individuals (such as departments of psychology), are willing to ignore the precepts of governing bodies such as the APA.

However firmly entrenched clinical psychology might be as an institution, it is apparent that outside forces are questioning its status and attempting to change the rules by which it operates. Depending on the environmental circumstances, all social institutions are vulnerable to such attacks, and clinical practice is no exception.

During the 1980s and 1990s, a dramatic change occurred in the ways in which health care and mental health care are provided. In many parts of the United States, managed care is now widely accepted as a mechanism for providing mental health services. But managed care does not merely mean utilization review; rather it encompasses a number of practices designed to regulate the utilization of health care (Dorwart, 1990; Tischler, 1990; Zimet, 1989). It "encompasses a wide range of organizational forms, financing arrangements, and regulatory devices that vary in their impact" on client care (Mechanic, Schlesinger, & McAlpine, 1995, p. 19).

From one point of view, the tools of managed care, including precertification requirements, utilization review, closed panels of providers, and reimbursement mechanisms (other than fee-for-service), threaten the taken-for-granted rules that previously guided practice. For example, many clinicians were trained to develop treatment plans with their clients that included the type and duration of treatment that seemed best given the client's presenting problem. It was taken for granted that the clinician could be the best judge of what treatment was required by the client. Under managed care, often, precertification requirements and utilization reviewers seem to be making those judgments with, at times, little input from the clinician.

In addition, insurance companies and other third-party payers, employers, and consumers of service are questioning whether the treatment provided is worth the cost. How can they be sure that the treatment provided is the "best" or most effective treatment? How do they know when an employee or a family member is "better"? Are treatment modalities that take longer superior to short-term treatments? When should hospitalization be used, and when are outpatient or partial care facilities more cost effective?

Finally, clinical psychologists who practice psychotherapy have found themselves under attack by other professions that provide this service: psychiatrists, clinical social workers, marriage and family counselors, and even other psychologists (e.g., counseling psychologists). For example, those psychiatrists who are biologically oriented question whether the use of psychosocial approaches to mental disorders are at all efficacious. And, because some disorders do tend to respond to approaches that have a biological orientation (e.g., medication for depression and schizophrenia), those practitioners who are oriented more toward a psychosocial approach often find themselves on the defensive.

On the other hand, some clinical social workers have argued that their education and training allows them to focus holistically on the entire gestalt of the client in his or her life situation rather than simply on individual psychological processes. And with that perspective, it is argued, they can better identify and treat more of the factors that facilitate or impede the treatment process. Furthermore, it is argued that this systems approach leads to improvements that persist longer and pervade the client's life more deeply. Nevertheless, because they also adopt a psychosocial approach to treatment, it would seem that clinical social workers would be natural allies as psychologists respond to attacks from biological psychiatry.

PSYCHOLOGY'S ROLE IN SHAPING THE MANAGED CARE OF THE FUTURE

There is no question that managed care represents a threat to the way clinicians have usually thought of themselves and to the way they are used to dealing with clients and patients. However, clinical psychologists and other social scientists have a role to play in setting the standards by which assessments and treatments are evaluated. In this way, clinical psychology has an opportunity to shape managed care.

With respect to managed mental health care, there indeed seems to be "more rhetoric than reason; more heat than light" (Feldman, 1992, p. 3). There is a faction in the managed care world that claims that much of psychotherapy is inefficient and ineffective. On the other hand, many practitioners can recount anecdotal horror stories about the ways in which managed care organizations have not necessarily served the best interests of the clients. In reviewing the problems that clinicians have with managed care, several themes tend to recur (Giles, 1993, p. 4).

1. Managed mental health care companies put dollars before patients.
2. Employees of managed mental health care companies merely feed the greed of the for-profit managed mental health care companies.
3. The quality and quantity of inpatient care is sacrificed to second-rate outpatient programs that rarely get the job done.
4. The quality of outpatient care suffers from managed care reliance on generic therapists with inadequate training and specialization.
5. Managed mental health care representatives are indifferent and hostile to provider opinions, preferring instead to make black-and-white decisions based on corporately derived cost containment rules.
6. In general, managed mental health care systems continuously place in jeopardy the lives of the very patients they are mandated to serve.

Feldman (1992) pointed out that because managed mental health care has not been around very long, there has been little in the way of dispassionate analysis and research. Much of the professional literature is replete with anecdotes and observations that tend to reflect the optimism of those who are seeking to manage mental health care and the unhappiness of those providers, both individuals and organizations, who find themselves being increasingly managed.

Practitioners have the opportunity to influence the way in which managed care organizations operate and managed mental health care is practiced in this country. The way in which clinicians can influence managed care has been a part of clinical training from the beginning. Having been trained in a scientific discipline, clinical practitioners have the education and skills to design studies that can demonstrate that what takes place in practice is efficacious and cost effective. By designing (or working with others to design) studies that examine outcomes and the differential effectiveness of treatment, clinical psychologists can assume an important role in mental health services research (Canter Kihlstrom, 1998; Woody & Canter Kihlstrom, 1997). By demonstrating a willingness to study their own practices, clinicians have a unique opportunity to effect change rather than merely react to it.

The management of mental health services has been inspired by the perceived (and real) increase in the cost of mental health and substance abuse services during the last decade (Feldman, 1992). However, it would be a mistake to assume that the debate about managed mental health care is just about economics. Cost and utilization have been the driving force of managed care in the past. Now, however, as rising costs have been contained (relatively), access to services, the outcomes of service, and quality of care must be the focus of any future system of service provision. And it is especially around the issue of quality that practitioners have the opportunity to make important contributions. By defining quality at a conceptual level, by constructing instruments by which to measure it, and by conducting studies of quality, including consumer surveys and other assessments, the field of psychology as a whole and clinical psychology in particular has much to contribute.

The debate over managed mental health care is also about professional status and autonomy. Many professionals fear that managed care threatens their autonomy. On the contrary, by responding positively to its demands, and making the case, through well-designed clinical studies, that specific mental health treatments are necessary, efficacious, and cost effective, clinical psychologists stand to *gain* status and autonomy, not lose it. On the other hand, if practitioners and clinical researchers refuse to conduct their own research on cost, quality, and access issues, managed mental health organizations will make these kinds of decisions with any information that is available—information that may not adequately represent the true outcome of the therapeutic encounter. Thus, somewhat paradoxically, positive, constructive responses to managed care can actually benefit clinical psychology.

Clinicians should take the opportunity to shape and control managed care, because health care and mental health care in the future will be managed. The emphases, the mechanisms, and even the rules for managing care will most certainly evolve, but the days of fee-for-service health care in the United States are numbered. Health care and mental health care will be managed in one form or another. Practitioners need to accept that the notion of managed care, broadly defined (Mechanic et al., 1995), will not simply wither away. It is a burgeoning institution in its own right, and its proponents are quite strong, vocal, and armed with studies reflecting short-term outcomes.

The Need for Regulation

Part of the concern about managed mental health care is that it is unregulated (Adelman, 1990, as cited by Giles, 1993). Until very recently, little was known about the ways in which managed mental health care organizations function. In addition, many state insurance commissioners have little or no authority to monitor these organizations or to intervene on behalf of consumers when problems occur. Alliances need to be formed between state psychological associations and other organizations, providers, and facilities to lobby for legislation to establish guidelines for managed care organizations (Adelman, as cited by Giles, 1993). Several states (e.g., California) have been at the leading edge in attempts to regulate managed care companies (e.g., health maintenance organizations, or HMOs).

Practitioner-Owned Managed Care Organizations

A second course of action is less political in nature but requires active participation and commitment by practitioners. Those involved in mental health treatment services might examine how medicine has responded to managed care. A small but growing number of physicians are offering to sell their services directly to employers, thereby bypassing the "middleman"—the HMOs, insurance companies, and others (Freudenheim, 1995, p. D1). In the last several years, physicians across the country organized many new medical groups (Freudenheim, 1995, p. D1) and have even begun their own HMOs. Bradman (1989, 1994) argued for this new generation of care in the mental health field.

Establishing Clear Guidelines for Treatment

This approach can only succeed if the practitioners can convince employers that particular therapeutic interventions actually work. To that end, practitioners must establish clear, formal standards and guidelines for practice through the research efforts that were discussed earlier in this chapter. In addition, practitioners must more clearly understand the position of most employers: If an employee becomes ill and requires treatment, most employers are willing to spend money, through health care benefits, to help the employee get the required treatment so that the employee can return to work and function productively on the job. In short, the employer wants to see value for the dollars spent. It is up to the practitioner to demonstrate that the services provided are indeed worth the dollars that are spent to purchase them. This is not necessarily a cold-hearted position. Most people are willing to spend money on services of all kinds, every day. However, no one wants to spend money on services that are ineffective.

The Institute of Medicine, a branch of the National Academy of Sciences, defines clinical practice guidelines as "systematically developed statements to assist practitioner and patient decisions about appropriate health care for specific clinical circumstances" (Field & Lohr, 1990, p. 38). Most clinical psychologists in practice would be interested in the Guidelines on *Depression in Primary Care* that have been developed by the Agency for Health Care Policy and Research (AHCPR; see, e.g., Munoz, Hollon, McGrath, Rehm, & VandenBos, 1994). The AHCPR guidelines consist of a review of the empirical literature on detection, diagnosis, and treatment of major depression, and they end with primary care practice guidelines. Other guidelines such as the diagnosis and treatment of anxiety and panic disorder in the primary care setting are slated for development and release. Although formal guidelines may seem to represent an encroachment on the freedom of the individual practitioner, it is important to recognize that guideline development will continue. Clinical psychologists must actively participate in the formulation of these guidelines.

Establishing the Efficacy of Treatment Through Research

The key to survival for clinical psychologists is understanding the nature of mental disorders and their treatment, which means having scientific data to support clinical practice. And, of course, data can only be obtained through carefully controlled study designs. Practitioners, together with researchers in clinical psychology and mental health services research, are in the best positions to design and conduct such studies because they have access to clients' presenting problems, ongoing treatment plans, and outcomes. The appropriate strategy, then, is to conduct such studies, gather clinical data into a reliable and valid database, and demonstrate that particular approaches are effective and efficient.

Some clinicians may turn to lobbying efforts to force the regulation of managed care. Such an approach will not address the fundamental issues that are clinical in nature. Other clinicians may seek to defeat managed care by simply resisting. That approach will not work either, for the simple reason that managed care will not go away. A more viable strategy is the formation of a strong, working alliance between science and practice through one or more of the broad mechanisms just discussed. As noted at the beginning of this chapter, it is necessary for practitioners to understand the environmental pressures (e.g., the penetration rate of managed care in a particular region, the supply of practitioners, contracting methodologies used by managed care companies in an area) in order to choose the proper strategy or combination of strategies.

CONCLUSION: FROM CONFLICT TO ALLIANCE

In the final analysis, it is not enough to say that there is no conflict between science and practice and conclude that science and practice can go their separate ways. Science needs practice to maintain contact with the living material of the field, and practice needs science to survive. Science can provide the means by which practitioners can understand which treatment works the best under what circumstance, what constitutes quality of care, and which treatments are cost effective. Armed with such information, clinicians can assume a more powerful position with respect to managed care and can maintain the status and autonomy that the profession seeks. Without these tools, the argument is too often reduced to the moral equivalent of a "he-said/she-said" argument between practitioners and managed care organizations.

Practitioners and clinical researchers can best focus energy on using scientific tools available to design studies, collect data, and draw valid conclusions that can contribute to the ongoing policy debate about what constitutes cost-effective and high quality mental health treatment. Managed care may seem like the enemy. And, indeed, some of its mechanisms and practices may not serve the clients or the therapeutic process. However, the real enemy is the reluctance to scientifically examine clinical practice and its outcome.

REFERENCES

Beck, A. T. (1967). Depression: Clinical, experimental, and theoretical aspects. New York: Harper & Row.

Benjamin, L. T. (1996). Introduction: Lightner Witmer's legacy to American psychology. *American Psychologist, 51,* 235–236.

Beutler, L. E., Williams, R. E., Wakefield, P. J., & Entwistle, S. R. (1995). Bridging scientist and practitioner perspectives in clinical psychology. *American Psychologist, 50,* 984–994.

Bradman, L. H. (1989). Contract directly for mental health care. *Business Insurance, 17,* 49–50.

Bradman, L. H. (1994, July–August). Direct contracts for substance abuse benefits. *Journal of Health Care Benefits,* 8–11.

Canter Kihlstrom, L. (1998). Mental health services research. In H. S. Friedman (Ed.), *Encyclopedia of mental health* (Vol. 2, pp. 653–663). San Diego, CA: Academic Press.

Davison, G. C., & Lazarus, A. A. (1995). The dialectics of science and practice. In S. C. Hayes, V. M. Follette, R. M. Dawes, & K. E. Grady (Eds.), *Scientific standards of psychological practice: Issues and recommendations* (pp. 95–120). Reno, NV: Context Press.

Dorwart, R. A. (1990). Managed mental health care: Myths and realities in the 1990s. *Hospital and Community Psychiatry, 41,* 1087–1091.

Ebbinghouse, H. (1885). *Memory: A contribution to experimental psychology.* Leipzig: Duncker & Humblot.

Ellis, A. (1962). *Reason and emotion in psychotherapy.* New York: Lyle Stuart.

Fagan, T. K. (1996). Witmer's contribution to school psychological services. *American Psychologist, 51,* 241–243.

Feldman, S. (1992). Managed mental health services: Ideas and issues. In S. Feldman (Ed.), *Managed mental health services* (pp. 3–26). Springfield, IL: Charles C Thomas.

Field, M., & Lohr, K. (Eds.). (1990). *Clinical practice guidelines.* Washington, DC: National Academy Press.

Freudenheim, M. (1995, March 7). Doctors, on offensive, form HMOs. *The New York Times* (p. D1).

Giles, T. R. (1993). *Managed mental health care: A guide for practitioners, employers, and hospital administrators.* Boston: Allyn & Bacon.

Hilgard, E. R. (1987). *Psychology in America: A historical survey.* San Diego, CA: Harcourt Brace Jovanovich.

Humphreys, K. (1996). Clinical psychologists as psychotherapists: History, future, and alternatives. *American Psychologist, 51,* 190–197.

James, W. (1980). *Principles of psychology* (Vols. 1 & 2). New York: Holt. (Original work published 1890)

Jepperson, R. L. (1991). Institutions, institutional effects, and institutionalism. In W. W. Powell & P. J. DiMaggio (Eds.), *The new institutionalism in organizational analysis* (pp. 143–163). Chicago: University of Chicago Press.

Maher, B. A. (1966). *Principles of psychopathology.* New York: McGraw-Hill.

Maher, B. A. (1992). A personal history of clinical psychology. In M. Hersen,

A. E. Kazdin, & A. S. Bellack (Eds.), *The clinical psychology handbook* (2nd ed., pp. 3–25). New York: Pergamon.

McFall, R. M. (1991). Manifesto for a science of clinical psychology. *The Clinical Psychologist, 44,* 75–88.

McFall, R. M. (1996). Making psychology incorruptible. *Applied and Preventive Psychology, 5,* 9–15.

McReynolds, P. (1996). Lightner Witmer: A centennial tribute. *American Psychologist, 51,* 237–240.

Mechanic, D., Schlesinger, M., and McAlpine, D. D. (1995). Management of mental health and substance abuse services: State of the art and early results. *The Milbank Quarterly, 73,* 19–55.

Munoz, R. F., Hollon, S. D., McGrath, E., Rehm, L. P., & VandenBos, G. R. (1994). On the AHCPR depression in primary care guidelines: Further considerations for practitioners. *American Psychologist, 49,* 42–61.

Ribot, T. (1882). *Diseases of memory.* New York: Appleton.

Routh, D. K. (1994). *Clinical psychology since 1917: Science, practice, and organization.* New York: Plenum.

Routh, D. K. (1996). Lightner Witmer and the first 100 years of clinical psychology. *American Psychologist, 51,* 244–247.

Routh, D. K. (1997). A history of Division 12 (Clinical Psychology): Fourscore years. In D. A. Dewsbury (Ed.), *Unification through division: Histories of the Divisions of the American Psychological Association* (Vol. 2, pp. 55–82). Washington, DC: American Psychological Association.

Shakow, D. (1969). *Clinical psychology as a science and as a profession: A forty-year odyssey.* Chicago: Aldine.

Tischler, G. L. (1990). Utilization management of mental health services by private third parties. *American Journal of Psychiatry, 147,* 967–973.

Witmer, L. (1996). Clinical psychology. *American Psychologist, 51,* 248–251. (Reprinted from *Psychological Clinic,* 1907, *1,* 1–9)

Woody, S. R., & Canter Kihlstrom, L. (1997). Outcomes, quality, and cost: Integrating psychotherapy and mental health services research. *Psychotherapy Research, 7,* 365–381.

Zimet, C. N. (1989). The mental health care revolution: Will psychology survive? *American Psychologist, 44,* 703–708.

AUTHOR INDEX

Numbers in italics refer to listings in reference sections.

31, 32, 33, 34, 36, 37, 38, 39, 40, 44, 45, 46, 47, 48, 50

Canobbio, R., 84

Canter Kihlstrom, L., 288, 292, 293

Cantwell, D., 258

Capaldi, D. M., 78, 90

Carey, G., 104, 120

Carr, A. T., 240, 258

Casanova, M. F., 30, 50

Cashman, L., 260

Cassady, S., 16, 22

Castellon, C., 214

Castle, D. J., 28, 48

Catanzaro, S. J., 101, 118

Cattell, R. B., 152, 160

Ceci, S. J., 90

Cerri, A., 20

Chambless, D. L., 223, 224, 230, 241, 245, 259, 263

Champoux, M., 106, 118

Chansky, T. E., 232

Cheslow, D. L., 237, 261, 263

Chorpita, B. F., 102, 103, 104, 107, 111, 116

Christensen, A., 267, 277

Christie, K. A., 54, 84

Christison, D. A., 30, 50

Chu, B., 228, 232

Chungani, H. T., 25, 46

Ciadella, P., 258

Cicchetti, D., 62, 73, 84

Clark, D. A., 104, 116

Clark, L. A., 67, 68, 92, 98, 99, 101, 104, 117, 120

Clarke, G. N., 54, 82, 84

Clarke, L., 97, 118

Clem, T., 21

Clements, C. M., 97, 115

Clements, M., 270, 278

Clementz, B. A., 8, 12, 13, 14, 15, 16, 17, 18, 19, 20, 22

Cloninger, C. R., 7, 19, 95, 117

Cobb, J., 250, 261

Cochran, S. D., 57, 84

Cohan, C. L., 267, 276

Cohen, D. J., 239, 261, 262, 263

Cohen, J., 172, 193

Colbus, D., 75, 88

Cole, D. A., 71, 78, 84, 111, 112, 117, 120

Coles, M., 260

Collins, A. C., 19

Colter, N., 44

Commenges, D., 21

Conley, J. J., 274, 277

Conners, C. K., xx, xxi

Conrad, A. J., 27, 42, 45

Constans, J. I., 241, 258

Cooley, C. H., 60, 62, 84

Coon, H., 19

Cooper, M. J., 171, 194

Corley, R., 19

Cornblatt, B. A., 33, 35, 46, 49

Corrigan, R., 63, 84

Corsellis, J. A. N., 44

Coryell, W. H., 54, 88, 238, 262

Cottraux, J., 252, 258

Cowell, P. C., 46

Cox, C., 259

Coyne, J. C., 56, 59, 84, 85

Cramer, G., 20

Craske, M., 97, 119

Creelman, D. D., 172, 179, 195

Crick, F., xv, xxi

Crits-Christoph, P., 157, 158, 160

Cronbach, L. J., 15, 19, 77, 84, 166, 194

Crook, K., 107, 120

Crouse-Novak, M., 88

Crow, T. J., 28, 44, 45

Csikszentmihalyi, M., 207, 213

Cuffe, S. P., 263

Cummings, E. M., 62, 73, 84

Cunningham, R. L., 176, 194

Cuthbert, B. N., 167, 194

Cutler, S. E., 110, 117

Cutrona, C. E., 57, 84

Czajkowski, S. M., 122, 140, 146

Dadds, M., 223, 230

Dagg, B. M., 26, 45

Dahl, R., 83

Damon, W., 61, 87

Dandoy, A. C., 66, 88

Darling, C., 120

Daslow, N. J., 88

Davidson, B., 26, 43

Davidson, R. J., xvi, xxi, 67, 84

Davies, M., 54, 88, 90, 259

Davis, A., 19

Davis, D., 35, 50

Davis, J. M., 19

Davis, K. L., 20

Davison, G. C., 282, 284, 292

Flashman, L., 30, *49*
Flaum, M., 30, *49*
Fleming, J. A. E., 13, *20*, 53, *85*
Flint, J., 11, *19*
Floyd, F. J., 270, *277, 278*
Flynn, C., 74, 76, 77, 79, 80, 86
Foa, E. B., 171, *196*, 236, 237, 239, 241,
    242, 243, 244, 245, 246, 249,
    250, 252, 253, 258, 259, 260,
    261, 263
Foerster, A., 34, *46*
Fontaine, R., *258*
Forsythe, S., 27, *45*
Frances, A. J., *22*
Frankenburg, F. R., *51*, 238, *260*
Franklin, M. E., 241, 256, 258, *260*
Franz, B. R., 27, *43*
Freedman, R., 17, *19*
Freud, S., 150, 154, 155, 158, *160*, 164,
    193
Freudenheim, M., 289, *292*
Friedlander, S., 63, 64, 65, 86
Friedman, J. H., *21*
Friedman, L., *22*
Frith, C. D., *44, 45*
Frost, R. O., 241, *263*
Fudge, H., 54, *86*
Fulker, D. W., *19*
Funkenstein, D., 122, 123, 124, 125, 126,
    145

Gallacher, F., *46*
Gambini, O., 16, *22*
Gammon, G., *92*
Garber, J., 56, 57, 58, 59, 66, 67, 71, 74,
    76, 77, 78, 79, 80, 81, 86, 87,
    90, 91, 111, *119*
Garrison, C. Z., 205, *213, 263*
Garvey, M. J., *85, 213*
Geer, J. H., 97, *117*
Gelder, M. G., 104, *115*
Gershon, E. S., 7, *19, 45*, 67, *84*
Gersten, M., *119*
Gibbons, R. D., 13, *19*
Giles, T. R., 287, 289, *292*
Gillham, J., 54, 58, 86, 88, 211, *213*
Gilliard, D., 70, *85*
Girgus, J. S., 56, 90, 110, *118*
Glover, G., 39, *49*
Goetz, D., *90*
Goetz, T. E., 70, *85*

Gold, J. M., *46*
Goldberg, T. E., 32, *46*
Goldbourt, U., 123, *145*
Golden, R., *46*
Goldin, L. R., 22, *45*
Golding, J., *45*
Golding, J. M., 237, *260*
Goldman-Rakic, P. S., 17, *21*, 25, 26, *46,*
    49, 50
Goodman, J., *21*
Goodman, S. H., 36, *46*, 59, 71, 78, *86*
Goodman, W. K., *260*
Goodnow, J. J., 175, *193*
Gordon, D., *87*
Gorman, J. M., *21*
Gotlib, I. H., 56, 57, 58, 68, 83, 84, *86*
Gottesman, I. I., 4, 6, 7, 8, *19, 21, 22,*
    30, *46*
Gould, S. J., 168, *194*
Grady-Fletcher, A., 266, *278*
Graham, S., 64, *92*
Granger, D. A., 114, *117*
Grawe, R. W., 16, *19*
Gray, J. A., *19*, 95, *117*
Grayson, J. B., 243, 244, *260, 263*
Green, J., 139, *145*
Green, M. F., 17, *19*
Gregory, S., *120*
Greist, J. H., 250, 253, 258, *260*
Greve, B., 26, *44*
Griffin, N. J., 107, *119*
Grimes, K., 35, *49*
Grimson, R., *45*
Grove, W. M., 12, 13, 14, 16, 18, *19,*
    20, 85, 213, 221, 227, 232
Gruenberg, E., *213*
Gruzelier, J., 33, *46*
Gunnar, M., 106, *118*
Gupta, S. M., *45*
Gur, R. C., *18*, 31, *44, 46, 50*
Gur, R. E., *18*, 27, 28, 29, 30, 31, 32,
    44, 46, 47, 50
Gursky, D. M., 97, *119*

Haaga, D., 56, *86*
Haas, G. L., 16, *22*
Hadzi-Pavlovic, D., 109, *120*
Hafele, E., 16, *22*
Hagerman, R. J., xiv, *xxi*
Hagman, J. O., *43*
Hahlweg, K., 267, 269, *277*

Jacoby, C. G., 29, 48–49
Jaenicke, C., 59, 71, 78, 87
Jagoe, R., *44*
James, W., 60, 87, 282, 292
Jang, K., *21*
Janoff-Bulman, R., 61, 66, 72, 88
Jansson, L., *21*
Jaycox, L. H., 54, 58, 86, 88, 211, *213, 214*
Jefferson, J., 250, *260*
Jenike, M. A., 238, 260, 262
Jepperson, R. L., 285, *292*
Jeste, D. V., *47*
Jody, D. N., *43, 45*
John, B., 8, *20*
John, K., *92*
Johnson, A. L., *120*
Johnstone, E. C., *44, 45*
Joiner, T. E., 57, 79, 81, 89, 92, 101, *118*
Jonas, J. M., 238, *260*
Jones, E. G., 25, *43, 47*
Jones, L. E., 175, *194*
Jones, P. B., 34, *47*
Jordan, C., 63, *90*
Just, N., 58, 59, 88

Kagan, J., 95, 113, 114, *118, 119,* 227, *231*
Kaij, L., 36, *48*
Kalikow, K., *259*
Kamen, L. P., 67, *91*
Kandel, D. B., 54, *88*
Kane, M. T., 219, 220, *231, 232*
Kaplan, B. H., 121, *145*
Kaprio, J., 30, *45*
Karney, B. R., 267, 269, 271, 272, 274, *276, 277*
Karno, M., 237, *260*
Kasell, E., *21*
Kashani, J. H., 66, *88*
Kaslow, N. J., 69, 76, 88, *91*
Kasvikis, Y. G., 238, *260, 261*
Katon, W., 99, 100, *118, 120*
Katsanis, J., 16, 17, *20*
Katz, D. B., 186, 187, 188, *197*
Katz, R., 67, 89, *258*
Katzelnick, D. J., 250, *260*
Kaufman, C. A., *21*
Kaufman, J., 54, *83*
Kauneckis, D., 114, *117*
Kazdin, A. E., 75, 88, 224, *231*

Keefe, R. S. E., 8, 17, 20, *22*
Keith, B., 265, *276*
Keith, D., 67, *91*
Keller, M., 54, 88
Kelly, E. L., 274, *277*
Kelly, G. A., 167, 175, 176, 177, 186, 193, *194*
Kelly, K. A., 97, *115*
Kelly, S., 270, *277*
Kendall, P. C., 99, 108, *118,* 120, 216, 217, 218, 219, 220, 221, 222, 223, 224, 225, 226, 227, 228, 230, 231, 232, *233*
Kendler, K. S., 14, 21, 22, 30, *47*
Kennedy, J. L., *21*
Keshavan, M. S., 40, 41, 42, 47, *49*
Kester, D. B., *50*
Kidd, K. K., *21*
Kiecolt-Glaser, J. K., 122, *146*
Kiesler, D., 224, *233*
Kihlstrom, J. F., 106, *118,* 167, 171, 176, 194, *195*
Kim, J. J., *43*
Kim, R., *232*
King, R. A., *263*
King, S. H., 122, *145*
Kingdon, D., *120*
Kinney, D. K., 17, *21*
Kinsley, H., 222, *233*
Kipps, B. R., *22*
Kirkpatrick, B., *21*
Klann, N., 267, *277*
Klann, R., 169, *195*
Klein, R. H., 33, *47*
Klerman, G. L., 53, *92*
Kobak, K. A., 250, *260*
Koby, E., *259*
Koch, R., 13, *20*
Koestner, R., 71, *88*
Kokenvuo, M., 30, *45*
Kortenkamp, S., 17, *20*
Kortlander, E., *232*
Kovacs, M., 55, 67, 68, 72, *88*
Kovelman, J. A., 26, *48*
Kozak, M. J., 236, 237, 241, 242, 243, 244, 245, 249, 250, 253, 259, 260, *261*
Kraemer, H., *120*
Kraepelin, E., 23, *48*
Kraft, R. W., 143, 144, *145*
Kremen, W. S., *19*
Kringlen, E., *20*

Kristbjarnarson, H., *21*
Kronmal, R. A., 13, *20*
Kruglyak, L., *19*
Kruschke, J. K., 174, *194, 196*
Kruskal, J. B., 173, *194*
Kuchna, I., 39, *48*
Kuck, J., *47*
Kulka, R. A., 265, *278*
Kun, A., 63, *88*
Kurtz, D., *45*
Kushner, M., *45*
Kwon, P., 79, *93*

LaFreniere, P. J., 108, *117*
Lahti, A., *21*
Laing, P., 39, *47*
Lamb, M. E., 65, *92*
Landau, P., *258*
Lang, M., 42, *50*
Lang, P. J., 167, 192, *194*
Lange, K., 14, 20, *21*
Larson, D. W., 56, *89*
Last, C., 222, *233*
Latimer, P., 243, *260*
Laurent, J., 101, *118*
Lavori, P. W., 54, *88*
Lawlis, G. F., 142, *145*
Lawrence, E., 270, *277*
Lazarus, A. A., 282, 284, *292*
Lease, A. M., 189, 190, 191, *194*
Lebow, B. S., *20*
Leckman, J. F., 239, 262, *263*
Lee, G., *45*
Leff, G., 73, *91*
Leite, P., *193*
Lelliott, P. T., 237, *261*
Lenane, M. C., 237, *259, 261, 263*
Lencer, R., *18*
Leon, A. C., 237, *261*
Leonard, H. L., 237, 255, *261, 262, 263*
Leonard, S., *19*
Lepine, J., *120*
Lerer, B., *22*
Lester, D., 75, *83*
Leutelt, J., *18*
Levander, S. E., 16, 18, *19*
Levin, S., *20*
Levis, D. J., 248, *263*
Levy, D., 12, *21*
Levy, D. L., 19, *20*
Levy, R., 242, *262*

Lewinsohn, P., 205, *213*
Lewinsohn, P. M., 53, 56, 57, 58, *84, 86,*
   88, 89, 91
Lewis, K. R., 8, *20*
Lewis, S. W., 34, 36, 37, 46, *48*
Li, S., 16, *22*
Licht, B., 70, *85*
Lichtermann, D., *22*
Lieberman, J. A., 43, *45*
Liebowitz, M., *120*
Liebowitz, M. L., 253, *261*
Liebowitz, M. R., 96, *116*
Lin, T.-Y., 13, *20*
Liotus, L., *84*
Lipsitt, L. P., 39, *44*
Lipton, D. N., 177, *194*
Lipton, R. B., *20*
Litman, R. E., 16, *21*
Litovsky, V. G., 71, 78, *89*
Liu, X., *21*
Livesley, W. J., *21*
Locke, B. Z., *84*
Loeber, R., 78, *89*
Loehlin, J. C., 22, *90*
Loftus, G. R., 172, *194*
Lohr, K., 290, *292*
Lonnqvist, J., 30, *45*
Lopatka, C., 241, *261*
Lorek, A., *49*
Lovaas, O. I., xx, *xxi*
Lovibond, P. F., 97, *118*
Lovibond, S. H., 97, *118*
Luborsky, L., 150, 151, 152, 153, 154,
   155, 156, 157, 158, 159, *160,*
   161, 203, 213, 214
Luce, R. D., 172, 179, *194*
Lucente, S., 238, *259*
Luiten, P. G., 39, *49*
Lukens, E., *90*
Lyonfields, J. D., 105, *116*
Lyons, M. J., *19*

Ma, J., *45*
Macciardi, F., *21*
MacDonald, J. P., 218, *232*
MacGlashan, T. H., 34, *48*
Macmillan, N. A., 172, 179, *195*
Maher, B. A., 282, 284, *292*
Maier, S. F., 106, *119*
Maier, W., *22*
Malamuth, N. M., 177, *195*

Malaspina, D., 16, *21*
Malatesta, V. J., 238, *258*
Malone, J., *278*
Manicavasagar, V., 109, *120*
March, J. S., 256, *261*
Marco, E. J., *18, 44*
Marcus, J., 35, *46, 48*
Margolin, G., 269, *277*
Markman, H. J., 270, *277, 278*
Marks, A., 247, *259*
Marks, I. M., 237, 238, 244, 245, 246,
        250, 251, *258, 260, 261*
Marris, P., 133, *145*
Marrs-Garcia, A. L., 217, 226, *232*
Marsh, L., *44*
Marten, P. A., 102, 105, *116*
Matthysse, S., 12, 14, *20, 21*
Mattick, R. P., 97, *118*
Mawson, D., 250, *261*
Maxwell, E., *45*
McAdams, L. A., *47*
McAlpine, D. D., 286, *293*
McCalley-Whitters, M., 29, *48*
McCauley, E., 58, 89, 107, *118*
McClelland, D. C., 172, *195*
McCleod, D. R., 105, *117*
McCormick, R. A., *120*
McCranie, E. W., 71, 78, *89*
McCubbin, H. I., 75, *89*
McDonald, R., 250, *261*
McDonel, E. C., 168, 177, 179, *194, 195*
McDowell, J. E., 16, 17, *18*
McEachin, J. J., xx, *xxi*
McFall, R. M., 165, 167, 168, 172, 177,
        179, 180, 181, 183, 184, 186,
        187, 188, 189, 190, 191, *194,*
        195, 197, 284, 293
McGrath, E., 290, *293*
McGue, M., 7, *21*
McGuffin, P., 67, *89*
McKeown, R. E., *263*
McKinley, S. C., 174, *196*
McLardy, T., 26, *48*
McLaughlin, J. E., 26, *45*
McLean, C. J., *22*
McNeil, T. F., 36, 38, 39, *48, 50*
McReynolds, P., 282, *293*
McSparren, J., *51*
Mechanic, D., 286, 289, *293*
Medalie, J. H., 123, *145*
Medin, D. L., 173, *195*

Mednick, S. A., 31, 33, 34, 35, 36, 37,
        39, *43, 44, 46, 47, 48, 49, 50*
Medoff, D., *21*
Medus, C., *20*
Meehl, P. E., 8, 15, *19, 21*, 77, 84, 165,
        167, 169, 172, *195*
Mehta, M., 247, *261*
Meichenbaum, D., 248, *262*
Mendelson, M., 68, *83*, 248, *258*
Mercier, M. A., *193*
Merhige, D., *22*
Merikangas, K., *92*
Merluzzi, T. V., 175, *196*
Messer, B., 75, *89*
Metalsky, G. I., 57, 81, 82, *89*, 110, *115,*
        203, 213
Metzger, R. L., 97, *118*
Meyer, J. M., *22*
Meyer, T. J., 97, *118*
Meyer, V., 242, 243, 244, *262*
Michelsen, N., 35, *48*
Miller, M. L., 97, *118*
Miller, N. E., 240, *258*
Miller, P. H., 63, *89*
Miller, S., *19*
Mineka, S., 97, 101, 106, 110, *115, 117,*
        118
Minichello, W. E., 238, *262*
Minshew, N. J., 41, *49*
Miranda, J., 58, 77, *89, 90*
Mischel, W., 167, *195*
Mitchell, J. R., 58, *89*, 107, *118*
Mitropoulou, V., *22*
Moberg, P., *18, 44*
Mock, J. E., 68, *83*, 248, *258*
Mohs, R. C., 20, *22*
Moises, H. W., 15, *21*
Mol, J. F. M. A., 16, *22*
Mollard, E., *258*
Monteiro, W. O., 237, *261*
Montemayor, R., 61, *89*
Montgomery, L. M., *278*
Moran, J. J., *21*
Moran, M., 16, *22*
Moras, K., 99, *116*
Moreau, M., 13, *20*
Moritz, G., *84*
Moroz, G., *258*
Moskowitz, J., *22*
Mowrer, O. A., 240, *262*
Mozley, D., 31, *50*
Mozley, L. H., 31, *50*

Pettegrew, J. W., 40, 41, *47, 49*
Peynirgioglu, Z. F., 241, *263*
Pfohl, B., 238, *262*
Phillips, J., 222, *233*
Piaget, J., 64, 65, *90*
Piasecki, J., *85*
Pickar, D., *21*
Pickles, A., 54, *86*
Pinnow, M., *18*
Platt, J. R., 172, *196*
Pogue-Guile, M. F., 34, 40, 41, *49*
Pollack, M., *88*
Pollack, S. L., 69, *88*
Polya, G., 169, *196*
Polymeropoulos, M., *19*
Pope, H. G., *51*, 96, *117*, 238, *260*
Popper, K., 165, 169, *196*
Portera, L., 237, *261*
Potkin, S. G., *43*
Powers, T. A., 71, *88*
Praestholm, J., *44*
Pribram, K. H., 25, *47*
Price, R. A., *18, 44*
Prusoff, B. A., 53, *92*
Puig-Antich, J., 53, *90*
Purmann, S., *18*

Quinn, D., 33, *47*
Quinn, P. O., *50*
Quitkin, F. M., *193*

Rabavilas, A. D., 245, *262*
Rachman, S. J., 97, *117*, 240, 241, 245,
    260, 261, 262, 263
Radke-Yarrow, M., 71, *90*
Rae, D. S., *84*
Ragland, J. D., *46*
Rajkowska, G., 26, *50*
Rakic, P., 25, *49*
Rapaport, K., 178, *196*
Rapee, R., 97, *119*, 223, *230*
Rapoport, J. L., 237, 259, *261, 262, 263*
Rapson, R. L., 133, *145*
Rasmussen, S. A., 237, 240, 259, *260,
    262, 263*
Raudenbush, S. W., 271, *276*
Rawlings, R. R., *50*
Ray, J. C., 112, 113, *119*
Redner, J. E., 58, *86*

Regier, D. A., *84, 214*
Rehm, L. P., 69, 88, 290, *293*
Reichler, R., *258*
Reid, J. C., 66, *88*
Reid, S. A., 16, *18*
Reimherr, F., *19*
Reiss, S., 97, *119*
Reivich, K., 54, 86, 88, 211, *213, 214*
Renick, M. J., 270, *278*
Retier, G., *43*
Rettew, D. C., *261*
Reveley, A. M., 37, *49*
Reveley, M. A., 37, *49*
Revenson, T. A., 65, *92*
Reynolds, M. L., 173, *196*
Reynolds, O. R., *49*
Reznick, J. S., 113, *118, 119*
Rheingold, A., *260*
Rholes, W. S., 63, 64, 77, *90, 91*
Ribot, T., 282, *293*
Rice, J., 22, 54, *88*
Richards, J., *120*
Riddle, M. A., 255, *263*
Riggs, D. S., 237, *263*
Riniti, J., 59, *86*
Risch, N., *22*
Riskind, J. H., 77, 90, 100, *119*
Roberts, G. W., 26, *46*
Roberts, R. E., 53, *88*
Robins, C. J., 77, *90*
Robins, L., 204, *213*
Robinson, N. S., 57, 59, 79, *86, 91*
Rodgers, A., 75, *88*
Rodgers, B., 34, *47*
Rogge, R. D., 274, *278*
Rohde, P., 56, 58, 86, *91*, 205, *213*
Roitman, S. E. L., 20, *22*
Ronan, K. R., 217, 218, *232, 233*
Roper, G., 240, 245, *262, 263*
Rose, D. T., 67, 72, 73, *91*
Rosenbaum, A., *278*
Rosenberg, A., *119*
Rosenberg, T. K., 66, *88*
Rosenthal, J., *19*
Ross, D. E., 14, 16, 21, *22*
Ross, J., 63, *91*
Roth, C., *84*
Rothberg, P. C., *83*
Rotter, J. B., 107, *119*, 175, *196*
Routh, D. K., xii, *xxi*, 282, *293*
Rowe, M., 217, *233*

Roy-Byrne, P., 99, 100, *118, 120*
Rozendaal, N., 16, *22*
Rubenstein, C. S., 241, *263*
Ruble, D. N., 63, 64, 65, 90, *91*
Rudy, T. E., 175, *196*
Rush, A. J., 58, *85*, 203, *213*
Russek, L. G., 122, 123, 125, 126, 128,
    130, 131, 135, 137, 138, 139,
    140, 141, 142, 144, *145, 146*
Russek, S. J., 122, *145*
Rutschmann, J., 33, *49*
Rutter, M., 54, 66, 86, *91*
Ryan, N. D., 54, *83*

St. Clair, D. M., 13, *18*
Sakuma, M., *45*
Salkovskis, P. M., 240, 241, *263*
Salzman, L. R., 33, *47*
Sandman, C. A., *43*
Sapolsky, R. M., 112, 113, *119*
Sarason, B. R., 122, 133, *146*
Sarason, I. G., 122, 133, *146*
Sarbin, T. R., 175, *196*
Savole, T., 35, *50*
Saykin, A. J., 31–32, *50*
Scahill, L., *263*
Scarone, S., 16, *22*
Sceery, W., *259*
Schaap, C., 270, *278*
Schaefer, E. S., 75, 78, *91*
Schafer, J., 247, *259*
Schaffer, M. M., 173, *195*
Schalling, D., 16, *18*
Scheibel, A. B., 26, 27, 45, *48*
Schiffman, S. S., 173, 183, *196*
Schlesinger, M., 286, *293*
Schludermann, E., 75, *91*
Schludermann, S., 75, *91*
Schmale, A., 155, *160*
Schmaling, K. B., 266, *277*
Schmidt, K. L., 78, *92*
Schmieding, A., 169, *195*
Schnurer, A., 242, *262*
Schroeder-Slomann, S., 169, *195*
Schulman, P., 67, *91, 214*
Schulsinger, F., 33, 35, 44, 46, 48, 49,
    50
Schulsinger, H., *49, 50*
Schurmann, M., *18*
Schwab, S. G., 15, *22*
Schwartz, G. E., 122, 123, 128, 130, 131,

133, 135, 137, 138, 139, 140,
    141, 142, 144, *145, 146*
Schwartz, J. E., *45*
Schweers, J., *84*
Schwinger, E., *18, 21*
Sears, L. L., 186, *196*
Seeley, J. R., 53, 56, 58, 84, 86, 88, *91*,
    205, *213*
Seeman, M. V., 42, *50*
Seeman, T. E., 123, *146*
Segal, Z. V., 58, *91*
Seidman, L. J., *19*
Seivewright, N., *120*
Selemon, L. D., 26, *50*
Seligman, M. E. P., 55, 56, 58, 67, 68,
    69, 72, 75, 76, 82, 82, 87, 90,
    91, 106, 109, 110, *115, 118,
    119*, 155, *161, 201*, 202, 203,
    204, *213*, 214, 266, *278*
Semmel, A., 67, *91*, 203, *213*
Serketich, W. J., 108, *117*
Serlin, R. C., 250, *260*
Sessa, F. M., *232*
Sexton, V. S., xi, *xxi*
Shadish, W. R., 266, *278*
Shaffer, D., *259*
Shafran, R., 241, *262*
Shakow, D., 282, *293*
Sham, P., 39, *49*
Shanley, N., 66, *86*
Shaw, B. F., 203, *213*
Shaw, P. M., 104, *115*
Shedlack, K., *45*
Sheeber, L. B., *84*
Shellenberger, R., 139, *145*
Shelton, M. R., 111, *119*
Shepard, R. N., 173, *196*
Shepherd, P. M., *45*
Sher, K. J., 241, *263*
Sherman, S. L., 8, *22*
Shields, G. W., *45*
Shields, J., 6, 8, *19*
Shinkwin, R., *22*
Shoda, Y., 167, *195*
Sholomskas, D., 53, *92*
Shtasel, D. L., 18, 44, *50*
Shumaker, S. A., 122, 140, *146*
Siegel, L. J., 107, *119*
Siever, L. J., 8, 16, 20, *22*
Silove, D., 109, *120*
Silverman, J. M., 8, 20, *22*
Silverman, W. K, 108, *120*, 219, *233*

Singer, D. G., 65, 92
Siomopolous, G., 65, 92
Siqueland, L., 108, 120, 232
Sjorgren, B., 21
Sluys, M., 258
Smeraldi, E., 16, 22
Smith, A. M., 45
Smith, J. C., 263
Smith, M. C., 182, 196
Smith, M. S., 152, 161
Smith, T., xxi
Snidman, N., 113, 118, 119, 227, 231
Snyder, D. K., 266, 269, 278
Soltys, S. M., 66, 88
Sorensen, I., 26, 43
Sorenson, S. B., 237, 260
Southam-Gerow, M. A., 218, 221, 226,
    228, 232, 233
Spinhoven, P., 263
Squire, L. R., 32, 50
Stafiniak, P., 50
Stampfl, T. G., 248, 263
Stanley, S. M., 270, 277, 278
Stark, D. D., 78, 92
Stark, K. D., 107, 120
Statfeld, A., 222, 233
Steer, R. A., 104, 116
Stefanis, C., 245, 262
Steinberg, L., 108, 120
Steinmetz, J. E., 186, 187, 188, 196, 197
Steinmetz, J. L., 56, 89
Steketee, G. S., 237, 243, 244, 245, 260,
    261, 263
Stern, R. S., 250, 261
Sternberg, R. J., 90
Stevens, J. R., 26, 50
Stevenson-Hinde, J., 133, 145
Stewart, A., 49
Stewart, J. W., 193
Stipek, D. J., 64, 65, 79, 92, 93
Stone, P. J., 152, 161
Straub, R. E., 15, 22
Strauss, M. E., 120
Street, L., 120
Strickland, B. R., 107, 119
Strupp, H., xx, xxi
Stuart, G., 228, 233
Stuart, R. B., 269, 278
Suddath, R. L., 30, 37, 50
Sugarman, A., 225, 232
Sullivan, K. T., 271, 278
Sun, C., 22

Swatling, S., 83
Swayze, V. W., 32, 43
Swedo, S. E., 237, 256, 261, 262, 263
Sweeney, J. A., 14, 16, 18, 22
Swets, J. A., 168, 172, 197
Syme, L., 123, 146

Taft, R., 175, 196
Takei, N., 39, 49
Tanenbaum, R. L., 91
Tapernon-Franz, U., 44
Targum, S., 28, 50
Taylor, E. I., xii, xxi, 50
Taylor, S., 63, 85
Teasdale, I., 202, 213
Teasdale, J. D., 55, 58, 82, 92, 109, 115
Teasdale, T. W., 49
Teherani, M., 120
Tellegen, A., 96, 98, 120
Tew, W., 45
Thacker, L. R., 14, 21
Thaker, G. K., 16, 21, 22
Thatcher, R. W., 25, 50
Thelen, M. H., 182, 196
Thode, H. C., 25, 46
Thompson, R. F., 197
Throdarson, D. S., 241, 262
Tien, A., 21
Tischler, G. L., 286, 293
Todak, G., 90
Tomarket, A. J., 67, 84
Torres, I., 49
Torrey, E. F., 30, 38, 46, 50
Towbin, K. E., 239, 262
Townsend, J. T., 167, 172, 193, 197
Treadwell, K. R. H., 217, 222, 226, 227,
    232, 233
Treat, T. A., 165, 172, 177, 180, 181,
    183, 184, 185, 186, 187, 188,
    189, 190, 191, 194, 195, 197,
    228, 233
Trestman, R., 22
Trojanowski, J. Q., 27, 43
Tsakiris, R., 238, 260
Tsuang, M. T., 19, 39, 44, 237, 263
Tuason, V. B., 85, 213
Tupling, H., 109, 119
Turetsky, B. L., 46
Turk, E., 69, 70, 76, 92
Turner, J. E., 111, 112, 117, 120
Turner, R. M., 243, 244, 260

Yu, M.-H., *21*
Yuh, W. T., *49*
Yurgelun-Todd, D., *51, 238, 260*

Zahn, T., *259*
Zahner, G. E., *239, 262*
Zhang, J., *22*
Zie, S., *45*
Ziegle, J. S., *22*

Zigler, E. F., 65, 92
Zimbalist, M. E., *21*
Zimet, C. N., 286, *293*
Zimmerli, W. D., 105, *117*
Zinbarg, R. E., 97, 99, 100, 102, *116,*
  120
Zisook, S., 17, *18*, 47
Zoega, T., *21*
Zorilla, L. E., *18*
Zupan, B., 87
Zuroff, D. C., 71, 88

SUBJECT INDEX

Australia, treatment of anxiety disorders in, 223, 224
Autonomic arousal (AA), 101, 102, 104–105
Avoidant disorder (AD), 219. *See also* Anxiety disorders
Aylward, E., 33

Bach, A. K., xvi
Barlow, D. H., xvi, 102
Barrett, J. E., 99–100
Bass, J. D., 71
BCT. *See* Behavioral Couples Therapy
BDD. *See* Body dysmorphic disorder
Bearden, C. E., xiv–xv
Beck, A. T., 54–55, 70
Beck Depression Inventory, 68
Beens, H., 249
Behavioral Couples Therapy (BCT), 266
Benes, F. M., 41
Bertelsen, A., 6
Bilder, R. M., 28
Binet, A., xii, 168
Body dysmorphic disorder (BDD), 239
"Bootstraps effect," 15
Bordin, E., 155
Boulder model, 282–284
Bowlby, J., 71
Bradbury, T. N., xix, 270n, 271–275
Brain
    hemispheric asymmetries and affect regulation and, xvi, 67–68
    neurodevelopment of schizophrenia and, 25–27
    normal development of, 24–25
    relation between cognition and, 169–171, 185–188
    structural abnormalities in schizophrenia and, 27–30, 41, 42
Brief psychodynamically oriented psychotherapy, xx
Brown, G. W., 73–74
Bry, B. H., 69

CAADC. *See* Child and Adolescent Anxiety Disorders Clinic
Cain, K. M., 69
Cannon, T. D., xiv–xv, 31, 32, 37–38
Canter Kihlstrom, L., xx

Category learning
    as cognitive dimension, 173–175
    sexually abusive behavior and, 176–181
Cattell, J. M., 168
Cattell, R. B., 150, 152
CCRT. *See* Core conflictual relationship theme
Charcot, Jean, xi–xii, xiii
Child abuse, 73
Child and Adolescent Anxiety Disorders Clinic (CAADC)
    description of, 219–220
    future priorities and, 227–229
    program of research at, 219
    treatment outcome evaluation at, 220–224, 227
    treatment procedures at, 220
Children. *See also* Depression in children; School contexts
    anxiety disorders and, 216, 217, 219–220, 222, 227
    MDS techniques and, 188–192
    onset of schizophrenia and, 33–36, 40–42
    treatment of OCD in, 255–257
    types of cognitive dysfunction in, 218
China, ancient, xiii
Chu, B., 228
Clark, L. A., xvi, 101
Classification, as cognitive dimension, 173–175
Clinical practice guidelines, 290
Clinical psychology
    application of MDS techniques in, 175–176 (*see also* Multidimensional scaling techniques)
    cognitive assessment and, 171–173
    cognitive revolution and, 166–167
    institutional status of, 285–287
    in managed care environment, 285–291
    origins of, 282
    pure practitioner model and, 283–285
    scientist–practitioner relationship and, 281, 282–283, 284–285, 290–291
    as term, xii
    transportability of research-based treatments and, 228
Clomipramine (CMI), 250–252

Cognition
  concept of, 169
  as experiential event, 165–166
  as process, 166
  relation between brain and, 169–171,
    185–188
  as thing, 165
Cognitive, as term, xvii
Cognitive–behavioral model, xix–xx,
    217–219. *See also* Cognitive
    therapy
  depression and, 54–60
  precursors to schizophrenia and, 33–36
  roles of therapist in, 217–218
  theories of OCD and, 240–242
Cognitive–behavioral treatment (CBT).
    See Cognitive therapy
Cognitive dysfunction, types of, 218
Cognitive processes. *See also* Multidimen-
    sional scaling techniques; Percep-
    tual organization
  bulimia and, 181–185
  key processes, defined, 173
  level of influence on information proc-
    essing, 185–188
  measurement of, 171–173
  sexually coercive behavior and, 176–
    181
  tools linking behavior and, 175–176
Cognitive revolution
  hybrid cognitive model and, 168–173
  two worlds of cognition and, 166–168
  views of, 163–166
Cognitive science. *See also* Scientist-
    practitioner relationship
  category learning and, 173–175, 176–
    181
  cognitive revolution and, 167, 168,
    171
  integration with practice, and managed
    care, 281–291
  prototype classification and, 181–185,
    192
  relation between brain and cognition
    and, 169–171
  tools of, and clinical problems, 171–
    173, 192–193 (*see also* Multidi-
    mensional scaling techniques)
Cognitive style
  attributional style and, 63–65, 109–
    110
  depression and, 66–74, 110

"Development of Depression" project
    and, 74–80
  effect of depression on, 55–60
  genetics and, 67–68
  interventions aimed at changing, 58,
    82
  optimism–pessimism and, 65–66
  relation between mother and child
    cognitions, 76–77
  self-worth and, 60–63
  stability of, 57–58
  vulnerability to depression and, 55–60
Cognitive therapy (CT)
  childhood anxiety disorders and, 220–
    227
  cognitive psychology and, 284
  depression and, 203–204
  OCD and, xix, 248–250, 253–255
Cole, D. A., 111–112
Community. *See* Social support
Community Mental Health Act of 1963,
    283
Comorbidity, 227, 237–238
Complexity theory. *See* "Dynamical en-
    ergy systems approach"
Congruence hypothesis, 177–181
Conners, C. K., xx
"Consilience," xiii
Construal process, 175–176
Constructive alternativism, 175n
Contingency. *See* Attributional style
Cooley, C. H., 60
Coping Questionnaire (CQ), 217, 226,
    228
"Coping template," 218
Core conflictual relationship theme
    (CCRT), xvii, 149–150
  new measure from old concept, 155–
    158
  symptom-context theme and, 153, 155,
    158
Correlational studies, and cognitive
    models, 56–57
Cost analysis, 288
Cottraux, J., 252
CQ. *See* Coping Questionnaire
Cronbach, L. J., 166
CT. *See* Cognitive therapy
Cure of mental disorders, 209–210, 229

Damon, W., 61

Davidson, R. J., 67
de Araujo, L. A., 244
"Decade of the Brain," xii, xv
Degreef, G., 28
DeLisi, L. E., 30
Delusional disorder, 239–240
Democritus, xi
Depression. *See also* Depression in children; Mood disorders
  absence of positive affect and, 101
  AHCPR guidelines and, 290
  anxiety and, xvi, 102
  cognitions in etiology of, 55
  cognitive models of, 54–60
  development of, 105–114
  epidemiology of, 204–205
  evidence of cognitive vulnerability to, 55–60
  GAD and, 102
  genetic risk and, 67–68, 68–70
  OCD and, 237
  pessimistic explanatory style and, 202–203
  prevention of, 209–212
  self-esteem movement and, 206–207
  sources of epidemic of, 205–206
  types of treatments for, 203
  uncontrollability and, 109–111
Depression in children
  "Development of Depression" project and, 74–80
  interventions and, xviii
  normative development and, 60–66
  origins of depressive cognitive style and, 66–74
  prevention of, 211–212
  psychosocial risk factors and, xv–xvi
  self-esteem movement and, 206–209
Depression in Primary Care (AHCPR), 290
Depressogenic cognitive schemata, 68
Developmental studies
  depressive cognitive style and, 60–66, 68–72
  precursors of schizophrenia and, 33–36
  "Development of Depression" project, 74–80
Diagnosis. *See also* Endophenotypes; Phenotype definition
  of anxiety disorders in children, 219–220
  diagnostic systems, 5, 217

of OCD, 236–237
role of therapist in, 218
of schizophrenia, 4–5, 15–17
structure of anxiety and mood disorders and, 99, 217
Diagnostic and Statistical Manual of Mental Disorders (4th ed.; DSM-IV; APA), 97, 100, 217
  OCD diagnosis and, 236–237
Diathesis–stress models of depression, 55, 57, 81, 111–112
Dollard, J., 240
Dossey, L., 121
Dumas, J. E., 108
Dusek, J. B., 71
Dweck, C. S., 70
"Dynamical energy systems approach," xvi, 142–143
Dysphoria, and failure, 207–209

Ebbinghaus, H., 282
Eisen, M., 61
Emmelkamp, P. M. G., 246–247, 248–249
Emotion, theory of, 192–193
Endophenotypes
  concept, 8
  eye tracking dysfunction and, 11, 16–17
  ideal qualities of, 9
  identification of, 8–10
  risk determination and, 11
  types of, 10–11
Experimental neurosis, 106
Explanatory style. *See also* Attributional style
  concept of, 201
  dimensions of, 202–203
Exposure, as OCD treatment, 244–246. *See also* Exposure and response prevention
Exposure and response prevention (EX/RP)
  cognitive therapy and, 248–250
  compared with other treatment approaches, 246–253
  family-based, 246–247
  group treatment and, 247–248
  pediatric OCD and, 255–257
  procedure, 242–243

relapse prevention techniques and, 249–250, 253

treatment variables, 243–246

Exposure orientation, and sexually coercive behavior, 179–181

EX/RP. See Exposure and response prevention

Eye-blink conditioning, and cognitive influences, 185–188, 192–193

Eye tracking dysfunction in schizophrenia, 12–17

as endophenotype, 11, 16–17

genetic models for transmission of, 12–15

Failure

depression and, 205

good uses of feeling bad and, 207–209

hopelessness and, 65

mechanisms underlying marital failure, 271–275

Fals-Stewart, W., 247

Families. See Family involvement in interventions; Genetic risk; Love and caring, perceptions of

Family involvement in interventions

anxiety disorders and, 223, 226, 228–229

depression and, 211

OCD and, 246–247

Fear, and OCD, 240, 241–242

Feedback, social, 70–72

Feinberg, I., 40–41

Feldman, S., 288

Fincham, F. D., 69

Fish, B., 35

Flow, 207–208

Floyd, F. J., 270

Fluvoxamine (FLU), 252

Flynn, C., xv

Foa, E. B., xix

Fragile X syndrome, xiv

Franklin, M. E., xix

Freud, S., 154, 158

GAD. See Generalized anxiety disorder

Garber, J., xv, 57, 59, 201

Gene–environment interaction model, 37, 39, 40

Generalized anxiety disorder (GAD). See also Anxiety disorders

in children, 219

depression and, 102

OCD and, 99, 102, 239

parenting styles and, 109

structure of anxiety and mood disorders and, 104, 105

Generalized Dysphoria, 99

Genetic risk, 3–18

competing genetic models, 14–15

depressive cognitive style and, 67–68

endophenotypes and, 8–11

facilitation of research on, 7–11

fit between endophenotype data and genetic models, 14–15

genetic heterogeneity and, 7

Huntington's disease and, 4–7

identification of gene carriers and, 6

mode of genetic transmission and, 7, 12–15

obstetric influences and, 37–38

phenotype definition and, 4–6

reproductive fitness and, 6–7

schizophrenia and, 8, 11, 12–18, 24, 30–31

theoretical considerations in, 17–18

Global/specific dimension, 202

Goldberg, T. E., 32

Goldbourt, U., 123

Goodman, S. H., 59, 71

Gottesman, I. I., 6

Graham, S., 64

Granger, D. A., 114

Green, J., 139

Growth curve modeling, 271–272

Gur, R. E., 30

Hahlweg, K., 267

Hall, G. S., xii

Harris, T. O., 73–74

Hart, D., 61

Harter, S., 60–61, 62

Harvard Mastery of Stress Study, xvi, 124–125

assessment of perceived love and caring and, 122–123

follow-up studies, 125–126, 143

LLC model and, 135–138

Harvard Parental Caring Scale, 123, 124, 138

Harvard Psychological Clinic, xii
HD. *See* Huntington's disease
Heaton, R., 29–30
Hecker, B., 66
Helping alliance counting signs method, 155
Helping alliance rating method, 155
Helplessness. *See* Hopelessness theory of depression; Learned helplessness
High-risk studies, and cognitive vulnerability to depression, 59–60
Hippocrates, xi, xiii, xv
Hiss, H., 249–250
Holzman, P. A., 16
Hopelessness theory of depression, 55, 79–80. *See also* Optimism-pessimism; Symptom-context theme
  development of cognitive style and, 65–66
  negative life events and, 79
Huntington's disease (HD), 4–7
Hypochondriasis, 239
Hypothalamic–pituitary–adrenocortical axis, 16, 114–115

Iacono, W. G., xiv
Identification, as cognitive dimension, 173–175
Imaginal exposure, and OCD, 244–246
Imipramine, 252–253
Impulsivity, 216
Individualism, and depression, 205
Institute of Medicine, 215, 290
Integrative theory, 217–219
Internal/external dimension, 202
Interpersonal model, and marital dysfunction, 271–275
Interpersonal psychotherapy, xx, 203
Interventions, xviii–xix
  anxiety disorders and, 219–227
  child characteristics and, 222
  effectiveness of, 224–225, 290–291
  empirical support and, 224–225
  families and, 211, 223, 226, 228–229, 246–247
  future research priorities and, 227–229
  marital dysfunction and, 265–276
  mediators of outcomes and, 226
  moderator variables and, 225–226

outcome evaluation methodology and, 220–224, 227
prevention of depression and, 209–212
research-based, transportability of, 228
In vivo imaging, xv, 27–33

Jacobson, N. S., xix, 266
Jaenicke, C., 59, 71, 78
James, W., xii, 60, 140, 282
Janet, P., xii
Janoff-Bulman, R., 66
Jerusalem Infant Development Study, 35
Johnson, M. D., xix
Journal of Abnormal Psychology, xii
Just, N., 58

Kagan, J., 113–114
Kaplan, B. H., 121
Karney, B. R., 271–275
Kaslow, N. J., 69
Katon, W., 100
Kelly, G. A., 175–176, 177, 186, 193
Kendall, P. C., 226
Keshavan, M. S., 41
Kihlstrom, J. F., xx, 106, 171
Klann, N., 267
Klein, D. F., xix
Koestner, R., 71
Kozak, M. J., 241–242, 243, 248, 249
Kraepelin, E., xii
Kruschke, J. K., 174–175
Kwon, D., 79

Lang, M., 42
Lang, P. J., 192–193
Last, C., 222
Latency models, and neurodevelopment of schizophrenia, 40–42
Lawrence, E. E., xix, 270n
Learned helplessness, 106, 155, 208–209
Learning, and "primacy" effect, xvii
Lease, A. M., 188, 189–192
Levels of love and caring (LLC) model, 133–135, 143
  Harvard follow–up data and, 135–138
Lewinsohn, P. M., 56
Lewis, S. W., 36
Lifetime prevalence of depression, 204–205

Litovsky, V. G., 71
Logical isomorphism, 170–171, 186
Lopatka, C., 241
Loss, 73
Lovaas, O. I., xx
Love, concept of, 141, 142–143
Love and caring, perceptions of
    application of findings on, 138–140
    Harvard follow-up data and LLC
        model and, 135–138
    levels of love and caring model and,
        133–135
    LOVE heuristic and, 139–140
    meaning of results on, 132–133
    measurement of, 122–124
    multiple-choice data on, 131–132
    narrative descriptions and, 128–130,
        136, 137
    numeric ratings and, 126–128, 137
Love and Survival (Ornish), 140–141
Luborsky, L., xvii

MAD. *See* Mixed anxiety–depression
Magnetic resonance imaging (MRI). *See*
        Neuroimaging studies
Maher, B. A., 284
Managed care environment
    need for regulation of, 289
    practitioner-owned organizations and,
        289
    psychology's role in shaping, 287–289
    as threat to clinical psychology, 285–
        287
Manual-based therapy, and therapist flexi-
        bility, 228
March, J. S., 256
Marcus, J., 35
Marital dysfunction
    competing models approach to, 271–
        275
    conflict behavior and, 268–269, 270n
    effects of therapy and, 266–267
    interventions with, 265–276
    link from basic research to interven-
        tion and, 267–271, 275–276
    prevention and, 269–271, 275
    research on causes of, 271–275
Marks, I. M., 246, 250–252
Mastery, vs. learned helplessness, 208–
        209
McClelland, D. C., 172

McCranie, E. W., 71
McFall, R. M., xvii
McNeil, T. F., 38
MDS photo-rating task, 182–183, 186
MDS techniques. *See* Multidimensional
        scaling techniques
Medalie, J. H., 123
Mediational model of depression, 111–
        112
Mednick, S. A., 37–38
Meehl, P., 169
Mehta, M., 247
Mental health services research, 288
Mental retardation, xiv
Metalsky, G. I., 57
Meyer, V., 242, 243, 244
Miller, N. E., 240
Mineka, S., 106–107
Mischel, W., 175n
Mixed anxiety–depression (MAD), 99–
        101
Modeling, and depressive cognitive style,
        68–70
Montemayor, R., 61
Mood disorders. *See also* Anxiety disor-
        ders; Depression; Depression in
        children
    DSM hierarchical structure and, 96–
        97
    factor analysis of models of, 97–105
    heritability and, 67–68
    mixed anxiety–depression, 99–101
    study of neuroticism and, 95–96
    tripartite model and, 101, 102–105
Mowrer, O. A., 240
MRI (magnetic resonance imaging). *See*
        Neuroimaging studies
Multidimensional scaling (MDS) tech-
        niques, 173
    bulimia and, 181–185
    children and, 188–192
    clinical application of, 175–176
    mapping of perceptual processing and,
        173–175
    schizophrenia and, 192
    sexually coercive behavior and, 176–
        181
Murray, R. M., 36

NA. *See* Negative affect
Nasby, W., 171

National Academy of Sciences, Institute of Medicine, 215, 290
National Institute of Mental Health (NIMH), xviii–xix, 204, 209–210, 215–216
Negative affect (NA)
   assessment of, 217
   MAD and, 100–101
   marital outcomes and, 274–275
   neurobiological factors and, 112
   structure of anxiety and mood disorders and, 97–99, 101, 105
Negative cognitions
   depressive disorders and, 56–57
   exposure to negative life events and, 72–74, 79
Negative cognitive triad, 54–55
Negative life events
   depressive cognitive style and, 72–74, 109–110
   "Development of Depression" project and, 74–80
Neufeld, R. W. J., 192
Neumann, L. S., 35
Neurobiological processes, and anxiety disorders, 113–114
Neurodevelopment of schizophrenia
   neuropathological abnormalities and, 25–27
   normal brain development and, 24–25
   obstetric complications and, 31
   postmortem neuropathology studies and, 24–27
   types of evidence for, 23–24
   in vivo imaging studies and, 27–33
Neuroimaging studies, xv, 27–33
Neuronal migration in brain development, 25–27
Neuroscience. See also Brain
   clinical problems and, 185–188, 192
   cognitive revolution and, 167, 168
Neuroticism
   anxiety and mood disorders and, 95–96
   depressive cognitive style and, 67–68
Newton, Sir Isaac, 142–143
NIMH. See National Institutes of Mental Health
Nolen-Hoeksema, S., 56, 73, 79, 110, 111, 112
Nopoulous, P., 30
Normative comparisons, 227

Nosofsky, R. M., 173–175, 176, 177
Not-otherwise-specified (NOS) diagnosis, 100
Nowicki, S., 107

OAD (overanxious disorder). See Generalized anxiety disorder
Obsessive–compulsive disorder (OCD), xix. See also Exposure and response prevention
   action–memory deficit and, 241
   assumptions characteristic of, 240–241
   in children, 255–257
   cognitive–behavioral treatment of, 235–258
   continuum of insight and, 236–237, 240
   course of, 237
   diagnosis of, 236–237
   differentiation from other symptoms, 238–240
   disorders associated with, 237–238
   GAD and, 99, 102
   prevalence of, 237
   role of responsibility in, 241
Obsessive Compulsive Responsibility Scale, 241
Obstetric complications (OC)
   mechanisms of, 38–39
   schizophrenia and, 31, 32, 36–40
OC. See Obstetric complications
OCD. See Obsessive–compulsive disorder
O'Leary, K. D., 270n
Optimism–pessimism. See also Attributional style; Explanatory style; Hopelessness theory of depression
   in college students, 210–211
   depression and, 202–203
   development of, 65–66
   therapy and, 203–204
Ornish, D., 140–141
Overanxious disorder (OAD). See Generalized anxiety disorder

PA. See Positive affect
Pandysmaturation (PDM), 35
Panic disorder, 109
Parental Bonding Instrument, 109

Parenting
  development of cognitive style and,
    71, 74, 77–79
  risk factors for depression and, 211
  uncontrollability and, 107–109
Parkinson's disease, 5
Parnas, J., 37
Pavlov, I. P., 105
PBO, 252–253
PDM. See Pandysmaturation
Peer relationships
  development of cognitive style and,
    70–71
  perception of, in children, 188–192
Perceptual organization
  mapping of, and MDS techniques,
    173–175
  sexually coercive behavior and, 176–
    181
  stability of individual differences in,
    185
  tools linking behavior and, 175–176
Perinatal hypoxia, 38–39, 40
Personality, and genetics, 67–68
Peterson, C., 68–69
PET (positron emission tomography). See
    Neuroimaging studies
Pharmacological treatment approaches,
    xix
  with children, 255, 257
  depression and, 203, 212
  OCD and, xix, 250–253, 253–255
Phenotype definition, 4–6, 15–17
Phenylketonuria (PKU), 8, 13
Phobia, specific, 246
Physical isomorphism, 170–171
Piaget, J., 64, 65
PKU. See Phenylketonuria
Polygenicity, 7, 12–14
Positive affect (PA), 101, 102, 104
Positron emission tomography (PET). See
    Neuroimaging studies
"Power of nonnegative thinking," 226
Practitioner-owned managed care organi-
    zations, 289
PREP. See Prevention and Relationship
    Enhancement Program
Prevention and Relationship Enhance-
    ment Program (PREP), 270
Prevention studies, and cognitive models,
    58–59
"Primacy" effect, xvii
Prince, M., xii

Professional organizations, 285
Professional status, 288–289
Prospective studies, and cognitive models,
    57
Prototype classification task, 182, 183,
    192
Psychological Clinic (journal), xii
Psychological control, 78
Psychology, and cognitive revolution,
    167, 168
The Psychology of Personal Constructs,
    175–176, 193
Psychosocial risk factors, xv
Psychotherapy sessions, assessment
    within, xvii
P-technique method, 150

Quantitative models, 172

Rachman, S., 241
Radke-Yarrow, M., 71
Rasmussen, S. A., 237
Rational Emotive Therapy (RET), 248–
    249
Recognition memory, 173–175
Regulation of managed mental health
    care, 289
Relapse prevention techniques, 249–250,
    253
Remission studies, and cognitive models,
    57–58
Repertoire grid technique (Rep Test),
    176
Replicability, 17
Responsibility, and OCD, 241
RET. See Rational Emotive Therapy
Rholes, W. S., 63–64
Ribot, T., 282
Risk factors, xiv–xvi
Ritual prevention, 243–244. See also Ex-
    posure and response prevention
Robinson, N. S., 59
Rogge, R. D., xix
Rose, D. T., 72–73
Rotter, J., 107
Roy-Byrne, P., 100
Ruminations, vs. obsessions, 238
Russek, H. I., 125, 126

SAD. *See* Separation anxiety disorder
Salkovskis, P. M., 240–241
Sapolsky, R. M., 112–113
Schizophrenia. *See also* Neurodevelop-
    ment of schizophrenia
    brain structure abnormalities in, 27–
        30, 41, 42
    diagnosis of, 4–5
    eye tracking dysfunction in, 12–17
    functional deficits and, 31–32, 34–36
    genetic risk for, 8, 11, 12–18, 24, 30–
        31, 40, 41–42
    Kraepelinian concept of, 23
    latency models and, 40–42
    MDS techniques and, 192
    neuropathological progression of, 29–
        30
    obstetric complications and, 31, 32,
        36–40
    OCD and, 240
    polygenicity and, 7, 12–14
    studies of first-episode patients, 28
Schizotypal personality disorder, 5
School contexts
    development of cognitive style and, 70
    prevention of depression and, 211–212
    self-esteem movement and, 206–107
Schulman, P., 67
Scientist–practitioner relationship
    Boulder model and, 281, 282–283
    redefinition of, 284–285, 290–291
SDT. *See* Signal detection theory
Seeman, M. V., 42
Seeman, T. E., 123
Self disclosure, as moderator variable,
    225–226
Self-efficacy, as mediator variable, 226
Self-esteem movement, and depression,
    206–207
Self-estimates task, 182, 184
Self-Instructional Training (SIT), 248
Self-talk, as mediator variable, 226,
    227–228
Self-worth, 55, 60–63, 78, 80, 81
Seligman, M. E. P., xviii–xix, 58, 67,
    68–69, 106, 109, 266–267
Separation anxiety disorder (SAD), 218.
    See also Anxiety disorders
Sertraline (SER), 257
Sexually coercive behavior
    exposure vs. affect orientation and,
        179–181

and perceptual organization, 176–181
Shellenberger, R., 139
Sidis, B., xii
Signal detection theory (SDT), 172, 183
Silove, D., 109
Simple additive influences model, 37, 39
Siqueland, L., 108
SIT. *See* Self-Instructional Training
Social learning, and depressive cognitive
    style, 68–72
Social phobia, 104
Social support
    assessment of, 122–123
    depression and, 205–206
Stable/unstable dimension, 202
Stark, K. D., 107
Stipek, D. J., 64, 65, 79
Stress. *See also* Uncontrollability
    development of emotional disorders
        and, 105–106
    neurobiological processes and, 112–
        114
Strickland, B. R., 107
Strupp, H., xx
Suddath, R. L., 30–31
"Surgency" factor, 152
Syme, L., 123
The Symptom-Context Method (Luborsky),
    150, 158, 159
Symptom-context theme, xvii, 149, 150
    basic components of, 153
    CCRT and, 153, 155, 158
    eight-stage theory of symptom forma-
        tion, 154–155
    new measure from old concept, 150–
        155
Systems theory. *See* "Dynamical energy
    systems approach"

Temperament, and depression, 66
Tic disorders, 239
Tourette's syndrome, 239
Tracey, S. A., xvi
Transference, concept of, xvii, 158. *See
    also* Core conflictual relationship
    theme
Treadwell, K. R. H., 226
Treat, T., xvii
Treatment. *See* Interventions
Tsuang, M. F., 237
Turk, E., 69

Turner, J. E., 111–112
Twitmeyer, E., 149n
Tyrka, A., 36

Uncontrollability
    anxiety in humans and, 106–107
    depression and, 109–111
    experimental neurosis and, 105–106
    parenting styles and, 107–109
Unitary construction of anxiety and
        mood disorders, 95–96
University of Pennsylvania, xiii, xvii,
        xviii, xx, 210–211

van Oppen, P., 249
Viken, R. J., xvii, 185

Walker, E. F., 35, 41–42
Watson, D., xvi, 67–68, 101
Weinberger, D. R., 40, 41–42
Weiner, B., 64
Weisz, J. R., 64
Whisman, M. A., 79
White, P. A., 63
Williamson, P. C., 192
Wilson, E. O., xiii–xiv, xix
Witmer, L., xii, xiii, xx, 149n, 163, 282
Women, and attributional style, 110–111
Wundt, W., xii

Young, J. E., 70

Zinbarg, R. E., 100, 102

ABOUT THE EDITORS

Donald K. Routh is Professor of Psychology at the University of Miami. He is President of the Division of Clinical Psychology of the American Psychological Association and President of the Division of Clinical and Community Psychology of the International Association of Applied Psychology. His current scholarly interest is in the history of clinical psychology and psychiatry. He is the author of the book *Clinical Psychology Since 1917* (1994).

Robert J. DeRubeis is Associate Professor of Psychology at the University of Pennsylvania. His research focuses on the role of cognition in emotion, especially in abnormal emotional states. He is the author of many articles, including a widely cited one by DeRubeis and his colleagues that appeared in 1990 in the *Journal of Consulting and Clinical Psychology*, "How Does Cognitive Therapy Work? Cognitive Change and Symptoms Change in Cognitive Therapy and Pharmacotherapy for Depression."